NOAH WEBSTER

PIONEER OF LEARNING

N Webster

NOAH WEBSTER

PIONEER OF LEARNING

BY

ERVIN C. SHOEMAKER

NEW YORK · MORNINGSIDE HEIGHTS

COLUMBIA UNIVERSITY PRESS

M · CM · XXXVI

FOREIGN AGENTS

OXFORD UNIVERSITY PRESS
HUMPHREY MILFORD, AMEN HOUSE
LONDON, E.C.4, ENGLAND

KWANG HSUEH PUBLISHING HOUSE
140 PEKING ROAD
SHANGHAI, CHINA

MARUZEN COMPANY, LTD.
6 NIHONBASHI, TORI-NICHOME
TOKYO, JAPAN

OXFORD UNIVERSITY PRESS
B. I. BUILDING, NICOL ROAD
BOMBAY, INDIA

PREFACE

SINCE it is usually conceded that we of the present can profit by the mistakes and successes of the past, an effort was made in this study to appraise the services of Noah Webster, who has been acclaimed by men of his age and the present as the chief proponent of American education following the Revolutionary War. What was his contribution to American education in general and to the teaching of English in particular? is the question this study has attempted to answer.

So far, a full portrait of Webster as an educator has not been given. Several works have appeared which have served to acquaint a small minority with his many activities, but to the masses he is known only as the compiler of "the dictionary," and even in this capacity he is often confused with his distant relative Daniel Webster. In 1881, Horace Scudder published *Noah Webster*, a biographical study. In 1912, Mrs. E. E. F. Skeel edited and published *Notes on the Life of Noah Webster*, compiled by her mother, Mrs. Emily Ellsworth Fowler Ford, Webster's granddaughter. This work contains Webster's diary, many of his letters, and other Websteriana. Several studies have been made which have explored certain fields in which Webster worked. Among these are Reeder's historical study of the school reader, Lyman's survey of the teaching of grammar, Leonard's study of correct usage in the eighteenth century, Neumann's dissertation on pronunciation in America according to Noah Webster, Mencken's and Krapp's works on the English language in America, and Tingelstad's treatment of the religious element in school readers.

In the present work an attempt has been made to present a full-length portrait of Webster, "the schoolmaster of our republic." A definitive biography by Professor Harry R. Warfel and an exhaustive bibliography by Mrs. E. E. F. Skeel are under preparation at this time. Numerous magazine articles on Webster have appeared within the last two years. These activities indicate that this long-neglected author is destined to be better known.

In attempting to form an estimate of Webster's contribution to education, the author has found it necessary to review what had been thought and done prior to Webster's day in the field of general education and in the teaching of spelling, grammar, reading, religion, morality, manners, and so forth, and in the compiling of dictionaries and in language reform. An exposition has been given of Webster's activities in these fields and an effort has been made to determine, if possible, Webster's influence on his contemporaries and successors. This survey, it may seem to the cursory reader, has at times taken the author far afield. Because of Webster's numerous activities and the abundance of material which is available, one of the chief problems has been that of selecting the materials which would contribute to the objectives of the study and eliminating that which was not pertinent. Because the sciences of pedagogy and psychology, the latter defined by Webster as a "study of the soul," were not developed in any sense of the word in Webster's day, no conscious attempt has been made to compare Webster's theories with those that are held today.

Since the study has led the author into many fields, the bibliography has tended to become unwieldy. In order to keep it from becoming burdensome and out of proportion to the remainder of the book, it seemed desirable that a selection should be made. The hundreds of school texts and dictionaries that were examined and in many cases referred to only casually by way of chronology or illustration are not listed. These are of course out of print and are not available except in the large libraries rich in Americana. Titles and dates of these publications have been given in the body of the work. Most of the Webster manuscripts referred to are in the New York Public Library.

The author takes this opportunity to thank the officials of the libraries at Columbia, Yale, and Chicago Universities, of the

Library of Congress, New Haven Colony Historical Association Library, Watkinson Library, and Newberry Library, for permission to use collections and for assistance in their use; also Mr. George Plimpton for permission to use his private collection, and members of the staff in the Rare Book Collection and the Manuscript Division of the New York Public Library. To Professors Allan Abbott, Franklin T. Baker, Edward H. Reisner, and the late George Philip Krapp of Columbia University he extends his most sincere thanks and appreciation for their encouragement and guidance.

ERVIN C. SHOEMAKER

NEW YORK CITY
June 4, 1935

CONTENTS

ILLUSTRATIONS

NOAH WEBSTER

PIONEER OF LEARNING

I

AMERICAN INTELLECTUAL PIONEER

WRITING in 1790, Noah Webster, a man of thirty-two, cast himself in the rôle of prompter, who would "prompt the numerous actors upon the great theater of life." In that he "wanted to whip vice and folly out of the country," he expressed his belief that "his only motive was to do good." [1] He played this rôle more or less consistently during a long and active life. There were times, however, when he left the prompter's box to act a part or to be the stage manager in the stirring drama that had to do with the birth of a nation and with more than half a century of its turbulent growth. In fact, at the risk of using the figure to the cracking point, it might be shown that he gave several sizable one-man performances through which he brought honor and profit to himself, as well as to his descendants and his country.

Because Webster gave the greater part of his life to lexicographical pursuits, to the compiling of spelling books and dictionaries, the only facts about his life that are generally known, people have come to look upon him as an exemplification of Johnson's definition of a lexicographer—"a harmless drudge that busies himself in tracing the origin and detailing the signification of words." Far from being a retiring, bloodless pedant, Webster was one of a group of shrewd, homespun, practical individuals like Benjamin Franklin, with whom, as we shall see, he had much in common. "He became in effect a kind of intellectual frontiersman, as fertile of ideas as the frontiersman is

[1] *The Prompter;* or a commentary on Common Sayings and Subjects, which are full of Common Sense, the Best Sense in the World (1790). This series of familiar essays, written in the "Franklin Style," went through many editions. They were imitated by Joseph Dennie in *The Lay Preacher* (1796). See Dennie's letter to Webster, dated "Walpole, New Hampshire, September 8, 1795." Webster MSS. Unless otherwise indicated, the Webster manuscripts referred to are in the New York Public Library. See also E. E. F. Ford's *Notes on the Life of Noah Webster* (1912), I, 299. This work is an invaluable source book of Websteriana. Many of the Webster MSS have been published in it.

fertile of mere material resources." [2] Schoolmaster, journalist, pamphleteer, lawyer, politician, historian, economist, scientist, and lexicographer, "he left some mark of his influence in almost every field of development in the age in which he lived." [3]

Webster's Patriotic Zeal Gave Impetus to His Versatility

THE amazing activity of Noah Webster in the numerous fields of endeavor and the many facets of his individual make-up, reflecting under varying circumstances lights of many hues, not always complimentary, presents something of an enigma. Several facts having to do with his ancestry and environment help, however, to explain some of the forces which were the mainspring of many of his activities and which shaped his rather odd assortment of personal characteristics. Foremost among these forces was his patriotic ardor. Many of his enterprises were undertaken and carried to completion because of his chauvinistic attitude toward the new Republic. He was a stanch patriot by inheritance as well as by conviction.

Born in 1758, Webster was the great-great-grandson of John Webster, who had emigrated from Warwickshire, England, and settled first near Boston; in 1636, as part of the famous Hooker band, he migrated from Massachusetts through the wilderness to Newe Towne, now Hartford, Connecticut.[4] On his mother's side, Noah Webster was the great-great-great-grandson of Governor William Bradford of Plymouth Colony. The marriage of Webster's father, Noah Webster, Sr., and his mother, Mercy Steele, was the union of Puritan and Pilgrim.[5] His forebears

[2] Edward Wagenknecht, "The Man behind the Dictionary," *Virginia Quarterly Review*, April, 1929, p. 247.

[3] T. W. Russell, "Webster, Word Arbiter for 100 Years," *New York Times Magazine*, April 15, 1928, p. 11.

[4] For facts pertaining to John Webster's life, see Noah Webster's *Biography for the Use of Schools* (1830), p. 117.

[5] For details concerning Webster's ancestry, see *Webster Genealogy*, compiled and printed by Noah Webster, 1836. According to Whitmore, this was the eleventh genealogy to be printed in America.—W. H. Whitmore, *American Genealogists* (1862), p. 37.

had rendered patriotic service in the French and Indian wars as well as in civil affairs, attaining some prominence, as is evidenced by the fact that they held such offices as those of magistrate, deputy governor, committeeman, representative, justice of the peace, and so forth.

Webster himself, although excused from military duty, marched with his two brothers, under the command of their father, who was captain in the alarm list, to meet Burgoyne when he came down from the north in 1777.[6] The summer before, he had gone with his brother Abraham to an army camp. Here, he reported, "The musketoes were so numerous that the soldiers could not sleep at night except by filling their tents with smoke. . . . At Mount Independence we found about half the soldiers sick with dysentery, and fever, so that the very air was infected." [7] In this experience, it seems logical to conclude, Webster first became interested in epidemiology, a field in which he later made a distinct contribution.[8]

While Webster was a student at Yale (1774-78) he endured many privations. At that time the dread disease of smallpox was running rampant in the army and spread to the civilian population, numbering Webster among its victims.[9] Then, provisions were scarce. Molasses made from cornstalks was a staple article of food.[10] In fact, it became so difficult to procure provisions that early in the year 1777 the classes were disbanded and many students were obliged to return to their parents. At that time it was feared that New Haven might be attacked by the British because of its strategic position along the coast. For that reason the Yale library, along with other college property, was removed to the country. In the summer of 1777, the classes were summoned to convene in various interior towns. The Junior Class, of which

[6] See Webster's account in Webster MSS. Also E. E. F. Ford's *Notes on the Life of Noah Webster* (1912), I, 20.
[7] *Ibid.*
[8] See pp. 27 ff.
[9] Webster MSS. Letter to Webster from Ichabod Wetmore, Jr., dated "Middletown, 24th May, 1774."
[10] Memo. by Noah Webster, E. E. F. Ford, *Notes on the Life of Noah Webster* (1912), I, 21.

Webster was a member, was stationed at Glastonbury, under the tutor, Rev. Joseph Buckminster,[11] whose early guidance and later friendship should be regarded as a potent factor in the molding of Webster's character. All these happenings, during those days that tried men's souls, made a strong impression on young Webster.

Webster's Puritan Home Training and Education Placed Strong Emphasis on Religion and Morality

THE Puritan tradition of religion and morality was another force which helps to explain the many activities of Webster. This inherited tradition found in the serious young Webster a congenial medium for growth and expansion. As the son of a deacon and a justice of the peace, he had been carefully trained in the Puritan faith of his age. The constant round of chores and hard labor in the fields on the ninety-acre farm at West Hartford, the numerous daily prayers at home and at school, frequent and regular church attendance, the strict observance of the Sabbath—all these put their stamp on the youth. "In the sterility of this poverty stricken life there was a certain iron which entered into the constitution of the people who lived it." [12]

When Webster was fourteen years old, he decided on a college career. It is not known just what forces worked to bring about this decision. It is likely that his intense interest in the life about him and his unusual intellectual vigor caused him to see in the college a means of realizing his ambitions for the future. Then, too, on his mother's side there was a tradition of education, beginning with the learned Governor Bradford [13] and extending to Webster's generation. At first the father opposed Noah's decision, but as he frequently found his determined son under a tree studying his Latin grammar instead of following the plow,

---

[11] *Yale College Register*, I, 213.

[12] Horace Scudder, *Noah Webster* (1882), p. 26. Houghton Mifflin Company.

[13] Bradford was "acquainted with Dutch, French, Latin, and Greek, and after sixty years of age was a diligent student of Hebrew . . . Some marked traits of his character seemed to descend to the fourth generation; his persistence, his justice, his vigour, and his patriotism, and even his linguistic tastes . . ." Ford's *Notes*, I, 8.

he engaged the Reverend Nathan Perkins to prepare the youth for college. Later Noah attended the Hopkins Grammar School in Hartford, but returned to Dr. Perkins to complete his preparatory studies.[14] In order to pay the expenses of the son at Yale College, which he entered in 1774, Noah Webster, Sr., mortgaged the homestead at West Hartford.

The foregoing account contains all that is known concerning Webster's early education. His descendants have said that his schooling up to his fourteenth year was limited to the "nurture and admonition of the lord," and there can be no doubt that his religious training, in compliance with the custom of the age, did overshadow the secular. His early training, however, was perhaps more extensive than has been generally supposed. It seems reasonable to conclude that his elementary education, because of the unusual industry and aptitude which he later exhibited, surpassed that of his elder brother, Abraham, who did not go to college, but whose letters indicate that he was far from illiterate. Webster must have gone to elementary school at least four months a year. According to a Connecticut school law passed in 1700, towns of more than seventy families were ordered to keep a school all the year and those of any number of families less than seventy to have one during half the year.[15] This provision does not mean, however, that one school would be in session the entire time. The town was divided into districts and each district had a school for four months.[16]

Just what Webster read as a boy would indeed be interesting to learn. We know that his schoolbooks were limited chiefly or wholly to Dilworth's Spelling Books, the Psalter, Testament, and Bible.[17] At home he assuredly had access to the Bible and the

[14] This account of Webster's early education is based on family tradition, as told by Webster's daughter, Mrs. Eliza Steele Webster Jones.—Ford, *Notes*, I, 15.

Perkins affords a good example of the prominent place the minister had in the scheme of colonial education. During his connection with the Church, he fitted for college more than one hundred and fifty young men.—Increase N. Tarbox, "Noah Webster," *Congregational Quarterly*, VII, Part I, 1.

[15] Bernard C. Steiner, *The History of Education in Connecticut* (1893), p. 30.

[16] Noah Webster, "On Public Schools," *The American Minerva*, January 8, 1794.

[17] Noah Webster, "Letter to Henry Barnard," dated "New Haven, March 10, 1840."—*American Journal of Education*, XIII, 1863, p. 123.

almanac, perhaps that of Nathaniel Ames,[18] "which was a 'best seller' preceding the Revolution." [19] The almanac was usually given a place in the colonial household on a shelf along with the Bible. It is probable, too, that he read the *Connecticut Courant,* which was started in Hartford in 1764. Because of the somber tone of his diary [20] and his writings in general, it seems reasonable also to conjecture that he may have read the "juveniles" of his day. "In the art of dying, as in that of living," writes Rosenbach, "example was thought better than precept, and the children of New England were therefore forced to read, mark, and learn, and inwardly digest the morbid accounts of the long-drawn-out illnesses and dying speeches of numbers of children who died pious deaths at an early age." [21] It would seem, however, that he did not read the juveniles which early in the last half of the eighteenth century were beginning to be written for the edification and amusement of children, by writers and publishers who no longer looked upon children as miniature adults.[22] Perhaps this lack of exercise in the field of childhood fancy helps to

[18] Published in Hartford, 1765–74. See A. C. Bates, "Check List of Connecticut Almanacs, 1709–1850." *Proceedings of American Antiquarian Society*, New Series, XXIV, pp. 96, 212.

[19] Clarence S. Bringham, *An Account of American Almanacs and Their Value for Historical Study* (1925), p. 5.

[20] Webster's MSS; also published in Ford's *Notes*, I–II.

From January 1, 1789, to May 15, 1794, Webster kept his diary rather religiously, there being an entry for practically every day. After the latter date, no entries were made until April 1, 1798. From that date until September 18, 1820 (1821 ?), the date of the last entry, he wrote intermittently, sometimes writing only a few times a month or a few times during the year. There are also lesser diaries, which he kept when traveling and from which he often copied into the main diary.

The entries are, on the whole, brief. There are short notes on his social interests, such as attendance at church, assemblies, lectures, and teas, accounts of his attentions to the ladies, his courtship, and finally his marriage to Rebecca Greenleaf on October 26, 1789. Many of the entries have to do with the weather, fruits and vegetables in season, diseases and remedies, births, marriages, deaths, burials, accounts of his lectures in various cities, and the compilation and publication of his numerous textbooks. Sometimes on his birthday the entry takes the form of a short essay or sermon on the vicissitudes of life and the need for resignation.

[21] A. S. W. Rosenbach, *Early American Children's Books* (1933), p. XIX.

The number of these books was very great, as is indicated by the numerous copies in such collections as the library of the American Antiquarian Society (Worcester, Mass.) and the private libraries of Rosenbach (Philadelphia) and Bates (Hartford, Conn.).

[22] See pp. 159 ff.

explain why, according to the record kept in his diary, Webster as a man read very few books of a purely literary nature, and why he joined so wholeheartedly in the current denunciation of novels and plays.[23] His comments on literature appearing in his diary, in the *American Magazine,* and elsewhere, are very wooden and puerile. All these facts tend to support Everett E. Thompson's statement that Webster had no real appreciation of literature.[24]

It is possible that some light on Webster's early training is shed by his remarks on various occasions concerning the education of the yeomanry of America, the class from which he sprang. These remarks should, however, be taken with the proverbial grain of salt, in that they illustrate Webster's tendency to build up an argument in order to prove his point when he was on the defensive, as he most assuredly was in his letters to Priestley.[25] There can be no doubt, however, that he was absolutely sincere, having convinced himself in the course of his reasoning that his contention was true. This tendency obviously exposed him to the charge of inconsistency, of which the critics in later years made much.

"These men [American yeomen] have considerable education," he explained to those who were inclined to compare them with the illiterate peasantry of England. "They not only learn to read, write, and keep accounts; but a vast proportion of them read newspapers every week, and besides the Bible, which is found in all families, they read the best English sermons and treatises upon religion, ethics, geography and history; such as the works of Watts, Addison, Atterbury, Salmon &C."[26] Again, in his letter to Priestley, he says that "in the Eastern States knowledge is more diffused among the laboring people than in any

[23] See p. 54.
[24] Everett E. Thompson, "Noah Webster and Amherst College," *Amherst Graduates' Quarterly,* August, 1933, p. 289.
[25] Priestley, an expatriated Englishman, addressed letters to the people of Northumberland, Pennsylvania, in which he lectured the citizens of the new republic in a rather condescending manner. Webster answered him in *Ten Letters to Dr. Joseph Priestley* (1800).
[26] *Dissertations on the English Language* (1789), p. 289.

country on the globe. The learning of the people extends to a
knowledge of their own tongue, of writing and arithmetic sufficient to keep their own simple accounts; they read not only the
Bible and newspapers, but almost all read the best English
authors, as the 'Spectator,' 'Rambler,' and the works of Watts,
Dodridge, and many others." [27]

The preparation for college which the youths of Webster's age
received extended little beyond the ability to read and write
easy Latin and a knowledge of some Greek.[28] Very little time was
spent in college in the formal study of Latin, but it was practiced daily in the classroom and in conversation. "Latin was the
key to knowledge, and the storehouse of wisdom was the college."
That the student might read the Bible in the original, Greek and
Hebrew were studied, and at one time Chaldee and Syriac were
also taught, but no modern language, such as French or German.[29] Logic, ethics, and politics were each taught for two years,
and lectures on physics, history, and botany were sometimes
given. The bachelor's degree was conferred upon those who
were "able to read the originals of the Old and New Testaments
into the Latin tongue, and to resolve them logically," provided
the students were "of Godly life and conversation." [30]

[27] *Ten Letters to Dr. Joseph Priestley, in Answer to His Letters to the Inhabitants of Northumberland* (1800), p. 22.

[28] Edward Emery Slosson, "The American Spirit in Education," *The Chronicles
of America*, XXXIII (1921), 49. Copyright Yale University Press. Clap has left a
record of what the entrant to Yale in 1766 was supposed to know, eight years before
Webster entered. "They are able well to construe and parse *Tully's* Orations,
Virgil and the Greek Testament; and understand the Rules of common arithmetic."—*The Annals or History of Yale College, 1700–1766* (1766), p. 81.

[29] To this list of Webster's linguistic equipment should be added French,
which he studied while teaching at Sharon (1781), with the Rev. John Peter
Têtard, later a professor of French in Columbia College.—Ford, *Notes*, I, 44.
It is possible that through Têtard Webster made his acquaintance with the
writings of Rousseau and other French liberals, which may have influenced his
ideas on education. Later, under the influence of the writings of Horne Tooke,
which Webster began to read in 1787, he studied Anglo-Saxon.

[30] The description of the early college curriculum in America was taken from
Slosson, *op. cit.*, p. 50. Again, President Clap has left a record of what the Yale
student studied in 1766:

First Year: Study of languages principally; Begin logic and mathematics.

Second Year: Study languages, "but principally recite Logick, Rhetorick, Ora-

The early religious and moral training which the, Puritan youth received was continued in Yale College, since the "Principal Design of the Institution of this college, was to educate Persons for the work of the Ministry." [31] The students were "obliged to attend the publick worship of God in the Chapel every Lord's Day" [32] and to attend daily the morning and evening prayers, "at which, occasion is frequently taken . . . to excite them to some particular Duty, and to Caution them against some particular Sin." [33] Special care was taken also to keep the students "from all Excesses and Extravagance; from all vain Affectations of Show . . . to instil in their Minds true Notions of Honor, Politeness, and a Love of Virtue." [34] It was impressed upon them that the special advantages which they enjoyed were meant "to qualify them for the special Service of God; and to render them most useful to their Fellow Men." [35]

Much emphasis was placed on disputation and oratory. According to the account given by Clap,

The two upper Classes exercise their Powers in disputing every Monday in the Syllogistick Form, and every Tuesday in the Forensick . . .[36] Twice a week five or six deliver a Declamation memoriter from the oratorical Rostrum . . .[37] There are also two Orations

tory, Geography and natural Philosophy." Some "make good Proficiency in Trigonometry and Algebra."

Third Year: Study natural Philosophy and most branches of mathematics. "Many of them will understand surveying, navigation and the calculation of the Eclipses and some of them are considerable Proficients in Comic Sections and Fluxions."

Fourth Year: Study principally metaphysics, ethics and divinity.—Clap, *Annals,* p. 81.

[31] *Ibid.*
[32] *Ibid.,* p. 83.
[33] *Ibid.*
[34] *Ibid.*
[35] *Ibid.*
[36] "A 'Syllogistic' disputation was conducted in the Latin language and with a strict adherence to the forms of the scholastic Logic, a thesis being proposed which the Respondent was to defend in mode of figure against all assailants. A 'forensic' disputation was a free debate in English."—Ford, *Notes,* I, 31.
[37] Among the Yale manuscripts is a Latin oration dated May 4, 1776, written and undoubtedly delivered by Noah Webster.—See T. A. Zunder, "Webster as a Student Orator," *Yale Alumni Weekly,* XXXVI (Nov. 19, 1926).

made every Quarter-Day, upon Examinations, and frequently on special Occasions.[38]

In these exercises Webster took an active part. In Ezra Stiles's diary we find this entry for July 14, 1778:

The Seniors disputed forensically this day in twofold Question, "Whether the Destruction of the Alexandrine Library, and the Ignorance of the Middle Ages caused by the Inund[a] of the Goths and Vandals, were Events unfortunate to Literature?" They disputed inimitably well; particularly Barlow, Swift, Webster, Gilbert, Meigs, Sage &C.[39]

The fact that President Stiles did not choose Webster as one of the five seniors who in his opinion would speak well at the public exercises in the afternoon following the examinations seems to indicate that Webster was not an especially effective speaker, a charge that was made later when he gave his lectures in Philadelphia.[40] An entry in Stiles's diary for July 23 records, however, that "Sir Webster" gave a Cliosophic Oration [41] at the exercises, the title being *A Short View of the Origin and Progress of the Science of Natural Philosophy, with Some Observations on the Advantages of Science in General.*[42]

Among the influences that helped to shape the character of Webster during the formative years, the association with members of his class at Yale was perhaps not the least. This class, says Zunder, was one of the most capable to be graduated from that institution before the Civil War.[43] Among the forty members, in addition to Noachus Webster, were Joel Barlow, Zephaniah Swift, Oliver Wolcott, Josiah Meigs, Uriah Tracy, Frederick William Hotchkiss, and others who later distinguished themselves in high places of trust. Then, too, President Ezra Stiles and the tutors Joseph Buckminster and Timothy Dwight exercised an influence which was lasting and far-reaching.

[38] Clap, *op. cit.*, p. 82.
[39] *Literary Diary of Ezra Stiles* (1901), II, 284.
[40] See p. 17.
[41] Stiles, *Diary*, II, 288.
[42] *New York Magazine*, I (June, July, 1790), 338–40, 383–84.
[43] T. A. Zunder, *The Early Days of Joel Barlow* (1934), p. 27.

Before 1874, when Yale established the requirements of at least one year of graduate study for the Master's degree, American colleges followed the custom of the English in granting the degree of Master of Arts "in course" to almost anybody who was willing to pay for it three years after graduating.[44] At the Yale commencement, September, 1781, the first to be held in seven years because of the state of the country, Webster took a part in the exercises and was given the degree of Master of Arts. His thesis was a "Dissertation in English on the universal diffusion of literature as introductory to the universal diffusion of Christianity." [45]

The foregoing pages relate practically all that is known of Webster's education—of the equipment with which he entered his many-sided career. Because of limited library and instructional facilities, his education was of course limited in scope. Certainly students of Webster's day "were not *over* educated ... Men were not educated *beyond* their moral service, and there were few literary prigs to the front. Patriotic, professional or religious ardor influenced the souls of the leaders of thought and action." [46]

In 1765, Yale's library consisted of about

four thousand volumes, well furnished with ancient authors, such as the Fathers, Historians, and Classics; many modern valuable books of divinity, history, philosophy, and mathematics; but not many authors who have wrote within these thirty years.

We have a good Air-Pump, set of Globes, Telescope, and small Astronomical Quadrant, Microscope, Thermometer, Theodolite, and an Electrical Machine; but no other apparatus of any consequence.[47]

During the first three years of Webster's college career, the faculty consisted of two professors and five tutors. Naphtali Daggett was professor of divinity and president *pro tempore* and Nehemiah Strong was professor of mathematics. Joseph Buck-

[44] Slosson, "The American Spirit in Education," *The Chronicles of America*, XXXIII (1921), 204. Copyright Yale University Press.
[45] Ford, *Notes*, I, 41.
[46] Ford, *Notes*, I, 37.
[47] Clap's *Annals* (1766), p. 86.

minster, "tongues and logic," was the tutor of Webster's class. During the senior years, the class was instructed by the newly-inducted president, Ezra Stiles.[48]

Such Personal Traits as Seriousness, Industry, Perseverance, and Aggressiveness Help to Explain Webster's Achievements

ASIDE from the inherited patriotic and Puritan traditions, there were certain personal characteristics which were strengthened by the privations of rugged pioneer existence. These set Webster apart from the rank and file of his contemporaries. Among his outstanding characteristics were seriousness and sincerity, industry, perseverance, and aggressiveness, together with an almost uncanny ability to appraise the present, to look ahead and anticipate the needs of future generations. These, combined with the courage to break with the past and to advocate a change from the established order, or, as in many cases, to become a ceaseless worker for a cause in which he believed, are the qualities that account for much of his achievement.

During Webster's youth, life was difficult. The rigors of pioneer days were not brightened by the Puritan outlook. As was later shown in the frontispiece to the "Old Blue-Back Spelling Book," the ambitious lad of Webster's day had to surmount the great rocks of difficulty which lay between him and fame. The attitude toward this life was serious and austere. Because of this moral earnestness, the test of right and wrong was applied in the solution of most problems. Sharing as he did in the belief, generally accepted in Europe as in the new world, that a millennium was at hand in America, that the new nation was set apart as a land where great things were to happen,[49] was it not his duty, his Puritan conscience told him, if he had in mind a plan to "new model" the government,[50] a plan to reform the language in such a way that children and foreigners could learn it with ease,[51] or

[48] T. A. Zunder, *The Early Days of Joel Barlow* (1934), p. 26.
[49] See p. 182.
[50] See p. 24.
[51] See chap. viii.

a plan to revise the Bible, purifying the language to render it inoffensive to those of the most tender sensibilities,[52] was it not his moral duty to the new republic to put these plans into operation?

His persistence and singleness of purpose usually did not permit him to waver after he had decided on a course of action, yet he was amenable to reason and did frequently change his mind. In modern parlance, he was thick-skinned and tough-minded. Although he winced at times at the flails of the critics, he seldom deviated from his charted course merely because of their criticism.

Webster's great output of school texts, pamphlets, and treatises on many subjects, often written while he was engaged in editing a magazine or a newspaper or while compiling a dictionary, can be explained only by his Herculean industry. He would be up half an hour before sunrise, in order to use all the natural light the day afforded. "How do you get thro' the cleaning all the Augean stables in the manner you do?" wrote his brother-in-law, Thomas Dawes, in regard to the *Minerva,* which Webster edited; "translating, transcribing, composing (tho' the last I know you can do when asleep) correcting other peoples' blunders, answering other peoples' absurdities, in short finding brains for people who, when they've got them don't know what to do with them? Mercy on me (or rather on *you*) how do you produce so many columns in a week, and so good ones? I don't believe you have kissed Beccy these six months." [53]

Webster's tendency to push himself forward, as his enemies would have it, is well illustrated by an incident which marks his introduction to Revolutionary society. While he was a freshman at Yale, in June, 1775, Washington and Lee passed through New Haven on their way to Charlestown. They reviewed the military company of the college and Lee "cried out with astonishment at their promptness." That company of Yale students, Webster reported, "had the honour of first escorting Gen. Washington,

[52] See pp. 243 ff.
[53] Webster MSS. Letter dated "Boston, 9th February, '95."—Ford, *Notes,* I, 396.

after his appointment to the American army. . . . It fell to my humble lot to lead this company with music." [54]

"This last sentence is a faint hint," says Scudder, perhaps a little unfairly, "at an amusing and pardonable vanity of Webster's, who . . . liked to think that he had a hand in pretty much every important measure in the political and literary history of the country in those early days, and remembered that when the great Washington appeared, Webster was ready with the prelusive fife." [55] To say merely that Webster "liked to think" that he had a hand in affairs shows a failure to consider the facts in the case. He did have a part in most of the happenings of his day. He did not merely lead the procession with his fife or carry a banner or wave a flag; frequently he was found battling in the front ranks. It was this forwardness, this aggressiveness, this rather angry championship of a cause in which he believed that frequently brought upon him criticism and dislike and at times meant the defeat of the cause for which he labored. He was, says Scudder, a "busy-body" (in the original sense of the word). "He rushed eagerly into pamphlet-writing both because he had something to say, and because he never stepped back to see if anyone else was about to say it." [56]

That "Institute Webster," as he was sometimes called,[57] was frequently criticized during his day for his petulance, by both friends and enemies, there is ample proof. In *Cuttgrisingwoldes*,[58] a sketch by William Dunlap, satirizing the members of the Philological Society, which Webster and some lesser lights had organized in 1788 [59] while he was publishing the *American*

[54] Ford, *Notes*, pp. 18 ff.
[55] Scudder, *op. cit.*, p. 6.
[56] *Ibid.*, pp. 114 ff.
[57] See, for example, letter written to "Institute Webster" by "Uncus" (William Blakely?), April 5, 1789.—Webster MSS.
[58] Dunlap's *Diary* (1930), I, 17.
[59] See entries in Diary for 1788. The identity of the members is more or less a matter of conjecture. In addition to Webster, Dunlap, and Joseph Ogden Hoffman, other members were, it is thought, Martin Hoffman, Edward Livingston, Leonard M. Cutting, and Dr. S. L. Mitchill.—See Dunlap's *Diary*, I, xvi ff., and Allan Walker Read's "The Philological Society of New York, 1788," *American Speech*, April, 1934, p. 131. See also p. 77 of this study.

Magazine in New York, Mars, one of the characters, says of Cobweb (Webster):

> What a curst boring fellow now that is,
> You may read Pedant in his very phiz.
> By Mars I swear and by the major-ship
> His very looks give gentlemen the hip.

In regard to this society and Webster's *American Magazine,* Ebenezer Hazard and Jeremy Belknap, two of the most critical intelligentsia of the day,[60] referred to him as "No-ur Webstur eskqier junier critick" and "coxcomb general of the United States," also as the "Monarch" and a "literary puppy," who "does not want understanding, and yet there is a mixture of self-sufficiency, all-sufficiency, and at the same time a degree of insufficiency about him." [61] Timothy Pickering, one of Webster's close friends, found him intolerably affected when reading his lectures in Philadelphia, and reminded him that "diffidence in a public lecturer, especially in a young man, was essential to the art of pleasing." [62] His former tutor, undoubtedly remembering the crudity and positiveness of Webster's youth, advised him not to be too forward in applying to persons with whom he had a slight acquaintance for a knowledge of the "genius, manners and police [policy?]" of his fellow citizens, which knowledge Webster had taken for his province, and not to be too frank with comparative strangers. "Such is the perverseness of human nature they will be disposed to ridicule you and perhaps set you down among those who have too high an opinion of their importance." [63] Another charge made was that Webster carried the dictatorial attitude of a schoolmaster into whatever he did. " 'Tho I view

[60] Belknap (1744–98) was educated at Harvard and later had a church in Federal Street, Boston. He is recognized as the father of the Massachusetts Historical Society. Hazard (1744–1817) was educated at Princeton. He was postmaster general (1782–89).

[61] "The Belknap Papers," *Massachusetts Historical Society Collections,* 1877, Series 5, III, 23.

[62] Ford, *Notes,* I, 102. Letter from Pickering to John Gardner, dated "Philadelphia, July 4, 1786."

[63] Letter from Buckminster to Webster, dated "Portsmouth, October 30, 1779."—Webster MSS; Ford, *Notes,* I, 33.

Webster as a mere pedagogue of very limited understanding and very strong prejudices and party passions," Jefferson wrote Madison, August 12, 1801, "yet as an editor of a paper and of the New Haven association, he may be worth striking." [64]

In discussing Webster's contribution to epidemiology, Dr. Warthin gives a more generous estimate of him.

Undoubtedly his youthful and vigorous enthusiasm exhibited along so many lines of mental activity made him appear conceited. That was inevitable and so he appeared to some of his less gifted contemporaries. One does not, however, get such an impression of the man from his own writings.[65]

Commenting on Webster's critics, Winslow says that

his later life, however, fully justified his youthful confidence and he moved easily in a larger world than that of the New England litterateurs. A friend of Franklin and Washington and Dickerson, dining and taking tea in Boston with Governor Bowdoin and Adams, in New York with Colonel Burr, his projects ardently supported by John Jay, he was truly a national figure.[66]

Posterity Has Sustained Webster's Opinions in Regard to Many of the Reforms He Advocated

IT WAS in the field of reform that Webster played the rôle of prompter most persistently. When one considers the reforms he advocated and worked to bring about, reforms having to do with copyright laws, slavery,[67] the English language, government,[68] and education, it is surprising to note in how many cases posterity has sustained his opinions. His greatest contribution to reform was probably his service in securing the passing of copyright laws. Before he published Part I of *A Grammatical Institute,* he was confronted with the necessity of procuring protection for his

[64] Paul Leicester Ford, *The Writings of Thomas Jefferson* (1897), VIII, 80.
[65] Aldred Scott Warthin, *Noah Webster As Epidemiologist* (1923), p. 18.
[66] C. E. M. Winslow, "The Epidemiology of Noah Webster," *Transactions of the Connecticut Academy of Arts and Sciences,* XXXII (January, 1934), 35.
[67] See *Effects of Slavery, on Morals and Industry* (1793).
[68] In addition to writing treatises on government, Webster served three terms as a member of the Massachusetts General Court and nine sessions as a member of the General Assembly of Connecticut.—Winslow, *op. cit.,* p. 32.

literary property. The states were to a very great extent independent of one another; none of them had made provisions for
the protection of literary products. In the autumn of 1782, Webster rode to Philadelphia for the purpose of showing his manuscripts to men of influence, and obtaining a law for securing to
authors the copyright of their publications.[69]

During the next five years he traveled to the capitals of various
states in behalf of copyright laws, usually arriving when
legislatures were in session, carrying letters of introduction to
governors and other influential men. Webster's home state,
Connecticut, led with the enactment of a copyright law in January, 1783. In March of the same year Massachusetts passed a
similar law, the acts in both states giving copyright for a term of
fourteen years with the right of a fourteen-year renewal if the
authors were living at the expiration of the first term. This action
was the result of a vigorous crusade by Noah Webster.[70] Webster's friend, Joel Barlow, and other interested men, presented
a memorial to Congress, petitioning that body to recommend to
the several states that copyright laws be enacted. Congress made
such a recommendation in a resolution passed in May, 1783.[71]
By May, 1786, ten more states had passed copyright acts for terms
of varying lengths, the acts being in principle and form similar to
the English Statute of 1710, called the Act of Queen Anne.[72] In
1790, Congress of the United States, influenced in large part by
the arguments of Webster [73] and other literary workers, passed
the first national copyright statute, which gave to authors who
were citizens or residents, and to their heirs and assigns copyright
protection for a term of fourteen years with the right to renewal

[69] Webster, "Origin of the Copy-right Laws in the United States," *Collection of Papers on Political, Literary, and Moral Subjects* (1843), pp. 173–78.
[70] *Encyclopedia Britannica* (14 ed., 1929), VI, 418.
[71] *Collection of Papers* (1843), p. 174.
[72] *Encyclopedia Britannica*, VI, 418.
[73] Webster's argument in the *American Magazine*, February, 1788, is typical:
"A man who has devoted the most valuable period of his life to the acquisition of
knowledge; who has grown 'pale o'er the midnight lamp;' who labors to decypher
ancient manuscripts, or purchases copies at three thousand per cent above the
usual price of books, is indubitably entitled to the exclusive advantage resulting
from his exertion and expenses."

for fourteen years more at the expiration of that time. But Webster continued to advocate better copyright laws [74] and it was largely through his efforts that the 1831 law was passed, extending the term to twenty-eight years, with the privilege of renewal for fourteen years to the author, his widow, or his children.

It is interesting to note [says Scudder],[75] that the earliest action by the States and Congress received its impulse from Webster's spelling book; the later and final form of the law was adopted in connection with Mr. Webster's indefatigable efforts, and the first book to take advantage of it was his "American Dictionary." [76]

Webster Pioneered in Many Fields on the American Intellectual Frontier

NOAH WEBSTER, like most of the members of the Yale graduating class of 1778, did not plan to enter the ministry, a profession which was pursued by most college graduates before 1750.[77] Yale graduates of his day were beginning to take up the professions of law and medicine.[78] He looked forward to a career as a lawyer, but finding it necessary to support himself, he turned to teaching. Boarding in the home of Oliver Ellsworth (later Chief Justice of the United States) while he taught in Hartford in 1779, he "picked up a little law." In the summer of 1780 he assisted

[74] See Webster's correspondence with Daniel Webster, a distant relative, in behalf of new copyright laws, 1826 and 1827. Webster MSS; Ford Notes, II, 297–301. Also Webster's letters to his wife, Rebecca Greenleaf Webster, 1830–31, from Washington, where he had gone to work for a new copyright law. Webster MSS; Ford, Notes, II, 319–26.

[75] Scudder, Noah Webster (1882), p. 67. Houghton Mifflin Company.

[76] "In my journeys to effect this object [passage of copyright laws], and in my long attendance in Washington, I expended nearly a year of time. Of my expenses in money I have no account; but it is a satisfaction to me that a liberal statute for securing to authors the fruits of their labor has been obtained."—Noah Webster, "Origin of the Copyright Laws of the United States," A Collection of Papers on Political, Literary and Moral Subjects (1843), p. 178.

[77] Scudder, Noah Webster (1882), p. 17.

[78] "An examination of the Yale catalogue shows that with some fluctuations, the proportion of clerical alumni to the whole number of graduates fell off pretty surely during the middle of the century. In the decades marked by Webster's graduation, the proportion was roughly as follows: in 1748, nearly one-half the class entered the ministry; in 1758, nearly one-third; in 1768, one-fourth; in 1778, one-tenth."—Ibid., p. 17.

Jedediah Strong, register of deeds in Litchfield, Connecticut.
During the following winter he continued his residence at Litchfield and at Salisbury, using his leisure time for the study of law
under the advice of the Honorable Titus Hosmer of Middletown. In the spring, Webster and twenty other young men
presented themselves at Litchfield on the same evening to be
examined for admission to the bar. To the surprise of the appli-
cants, the examiners refused to recommend any of the candidates.
With his usual persistence and resourcefulness, Webster immediately returned to Hartford, where he and Chauncey Goodrich
were examined in April and were admitted to practice. However, as people were "too poor to go to law," he went back to
teaching in the fall of 1781, this time at Sharon, Connecticut,
where he continued his law studies in the office of the Honorable
John Canfield.[79] After his marriage to Rebecca Brown Greenleaf
in 1789, he settled at Hartford, where he built up a lucrative
practice. Through the influence of his friend Timothy Pickering, then Postmaster General of the United States, he was made
prosecutor for mail robbery cases, and he defended the Connecticut land claims against Pennsylvania.[80]

Not least among his talents was a flair for journalism. From
December, 1787, to November, 1788, he published *The American Magazine,* Containing a Miscellaneous Collection of Valuable Essays in prose and verse, and Calculated both for Instruction and Amusement, with the motto, "Science the Guide, and
truth the eternal goal." The interests of America were represented by patriotic poems from Dwight, Barlow, and Trumbull.
Even Webster contributed verse, but the muses were apparently
wooed in vain. The first stanza of a six-stanza poem, which
appeared in the January number, 1788, under the title "On the
New Year," indicates his stature as a poet.[81] It is evident, as he

[79] Ford, *Notes,* I, 39–45.
[80] See Webster and Pickering Correspondence, Webster MSS; Ford, *Notes,* I, 269,
317–24.
[81] The author of this poem was not indicated. However, in Webster's personal
copy of the *American Magazine* (N.Y.P.L.), this poem is autographed by Webster.
Other poems are marked with a sign frequently used by Webster, indicating that
they also were probably written by him.

once said of the efforts of a contributor, that the lines had not "descended from Jove."

> The circling Sun, bright Monarch of the day,
> Who rules the changes of this rolling sphere
> With the mild influence of his favoring ray,
> From shades of night calls forth the opening year.

Although Webster was meeting success in his law practice at Hartford, in 1793 he sold his law library and moved to New York. At this time the French minister Genêt was organizing a party in America to make a common cause with France in the Revolution. Washington's administration was being assailed by the *Aurora, National Gazette,* and other organs of what became the Republican Party, and by the partisans of France. The administration was supported by Hamilton, but was increasingly embarrassed by Jefferson. Newspapers were established by both parties in an effort to carry out their policies. Noah Webster was considered the man best fitted to aid the Federalists and he was requested to establish a newspaper in New York, in order to oppose the designs of Genêt and maintain neutrality.[82] On December 9, 1793, the first number of Webster's daily, *The American Minerva,* appeared, "Patroness of Peace, Commerce and the Liberal Arts." It was to be the "Friend of Government, of Freedom, of Virtue and every Species of Improvement." In connection with the publication of the *Minerva,* the resourceful Webster introduced an ingenious device, common enough since his day, by publishing a semi-weekly made up from the columns of the daily without recomposition of the type. This semi-weekly was called the *Herald.*[83] Webster retired from active editorship in 1798.[84] During the first years as editor of the *Minerva,* he

[82] For a summary of the political situation in the 90's and the part the newspapers played, see Frederic Hudson, *Journalism in the United States* (1873), pp. 191–92.

[83] In October, 1797, the names of the *Minerva* and the *Herald* were changed to *The Commercial Advertiser* and *The New York Spectator* respectively.

[84] Letter from Webster to Rufus King, dated "New Haven, Nov. 1, 1798," Ford's *Notes,* I, 454. In 1803, Webster retired in favor of Zachariah Lewis. Hudson, *Journalism in the United States* (1873), p. 192.

labored incessantly, writing editorials and political essays, supplying general or commercial intelligence, translating from
French papers, and writing to foreign correspondents, among
them the German orientalist and historian, Daniel Ebeling,[85]
regarding European politics. Twice he sank under exhaustion.

In reply to complaints from some of his readers, he later had
this to say:

I have defended the administration of the national government, because I believe it to have been incorrupt and advocated the Constitution because if not perfect, it is probably the best we can obtain,
and because experience teaches us, it has secured to us important
rights and great public prosperity . . . I have cautioned my fellow-
citizens against all foreign intrigues, because I am aware of the fatal
dissensions they would introduce into our councils, and because I
hold it proper for us to attach ourselves to no foreign nation whatever, and be in truth and spirit *Americans*.[86]

Hand-in-hand with Webster's editorship went his career as
pamphleteer. The pamphlet, which was a forerunner of the
modern editorial,[87] made up the greater part of the ephemeral
literature which flourished during the first years of the Republic.[88] In respect to his literary output, the variety of his interests,
and his anonymity, Webster resembles the prolific Daniel Defoe.
Webster was, of course, more sincere and more naïve than his
astute predecessor, but he did not possess the literary skill of the

[85] Webster MSS; Ford, *Notes*, I, 399.

[86] Hudson, *op. cit.*, p. 192.

In 1801 Webster sent out a circular letter in the form of a questionnaire to
newspaper offices, requesting information which he planned to use in writing a
history of American newspapers. Only a few editors replied (see Webster MSS).
There is no record to indicate that Webster put this material to use. He probably
gave it to Rev. Samuel Miller to use in his *Brief Retrospect of the Eighteenth
Century* (1803). See Allan Walker Read, "Noah Webster's Project in 1801 for a
History of American Newspapers," *Journalism Quarterly*, XI (Sept., 1934), 258.

[87] Allan Nevins, *American Press Opinion* (1928), p. 4.

[88] "It is in the orations and pamphlets and state papers inspired by the Revolutionary agitation that we find the most satisfactory expression of the thought and
feeling of that generation. Its typical literature is civic rather than aesthetic, a
sort of writing which has been incidental to the accomplishing of some political,
social, or moral purpose, and which scarcely regards itself as literature at
all."—Bliss Perry, "The American Spirit in Literature," *The Chronicles of America*, XXXIV (1918), 72. Copyright Yale University Press.

latter. Some of his articles appeared first in newspapers, such as
the *Curtius* papers,[89] which were written in defense of Jay's
treaty with England and whose authorship was ascribed by the
wary Jefferson to Hamilton.[90] In the writing of political articles,
Webster had had much experience. Beginning as early as 1780,
he contributed such articles to the *Connecticut Courant*.[91]

His first pamphlet of note was *Sketches of American Policy*
(1785), in which he proposed that a constitution should take the
place of the Articles of Confederation under which the war had
been carried on. This proposal he carried to Mt. Vernon and
showed to Washington; Madison saw it later. In 1804, Webster
corresponded with Madison regarding the originality of the
plan Webster proposed. Webster took the stand that his was
the first proposal and that it was his *Sketches* that led to the
Annapolis Conference (1786), which in turn led to the Philadelphia Convention (1787). Madison, on the other hand, regarded Webster's proposal as an expression of thought that was
commonly held.[92]

While Webster was a schoolmaster in Philadelphia in 1787,
the Constitutional Convention met in that city. After the work
of the convention had been completed, Webster published
anonymously *An Examination into the Leading Principles of
the Federal Constitution Proposed by the Late Convention Held
at Philadelphia. With Answers to the Principal Objections That
Have Been Raised against the System*. This is perhaps the most
magniloquent of all Webster's writings. It "shows rather zeal

[89] Published in the *Minerva*, 1795. There were twelve numbers. Numbers six
and seven were written by James Kent. These were widely copied in the journals
of the day. Webster later published them in pamphlet form. See *Vindication of the
Treaty of Amity . . .* (1795).

[90] Jefferson's letter to Madison, dated "Monticello, Sept. 20, 1795."—Ford, *Notes*,
I, 394.

[91] His first contributions were remarks on Benedict Arnold. For the next four
or five years following 1780 he was an occasional contributor upon subjects of
finance, banking, the pay of soldiers, congressional action, events of the war, and
copyright.—Scudder, *op. cit.*, p. 112.

[92] For Webster's correspondence with Madison on this subject, see *Old South
Leaflets*, VIII, No. 197, 19 ff.

On the flyleaf of Webster's personal copy of the *Sketches*, the claim that his
was the first proposed to "new model" the government is set forth in his own hand.

and fervor than acuteness, and seems to have been hastily written to serve some special and temporary purpose." [93] Other political pamphlets which did service in their day were *An Enquiry
into the Excise Laws of Connecticut* (1789), *The Revolution in
France* (1794), and *The Rights of Neutral Nations* (1802). In the
field of Economics,[94] such writing as *The History of the Present
State of Banks and Insurance Companies in the United States,*
1802, and *A Letter to the Secretary of the Treasury on the Commerce and Currency of the United States* (by Aristides),[95] 1819,
were of importance to his age. It was, however, in the field of
language reform, a subject to be considered later, where Webster
was most prolific as a pamphleteer.

Webster also indulged in those other forms of transient literature for which his age was noted, speechmaking and oratory. As
an orator, he of course never reached the heights or acclaim of
such men as Otis or Henry, but characteristically he entered the
lists in this field of endeavor. Excepting the lectures he gave in
the 80's on language reform, most of his speechmaking was done
in the nineteenth century, after the intense patriotic fervor
which immediately followed the Revolution had subsided. He
seems to have been given to occasional addresses [96] rather than
to outpourings prompted by spontaneous feelings incidental to
the accomplishment of some great purpose. In comparison to
his pamphlets, his addresses are noticeably lacking in vigor and
vitality.

As shown in his diary and his correspondence, it is evident
that Webster had a keen practical interest in the life about him.
He was much interested in fruits and vegetables and whenever
possible he lived in premises where he could have a garden and
orchard. Space forbids a lengthy consideration of the idyllic life

[93] Scudder, *op. cit.*, p. 129.
[94] According to W. H. H. Lecky, Noah Webster was one of the best of the early
economists of America. *History of England in the Eighteenth Century* (1892–93),
III, 311.
[95] The authorship of this pamphlet is a matter for dispute. Those who ascribe
it to Webster base their claims largely on the fact that Webster signed a letter to
General Hamilton "Aristides," in 1800.
[96] See Bibliography for titles of Webster's addresses and orations.

he lived with his growing family at various places. He set up
housekeeping at Hartford in 1789, moving to New York in 1793.
He lived first on Queen's Street and later "in the country at
Corlaer's Hook," where he had a garden (imagine a garden at
Corlear's Hook today!). Moving to New Haven in 1798, he re-
sided in the Benedict Arnold house, where he enjoyed working
in the garden and orchard on the sound.[97] Taking his family to
Amherst in 1812, he bought land, made a fine garden and planted
an orchard. He returned to New Haven in 1822, where he lived
the remainder of his life. The nutritional value he attached to
fruits and vegetables is more in keeping with present-day beliefs
than with those of his day, when meats occupied the most important place among articles of food.[98] He was also interested in
such practical subjects as brick making[99] and decomposition of
white lead paint.[100]

Webster took delight in figures and statistics. It is said that
the collecting of data interested him, even when there was no
apparent purpose to which it could be put.[101] "There must have
been in his constitution an inordinate love of detail, intensified,
perhaps, by much contemplation of those battalions of words
which make his spelling-book pages look like spiritual armies
marching against ignorance."[102] When traveling in behalf of the
copyright law, he not only observed and took notes on the state
of the language; he also counted the houses,[103] examined town
lists of votes, consulted records of births and deaths,[104] and noted

[97] Here, Webster's daughter reported, Webster would often return from the
orchard bringing a great basket of fresh apples or plums, saying, "Now children,
eat your peck of fruit today."—Ford's *Notes*, I, 451.

[98] For a summary of accounts given by foreigners relative to the extent meats
were eaten in America during the first half of the nineteenth century, see
Catherine MacKenzie's "Our Food Habits Changed by Time," *New York Times
Magazine*, February 24, 1935, p. 14.

[99] See Webster's correspondence with Timothy Pickering, 1792. Webster MSS;
Ford, *Notes*, I, 312.

[100] See Webster's "Decomposition of White Lead Paint," *Memoirs of the Connecticut Academy of Arts and Sciences*, I, Pt. I, No. 111, 1810, 135–36.

[101] Wagenknecht, "The Man behind the Dictionary," *Virginia Quarterly Review*,
April, 1929, p. 248.

[102] Scudder, *op. cit.*, p. 162.

[103] See diary. Also *Description of New York* (1786).

[104] See, for example, *Number of Deaths in the Episcopal Church in New York*,

weather conditions,[105] thus anticipating in a way the census and weather bureaus, and other appurtenances of modern life.

Webster's acumen in the direction of scientific research is best illustrated by his interest and work in the field of epidemiology. Although he had had practically no scientific training, "he had a wonderful natural power of clinical observation and a facility of description that would have taken him a long way had he elected to become a physician rather than a writer of dictionaries." [106]

During a period of years, 1793-96, the country suffered from epidemics of yellow fever in such cities as Philadelphia, New York, New Haven, and Baltimore. The epidemic was found as far south as Norfolk and Charleston and as far north as Newburyport, Massachusetts. The physicians of the country were divided into two hostile camps: those headed by Dr. William Currie, of Philadelphia, who believed the disease to be imported and contagious; and those who, like Dr. Richard Rush, also of Philadelphia, believed it was of local origin, depending on a local or general atmospheric state.[107]

Webster cast his lot with those of the second group, believing as he did that a close relationship existed between epidemics and natural phenomena. His diary shows that he became more than ever cognizant of meteorological conditions. Take, for example, the month of October, 1793:

4. Rain. Circuit Court rise.
5. Cool. Vines first killed by frost.
6. Sunday. Pleasant. Cool.

---

in Each Month for Ten Years from January 1, 1786 to Dec. 31, 1795. Taken from Sexton's Books . . . (1810). Webster read this and other treatises before the Connecticut Academy of Arts and Sciences, of which he was a member.

[105] See Dissertation on the Supposed Change in the Temperature of Winter (1810) and Experiments Respecting Dew, Intended to Ascertain Whether Dew Is the Descent of Vapour . . . or . . . the Effect of Condensation (1809). In this experiment Webster anticipated the conclusions of Dr. William Wells, 1814. When C. F. Volney, a distinguished French scientist, sent a circular letter to the Herald in 1796, asking for facts in regard to winds, Webster sent his observations on the subject for a score of years in the several states in which he had lived.—Ford, Notes, I, 406.

[106] Dr. Aldred Scott Warthin, Noah Webster as Epidemiologist (1923), p. 17.

[107] Ibid., pp. 20-24.

7. d°. No favorable news from Philad[a] as to the fever, it still rages.
8. City Court. Pleasant.
9. Pleasant. Very warm.
10. Very warm like June.
11. do. fever in Phila[d] carries off 159 in a day.
12. Cloudy.

. . .

15. Wind changes, cool.
16. My birthday, completing 35 years, half the life of man. Very cold.
17. Cold; disorder in Philad: abates.

. . .

19. Cloudy. M[r] Strong's mother dies; a Shower & thunder this evening.

. . .

21–22. Warmer.

. . .

24. Pleasant.

. . .

29. Snow.

In his search for the facts, Webster, "America's first professional scholar," used a technique worthy of a later age when the scientific method was more generally employed. In the Advertisement to his *Collection of Papers on Bilious Fever,* he says,

as *facts* are the basis of human knowledge, it is of great importance to collect them. There are probably in every profession, facts enough which occur *every year,* in an extensive country, to constitute a mass of information, if collected, equal to what a long life of experience would be necessary to acquire for *one man.*

He sent out a circular letter to the physicians of Philadelphia, New York, Baltimore, Norfolk, and New Haven. This was in effect an informal questionnaire. The doctors were requested to answer the questions and include any other information that might shed light on the origin, nature, and cure of the disease. Eight doctors responded. In 1796, appeared *A Collection of Papers on the Subject of Bilious Fevers, Prevalent in the United States for a Few Past Years.* In this work he published the reports received from the physicians, concluding the treatise with the remarks on cleanliness and ventilation. The next year, 1797, Webster published a series of twenty-five letters in the public press, addressed to Dr. William Currie, of Philadelphia. In 1798, after he had retired from the active editorship of the *Minerva*, he went to work on his history of epidemic diseases, a historical study of the relations existing between epidemics and natural phenomena. He consulted the libraries in New York and Philadelphia as well as the Yale and Harvard libraries, collecting all the available material bearing on the occurrence of epidemic diseases at all times and places. He also took depositions from people in all walks of life in regard to their experience with such diseases. With his usual indefatigable industry he arranged systematically and analyzed the voluminous material which accrued from these efforts. He collated these results with records of such natural phenomena as comets, meteors, eclipses, earthquakes, famines, and storms. In 1799, appeared his *History of Epidemic and Pestilential Diseases*, his chief theorem being that "the principle which gives to fevers the pestilential quality consists in the insensible properties of the atmosphere." We know today "that these early strivers for the truth were all wrong; that the intangible something in the atmosphere was a mosquito, *Stegomyia*, and the organism of yellow fever carried by it and injected into human beings bitten by it." [108]

Webster [says Winslow], was a pioneer in appreciating the importance of statistics and in planning for and indeed initiating their collection. He was perhaps the first protagonist of vital statistics in this country. Yet he had not the slightest grasp of statistical method or of its essential principle—the use of adequate controls . . . He understood, however, the vital importance of factual data.[109]

Webster's name is frequently found in the indexes of the earliest volumes of the Medical Repository, and as late as 1855 he was quoted as an authority on epidemics.[110] His history of epidemics, like its humble contemporary, the "Old Blue-Back

[108] Warthin, *op. cit.*, p. 29.
[109] C. E. M. Winslow, "The Epidemiology of Noah Webster," *Transactions of the Connecticut Academy of Arts and Sciences*, XXXII (Jan., 1934), 21–109.
[110] Warthin, *op. cit.*, p. 16.

Spelling Book," was often imitated and pirated during the nine-teenth century.[111]

Another respect in which posterity has supported Webster is his interest in old documents. In 1788 he negotiated for the pur-chase of Ebenezer Hazard's state papers, which he planned to publish in the *American Magazine,* then in its last number, which was to appear in a new form as the property of "a society of gentlemen." [112] Nothing came of the plan, however.[113] In 1790 Webster saw a copy of Winthrop's Journal in possession of Gov-ernor Trumbull. Recognizing the value of this document to future generations, he employed a secretary to make a copy of the copy and compare it with the original, which Webster never saw. Deficient as the publication was, Webster deserves credit for being able to carry the enterprise through successfully at a time when few people realized the value of such papers. So zealous was he in the undertaking that he risked his entire property and in the end lost money.

[111] Edward Bascome, in his *History of Epidemic Pestilence* (1851), carried the same method of investigation up to 1848. "Much of this work and conclusions are taken bodily from Webster, but his name is not even mentioned."—(Warthin, *op. cit.,* p. 29.)

[112] "Belknap Papers," *Massachusetts Historical Society Collections* (1877), Ser. 5, Vol. III.

[113] Hazard later published the papers. See *Historical Collections Consisting of State Papers and Other Authentic Documents* (1792–94), 2 vols.

II

THE SCHOOLMASTER OF THE REPUBLIC

It is an object of vast magnitude that systems of Education should be adapted and pursued, which may not only diffuse a knowledge of the sciences, but may implant, in the minds of the American youth, the principles of virtue and of liberty; and inspire them with just and liberal ideas of government, and with an inviolable attachment to their own country.[1]

FROM Revolutionary days until the end of the century Webster's theories concerning education and government were more or less intertwined, since it was the concern of the day that a system of education be established which would be relative to the democratic form of government that most of the leaders desired to establish. During this time he put his faith in openminded investigation and experimentation; he, like most thinkers of his day, was a foe to existing institutions, since, it was reasoned, they belong to the inertia of the past, being the creation and instrument of the monarchies of Europe, designed to exploit the masses and keep them in ignorance. Although during this time he was engaged in many pursuits in many fields, he was in close touch with the efforts that were being made to lay the foundation of American education, in that he taught school and compiled textbooks. His theories concerning the education that would meet the peculiar needs of the new democracy were in the main set forth in his *Sketches of American Policy* (1785) and his essay *On the Education of Youth in America,* which appeared first in his *American Magazine*[2] and later in his *Collection of Essays and Fugitiv Writings on Moral, Historical, Political and Literary Subjects* (1790).

From the beginning of the nineteenth century until his death in 1843 Webster became more and more conservative. It was dur-

[1] Noah Webster, "On the Education of Youth in America," *A Collection of Essays and Fugitiv Writings, on Moral, Historical, Political and Literary Subjects* (1790), p. 3.

[2] December, 1787, to May, 1788.

ing this period that he compiled his dictionaries, and his theories regarding education, in so far as they were voiced, were expressed along with his ideas concerning language reform. Near the end of his long life, however, he set forth some of his ideas on education in *A Collection of Papers on Political, Literary and Moral Subjects* (1843).

Webster Laid the Foundation for His Theories on Education in the Schoolroom

NOAH WEBSTER was like Ichabod Crane in that he was a schoolmaster from Connecticut, a state, says Irving, "which supplies the union with pioneers for the mind as for the forest, and sends forth yearly its legions of frontier woodsmen and country schoolmasters." Being graduated from Yale in 1778, Webster planned to study law, but it was at this time that his father gave him an eight-dollar bill in continental currency and told him he would have to earn his own living. Facing the facts thus thrust upon him, he retired to his room, where he spent three days planning the future and reading the *Spectator* and Johnson's *Rambler*.[3] It was then, he later wrote his brother-in-law Dawes, that he "formed a firm resolution to pursue a course of virtue through life, and to perform moral and social duties with scrupulous exactness . . ."[4]

The following winter he taught school in Glastonbury,[5] Connecticut, where he had been stationed during his junior year in college. Returning to Hartford, he took charge of a school there during the summer of 1779.[6] The following year he taught in his native parish of West Hartford, walking for three months nearly four miles a day during a memorable winter which for extremity of cold and depth of snow had not been equaled in that section

[3] E. E. F. Ford, *Notes on the Life of Noah Webster* (1912), I, 38.
[4] Letter dated "New Haven, December 20, 1808."—Webster MSS; Ford, *Notes*, II, 42.
[5] Ford's *Notes* (1912), I, 39.
[6] On a letter from his classmates, Wetmore and Meigs, dated "Middletown, August 20, 1779," is Webster's endorsement: "The summer of 1779, I taught in

SOUTH VIEW OF GOVERNOR SMITH'S HOUSE, SHARON

According to tradition Webster began to compile his spelling book in the attic of this house.

by any season on record.[7] During these early years of teaching he had been studying law, and was admitted to the bar in April, 1781, but as there was no immediate prospect of business, he went back to teaching, this time at Sharon, Connecticut.

While in Sharon, Webster conducted a singing school. Tradition has it that he fell in love with Miss Rebecca Pardee, the belle of Sharon, who attended this school. Contrary to the fact that Webster's correspondence and diary show that he was much interested in "the ladies" and was somewhat of a favorite among them,[8] he, again like Ichabod Crane, met his Brom Bones, a certain Major Patchin. The story goes that for a long time the girl was undecided which of the two suitors to accept. Becoming impatient of her vacillation, the elders and deacons of the church took the matter up and solemnly decided that she ought to accept the first claimant, who was away fighting for his country. According to tradition, she dutifully abided by this decision and Webster closed the singing school and not long after left the community.[9]

From Sharon Webster went to Goshen, New York, where he kept a classical school [10] and compiled, or perhaps finished compiling, his speller and grammar. He returned to Hartford in 1783, where he published the speller, *Part I of the Grammatical Institute*. On December 30 of that year and again the following week Webster advertised in the *Connecticut Courant* his plan to

the brick school house in Hartford, and boarded at Mr. Ellsworth's, N. W."—Webster MSS.

[7] Reminiscences of Webster's daughter, Mrs. Jones.—Ford, *Notes*, I, 40.

[8] See letter to Webster from Zephaniah Swift, dated "New Haven, December 13, 1776."—Webster MSS; Ford, *Notes*, I, 23. This letter is a good example of the epistolary style in which many of the letters of the day were written.

[9] Joel Benton, "An Unpublished Chapter in the Life of Webster," *Magazine of American History*, X (1883), 52.

[10] "In the year 1782, while the American army was lying on the bank of the Hudson, I kept a classical school in Goshen, Orange County, New York."—N. Webster, *A Collection of Papers* . . . (1843), p. 173.

On a letter written by John Smith to Webster at Sharon, dated "New Haven, January 31, 1782," this endorsement appears in Webster's hand: "In 1781, I kept school at Sharon. I left it for the South in May, 1782. I went to Goshen, Orange Co. N. York."—Webster MSS.

open a "Rhetorical School" in Hartford. Apparently nothing came of the plan.[11]

In December, 1786, Webster went to Philadelphia to consult with Benjamin Franklin concerning a proposed scheme for a new alphabet. In April, 1787, he accepted the position of instructor, first in mathematics and later in English in the Episcopal Academy in that city, in which post he remained six months. While in this position, Webster was attacked in the newspaper by "Seth," a foreigner, who had previously been a teacher in the academy and who bore a grudge against the principal.[12] In Webster's spirited answer he defends the American cause with his customary championship, saying that he "was bred in a part of America, where no men but of the best character and education are permitted to take schools . . . America has not arrived at that pitch of refined taste which places the first business in society in the worst hands, and directs that drunkards and clowns should form the minds of youth for good citizens and legislators." Undoubtedly Webster himself was a living example of this high type of teacher. But if we are to believe other records, some of them Webster's own accounts, he was an exception to the rule. Undoubtedly he did something toward putting the profession on a higher plane.[13]

Webster's defense of the American schoolmaster shows his reluctance to wash America's dirty linen in the presence of a foreigner. Then, too, he was living up to one trait of the popularly conceived American character, a conception which was reflected in the literature of the day and of which Colonel Manly in *The Contrast* is the prototype.

There is a laudable partiality [says Colonel Manly], which ignorant, untravelled men entertain for everything that belongs to their native land . . . I love my country; it has its foibles undoubtedly; some

---

[11] Ford, *Notes*, I, 64. R. L. Lyman says, however, that the school opened.—*English Grammar in American Schools before 1850* (1922), p. 77.

[12] Ford, *Notes*, I, 119 ff.

[13] An entry in Webster's diary for April 30, 1787, sheds light on the kind of masters that were employed in this school: "Busy enough with the Boys of the Academy, they have been managed, or rather not managed, by poor low Irish

foreigners will with pleasure remark them—but such remarks fall very ungratefully from the lips of her children.[14]

Webster was, of course, aware that the usual American schoolmaster was a very low character.

Many of our inferior schools . . . [he wrote in 1788], are kept by men of no breeding, and many of them, by men infamous for the most delectable vices. . . . Many of the instructors of youth . . . are often found to sleep away, in school, the fumes of a debauch and to stun the ears of their pupils with frequent blasphemy.[15]

Much has been written about the floggings administered by the Ichabods of long ago. "The American boy began the practice of liberty and equality rather too early in life for the peace of mind of the old-time pedagogue . . . "[16] Admitting that the master must be in full authority and that it might be necessary to use the rod, Webster anticipated modern theories and practices by declaring that "Respect for an instructor will often supply the place of a rod of correction."[17] In one of the naïve dialogues in his first text, the speller, 1783, Webster shows the relation that should exist between master and pupil:

How do you like your master?
Exceedingly well; he is an agreeable man.
Is he pleasant and good-natured?
Always so: I never saw him angry.
Is he strict in keeping orders in school?
Very strict indeed. He will not permit us to whisper or play or be idle a single moment.
Does he scold and fret and find fault at trifles?
Not in the least. If one breaks a law, he is sure to be punished. But the master, though he is very severe, never appears to be in a passion.
You esteem it a pleasure as well as an advantage to be under the care of such a man?

---

masters. 'O habit! O Education!' Of what Importance that our first examples be good, and our first impressions virtuous."

[14] Royall Tyler, *The Contrast* (1790), produced in New York in 1787.

[15] *American Magazine,* March, 1788, p. 210.

[16] E. E. Slosson, "The American Spirit in Education," *The Chronicles of America,* XXXIII (1921), 108. Copyright Yale University Press.

[17] *Essays* (1790), p. 17.

Indeed I do and so do all in the school. I hardly know which we love most, the master or our books.[18]

In 1788 Webster declared that "the principal defect in our plan of Education in America, is the want of good teachers in the academic and common schools." [19] He was an advocate of specialization. Admitting that in new settlements the practice of having the master teach many subjects is unavoidable, he asserted that in populous towns it is a better plan "to appropriate an apartment to each branch of Education, with a teacher who makes that branch his sole employment," [20] following the custom of the principal academies in America and Europe. In 1789 Elisha Tichnor urged in the *Massachusetts Magazine* that a system of country schools be established to fit young gentlemen for college and schoolkeeping. Without doubt, says Boone, these remarks by Webster and Tichnor "were the expression of a common feeling, whose development and realization belong to the present century." [21]

With his position in the Episcopal Academy in 1787, Webster's career as a teacher came to a close. At this time he was becoming well known as a writer on political questions and a compiler of textbooks. Already his speller, grammar, and reader had passed through several editions, and he was beginning to introduce other subjects into the schools. "No geography was studied," he wrote in 1840, "before the publication of Dr. Morse's small books on that subject, about the year 1786 or 1787.[22] No history was read, as far as my knowledge extends, for there was no abridged history of the United States . . . " [23] In

[18] *A Grammatical Institute*, Pt. I (1783), p. 109.
[19] *American Magazine*, March, 1788, p. 210; *Essays* (1790), p. 15.
[20] *Ibid.*, pp. 10f.
[21] Richard G. Boone, *Education in the United States; Its History from the Earliest Settlements* (1890), p. 127.
[22] Jedidiah Morse's *Geography Made Easy* was published in 1784.—Evans, 18, 615.
[23] Letter from Webster to Henry Barnard, dated "New Haven, March 10, 1840."—*American Journal of Education*, XIII (1863), 123.
The History of the United States appeared in the 1787 edition of *An American Selection* and in many successive issues of that text. See *Old South Leaflets* VIII, No. 198, p. 425. In 1789 Webster's *History of the Late War* was published anonymously in Morse's geography.

some of the early editions of the Third Part of the *Institute,* says Webster, "I introduced short notices of the geography and history of the United States and these led to more enlarged descriptions of the country." [24]

During the age in which Webster lived, especially at the beginning of his career, subjects were not clearly defined. His treatment of subjects often shows a correlation comparable to the ideals held by progressive educators today. He was aware that the geographer's task extended beyond a mere "enumeration of the latitude and longitude of a place, its boundaries, magnitude and population." [25] In his effort to excite curiosity and prompt the student to further inquiry, he interwove topographical description with historical facts.[26] It is the duty of the historian, he declared,

not merely to collect accounts of battles, the slaughter of the human race, the sacking of cities, the seizure and confiscation of shipping, and other bloody and barbarous deeds . . . [but to show] the causes of great changes in the affairs of men; the springs of those important movements, which vary the aspect of government, the features of nations, and the character of man.[27]

Webster Was More or Less Familiar with Educational Theories, Both Past and Present

WE SEE then that the beliefs Webster held with regard to education in America were at least in part based on his experience as

[24] *Ibid.*

Early in the eighteenth century his *Elements of Useful Knowledge* began to appear: Vol. I (1802) and II (1806), containing a historical and geographical account of the United States; Vol. III (1806), a historical and geographical account of the empires and states in Europe, Asia, and Africa, with their colonies, to which was added the principal islands in the Pacific and Indian Oceans; Vol. IV (1812), a history of animals, all "for the use of schools." Webster's early dictionaries, 1806 and 1807, contained short historical outlines. In 1832 Webster published the *History of the United States,* to which was prefixed a "Brief Historical Account of Our Ancestors from the Dispersion at Babel to their Migration to America and of the Conquest of South America by the Spaniards."

[25] *Elements of Useful Knowledge* (1812), III, 3.

[26] *Ibid.*

[27] "The Revolution in France" (1794), in *A Collection of Papers* . . . (1843), p. 1.

a teacher. Another force which must have had some influence on Webster is the fact that during the eighteenth century there was in both Europe and America a large body of theories concerning what philosophers, theorists, and reformers of the past had thought, as well as what those of Webster's day were thinking, concerning man and his environment.

During the seventeenth century such men as the English philosopher and statesman Francis Bacon (1561–1626),[28] the French philosopher René Descartes (1596–1650),[29] and the English philosopher John Locke (1637–1704)[30] had speculated on the nature of man and the part that environment plays in his progress. These men "had prepared the way for a critical evaluation of institutions in their relation to human progress. . . . They had raised not only the question of the nature of man but they had indicated the need of a science of human development."[31]

These ideas of the seventeenth-century philosophers, along with the attendant implications and ramifications, filtered down to the eighteenth century and influenced the thinking of the philosophers who were a part of the Intellectual Revolution which spread throughout Western Europe in that century. In England this revolution was associated with the names of Boling-

[28] Bacon's *New Atlantis* (written 1617 and published 1627) exhibited a "model of description of a college, instituted for the interpreting of nature and the producing of great and marvellous works for the benefit of man."

[29] In Descartes's *Discours de la methode* (1637), which is the history of the inner life of the author, he based his reasoning on the well-known maxim *Cogito, ergo sum,* concluding that truth can be discovered only by reason. The Cartesian philosophy was echoed in the eighteenth century when reason became enthroned. The fact that Descartes originally proposed to give his book the title "The Project of a Universal Science Which Can Elevate Our Nature to Its Highest Degree of Perfection" is significant.

[30] In Locke's *Essay Concerning Humane Understanding* (1690) he contributed his famous theory of "sensationalism." All ideas, he reasoned, take their origin from experience coming through the senses from the natural and social world and from reflection on these sensations. Man's environment determines what he thinks and does; hence the need of adjusting social institutions to further the progress of man. Locke's *Treatises on Government* (1690) and *Some Thoughts Concerning Education* (1693), especially the former, exerted a strong influence on eighteenth-century thought.

[31] Allen Oscar Hansen, *Liberalism and American Education in the Eighteenth Century* (1926), p. 4. The Macmillan Company.

broke, Hume, Gibbon, Adam Smith, Godwin, and Bentham; in Germany, with Kant, Lessing, Herder, and Goethe; in Italy, with Vico and Beccaria. But the head and center of the movement was France, where it was known as the "age of reason."[32] The most important of the French *philosophes* were Voltaire, Rousseau, Diderot, Montesquieu, Turgot, Condorcet, d'Alembert, Helvetius, von Holbach, Abbé Saint-Pierre, Abbé Raynal, and Abbé Mably.[33]

Taking as a foundation on which to build the body of theories which the eighteenth century inherited from the past, the thinkers of the century defined the doctrine of the indefinite perfectibility of man and of institutions, the dominant motif of enlightenment and of the revolutionary democratic movements in America and France, and elaborated its implications.[34] It is a law of nature, they reasoned, that man should progress. The natural law that controls his development can be discovered and the lines of his progress can be scientifically determined only through a system of education which will take the scientific, experimental attitude, a system that will discard or change the narrow, fixed, obsolete institutions of the past insofar as they hinder man in his development.[35]

The extent to which eighteenth-century thought in America was influenced by French thinkers has been a question for dispute.[36] There are those who maintain that the influence up to 1776 was essentially English, principally that of Locke.[37] It has also been maintained that between 1776 and 1789 "America influenced France so powerfully . . . that the American Revolution may safely be called a proximate cause of the French Revolution."[38] Condorcet, "who elaborated a scheme of public

---

[32] J. S. Schapiro, *Condorcet and the Rise of Liberalism* (1934), pp. 23f. Harcourt, Brace and Company.
[33] *Ibid.*, pp. 28f.
[34] Hansen, *Liberalism and American Education*, p. 20. The Macmillan Company.
[35] *Ibid.*, p. 21.
[36] See Schapiro, *Condorcet* (1934), Note 13, p. 302.
[37] Carl L. Becker, *The Declaration of Independence* (1922), p. 27.
[38] L. Rosenthal, *America and France* (1882), p. 297.

instruction (1792) which is the foundation of the present system of education in France," [39] praised America as the "inspiration of the ideas that he advocated for France." [40] He beheld in America "a figure reflected in the shining mirror of the generous principles of the eighteenth-century philosophy. . . . It was a figure drawn by Franklin, Paine, and Jefferson, who so deeply influenced the views of the French intellectuals regarding America." [41]

Be that as it may, there is undoubtedly much truth in the statement that "a definite application of French ideas may be noted as demonstrable or probable" after America formed an alliance with France in 1778. In support of this contention it is pointed out that (1) academies of arts and sciences founded in Boston (1780) and Richmond (1786) were apparently more in sympathy with the Royal Academy of France than with the Royal Society of England; (2) that the ideas embodied in the provisions for state universities in New York, Georgia, and Michigan were unknown in England and America, but were at least ideals in France; (3) that Jefferson's idea of a system of education crowned by a university shows the French influence.[42]

The question as to the source of the eighteenth-century ideas which were held in America is not of prime importance to this study. That they were here is, however, important. To what extent was Webster familiar with the thought of his day and influenced by it? Commenting on Webster's education, Scudder says that he "was not so much opposed to foreign culture as he was ignorant of it." [43] We know, however, that he studied the classic authors [44] and Locke while in Yale College,[45] and he refers to Plato, Pythagoras, Tacitus, Cicero, and Quintilian in his dis-

[39] *New International Encyclopaedia* (1923), II, 219.
[40] Schapiro, *Condorcet* (1934), p. 219. Harcourt, Brace and Company.
[41] *Ibid.*, p. 232.
[42] *Cyclopedia of Education* (1911), II, 708.
[43] *Noah Webster*, pp. 50f.
[44] See p. 10.
[45] Locke's *Essay Concerning Humane Understanding.* Zunder, *The Early Days of Joel Barlow* (1934), p. 48.
"The seniors finished 2 vol. of Locke."—*Literary Diary of Ezra Stiles*, July 22, 1778, II, 287.

cussions of government and education in the *Sketches* (1785) and
the *Essays* (1790). From these works we learn that he knew the
writings of Ascham, Rousseau,[46] Price, and Montesquieu. Then
there were certain men on the American scene whom he knew
personally, among them Benjamin Franklin,[47] George Washington,[48] Thomas Paine,[49] David Rittenhouse,[50] and Dr. Benjamin
Rush.[51] The list of names of men who subscribed to his *Essays*
(1790), most of them men with whom Webster became acquainted
while traveling from state to state in behalf of the copyright law,
reads like a roster of men of affairs during the last quarter of the
eighteenth century.

In his *Revolution in France* (1794) and in his *Ten Letters to
Dr. Joseph Priestley* (1800), he shows that he was familiar with
French history and with contemporary thought in France and
England. Among the men discussed and referred to in these
writings were Voltaire, Rousseau, Hume, Brissot, Neckar,
Raynal, Helvetius, Turgot, Perthion, Condorcet, the Duc de
Rochefoucauld, Godwin, and Adam Smith.[52] These treatises
were written after Webster, like many men of his age, began
to be disillusioned because of the excesses of the Revolution in France and the machinations of Genêt in America.
While he was an active editor of the *Minerva* (1793–98), he spent
countless hours translating from French books, pamphlets, and
newspapers, making abstracts and writing editorials for his
columns. Because of this close application to French affairs, he
of course acquired a knowledge of French thought during the
90's that he did not possess when he wrote on education and
government in the 80's.

[46] In the *American Magazine*, Jan., 1788, p. 86, and the *Essays* (1790), pp. 19,
20, 21, 22, 23, 25, 27, 30, there is evidence that Webster was familiar with *Emile*
and the *Contrat social*. Then, too, he was influenced by the writings of Richard
Price and Thomas Paine, who, says Hansen, carried Rousseau's doctrines to
America. *Op. cit.*, p. 5.
[47] See pp. 254 ff.
[48] See pp. 51 f.
[49] *Diary*, Feb. 27, 1786.
[50] *Ibid.*; see *Minerva*, July 19, 1796, for Webster's obituary of Rittenhouse.
[51] *Diary*, Feb. 21, 1786.
[52] *Letters to Priestley* (1800), pp. 10 and 21.

*Leaders of Webster's Day Proposed Many Plans for Educa-
tion in America, a Country Which Was Looked upon as
the Ideal Commonwealth about Which Men Had Dreamed*

MAN has always dreamed of an ideal existence, either in a
future life or in an ideal commonwealth. Such works as Plato's
Republic, St. Augustine's *City of God,* More's *Utopia,* Bacon's
New Atlantis, Butler's *Erewhon,* bear testimony to this craving
of the human soul. During the last quarter of the eighteenth
century, all eyes were turned to America as a place where dreams
were being realized. "Popular sentiment, elated at the triumph
of American ideas throughout the entire world and proud of its
new country, demanded a practical and democratic education
suited to the needs of the country." [53]

Noah Webster shared in this enthusiasm. Contrary to the
manner in which the constitutions of other governments had
been formed, America, he declared, had the advantage of science
and human experience and would be able to "lay a broad foundation for the perfection of human society." American legislators
are not swayed by a blind veneration for an independent clergy
nor awed by the frowns of a tyrant. The civil power is or ought
to be the collected wisdom of all nations and the religion that
of the Saviour of mankind. Nature has given America every
advantage.[54]

Hand-in-hand with this concern for a government that would
serve the needs of democracy went the interest in establishing a
system of education which would be relative to the principles of
the government. Numerous plans were proposed and published,
which, their authors thought, would fit the needs of the new
republic. No one of these plans makes a wide departure from the
thought of the others. In the main they agree on three points:
(1) the approach to education should be scientific; (2) all children should be indoctrinated with a love of and a reverence for
all things American; (3) since there is to be no aristocracy, education should be pragmatic.

[53] B. Faÿ, *The Revolutionary Spirit in France and America* (1927), p. 341.
[54] *Sketches of American Policy* (1785), p. 23.

The first of these plans to be proposed after the Revolution [55] was published by Dr. Benjamin Rush in 1786.[56] He also proposed a system of public education for Pennsylvania, somewhat similar to the one outlined by Jefferson in 1779. According to his plan, each township of a hundred families should support a free school and each county an academy. There were to be four colleges distributed throughout the state, and the whole system was to be crowned by a state university.[57] Youths, according to the theories of Rush, should be educated in America rather than in foreign countries. Here a love of country should be instilled, based on an understanding of republican principles,[58] and nationalistic culture should be attained through the study of national history.[59] In order to assist American progress, manners and institutions should be made indigenous.[60] Since the principal business in any new country is to develop its resources,[61] time should be devoted to science and human affairs rather than to Latin and Greek.[62] Women should receive education of a utilitarian character, which would prepare them to perform their peculiar duties in a democracy.[63] Education should receive national support and teachers should be well trained.[64]

Second in point of time was the plan proposed by Noah Webster, *On the Education of Youth in America.*[65] Webster's plan

[55] Among the plans for education in America that had appeared earlier were: William Penn's *Charter of ye Publick School Founded in ye Town and County of Philadelphia in Pennsylvania;* Benjamin Franklin's *Proposals Relating to the Education of Pennsylvania* (1749) and *Sketch of an English School* (1750); and Thomas Jefferson's measure introduced into the Assembly of Virginia proposing the establishment of a state school system (1779).

[56] *Thoughts upon the Mode of Education Proper in a Republic* (1786).

[57] *A Plan for Establishing Public Schools in Pennsylvania* (1786), pp. 1–4.

[58] *Thoughts upon the Mode of Education* (1786), p. 22.

[59] *Ibid.,* p. 29.

[60] *Thoughts upon Female Education* (1798), p. 87.

[61] *Essays, Observations upon the Study of Latin and Greek* (1798), p. 25.

[62] *Ibid.,* p. 43; *Thoughts on the Mode of Education,* p. 28.

[63] *Thoughts on the Mode of Education,* p. 33.

[64] *Ibid.,* p. 32.

[65] Published first in the *American Magazine* (1787–88). In 1790 it appeared in Webster's *Collection of Essays and Fugitiv Writings on Moral, Historical, Political and Literary Subjects.* Since Webster expressed his ideas on education in other writings the discussion of Webster's plan is not limited to this one essay.

has much in common with that of Rush, whom Webster had met in Philadelphia in 1786. They both embody the thought of their age.

Education is a subject which has been exhausted by the ablest writers, both among the ancients and moderns [wrote Webster]. I am not vain enough to suppose I can suggest new ideas upon so trite a theme as Education in general; but perhaps the manner of conducting the youth in America may be capable of some improvement.[66]

The following discussion includes the most salient points in his proposed plan:

THE APPROACH TO EDUCATION SHOULD BE SCIENTIFIC [67]

Writing in 1785, Webster summed up very succinctly his ideas concerning the place that science should have in American education:

It is scarcely possible to reduce an enlightened people to civil or ecclesiastical tyranny. Deprive them of knowledge, and they sink almost insensibly in vassalage. Ignorance cramps the powers of the mind, at the same time that it blinds men to all their natural rights. Knowledge enlarges the understanding, and at the same time, it gives a spring to all intellectual faculties, which direct the deliberations of the cabinet and the enterprises of the field. A general diffusion of science is our best guard against the approaches of corruption, the prevalence of religious error, the intrigue of ambition, and against the open assault of external foes.[68]

In order to put instruction on this scientific basis, Webster recommended that schools be endowed, that professors of the first rank be employed, and that complete apparatus for establishing theories by experiment be supplied. If this country "should long be indebted to Europe for the opportunities of acquiring any branch of science in perfection, it must be by

---

[66] *Essays* (1790), p. 3.

[67] The predominant thought represented in the plans proposed after the Revolution, says Hansen, stressed chiefly the development of an unbiased scientific attitude which was to be openminded to whatever contributions might be made to human progress, regardless of source.—*Liberalism* (1926), p. 45. See Rush, *Thoughts upon the Mode of Education in a Republic* (1786), p. 28.

[68] Noah Webster, *Sketches of American Policy* (1785), p. 27.

means of a criminal neglect of its inhabitants." [69] Enthusiastic as he was with regard to the teaching of sciences, he warned against the practice of putting boys into difficult sciences too early. "Years of valuable time are sometimes thrown away, in a fruitless application to sciences, the principles of which are above the comprehension of the students." [70]

Since, then, education in the new democracy was to be put on a scientific basis, what was to be the place of religion, that stern preceptor which had heretofore been the be-all and the end-all in matters educational? Religion, by which he meant "superstition or human systems of absurdity," Webster declared, is "an engine used in almost all governments and has a powerful effect where people are kept in ignorance." [71] In his summary of the situation with regard to ecclesiastical policy in America, Dr. Richard Price [72] rejoiced to find that the new American states are strangers to civil establishments of religion. Religious establishments, he declared, tend "to impede the improvements of the world. They are the boundaries prescribed by human folly to human investigation; and inclosures which intercept the light and confine the exertion of reason." [73]

If sound sense is to be found on earth, Webster declared, it is Price's reasoning on the subject of ecclesiastical policy.[74] But Webster proceeds to show that there are still vestigial traits of religious tyranny in America in that a profession of faith is necessary in the states to entitle a man to hold office. In his "Federal Catechizm, containing a short explanation of the Constitution of the United States, for the use of schools," Webster's last question and answer, run as follows:

[69] Webster, *A Collection of Essays and Fugitiv Writings* (1790), p. 34.

[70] *Ibid.*, p. 10.

[71] *Sketches of American Policy* (1785), p. 30.

[72] Of Dr. Price's influence Webster has this to say: "Many of my observations, particularly on religious tests and establishments, and on liberty of discussion, have been anticipated by that respectable writer, so distinguished by the justness and liberality of his sentiment and by his attachment to America."—*Sketches* (1785), prefatory Advertisement.

[73] *Observations on the Importance of the American Revolution* (1785), p. 37.

[74] *Sketches of American Policy* (1785), p. 27.

Q. Why is it not best that every man should take an oath of his belief in religion, in order to be admitted into office?

A. Because such an oath would not prove him to be an honest man, or better qualified to discharge his duty in any office of government.[75]

Since Webster's utterances at various times and places are not all in accord with the stand he took in the 1780's, during the time he wrote the *Essays* and the *Sketches,* a brief survey of his religious life may serve to clarify his pronouncements. Writing to Dawes in 1808,[76] he says in the epistolary manner of the day into which he at times lapsed,

Being educated in a religious family, under pious parents, I had, in early life some religious impressions, but . . . falling into vicious company at college, I lost those impressions and contracted a habit of using profane language. . . . Being set afloat in the world at the inexperienced age of 20 . . . my mind was embarrassed with solicitude, and overwhelmed with gloomy apprehension. In this situation I read Johnson's *Rambler,* with unusual interest and with a visible effect upon my moral opinions. . . . I now perceive I ought to have read my bible first, but I followed the common mode of reading, and fell into the common mistake of attending to the duties which man owes man, before I had learned the duties which we all owe to our Creator and Redeemer.

Webster's references in his diary to church attendance and various aspects of life indicate that the unorthodox views expressed in the *Sketches* and *Essays* were not very deep-seated. In the 90's we find that he began to show signs of conservatism in religions and politics. In his *History of the French Revolution* (1794), he deplored that the philosophers, under the championship of Voltaire and Rousseau, had attempted to demolish the whole fabric of national religion in France and to erect the throne of reason. Admitting that science and education had illuminated a portion of the inhabitants, they had not, he declared, dissipated the gloom that was spread over the mass of the nation.[77]

[75] *Little Reader's Assistant* (1790), p. 69.
[76] Webster MSS; Ford, *Notes* (1912), II, 42 ff.
[77] "The Revolution in France," *A Collection of Papers on Political, Literary and Moral Subjects* (1794), p. 9.

In 1807 Webster embraced Calvinism by uniting with the Congregational Church at New Haven.[78] During the remainder of his life, he frequently referred to the importance of a "well grounded faith in the doctrines of the Christian Religion." [79] Writing to David McClure in 1836 on the subject of the proper course of study in Girard College, in Philadelphia, he says, "In my view, the Christian religion is the *most important and one of the first things* in which all children, under a free government ought to be instructed." This view at first appears to have the marks of an orthodox conservatism, accompanying the twilight of old age, but continuing, he says, "I do not mean an ecclesiastical establishment, a creed, or rites, forms, and ceremonies, or any compulsion of conscience. I mean primitive Christianity, in its simplicity, as taught by Christ and his Apostles." [80]

EDUCATION SHOULD BE UNIVERSAL [81]

Taking as a text Montesquieu's dictum "that the laws of education ought to be relative to the principles of the government," Webster declared that

In our American republics, where government is in the hands of the people, knowledge should be universally diffused by means of schools. Of such consequence is it to society, that the people who make laws, should be well informed, that I conceive no Legislature can be justified in neglecting proper establishments for this purpose.[82]

A system of education, he insisted, should give every citizen an

---

[78] Letter to Dawes, 1808.

[79] *Letters to a Young Gentleman Beginning His Education* (1823), p. 63.

[80] Noah Webster, *Papers on Political and Literary Subjects* (1843), p. 291. Letter dated, "New Haven, Oct. 25, 1836."

[81] This ideal was held by many prominent men of affairs of the day, among them Washington and Jefferson. These men were not in agreement, however, in that "Jefferson wanted to unify the mind of the individual state; Washington to unify the mind of the whole nation by educating the youth together."—Slosson, "American Spirit in Education," *The Chronicles of America*, XXXIII (1921), 94. Copyright Yale University Press.

[82] *A Collection of Essays* (1790), p. 24.

opportunity to acquire knowledge and fit himself for places of trust.[83] "A constitution is an *ark of safety* only, when under the management of *skillful pilots*. These pilots must be the *substantial yeomen* . . . not an ignorant populace, for when they take the helm, shipwreck is their certain doom."[84] Educated people, he held in opposition to Jefferson, do not need a bill of rights, "a declaratory article for a knowledge of their rights. They carry that knowledge in their heads."[85] He declared further that insofar as the states were passing laws which established provisions for colleges and academies where people of property may educate their sons, but which made no provisions for the instruction of the poorer rank, even in reading and writing,[86] where citizens worth a few shillings annually are permitted to vote for legislators, the laws of education may be said to be *monarchial,* which condition is a solecism in government, since the Constitution is *republican.*[87]

In recommending a system of education that would embrace every part of the community, Webster held that women should be educated,[88] because they are not generally above the care of educating their own children and because they should be able "to implant in the tender mind, such sentiments of virtue, propriety and dignity, as are suited to the freedom of our governments."[89] Another strong reason for educating women, he continued, was that through their influence they held great power to kindle or restrain. "There are innumerable instances of men, who have been restrained from a vicious life, and even of very

[83] *Loc. cit.*
[84] *Minerva,* Jan. 8, 1794.
[85] *Ibid.*
[86] In 1796 Webster declared he had been "attentive in particular to the instruction of the *common laboring people* in the more necessary and useful sciences, by annexing to his Institute, or publishing in some cheap form, the most general truths in agriculture, morals, and politics."—The *Minerva,* July 19, 1796.
[87] *Essays,* p. 24.
[88] For a discussion of "female education" see, Slosson, *op. cit.,* pp. 18 and 234 ff. Rush was also a strong advocate of the education of women. See *Thoughts upon Female Education* (1787).
[89] *Essays,* p. 27.

abandoned men, who have been reclaimed, by their attachment to a lady of virtue."

"In all nations," Webster declared, "a *good* education, is that which renders the ladies correct in their manners, respectable in their families, and agreeable in society. That education is always wrong, which raises a woman above the duties of her station." Contrary to the practice in monarchial Europe, women should be taught that which is useful, "to speak and write their own language with purity and elegance" and some arithmetic and geography. "Belles Letters learning seems to correspond with the dispositions of most females. . . . The *Spectator* should fill the first place in every lady's library," and some of the best histories should be read.[90]

As for the so-called finishing-school subjects, such as music, drawing, and dancing, they hold a subordinate rank. It is to be remembered, too, that "No man ever marries a woman for her performance on a harpsichord, or her figure in a minuet." [91]

Radical as Webster's theories regarding the education of women may have seemed to the masses of his day, yet on every hand we find traces of the traditions of the past:

A strong attachment to books in a lady often deters a man from approaching her with the offer of hiz heart. . . . One sex iz formed for the more hardy exercises of the council, the field and the laborious employments of procuring subsistence. The other, for the superintendence of domestic concerns, and for diffusing bliss thro social life. . . . To be *lovely* then you must be content to be *wimen;* to be mild, social and sentimental; to be acquainted with all that belongs to your department, and leeve the masculine virtues, and the profound researches of study, to the province of the other sex. . . . A man is pleezed with the deference hiz wife shows for hiz opinions; he often loves her even for her want of information, when it creates a kind of dependence upon hiz judgement.[92]

[90] *Essays,* p. 28. In 1839 Webster wrote a chapter on "Laws Respecting Females," in order that they might have some knowledge of their legal rights in case they be left without a father, a husband, or other protector.—*Manual of Useful Studies,* pp. VI and 79.

[91] *Essays,* p. 29.

[92] "An Address to Young Ladies," *Essays* (1790), pp. 410f.

YOUTHS SHOULD BE EDUCATED IN AMERICA [93]

In his zeal to further the interests of his country, Webster denounced the practice of sending youths to Europe to be educated,
a custom followed by all well-to-do men in all the colonies, but
especially in the South.[94] This custom, he reasoned, was right
when the colonies were dependencies of Britain, but now that
this dependency no longer exists and America has a government,
society, and manners peculiarly her own, it is wrong.[95] Because
a foreign education is opposed to the political interests of
America, it "ought to be discountenanced if not prohibited."
The years from twelve to twenty are the most impressionable.[96]
The impressions received in early life form the characters of the
individuals, which in turn form the general character of a nation.[97] European and American governments differ widely, and
men form modes of reasoning or habits of thinking on political
subjects in the country where they are bred. "Before a man can
be a good Legislator, he must be intimately acquainted with the
temper of the people to be governed. No man can be thus acquainted with a people, without residing amongst them and
mingling with all companies." [98]

The refinement of manners in every country, he believed,
should keep pace exactly with the increase of its wealth. A foreign
education, he declared, "gives young gentlemen of fortune a
relish for manners and amusements which are not suited to
this country." [99] Then, too, "there are vices predominant in most
polite cities in Europe, which are not only unknown, but are
seldom mentioned in America; and vices that are infamous

---

[93] George Washington shared the belief that youths should be educated in
America. One of his cherished ideals was the establishment of an American university. See Slosson, op. cit., pp. 95 f. It is apparent that Webster leaned heavily
on Rush in his discussion of foreign education. See Rush, Thoughts (1786),
pp. 13 f.

[94] Slosson, op. cit., p. 44.

[95] Essays, p. 30.

[96] Ibid., p. 31.

[97] Ibid., p. 1.

[98] Ibid., p. 34.

[99] Ibid., p. 32.

beyond conception." [100] Throughout Webster's writings he gives full cognizance to the force of habits formed in early life—to the fact that "kegs retain the flavor of their first wine." Not giving full recognition to the fact that the consequences of our acts play an important part in the formation of habit, he warned that the "man who begins life with sowing *wild oats,* seldom sows a better kind, in middle life and old age." [101]

In answer to the contention that American schools are inferior to European schools, he admitted that in regard to the sciences, especially "chymistry," this may be true, and that in some special cases it might be useful for students to cross the Atlantic to complete a course of studies; but it is not necessary for them to go early in life or to continue a long time. If our universities and schools are not so good as the English or Scotch, it is the business of the rulers to improve them. Since "nature has been very profuse to the Americans, in genius, and in the advantages of climate and soil," Americans can remain long indebted to Europe for opportunities of acquiring perfection in the sciences only by a criminal neglect of its inhabitants.[102]

SCHOOLMASTERS SHOULD BE AMERICAN

Not only were American children to be educated in America, but they were to be educated by American instructors. "It is very little to the reputation of America to have it said abroad, that after the heroic achievements of the late war, these independent people are obliged to send to Europe for men and books to teach their children their A B C."

Webster's insistence on the native product is well illustrated by a conversation he had on one occasion with George Washington. On his way to Richmond, Virginia, in November, 1785, Webster stopped at Mount Vernon and spent the night. Wash-

---

[100] "Remarks on the Manners . . . of the United States," *Essays* (1790), p. 85.
[101] *The Prompter* (1802), p. 63. See also "Letter to the Author" and "The Answer," *Essays* (1790), pp. 245–48.
[102] *Essays,* p. 34.

ington casually remarked that he was thinking of sending to Scotland for a man to act as his secretary and as teacher to the Custis children. Webster ventured to ask what European nations would think of this country if after our military triumphs we should send to Europe for secretaries and men to teach the rudiments of learning. Webster said he believed any of the northern colleges could supply a person qualified for the position and agreed to try to find a suitable person when he returned North. Later Webster corresponded with Washington regarding his taking the position. One motive he had in making the proposal was the hope that he might have leisure to write and that he could "execute a work" under Washington's inspection, obtaining from him or from official letters personal intelligence that could not be obtained in any other way. Webster finally decided not to take the place, and it was later filled by Tobias Lear of New Hampshire.[103]

TRAVEL IN AMERICA

From this denunciation of foreign education and residence abroad, Webster goes on to the subject of travel. He recommends that when young gentlemen have finished their academic education, they should spend "twelve or eighteen months in examining the local situation of the different states; the rivers, soil, the population, the improvements and the commercial advantages of the whole." Such a tour, he reasoned, would enable citizens of the different parts to become acquainted, would remove jealousies, and establish mutual respect and confidence, and a harmony of views and interests would result. Later, if time and fortune permitted, a tour through Europe might be of value, but if a tour cannot be made through both countries, that in America is certainly to be preferred, for the people of America, with all their information, are yet extremely ignorant of the geography, policy, and manners of their neighboring states.[104]

[103] Ford, *Notes*, I, 104 ff.
[104] *Essays*, p. 36.

SCHOOLBOOKS SHOULD BE AMERICAN; BOOKS FOR READING
SHOULD BE SELECTED WITH CARE

Another defect that Webster observed in the schools, a defect
which he did more than anyone else of his age to remedy, was the
want of suitable books. The collections then in use consisted of
"essays that respect foreign and ancient nations. . . . These are
excellent specimens of good sense, polished stile and perfect
oratory; but they are not interesting to children. . . . A selection of essays, respecting the settlement and geography of
America; the history of the late revolution and of the most remarkable characters and events that distinguish it, and a compendium of the principles of the federal and provincial government,[105] should be the principal schoolbook in the United
States." [106] In fact, one of the arguments Webster advanced in
favor of language reform was that the necessary alterations in
spelling, however small, would encourage the publication of
books in America.[107]

Webster's break with the past can perhaps best be shown by
his attitude toward the use of the Bible as a textbook in the
schools.[108] The opening shot protesting against the practice was
fired in the Preface to his first text, the speller, in 1783, by his
declaration that sacred things should be appropriated to sacred
purposes. In the Preface to *The Little Reader's Assistant* (1790)
he declared that the practice had in it an element of the sacri-
legious as it was a "prostitution of divine truth to secular
purposes."

The Bible was used universally in the schools, Webster pointed
out, because it was the only book some families possessed and
because the readers and speakers used in the academies and col-

---

[105] In some of Webster's readers, notably *The Little Reader's Assistant* (1790),
he published "A Federal Catechism," with questions and answers regarding some
of the salient features of American government.

[106] *Essays*, p. 23. The ideal set forth in this paragraph seems to be the one he had
in mind when he compiled his reader, Part III of *A Grammatical Institute*.

[107] *Dissertations on the English Language* (1789), p. 397.

[108] In this respect he did not agree with Rush. See *Thoughts* (1786), pp. 15–18.

leges were too large and expensive.[109] Then, too, the use of the
Bible in schools was thought to be an efficacious means of im-
pressing important truths of religion and morality upon the
minds of youth. He argued that the practice was a mistake, just
as it was a mistake for the Puritans to place burial grounds in a
prominent place, thus ridding the living of their terror of death.
"Those parts of the scripture therefore which are calculated to
strike terror to the mind lose their influence by being frequently
brought to view." [110]

Throughout Webster's writings he has much to say against the
reading of novels and plays and attendance at the theatre. Novels
are, he declared, the "toys of youth"—the "rattleboxes of sixteen." [111] Writing in 1823, he admitted that a small portion of
time might be given to reading that relaxes the mind, but warned
"against the fascination of plays, novels, romances," and highly-
embellished descriptive writings.[112] Many of the plays, he complained, "abound with ribaldry and vulgarity, too gross for
exhibition before persons of delicacy and refined manners." [113]
Vice, he reminded, "always spreads by being published—young
people are taught many vices by fiction, books or public
exhibitions." [114]

EDUCATION SHOULD BE PRAGMATIC

In that there was to be no leisure class in America, Webster insisted that education should be practical—utilitarian. One serious
criticism Webster made of the prevailing tendency in education,
was that there was "a too general attention to the dead languages,
with a neglect of our own." [115] There was a long period of time
when Greek and Latin were the only repositories of science in
Europe. English translations now make it possible to dispense

[109] *Grammatical Institute,* Part II (1785), Preface.
[110] *Essays,* p. 8.
[111] *Ibid.,* p. 29.
[112] *Letters to a Young Gentleman* (1823), p. 13.
[113] *Ibid.,* p. 14.
[114] *American Magazine,* March, 1788, p. 210.
[115] *Essays,* p. 3.

with the original works in these languages. "The English language," he declared, "perhaps, at this moment, is the repository of as much learning, as one half the languages of Europe." [116]

"What advantage," he asks, "does a merchant, a mechanic, a farmer, derive from an acquaintance with the Greek and Roman tongues?" [117] We have an elegant and copious language of our own, with innumerable writers upon ethics, geography, history, commerce, and government.[118] A system of education which does not include these languages might be completed by the age of fifteen or sixteen, and time would be left for the student to serve a regular apprenticeship, an ordeal through which the gentleman graduate of universities is, because of his age and his pride, unwilling to go.[119]

According to Webster's belief, a *liberal* education disqualifies a man for business. Since business is in some measure mechanical, every person should be exercised in his employment early before his habits are formed. A university education interferes with these habits; in fact, opposite habits, such as a fondness for ease, pleasure, or books, may be formed. The method pursued in our colleges, he concluded, is better calculated to fit youth for the learned professions than for business.[120]

Another practice Webster criticized was that of restricting all students to the same course of study. "Young gentlemen are not all designed for the same business, and why should they pursue the same studies?" he asked.[121] "Every man should be able to speak and write his native tongue with correctness; and have some knowledge of mathematics." Each lad should, then, pursue those studies which are more directly concerned with the business for which he is destined.[122] He therefore urged a closer attention to dead languages among young men who are designed for the learned professions, such men as poets, orators, philosophers, and the historians who write of Greece and Rome.[123]

[116] *Ibid.*, p. 4.
[118] *Ibid.*
[120] *Ibid.*
[122] *Ibid.*, p. 13.

[117] *Ibid.*
[119] *Ibid.*, p. 14.
[121] *Essays*, p. 5.
[123] *Loc. cit.*, p. 5.

Plans were also proposed by Robert Coram,[124] James Sullivan,[125] and Nathaniel Chipman.[126] These men were in agreement in that they believed education in a democracy should be a function of the state and that it should be universal. Chipman was emphatic in his insistence that education should be placed on a scientific basis.

One of the agencies that was prominent in molding American thought was the American Philosophical Society, which grew out of a union in 1769 of the Junto (1727) and the American Philosophical Society (1743), both of which were organized by Franklin and his contemporaries.[127] Its members were the leading Americans and Europeans of the day, among them being Frenchmen who were refugees in America. Thus we see another avenue whereby the liberal French philosophy of the eighteenth century and also the reactionary philosophy of royalty were brought to America. Among the many interests of this organization was that of American education. A prize was offered for "the best system of liberal education and literary instruction, adapted to the genius of the Government of the United States; comprehending also a plan for instituting and conducting public schools in this country, on principles of the most extensive utility." In answer to this offer, many essays were submitted, but the premium was divided between the two best, those of Samuel Knox [128] and Samuel Harrison Smith,[129] the only plans that now exist of the many submitted.

Knox's thesis was that education should be "adapted to the genius of the government of the United States." Education was to be universal as to benefits and support. It was to be based on

[124] *Plan for the General Establishment of Schools throughout the United States* (1791). In this work Coram says, "I had the present work in Idea, sometime before Mr. Webster's essays made their appearance; and was not a little pleased to think he had anticipated my idea."—Preface, p. 76.
[125] *Observations upon the Government of the United States of America* (1791).
[126] *Sketches of the Principles of Government* (1793).
[127] *Proceedings of the American Philosophical Society* (1843), III, 3–37.
[128] Samuel Knox, *Essay on Education* (1797).
[129] Samuel H. Smith, *Remarks on Education* (1798).

science instead of the superstitions and prejudices of the past. It was to educate for leadership and be free from religious dominance. Smith's plan, it is said, was composed of the thoughts of the leading statesmen and scholars in the American Philosophical Society. According to these minds, education should be "of the most extensive *utility*." To inculcate the scientific attitude was to be the chief aim of American education. It should be universal, and flexible enough to permit growth. America was to set an example before the world by evolving a humanitarian, scientific type of education.

We have previously noted the French influence in the United States. The plans of Lafitte du Courteil [130] and DuPont de Nemours [131] are representative of this influence on American thinking during the last quarter of the eighteenth century. Lafitte advocated a system of national education that would give equal opportunities to country and city children. Family pride was to be replaced by national pride. According to his belief, by the developing of the rural life and resources, America would be independent of European monarchial influences.

DuPont advocated a highly-centralized system of education, nationally controlled and supported, one that would permit constant growth, that would select and educate geniuses for leadership. The system was to be directly related to immediate economic and social problems.

Webster's Works and Remarks after 1800 Show His Growing Conservatism

ON JULY 19, 1796, Webster's *Minerva* carried an article entitled "From the Aurora," in which the *Aurora* was quoted as saying, "There are but few numbers of the New York *Minerva*

[130] *National Plan of Education* (1797).

[131] *National Education in the United States of America* (1800). It is said that DuPont's plan "probably contains the theories of both Jefferson and DuPont de Nemours modified to form one carefully detailed plan."—*National Education in the United States of America*, translated (1923) by Bessie Gardiner DuPont, Preface, p. iii.

that do not contain a column or more devoted to the cause of
aristocracy . . . reflections the most insulting are made on the
poorer classes of citizens, who are stigmatized as an ignorant
set . . . " In Webster's reply he shows that many of his efforts
have been directed toward the education of the masses, believing
as he did that an enlightened citizenry is indispensable to a free
government. He speaks of the "misfortune of the poor in being
deprived of the advantage of education . . . as a *matter of regret,* as it is this which renders them more easily the *dupes* of
designing factious men . . ."

This article is a fair and complete summary of Webster's
labors for the cause of democracy up to that time. But toward the
end of the century there were signs that his earlier democratic
convictions were on the wane. He had lost faith and interest in
the French Revolution,[132] and there is evidence that he deplored
the excessive spread-eagle enthusiasm displayed in some quarters.[133] When the Federalist Party split, in 1798, Webster was on
the side of the minority against Hamilton. At that time he retired from the active editorship of the *Minerva* and from partici-
pation in national politics.[134] He remained, it seems, a Federalist
at heart during the remainder of his life. During the following
century he became more and more conservative, frequently
showing his dissatisfaction with the republican form of government which had once promised so much.[135] In 1802 he published
an "Address to the President of the United States on the Subject
of His [inaugural] Address," attacking the budding spoils system
with vitriolic invective.[136]

[132] See *The Revolution in France* (1794).
[133] Because of the intense Americanism of the times the corporation of New York
changed "Queen" Street to "Pearl" and "Crown" to "Liberty." Webster suggested
satirically that the "vile aristocratical name New York" should be changed.
"What is to become of Kings, Queens, and Orange Counties?" he asked.—*Minerva,*
April 19, 1794.
[134] See *A Letter to General Hamilton, Occasioned by His Letter to President
Adams* (N. Y., 1800 ?), signed "Aristides."
[135] "A Brief History of Political Parties in the United States," *A Collection of
Papers* . . . (1843), p. 311. *Letters to a Young Gentleman Beginning His Education* (1823), p. 17.
[136] Scudder, *Noah Webster* (1882), p. 144. Houghton Mifflin Company.

That Webster's theories regarding democracy suffered a considerable slump as the nineteenth century advanced is shown by one of the criticisms of plays, which he offered in 1823:

What sort of entertainment is that in which a partition only separates the nobleman from his lackey, and the duchess from her kitchen-maid; in which the gentleman and the lady associate at the same board with the footman, the oysterman, and the woman of the town, and all partake of the same fare! [137]

So little in sympathy was he with the democracy for which Andrew Jackson stood in 1832, realizing Jackson would be re-elected, he sent away the carriage which came to take him to the polls.[138]

Later in life (1838) Webster wrote of his early writings with disparagement: "My Dissertations and Essays were written at an early period of life, and although they may contain much truth, yet many of them at least, are too incorrect for republication." [139] Commenting in 1838 on the inaccuracies of authors, Webster admitted that

[he] had begun to publish his opinions prematurely; a circumstance which is now regretted. Possibly this example may operate as a caution to young men, ambitious of authorship, not to Hazard the publication of their opinions, till time, long study, observation, and experience, have matured their judgment.[140]

In Webster's personal copy of the *Sketches of American Policy* (1785), there are many indications that he found in them much with which he no longer agreed in 1800.[141] The parts referring to religion, most of which were taken from Richard Price, he crossed out so effectively that they can be read only with difficulty.[142] Then, there are other remarks in Webster's hand: "The Three first Sketches contain many chimerical notions—adopted in the enthusiasm of the revolution; but which can never be re-

[137] *Letters to a Young Gentleman* (1823), p. 14.
[138] Scudder, *Noah Webster* (1882), p. 145.
[139] Ford, *Notes*, I, 469.
[140] *A Manual of Useful Studies* (1839), p. v.
[141] The copy is in the New York Public Library. See title-page.
[142] The "Sketches" were published widely in newspapers. See *Maryland Gazette*, December, 1785, and January, 1786.

duced to practice"; [143] "Many of these notions taken from Rousseau's *Social Contract*, are found to be chimerical"; [144] and "These ideas are too democratic and not just. Experience does not warrant them," [145] and so forth.

After 1800 Webster devoted his time in the main to lexicographical pursuits and the little he had to say about education appeared in the prefaces to his books and in pamphlets. In a letter written in 1842 to the Reverend Alfred Saxe, who had requested that Webster suggest a course of English study for the instruction of young men preparing themselves for teachers, Webster stated that for a "series of years" his labors had been directed "to find what should be taught, rather than how it should be taught." [146]

The following year Webster formulated some of his ideas in "Modes of Teaching the English Language." [147] Although this disquisition has to do with the teaching of spelling and reading by the alphabet method, along with the implications involved, insofar as he was aware of them, he says that the same principles are applicable in the teaching of other languages and the sciences. He points out three mistakes that are very common: (1) Children are put to their studies too early. "A child that begins at *three,* will be two or three years learning to read; but one that begins at *five,* may be taught to read well in six or eight weeks." (2) The study of some subjects requires maturation more than that of others. A child put to the study of geography, arithmetic, or history at the age of nine or ten will learn as much in two months as the same child would have learned in two years at the age of five or six; and will better understand and retain what he learns. (3) An attempt is made to instruct young people in *too many things at once.* "The most important point perhaps in a system of instruction . . . is, *to do one thing at a time.*" [148]

[143] Written on flyleaf.
[144] Page 7.
[145] Page 6.
[146] Webster MSS.
[147] Published in *A Collection of Papers* (1843), p. 307.
[148] See p. 122.

It has been pointed out that Webster's ideas on education were liberal and aggressive in the eighteenth century. But this estimate does not apply to his opinions with regard to methods of teaching. He accepted the alphabet method in 1783, apparently without even thinking that spelling and reading could be taught in any other way.[149] We find that in 1843 he still had the beliefs he held in the eighteenth century. The statement of what education meant to him, which formed a part of his "Modes of Teaching," has about it, however, a serene quality which is in contrast to the fiery tone often found in his earlier remarks concerning the education of youth in America:

Education, in the most comprehensive sense of the word, consists in the instruction of the young and the ignorant in what is necessary or useful for them to know in order to be qualified to procure their subsistence, to correct their evil propensities, to direct their minds to the proper objects, and to form their moral, social, and religious characters. In short the objects of education are to furnish pupils with the best means of providing for themselves; in being useful in all the relations of life; and prepared for a future state of happiness.[150]

Because of His Textbooks Rather Than Because of His Theories, Webster Has Been Called the Schoolmaster of Our Republic

THE extent to which Webster influenced education in America is difficult to determine. His influence was perhaps considerable. That he was one of the most prominent educators of the late eighteenth century has been acceded by writers of his day as well as by those of the present. Coram wrote, in 1791,[151]

Mr. Noah Webster is the only American author, indeed the only author of any nation, if we except perhaps Montesquieu, who has taken up the subject of education upon that liberal and equitable scale which it deserves.

[149] See p. 92.
[150] A Collection of Papers (1843), p. 307.
[151] Plan for the General Establishment of Schools throughout the United States (1791), Preface, p. 76f.

Writing in 1926, Hansen says,

Noah Webster was the chief proponent of and worker for educational reconstruction during this period.[152]

Many of the fine views of education advocated by Webster and his contemporaries as a means of progress and for the service of mankind are now realities. They were not, however,

caught by the governing authorities of the time. Owing in part to the deadliness of indifference, which has always acted upas-like upon new suggestions for social reform, the proposals of these thinkers were to remain only the visions and theories which all except a few people considered them to be at the time.[153]

It was perhaps through his textbooks that Webster performed his greatest service to American education, rather than through the theories he set forth regarding education and government.

His principal claim to lasting fame [says Russell], is probably that he holds the title of America's greatest schoolmaster. His speller, grammar, and dictionary were carried from the hillsides of New England to the parts of the country as the tides of migration and settlement flowed through the valleys of the Alleghanies, through Ohio and Indiana, to the prairies of Illinois and on West . . .[154]

The estimate which has been made of the contribution of one of Webster's contemporaries is equally applicable to Webster: "What Jefferson actually accomplished in education was little; but what he aspired to and inspired others to was immense. The appraisal of his achievement depends upon whether the balance sheet is drawn during his life or a hundred years later." [155]

Summary and Conclusions

ASIDE from the moral and patriotic zeal that colored much of Webster's thinking, the two main forces which influenced his ideas concerning education were his experience as a teacher and

[152] Allen Oscar Hansen, *Liberalism and American Education in the Eighteenth Century* (1926), p. 200. The Macmillan Company.

[153] Edgar Wallace Knight, *Education in the United States* (1934), p. 147.

[154] T. W. Russell, "Webster, Word Arbiter for 100 Years," *New York Times Magazine*, April 15, 1928, p. 11.

[155] Edwin E. Slosson, "The American Spirit in Education," *The Chronicles of America*, XXXIII (1921), 79. Copyright Yale University Press.

the theories concerning man and his environment, which were prevalent in the eighteenth century and with which he was more or less familiar. In order that man might progress indefinitely toward perfectibility, an aim which held a prominent place in the thinking of the age, Webster proposed that (1) the approach to education should be scientific; (2) in order that youths might be indoctrinated "in those things that were thought to be peculiarly characteristic of American thinking and life," education should be universal, youths should be educated in America, by American schoolmasters, from American books, and should travel in America rather than in Europe; and (3) since there was to be no aristocracy in America, education should be pragmatic. These views were held in common by many men of Webster's day and were expressed by some of his contemporaries in the plans they proposed. Many of these views have since become realities. Since Webster has been regarded by some as the most important worker for the cause of American education during the last quarter of the eighteenth century, it seems reasonable to conjecture that his theories, which he kept constantly before the public for a period of years, bore fruit later when the public-school systems of America were born.

After 1800, Webster became increasingly more conservative in matters pertaining to education and government. The views which he expressed on education are to be found mostly in the prefaces to his texts and in pamphlets having to do with his lexicographical interests. He denounced many of his eighteenth-century opinions as the enthusiasms of a youth, who, under the excitement of post-Revolutionary days, hastened to utter thoughts that were erroneously formed. In 1843, the year of his death, he set down some of his ideas concerning method in teaching. These were few in number and were based on the traditional methods which were in vogue when he compiled his speller in 1783. As we shall see, it was perhaps through his texts, especially his spellers and dictionaries along with the universal interest in language which they aroused, that he made his greatest contribution to American education.

III

WEBSTER'S BLUE-BACK SPELLING BOOK

The spelling-book does more to form the language of a nation than all other books.[1]

ALTHOUGH spelling, which was the natural outcome of the A B C method in learning to read,[2] came to occupy a very prominent place in the early American school,[3] at first it was largely incidental to reading in both England and America. It was not until Dilworth's *New Guide to the English Tongue,* a composite text in which Parts I and II contained words for spelling, was published in England in 1740 and in America in 1747, that the formal spelling lesson began to be universally a thing apart from reading.[4] There are records, however, of earlier texts. Littlefield records, for example, that Stephen Day printed spelling books in Cambridge, Massachusetts, as early as 1642. This may refer to Coote's *The English Schoolmaster* (1590), another composite text which was widely used in New England.[5] Then, there was George Fox's primer or spelling book, *Instructions for Right Spelling, and Plain Directions for Reading and Writing True English,* published in England in 1674 and republished in Philadelphia in 1701.[6] In 1731 Henry Dixon published *The*

---

[1] Webster, *A Collection of Papers on Political, Literary and Moral Subjects* (1843), p. 309.

[2] Rollo La Verne Lyman, *English Grammar in American Schools before 1850* (1922), p. 19.

[3] Spelling, says Lyman, "became a craze in the first quarter of the nineteenth century and came to occupy an undue proportion of attention. Elaborate school instruction was supplemented by evening spelling schools and spelling matches."— *Op. cit.,* p. 8.

[4] Lyman, *op. cit.,* p. 19.

[5] G. E. Littlefield, *Early Schools and School Books* (1904), pp. 118f.

[6] J. P. Wickersham, *A History of Education in Pennsylvania* (1886), p. 194. Other editions followed; Philadelphia (1702); Boston (1743); and Newport, Rhode Island (1737 and 1769). The tendency for the early texts to be of the omnibus variety is well illustrated by this text. In addition to the usual fulsome exposition and discussion of the alphabet, there were lessons in spelling, reading, and defining; explanations of scriptural names; rules of pronunciation; examples of words

KNOWLEDGE and FAME are gain'd not by surprise;
He that would win, must LABOR for the prize:
'Tis thus the youth, from lisping A, B, C,
Attains, at length, a Master's high degree.

FRONTISPIECE OF THE ELEMENTARY SPELLING BOOK (1829)

English Instructor; or, The Art of Spelling Improved. This compilation ran through many editions until 1750, when the title was changed to *The Youth's Instructor in the English Tongue.* The book was in use up to the Revolution. Anthony Benezet, another Quaker, who was a teacher in Philadelphia, compiled both a primer and a spelling book, the second edition of which appeared in 1782.[7] In 1777 *The Only Sure Guide to the English Tongue,* the compilation of William Perry, Webster's most formidable rival in the spelling-book field, was published in Edinburgh. Whether or not this work was printed in America before the Worcester edition of 1785 is doubtful.[8]

Speaking of these early texts, which were the forerunner of Webster's spelling book published in 1783, Meriwether says,

They all were a jumble of the Bible, morality, and religion luxuriously interlarded with the alphabet and with words of 1, 2, 3, 4, 5, 6, and more syllables. When it came to longer ones, the pedant and the preacher vied with one another in such words as "cocolico," "euroclydon," and "antitrinitarian." It was such hopelessly unfit specimens that youthful tongues had to stumble over until Noah Webster earned the gratitude of all with his blue spelling book, which is an opulent enlargement of the New England Primer . . .[9]

Recognizing That American Texts Were Needed, Webster Compiled His Spelling Book while Teaching at Sharon and Goshen

When Noah Webster was in Sharon, Connecticut, a hundred years ago [writes Benton], beginning what was to be a great career, he

---

pronounced alike but spelled differently; Roman numerals and lessons in arithmetic; an almanac; and a catechism setting forth the authors' interpretation of the religious doctrines of the Friends.

[7] Neither Fox's nor Benezet's books were much used outside the Society of Friends.—Wickersham, *op. cit.,* p. 194. In the introduction, Fox says that it was his view not only to make spelling more easy, familiar, and agreeable than usual, "but also to cause the bent and aim of all the lessons from the beginning to the end to be such as tended to mend the heart as well as convince the judgment by raising in the tender mind principles of compassion and tenderness, as well to the brute Creation as to their fellow-men, a nobility of mind and a love of virtue."

[8] Oscar Adolph Tingelstad, *The Religious Element in the American School Reader up to 1830* (1925), p. 137.

[9] Colyer Meriwether, *Our Colonial Curriculum* (1907), p. 34.

undoubtedly did not imagine what his little makeshift of school-teaching would, in time, lead to. One of his perplexities, as he told Governor Smith,[10] was the difficulties he had in teaching scholars to spell. This difficulty induced him to project a book which should make the acquirement of orthography easier, and also reduce the teacher's toil and trouble with his pupils.[11]

The fact that Webster included in his spelling books the names of such Connecticut towns as Amenia, Kent, Salisbury, and Cornwall, all in the vicinity of Sharon, tends to substantiate the tradition that the book had its inception in Governor Smith's attic. Benton says it was here where Webster "pursued diligently those meditations and studies which have been connected with the education of more Americans than have the studies of almost any other dozen men." [12]

In May, 1782, Webster left Sharon, crossed the Hudson and went to Goshen, New York, where he taught a classical school during the following winter while the American army was lying on the bank of the Hudson.[13] "The country was then impoverished," Webster explained; "intercourse with Great Britain was interrupted; school-books were scarce and hardly obtainable; and there was no certain prospect of peace." [14] Although Webster says that it was here where he compiled two small elementary books for teaching the English language,[15] it is probably true that he began his compilations the year before while at Sharon, since the spelling book was well under way in October, 1782.[16] Then, too, in that fall he traveled to New Jersey and Pennsylvania in behalf of a copyright law, which would protect his literary property, meeting such "gentlemen of influence" as Governor Liv-

[10] The Hon. John Cotton Smith, the last Governor of Connecticut under the old charter and an early President of the American Bible Society, with whom Webster lived at Sharon.
[11] Joel Benton, "The Webster Spelling Book," *Magazine of American History*, X (1883), 299.
[12] *Ibid.*, p. 299.
[13] *A Collection of Papers on Political, Literary, and Moral Subjects* (1843), p. 173.
[14] *Ibid.*
[15] *Ibid.*
[16] In a memorial dated "Hartford, October 24, 1782," Webster describes the speller.—Webster MSS.

ingston of New Jersey and the Rev. Samuel Stanhope Smith, the professor of theology in Nassau Hall, and afterward president of that institution.[17]

In October following [Webster wrote], I went to Hartford, with a view to petition the Legislature . . . The petition was presented but too late in the session to obtain a hearing. I then returned to Goshen, and devoted the winter to a revision of my manuscripts, and the introduction of some improvements which had been suggested by gentlemen in Princeton and Philadelphia.[18]

Webster's spelling book, like most of the texts that he published later, was not original, but was a combination of and an "improvement" on two English texts, Daniel Fenning's, *The Universal Spelling Book*,[19] and Thomas Dilworth's *The New Guide to the English Tongue*,[20] a very popular text in both England and America. Dilworth's book was a composite text containing, among other things, a speller, a grammar, and a reader. It was Webster's plan, which he later carried to execution, to publish three separate books to take the place of these three main divisions in Dilworth.

From a letter written to John Canfield[21] we learn that Webster, "America's first professional scholar," soon discovered what has since often proved to be the bane in the life of the schoolmaster, that is, the necessity of teaching while engaging in scholarly pursuits.

I find the plan I now propose, will cost still more labor; I have been indefatigable this winter; I have sacrificed ease, pleasure, & health to the execution of it, & have nearly compleated it. But such close application is too much for my constitution. I must relinquish the school or writing Grammar. I shall not pursue the plan any

[17] Webster, "Origin of Copy-right Laws," *Collection of Papers* (1843), p. 173.
[18] *Ibid.*, p. 174.
[19] Daniel Fenning, *The Universal Spelling Book; or, a New and Easy Guide to the English Language*. London, 1756.
[20] Thomas Dilworth, *A New Guide to the English Tongue*, New York, 1754. "First issued in London, 1740, popular till after 1800. A reprint of the eighth English edition, Philadelphia, 1747, appears to be the first American edition."— Evans, *op. cit.*, p. 183.
[21] From Noah Webster, Goshen, N. Y., Jan. 6, 1783, to John Canfield, Esq., Sharon, Connecticut.—Webster's MSS.

further, unless it shall meet with public approbation, encouragement & security. On the decision, therefore, of these two Legislatures, depends, the further prosecution of my design.[22]

In this letter to Canfield, Webster showed that he realized that custom has a strong hold on the people—a realization that was brought home to him often in the succeeding years, when he tried to introduce his linguistic reforms.

Popular prejudice [he wrote], is in favor of Dilworth, & because he was universally esteemed in G B-n half a century ago, people are apt to slumber in the opinion that he is incapable of improvement. But he is not only out of date; but is really faulty and defective in every part of his work.

Added to the dislike of Dilworth's "guide" was Webster's prompt recognition of the need of American texts for American schools. This stand is shown in his memorial addressed to the General Assembly of Connecticut.[23]

Instead of those proper names which belong to Great Britain, which we are incapable & unwilling to learn, & which are totally useless in America, your memorialist has inserted those words only which occur in the sacred or other writings, which are of obvious use & different pronunciation together with the names of the Kingdoms of Europe, their Capital Cities & the United States of America, the Counties, principal towns & rivers in each seperate [sic] State—with other improvements of obvious utility.[24]

[22] The grammar was the second part of the series to be published (1784).

[23] Op. cit.

[24] When the work appeared in 1783, in a long introduction, the author showed that however useful 12 or 15 pages which Dilworth had devoted to the names of English, Scotch, and Irish towns and boroughs may be to the school children of England, they were certainly useless in America. Not all of Webster's friends agreed with him in his denunciation of Dilworth. "I am pleased with the Spirit and stile of your Introduction," wrote his old friend and tutor, Joseph Buckminster, "think however you are a little too severe upon our Friend Mr. Dilworth. His Guide to the english tongue was an improvement upon all that had gone before him and he has deserved well of the english nation, in carrying us a little farther than we would have gone without him, and it is a wonder if an ill natured world does not ascribe some of the observations not so much to his deficiencies as to a desire to give currency to your institute." Letter dated "Portsmouth, November 17, 1783."—Ford, Notes, I, 62. Elizur Goodrich wrote Webster, "I cannot pass so hard a censure on it [Dilworth] as you do . . . The censure you pass on the authors of Spelling-Books and Dictionaries are, in my opinion,

The belief that America should be as independent of Great
Britain in all matters as she was independent politically was
beginning to take shape in the mind of Webster, as was shown
later in his aggressive advocacy of an independent American
literature and language.[25] "America must be as independent in
literature as she is in *politics,* as famous for *arts* as for *arms*,"
Webster wrote to Canfield in 1783.[26] His attitude was well
summed up in an unpublished discourse in 1788:

My young friends . . . At the close of the revolution, but before the
American army disbanded, I set myself to favor the independence of
my country, by compiling books for the instruction of youth; & with
one express purpose of lessening the dependence of this country on
foreign supplies.[27]

At the outset of his career as a compiler of textbooks, Webster
expressed a desire to do good in the world.

A Folio upon some abstruse philosophical subject might [he wrote],
at first thought, appear to be a work of some consequence, & attract
the public attention; But this would be read only by a few & its
utility seldom reach further than the Philosopher's head. While a
little fifteen penny volume, which may convey much useful knowledge to the remote obscure recesses of honest poverty, is overlooked
as a matter of trivial notice.[28]

Again, in the preface to his first speller (1783), he says:

The author's intention is certainly good—he wishes to render the
acquisition of our language easy and the pronunciation accurate and
uniform. The necessity of reforming our present method of instruction was suggested by his own experience. . . .[29]

---

too undistinguished; for, though they may be applicable to some, yet not to all
indeterminately. However deficient, or even erroneous they may really be in some
things, yet literature and the system of education have been much improved by
them . . . Mr. Dilworth followed the rules of spelling long established: He only
improved on a system, that had been in being for ages before he was born . . ."
Letter dated "Durham, Conn., September 29, 1783."—Webster MSS.

[25] See chap. v.
[26] *Op. cit.*
[27] Webster's MSS. Miscellaneous papers.
[28] Letter to Canfield, *op. cit.*
[29] Page 13.

Part I of a Grammatical Institute, the Parent of the Old Blue-Back Speller, Appeared in 1783

IN THE spring of 1783 Webster returned to Hartford to arrange for the publication of his speller. Since copyright laws had been passed in several states, he was assured of at least a measure of protection. The next difficulty he encountered was in interesting friends and publishers in the work. "I could find two gentlemen only," Webster wrote to the editor of the *Recorder,* "who gave me the least encouragement of success. These were the late Judge Trumbull & Joel Barlow." [30] "I was obliged to print the books at my own risk & give my note for more than I was worth." [31] A contract for five thousand copies was let to Hudson & Goodwin, Hartford printers.[32] In the *Connecticut Courant,* October 7, 1783, this announcement appeared: "Just published 'The First Part of a *Grammatical Institute of the English Language . . . .*' by Noah Webster, A.M., 10ˢ per dozen or 14ᵈ per single book."

On reading this announcement, perhaps no one, not even Webster himself, realized that it announced to the world the beginnings of the banner text of all times and places. The full title of the first edition was *A Grammatical Institute of the English Language, Comprising An Easy, Concise, and Systematic Method of Education, Designed for Use of English Schools in America. In Three Parts. Part I. Containing a New and Accurate Standard of Pronunciation.*[33] This very formal, dignified title, "was the tribute which Webster paid to old-fashioned scholarship." [34] In keeping with the increasing patriotic ardor which followed the Revolution, the title was changed in the 1786 edi-

[30] Webster MSS. See also letter from Webster to Barlow, dated "New Haven, Oct. 19, 1807."—Todd's *Life and Letters of Joel Barlow* (1886), p. 244. It is said that Barlow gave Webster financial aid in the undertaking.—Ford's *Notes,* I, 59; II, 30.

[31] Webster MSS. Miscellaneous papers, undated.

[32] This firm remained Webster's Hartford printers for years. Webster's correspondence with Hudson and Goodwin was voluminous. See Webster MSS.

[33] According to the memorial addressed to the General Assembly of Connecticut, Oct. 24, 1782, the proposed title was *The American Instructor.*—Webster MSS.

[34] Scudder, *op. cit.,* p. 34.

tion to *The American Spelling Book*. With the 1829 revision the book was called *The Elementary Spelling Book*. Five generations of school children simplified these titles further to "The Blue-Back Speller" and "Webster's Old Spelling Book," the latter title having been actually used as a title to at least one printed edition.[35]

Part I of *A Grammatical Institute* was published in duo-decimo volumes, bound in contemporary calf. In the general plan of this speller, as well as in externals, Webster's "Part I," as it was frequently called, is similar to Dilworth's "Guide." The text was printed in type of medium size on cheap paper similar to that used in the printing of other early American texts. Of this practice Timothy Pickering complained, saying "The leaves should be thick, strong paper, & of tolerable fineness, to take a fair impression from a large & good type. For the letters ought to be perfectly fair and accurate to enable a child to distinguish them."[36] In Pickering's remarks we perhaps have the first concern shown in America over the format of a textbook, a concern of great importance among educators today.

In 1890 Colton described the traditional blue-back speller known to his generation and undoubtedly to some people living today:

The back of the cover is of coarse linen cloth—very coarse—threads within sight of each other. The sides of the cover are of layers of brown paper, with an over-all of thin blue paper. The paper and pages within look as if they might have come from a mill using bleached straw and slacked lime, with a little sulphur thrown in to give it tinting.[37]

As in Dilworth's *New Guide*, the alphabet in Part I was given in "small and great" Roman and Italic letters, which were followed by the pronunciation of the letters of the alphabet.[38] The

[35] Sanbornton, N. H. (1817 ?).

[36] Letter from Timothy Pickering to Noah Webster, Philadelphia, Oct. 19, 1785.—Ford's *Notes*, I, 97 f.

[37] A. M. Colton, "Our Old Webster Spelling-Book," *Magazine of American History*, XXIV, 467.

[38] One difference between the English and American pronunciation of the letters of the alphabet lies in the pronunciation of the letter *z*, which was pro-

syllabarium followed next, containing tables of nonsense syllables, two letters in length, such as *ba, be, bi, bo, bu;* these tables
were followed by tables of three-letter syllables, such as *bla, ble,
bli, blo, blu,* and so forth. Then appear the tables of words. Both
Dilworth's and Webster's spellers have lists of words ranging
from one to six syllables in length. In Webster's arrangement,
however, he proceeded with a gradation of easy words from one
to four syllables long. He then included some monosyllabic
words that are hard to spell and pronounce, such as "height,"
"wedge," "bough," and so forth, before he introduced the longer
words of five and six syllables.[39]

Webster made an effort to make his text practical. "The names
of domestic articles, animals, fruits, &C," he explained, "are collected for the use and pleasure of children, who are usually
taught to be better acquainted with all the words in the language, than with the written names of articles with which they
are most familiar." [40] He included a few six-syllable words, but
be it said to his credit that such useless and retired proper names
as Dilworth's "Abelbethmaachah" and "Berodachbaladan" were
not among them.

Dilworth's classification of words was arbitrary and confusing.
It was made according to the number of letters the words contained—the number of vowels and consonants, as indicated in
the heading, "Words of five, six, etc. letters, viz.: two vowels
serving only to lengthen the sound of the former, except where it
is otherwise marked," which explanation, says Scudder, "is

---

nounced "zed" by Dilworth and "zee" by Webster. It has been said that the
alphabet has been used as a shibboleth by immigration officers between the
United States and Canada, the English and Americans still using "zed" and
"zee" pronunciations, respectively. In the 1783 speller (p. 33) Webster declared
that "It is an errour universal among inaccurate speakers to sound *e* before *r*
like *a*," as in "mercy," "derby," and so forth. He concluded by saying, "I therefore request, once for all, that it may be attended to." He nevertheless gave *ar*
as the pronunciation of *r* in the alphabet. In the 1787 edition (Hartford), however, he gave *er* as the pronunciation of the letter *r*.

[39] *Institute*, Pt. I (1783), p. 10.
[40] *Ibid.*, p. 11.

nearly as luminous as a direction in knitting." [41] In compiling his tables, Webster "endeavoured to associate words of the same class in the same table that persons may know where to find them and learn their true pronunciation." [42] These tables, made up of words with such similar elements as sound, accent, and syllabication, enabled the pupils to generalize, a step in the learning process which is held desirable by modern educators.

As Webster did not believe that pupils should begin to read until they had learned to spell all the words,[43] his first reading lesson in the 1783 speller began on page 101. It contained no word of more than three letters. The sentences are either taken verbatim or adapted from Dilworth's. The manner in which Webster adapted these sentences shows that his tendency to secularize his text consisted largely in the expurgation of the word "God."

Dilworth's Version	*Webster's Version*
No man may put off the law of God	No man may put off the law of God
The way of God is no ill way	My joy is in his law all the day
My joy is in God all the Day	O may I not go in the way of sin
A bad man is a Foe to God.	Let me not go in the way of ill men.

He imitated Dilworth and Fenning also in that he used selections from the Psalms for the reading lesson. In like manner he adapted from Fenning such moral precepts as "A good child will not lie, swear nor steal. He will be good at home and ask to read his book; when he gets up he will wash his hands and face clean; he will comb his hair and make haste to school; he will not play by the way, as bad boys do." [44] Another borrowing from Fenning was the highly moral "Story of Tommy and Harry," in which

[41] *Op. cit.*, p. 36.
[42] *Institute* (1783), p. 10.
[43] As soon as a child can spell all the tables with the help of this book . . ." Webster advised, "let him spend one part of the day in reading the easy lessons; and the other part in getting the tables by heart." *Institute* (1783), I, 26.
[44] For further examples of selections intended to inculcate high moral standards in the minds of the young, see chap. v.

Webster, according to his own statement, made the original "flat, puerile, ungrammatical language" used by Fenning more grammatical and made the style plainer and simpler, free from vulgar expressions and "fitted to the capacities of youth."

As an aid in his attempt to make the orthography easier, and also to reduce the teacher's toil and trouble with his pupils, Webster introduced several devices to indicate the pronunciation. In the first place, he divided the words into a "natural division" of syllables, that is, as he thought they were pronounced. Dilworth's "clu-ster," became "clus-ter"; "ha-bit," "hab-it"; "nost-ril," "nos-tril"; "bis-hop," "bish-op," and so forth.[45] He also used a system of ten numerals, later increased to eleven, to indicate the vowel sounds in monosyllabic words and stressed syllables,[46] thus indicating the accent as well as the vowel quality, as illustrated by such words as "hă ven," "hăm let," "fȧll ing," "pȧrt ly," and so forth.[47] Silent letters were written in italics and italicized "s" was to be given the sound of "z." [48]

In his first speller, 1783, and in some of the later editions,[49] Webster included footnotes which served as warnings "calculated to extirpate the improprieties, introduced by settlers from various parts of Europe; to reform the abuses & corruptions which, to an unhappy degree, tincture the conversation of the polite part of the Americans . . ." Readers were told to say "burst," not "bust"; "chimney," not "chimbley"; "cover," not

[45] *A Grammatical Institute,* Part I (1783), p. 9.

[46] See Appendix I for Webster's Key or Index. Similar devices had been used in dictionaries by Kenrick (1773), Perry (1775), Sheridan (1780). Webster claimed, however, that these works were unknown to him in 1783.

[47] "In spelling and accenting," Webster wrote, "I have generally made Dr. Johnson's dictionary my guide; as in point of orthography this seems to be the most approved authority."—*Institute* (1783), p. 11.

[48] See p. 307. Italics were not consistently used, however. With regard to the devices used to indicate pronunciation, Webster gives this advice, following the four syllable words (page 45):

"Having carried a child through several tables of easy words, let him proceed to those which comprise more difficult and irregular words. Let him learn the use of the Italics, and to distinguish letters that are sounded from those that are silent. Let him be taught to use the Index; that is, to annex to every figure its proper sound."

[49] Improprieties were given in the 1787, 1792, 1799, 1801, and 1802 editions.

"kiver"; "asparagus," not "sparrowgrass"; "raspberry," not "roz-berry," and so forth.[50]

The 1783 speller imitated Dilworth further and on a much larger scale by including encylopedic material. As books were scarce in Webster's day, an informative book of this nature met a wide demand. This material includes abbreviations, names of principal kingdoms and states of Europe with their capital cities and population, names of the Islands of the West Indies, the thirteen original states with their capital towns, the provinces of Canada, some New England states with their counties and principal towns, principal counties in states and the principal towns in some counties, and an explanation of the length of pauses in reading. At the end of the book is given a short chrono-logical account of remarkable events in America, beginning with the discovery of America in 1492, recording forty events, and concluding with the General Pacification, January 29, 1783. In later editions this account was expanded to include many more events.

In this encyclopedic material, the author shows that his hori-zon does not extend far beyond his native state, Connecticut. Webster's *Institute* was plainly meant for the farmer boys and girls of his country. He shows his provinciality by listing the principal towns of Connecticut with the number of inhabitants and the distance of each town from Hartford. This trait is further shown, as has been noted, in that he included in the tables the names of small towns in the neighborhood of Sharon where he taught in 1781.

Several Revisions and Numerous Editions of Webster's Spelling Book Appeared during the Eighteenth and Nineteenth Centuries

THE foregoing is descriptive of some of the salient features of *A Grammatical Institute of the English Language, Part I,* first published in 1783, the speller upon which Webster based later

[50] For a discussion and complete list of Webster's improprieties see pp. 277 and 308 f.

editions. It is difficult to describe the traditional Webster speller
known to many generations. Such a description would involve
the extraction of the common denominator of many texts, varying according to the edition, the year, or the states in which they
were published.

In the preface of this first edition of the *Institute,* Webster
says that the author is "sensible that in words of this kind many
errours will escape the most critical observation." Immediately
after the publication of this speller he sought the advice of
friends in order to further his desire to improve succeeding editions.[51] Among those making suggestions were, as we have seen,
Elizur Goodrich and Timothy Pickering. The most thorough
criticism of Webster's first speller was made, however, by Samuel
Baldwin,[52] whom Webster had met in 1785 when he was in
Charleston, South Carolina,[53] in behalf of the copyright law and
whom Webster had asked to examine the text and communicate
to him such remarks and observations as might suggest themselves to him on a critical perusal of the work. Appended to
Baldwin's letter were the comments, which numbered more
than one hundred and fifty, having to do with spelling, pronunciations, usage, parts of speech, typographical errors, and so
forth.

As the many editions still extant testify, Webster set about at
once to improve his speller as well as to supply the demand which
it had created. The use that he made of the dictionaries is set
forth in an article published in 1785:

As to the first part, the plan of the speller of 1783, I solemnly declare
it was my own. I never heard the name of Sheridan, Kenrick or Perry
till I had prepared my copy for the press; and never consulted their

[51] Apparently, in at least one case, Webster sought advice before the book was
published on October 5, 1783. On August 27 of that year, he wrote the Reverend
Elizur Goodrich at Durham, Connecticut, sending him some sheets of the *Institute.* On September 29, Goodrich wrote him at length, commenting and criticizing
freely.

[52] Webster MSS; a letter to Noah Webster from Samuel Baldwin, dated
"Charleston, Dec. 30, 1785."

[53] This entry appears in Webster's diary for July 3, 1785: "Sunday. Read Beattie's
Theory of Language, lent me by Mr Sam^1 Baldwin."—Ford, *Notes,* I, 136.

works till I had published my first edition. But I acknowledge myself
much indebted to them for the improvements in the last editions.[54]

An important revision of the *Institute* took place in 1788
when the title was changed to *The American Spelling Book.*
From a letter [55] dated New York, July 4, 1788, and signed by
Josiah Hoffman, president of the Philological Society,[56] we learn
that Webster's *American Spelling Book* was approved by that
organization and recommended "to the use of schools in the
United States, as an accurate, well digested system of principles
and rules, calculated to destroy the various false dialects in pronunciation in the several States, an object very desirable in a
federal republic." In a letter written September 7, 1788, to
Russel and Hopewell, publishers, at Bennington, Vermont, Webster stated that the work in the future "must be copied from the
last edition, which is corrected by the Philological Society &
recommended as the elements of a *federal* language. I shall in-
sist upon it that all the future editions be alike. The works must
also be correct and well executed. . . ." [57] Other important revisions were made in 1792 and 1803. These had to do in the main
with the rearrangement and addition of words. More reading
lessons were added and these were placed earlier in the texts.

A valuable addition to the revised texts was the inclusion of
fables. In a letter dated at Lansingburgh, Vermont, May 14,
1788, Sam Cogswell,[58] made this suggestion:

I wish your first part had a little more reading in it than it has—
Do you not think that a few easy fables, and familiar allegories,
where the application is so readily understood, that while the little
mind is delighted with the story, it cannot fail of being benefited by
the moral, would render it more serviceable than it is now?

This letter may have suggested to Webster that fables be included for reading lessons. Since his plan from the first included

[54] Noah Webster's Reply to *Dilworth's Ghost, Weekly Monitor*, Feb. 15, 1785.
[55] Advertisement in *American Spelling Book*, Boston, 1790, VIII. This letter
along with many others was frequently quoted in advertising Webster's books.
[56] See pp. 16f.
[57] Webster MSS.
[58] *Ibid.*

the reader as a separate part, he perhaps had not planned to include as many reading lessons in the speller as the fables supplied. At any rate, soon after Cogswell's letter was received, Webster included in his speller [59] such fables as "Of the Boy That Stole Apples," "The Country Maid and Her Milk Pail," "The Fox and the Swallow," "The Two Dogs," "The Partial Judge," "The Cat and the Rat," "The Fox and the Bramble," "The Bear and the Two Friends," and "The Boy who Went to the Woods to Look for Birds' Nests When He Should Have Gone to School." These fables did not appear in all of the various editions, and at times only part of them were printed; but whenever fables appeared, "Of the Boy That Stole Apples" and "The Country Maid and Her Milk Pail," because of their popularity, were always sure to be included.

In adding these fables Webster again followed the example of Fenning and Dilworth, although, with the exception of "Of the Boy That Stole Apples," which was taken from Fenning's Speller, he did not print the fables found in the books of these authors. Excepting the first and last of the stories named, they were taken verbatim from Robert Dodsley's *Select Fables of Esop and Other Fabulists* (1761).[60] Webster perhaps did more to popularize these fables than has any other agency. The authorship of the dull, highly moralistic story, "The Boy Who Went to the Woods to Look for Birds' Nests When He Should Have Gone to School," is unknown. It may have been written by Webster and may have been "inspired" by Fenning's "Of the Boys that Went into the Water, Instead of Being at School, or at Home." Imitating Dilworth and Fenning again, Webster had his stories illustrated, at first with crude illustrations by such en-

[59] The earliest edition I have seen which includes the fables is the Hartford, 1792, edition. This is one of the earliest editions, if not the first edition, in which appeared the maxims, which later became an important part of the work.

[60] Dodsley is the acknowledged source of the fables used by William Scott in his *Lessons in Elocution* (1779), a book to which Webster refers in the preface to his Part III of the Institute. Since the language in the stories and the morals is identical to that used by Dodsley, Webster undoubtedly drew from that source also. See pp. 314 f.

gravers as Asa W. Lay,[61] Z. Howe, and W. Wadsworth.[62] In 1795 Alexander Anderson, the first American engraver of note, did the engravings, and these excellent pictures appeared from time to time throughout the nineteenth century; however, not all the illustrations that appeared after 1795 were Anderson's. Sometimes those by Lay, Howe, Wadsworth, or some other crude engraver were used.

In 1829, *The American Spelling Book* passed through a thorough revision and the title was changed to *The Elementary Spelling Book*.[63] The object of a work of this kind, Webster stated in the Preface, is to teach orthography and pronunciation; and for that reason it was "judged most proper to adapt the various tables to these specific objects, and omit extraneous matter. In short, this little book is so constructed as to condense, into the smallest compass a complete *System of Elements* for teaching the language." At this time, more than ever, Webster seemed conscious of the importance of the work. "However small such a book may appear," he declared, "it may be considered as the most important Class-book, not of a religious character, which the youth of our country are destined to use." [64]

Writing in 1831,[65] Lyman Cobb, a rival compiler of school texts who was indefatigable in his attacks on Webster, says that the 1829 revision was made not by Webster but by Aaron Ely.[66] Webster denied this charge,[67] but papers show that at least a contract between Webster and Ely was made.[68] Cobb says further

[61] See Hartford, 1792, edition.
[62] See Hartford, 1799, edition.
[63] *The American Spelling Book* was again revised in 1833 and sold under the title "*The New American Spelling Book* for the use of Primary Schools in the United States."
[64] In 1836 Webster published *The Teacher; or Supplement to the Elementary Spelling Book.* A second edition was published in 1837.
[65] *A Critical Review of the Orthography of Dr. Webster's* . . .
[66] *Ibid.*, p. vi.
[67] Webster MSS. In a printed statement to the public Webster says, "His [Cobb's] unfounded conjectures, and one palpable falsehood, respecting the authorship of my *Elementary Spelling Book*, I will not particularly notice."
[68] This contract was written in Webster's hand and signed by both Webster and Ely. There are two identical copies among Webster's papers. The fact that Web-

that it was his attack of Webster in 1828 [69] that made the revision of the spelling book imperative. Be that as it may, it seems to have been the policy of Webster to revise his spellers from time to time, thus renewing the copyrights and securing the benefits for himself and his heirs for another term of years. It was this plan which he purposed to follow and which he advised his heirs to follow with regard to the dictionary.[70] During the five years following the 1829 revision, Webster's speller achieved substantially its final form, the form which was used during the remainder of the century. More words were added, the ensemble was changed, and more selections for reading were included. The variations which were noticeable toward the end of the century were on the last twenty or thirty pages.

Another interesting edition of the *Elementary Spelling Book* was the *Pictorial Elementary Spelling Book* [71] in which the "old quaker dress" of former editions was laid aside and a more colorful one donned. This edition contained one hundred and sixty engravings by Alexander Anderson [72] and his pupil, W. F. Morgan. Like the old almanacs of the period, it had running pictures at the top of the page, over such captions as "A tribunal is a court for deciding causes," "An orator makes orations," "The farmer likes to have plenty of hay for his cattle," and "Autumnal fruits are fruits that ripen in the autumn," all sentences taken from the reading lessons. Then there was a frontispiece, a sort of glorification of the usual one found in Webster's spellers, representing the temple of Fame on the hill of Science and groups of young urchins struggling up the eminence.[73] The text

ster retained both copies tends to substantiate Webster's claim that Ely did not compile the book.

[69] *Critical Review of Noah Webster's Spelling Book.* First published in a series of articles in the Albany *Argus* in 1827 and 1828, by "Examinator" (Lyman Cobb). Printed in pamphlet form in 1828. Many held this review "was inspired by malice and a desire to increase his own sales. This he stoutly denied."—*Dictionary of American Biography,* IV, 244.

[70] William Chauncey Fowler, *Printed, but Not Published,* n. t., n. p. (after 1846), p. 6.

[71] Published by George F. Cooledge & Brother, New York [1844 ?].

[72] For examples of Anderson's work see pp. 64, 80, 314-15.

[73] See p. 31.

SEE where FAME's Temple stands,
Like beacon from afar;
Press on, ye youthful bands,
Let no true heart despair.

FRONTISPIECE OF THE PICTORIAL ELEMENTARY SPELLING BOOK [1844?]

of the *Elementary Spelling Book* was unaltered, except that it was compressed to give the needed space for the pictures. The fact that the book was "printed with a new and clear type on good paper" indicates that authors and publishers of that age were beginning to realize the importance of these elements in the make-up of a textbook for children. This edition was perhaps one of the most elaborate attempts at illustrating a schoolbook in order to "interest children and help them over the shoals and quicksands of learning their first lessons" that had been made up to that time.

The Great Extent to Which Webster's Speller Was Used and the Enthusiasm with Which It Was Remembered Indicate the Scope of Its Influence

THESE outstanding editions, however significant, are only a few of the many editions of this very popular textbook, which, it is said, had in it from the first the promise of success.[74]

The first edition of five thousand copies was exhausted in the course of the following winter. These five thousand copies were probably a greater supply of spelling books for schools than the whole country contained when Webster took his first lesson in reading at a common school some twenty years before.[75]

The demand for a spelling book and the importance which prominent men of the post-Revolutionary days attached to its publication is well shown by a letter written in 1783 by Timothy Pickering. This letter was written after Pickering, then stationed at Newburgh waiting for the army to be disbanded, had sat up all night to read the speller through, having received it by post the day before. Of the book he wrote to his wife:

I am much pleased with it. The author is ingenious, and writes from his own experience as a schoolmaster, as well as the best authorities; and the time will come when no authority, as an English grammarian, will be superior to his own. It is the very thing I have so long wished for, being much dissatisfied with any spelling-book I had seen before . . .

[74] Scudder, *op. cit.*, p. 52.
[75] Ford, *Notes*, II, 447.

The propitious reception which the speller received is further shown by the letter written by Elizur Goodrich (1734-97), a Congregational minister, then pastor at Durham, Connecticut. Goodrich heartily approved of the part submitted to him, not without reservations, however, and expressed his hope that the "other parts may be so well executed, as that the work may answer the excellent purpose of its general title, in the education of youth, and be of eminent use and service not only in the lower schools but also in the higher seminaries of literature throughout America." [76]

From the very beginning Webster shows that he deemed it a matter of great importance that he should know the right people and that they should endorse his opinions. He accumulated a vast collection of testimonials from prominent men and groups of prominent men, with whom he was in most cases personally acquainted—101 members of Congress, the Philological Society, publishers, authors, educators, and so forth. These testimonials were frequently appended to his texts and his pamphlets. Perhaps not all of his acquaintances and friends were as frank as George Washington, who wrote in answer to Webster's discreet suggestion that his name "as a patron of the *Institute,* would be very influential in introducing it to notice in these States [Southern] . . . if it can be done, consistently with the sentiments of your heart and the delicacy of your feelings. . . ." To this request Washington replied that he was willing to write letters recommending the author to some of the first Gentlemen of his acquaintance in Charleston on the basis of the favorable impression Webster had made on him, but as to the utility of the work he wished to decline from comment. "I haven't the leisure to examine the *Institute* with that attention which ought, always, to precede a certificate, and because I do not think myself a competent judge, if I had." [77]

It would be a Herculean task indeed to give an accurate account of the numerous editions and issues, including dates and

[76] Webster MSS. Letter dated "Durham, Sept. 29, 1783." See p. 76.
[77] Letter dated "Mount Vernon, July 30, 1785."—Ford, I, 93.

places of publication. Webster's *Spelling Book,* like the *New England Primer* and the *English Reader,* once printed by the million, has taken its place among the rare books of America. With the shifting of the frontier came the establishing of new centers of publication. Webster's unpublished manuscripts are replete with letters to and from publishers throughout the East, the South, and the Middle West. In one of Webster's account books [78] are given one hundred names of publishers who had secured the rights of publication for certain districts. The manner in which Webster sold the rights for the early editions of Part I is indicated by a sworn affidavit [79] charging Samuel Campbell, who had the sale rights in New York, with bootlegging the *Institutes* into Connecticut. According to this sworn statement, in 1786 Webster disposed of the sale rights of the speller, the grammar, and the reader, to Hudson and Goodwin, printers and booksellers in Hartford, Connecticut, for a "good and valuable consideration." [80] This contract gave the firm the "exclusive privelege [*sic*] of printing & vending said *Grammatical Institute* & all parts of it, in Connecticut, New Hampshire, Massachusetts, & Rhode Island, for the whole term granted & secured to him the deponent by the laws of the several States aforesaid." [81] The rights of printing and selling the three parts in Pennsylvania, Delaware, Maryland, and Virginia were sold to William Young, bookseller in Philadelphia, in 1787, for a period of three years; also a "concurrent right of vending s^d Institute in New York, New Jersey, North Carolina, South Carolina & Georgia." During the same year (1787) Webster sold to "Samuel Campbell, book-

[78] Webster MSS.

[79] Webster MSS. "The Charge against Campbell, Feb. 28, 1789."

[80] The amount of this "consideration" varied; usually it ranged all the way from five mills to a cent a copy. In some cases a flat sum was paid for the rights during a term of years. Such a contract was made in 1818 between Webster and the firm at Hartford, Hudson and Goodwin, who were to pay him $3,000 during a term of fourteen years.—Scudder, *op. cit.,* p. 70.

[81] In a 1790 edition of the *American Spelling Book,* Thomas and Andrews, Boston printers, made this announcement: "The very favourable reception has induced us to purchase the exclusive right of printing all the Three Parts of said *Institute,* in the states of Massachusetts, New Hampshire, and Rhode Island for a Term of Fifteen years."

seller in New York, the sale right of *printing* & a *concurrent right* of vending the first part of said Institute, in the States of New York, New Jersey, North Carolina, South Carolina & Georgia, for the term of five years," to commence the first of May, 1788.

"His desire 'to correct popular errors,' " says Krapp, "and his patriotism were beyond question both sincere, but these ideals were combined in his character with a very keen business sense and an ear for popular approval which sometimes served to check the purer impulses." [82] At no place are the traits of Webster the shrewd Yankee business man more apparent than in his correspondence relative to the publication of his texts: Now it is a letter to publishers accused of printing pirated editions, making an offer permitting them to print and sell as "many of the books as you please & where you please; provided you pay me ten pounds, L M, the present year . . . and fifteen pounds a year for the four succeeding years—at which time a new contract shall commence"; [83] again a letter to publishers whose contract is about to expire, saying that "a reputable Bookseller here informs me, he understands you are printing an unusual number of copies with a view to supply the market beyond the term for which you have the exclusive right of printing & vending—I cannot believe this information as such a step is not only illegal (& I have recovered damages agt one Bookseller for a like measure after a contract for five years.)"; [84] and now a letter to booksellers proposing to dispose of the copyright of the spelling book to a single purchaser for the whole term of fourteen years at the price of one cent a copy or ten dollars a thousand.[85]

Many pirated editions of the *Elementary Spelling Book* appeared,[86] especially in the South after the Civil War, where

[82] George Philip Krapp, *The English Language in America* (1925), I, 335.

[83] Webster MSS. Letter from Webster to Russel & Hopewell, Bennington, Vt., dated "New York, Sept. 7, 1788."

[84] Webster MSS. Copy of letter sent by Webster to Messrs. Bonsal & Niles, Wilmington, Del., dated "Philadelphia, Nov. 24, 1803."

[85] Webster MSS. Dated "Amherst, Mass., Nov. 20, 1815."

[86] "The spelling book was repeatedly published in a pirated form without any acknowledgement to the author. Indeed both in England and America this trespassing and pirating was the frequent accompaniment of Webster's successful school books. Many attacks of piracy and criticism followed during his later years.

"Webster's book had been more generally accepted than at the North." [87] Slosson states that "When the South attempted to establish its Confederacy, it declared at the same time its independence of the New England text-book." [88] The pirated editions of Webster's spelling book show, however, the hold which the book had on the schools of the South. One edition was entitled *"The Elementary Spelling Book,* Revised and adapted to the youth of the Southern Confederacy, interspersed with Bible Readings on Domestic Slavery." [89] The Preface states that for many years Webster's spelling book "has been almost the only Spelling-book used in the Southern States, as well as in other sections of the old union; and his dictionary may be found in almost every family, occupying, as it deservedly does, a preeminence over all others." The editor says further that the orthography of Webster has been invariably retained and that only in a few cases has his pronunciation been rejected. An interesting feature of this speller, as the title indicates, is the quotations from the Bible, justifying the rebellion and the institution of slavery.[90] Included in the encyclopedic material are the names of the Confederate States along with their capitals, populations, and dates of secession. Then follow the names of the Federal States, their capitals, their populations in 1860, and a short biography of Washington.

This illicit traffic in Webster's spellers did not supply the entire demand during and following the Civil War. In 1880

The complaints, remonstrances and even suits, some libelous, some for violation of copyright, some for downright dishonesty which progressed for forty years would fill a volume by themselves, and the strangest contradictions were seen of bookmakers who struck at Webster's system with one hand, while they pillaged his ideas with the other."—Ford, *Notes,* II, 449.

[87] Scudder, *op. cit.,* p. 71.

[88] "The American Spirit in Education," *The Chronicles of America,* XXXIII (1921), 120. Copyright Yale University Press.

[89] Copyrighted in 1863 by Robert Fleming in the clerk's office of the District of the Confederate States of America, for the Southern District of Georgia.

[90] The following quotations are typical: "When the enemy shall come in like a flood, the spirit of the Lord shall lift up a standard against him."—Isaiah 59:19.

"Servants, be obedient to them that are your masters according to the flesh, with fear and trembling, in singleness of your heart, as unto Christ."—Eph. 6:5.

William H. Appleton stated that "The year following the eman-
cipation of the slaves we sold one million five hundred thousand,
because every negro in the South thought it only necessary to
have a Webster's Speller to learn to read. After that year it fell
back to the original million and has never varied." [91]

Such a common commodity did Webster's spelling book become that country merchants, it is said, laid in supplies of them
when they came to the nearest trading town, as confidently as
they bought West India goods or English tools. It is interesting
to note that during the twenty years Webster was preparing the
American Dictionary, published in 1828, the royalty obtained
from the sale of the spelling book, usually five mills a copy, was
the chief source of his income for the support of his family,[92]
although some of his letters reveal the fact that at times in the
earlier years he was in straitened circumstances and the prophecy made by one of the "Hartford Wits" [93] at the time of Webster's marriage, that he would perhaps breakfast on institutes,
lunch on dissertations, and go supperless to bed, almost came
true.

As money was scarce in those days and there was much barter
of merchandise, Webster, at least on one occasion, met a financial
obligation with spelling books. The records of Christ's Church
at Hartford show that although he was a Congregationalist Webster subscribed three pounds toward the building fund, which
amount he paid in seven dozen spelling books—a strange payment in kind to be found in the company of the other donations

---

"Knowing that whatsoever good thing any man doeth, the same shall he receive
of the Lord, whether he be bond or free."—Eph. 6:8.

[91] *Youth's Companion,* May 27, 1880.

[92] Webster's MSS. In an open letter addressed to "Messrs. A. Picket and J. W.
Picket" (formerly the editors of the *Academician* (1818) and text books), dated
"Nov., 1836," Webster accuses the brothers of plagiarism. "This work has," he
informed them, "during nearly forty years, been the chief means of my support,
and has been the only source from which supplies for my family were drawn while
I was compiling my large dictionary. It is now the principal means of my subsistence in old age."

[93] John Trumbull in a letter to Oliver Wolcott, Hartford, Dec. 9, 1789. See
Ford's *Notes,* I, 269.

mentioned: ten pounds of "pure spirit," donated by Major Cald-
well, and a hogshead of molasses, given by John Chenevard, the
right ingredients for "black strap," a beverage then popular in
the best class of society.[94] Also, he expressed his willingness to
take commodities in payment for spellers. "To make the payment easy," he wrote to Russel & Hopewell, "for I know the difficulty of raising cash, I will take wheat, or any merchantable
produce, delivered at the store of Messrs. Jones & Dale in Lan-
singburg at cash price; or such articles as they suppose will find
a ready market in New York." [95]

Perhaps no textbook has ever had a longer life of usefulness
than Webster's speller. The results of his efforts in the field of
textbook compilation "were prodigious, perhaps unparalleled
in the history of American elementary education." [96] At least in
some quarters the speller was looked upon as a great civilizer.
For this reason, at one time an appeal was made to leading Bap-
tist missionaries in Burmah asking them to devote their time to
the preparation of texts. "School books, too," it was declared,
"will be missionaries. Webster's spelling-book helped to make
this nation. Let something of the kind be made a corner-stone in
Burmah." [97]

Writing in 1883, Benton says, "The hundredth birth-year of a
school-book still in successful life, is not an ordinary affair. But
this year the friends of Webster's *Spelling-Book* can celebrate
that anniversary. Few among those that are now happening are
more worthy." [98]

[94] Wilbur Webster Judd, *Connecticut Magazine,* n. d., Book of Pamphlets on
Education, Teachers College, Columbia University.

[95] *Op. cit.*

[96] Old South Leaflets, VIII, 424. "The success of these undertakings of Webster
[the Spelling Book] and Morse [the Geography] is to be classed among the
wonders in literary history . . . It is not saying too much that these books were
great books for the advancement of popular knowledge."—J. W. Frances, *Old
New York,* 1858, p. 341.

[97] "The Spelling Book as a Civilizer," *New York Evangelist,* March 24, 1873.
One reason Webster gave for his desire to reform the English language was that
its anomalies hinder the spread of the gospel.

[98] Joel Benton, "The Webster Spelling-Book," *American Magazine of History,*
X (1883), 299 ff.

Other writers have commented on the longevity of the book. Sullivan says,

More than five generations of Americans learned from it. The first studied it before there was any United States. . . . Boys learned from the Blue-Back Speller, grew up, became Presidents of the United States, died, and were relatively forgotten, while the presses of D. Appleton & Company ground out new editions for second, third, and fourth generations.[99]

Colton says that

It has trained and strained more heads than any other book of the kind ever did, or perhaps ever will.[100]

Writing in the *Congregational Quarterly,* the Rev. I. N. Tarbox declares that

There can be no doubt that this little work is intimately associated with the primary education of a greater number of minds than any other book ever used in this country. The present generation (1865) of living men and women, in almost every part of the land, when they go back in memory to their early school days find their thoughts resting upon this, as their only and all important text-book. Many a gray haired man or woman can remember the time when every hard word in its columns on which they were liable to stumble was mapped out in their minds . . .[101]

As to the number of spellers published, we have no exact figures, as records were not kept during the early years of its career. Estimates made by Webster and by the publishers, along with advertisements which have appeared in the various editions from time to time, tell all that is known. The estimates all point to the conclusion that the number of books published and used is stupendous. In 1807 Webster estimated the annual sale at 200,000 copies.[102] Scudder reports that "In 1814, 1815, the sales averaged 286,000 copies a year."[103] In 1837, Webster estimated that the number of copies sold to that date was at least fifteen millions.[104]

[99] Mark Sullivan, *Our Times* (1927), II, 89. C. Scribner's Sons.
[100] A. M. Colton, "Our Old Webster Spelling-Book," *Magazine of American History,* XXIV (1890), 467.
[101] Vol. VII, Pt. I, p. 4. See Ford's *Notes,* II, 448.
[102] Todd, *Life and Letters of Joel Barlow* (1886), p. 244.
[103] *Op. cit.,* p. 71.
[104] Letter to William D. Williamson.—Ford, *Notes,* II, 448.

During the year of his death, Webster wrote, "The whole estimates nearly 19,000,000 copies—and selling almost a half million yearly, at present time, 1843." [105] By 1865 the estimate had risen to 42,000,000,[106] and an advertisement in an 1889 edition says that 62,000,000 copies of the book had been sold.[107] As we have seen, the sales of the book reached the peak immediately following the Civil War.

When D. Appleton & Company took over the plates of the speller in 1855, the book was seventy-two years old. But this company, reports Sullivan, "took it up with as much enthusiasm as if it were the newest and most up-to-date manuscript." [108] When in 1880 an interviewer asked William H. Appleton what was the best selling book published by his firm, he replied,

Webster's Speller . . . and it has the largest sale of any book in the world except the Bible. We sell a million copies a year. Yes, and we have been selling it at that rate for forty years . . . we sell them in cases of seventy-two dozen, and they are bought by all the large dry-goods houses and supply stores, and furnished by them to every cross-roads store.[109]

The first edition of this remarkable book antedated the presidency of Washington and the last was contemporary with Theodore Roosevelt. The first edition was printed on a hand press and the last on the most modern Hoe.[110] One of the largest presses in the Appleton plant ran day after day, on this book, until it was completely worn out.[111]

Several writers have commented on the most unusual popularity of this book. Krapp says that its popularity was undoubtedly due in large measure to the fact that it presented an orderly,

[105] Webster MSS. Miscellaneous papers relative to Webster's Spelling Book. It was also during 1843 that the copyright privileges of the speller along with those of the dictionary were bought by the G. & C. Merriam Company of Springfield, Mass.

[106] Ford, *Notes*, II, 448.

[107] "It is computed that more than 80,000,000 copies of this spelling book were sold before 1880."—Evans, *American Bibliography*, VI, 263.

[108] *Op. cit.*, II, 128.

[109] *Youth's Companion*, May 27, 1880.

[110] Sullivan, *op. cit.*, II, 89.

[111] *Ibid.*, II, 128.

and as far as convention at all permitted, an economical and systematic guide to English spelling, and he believes the book is historically significant not as a radical book but as a book that was widely used.[112] Scudder believes that there were several contributory causes for the popularity of the book—the great demand for elementary schoolbooks, the real advance of Webster's speller over any other existing, the promptness with which he met the first call—all these causes combined, he believes, gave a great impetus to the little book.[113] Thompson is of the opinion that the effective moral training which it gave "had not a little to do with the unexampled continuous success of the speller." [114]

Undoubtedly the great popularity of the book was due in the main to these causes. But that there were certain intrinsic qualities which captured the imagination and the sentiments of succeeding generations and held them is made clear by writers who used the book and who in after years wrote of it with affection.

But what pleasant memories remain with those who long ago studied Webster's Spelling Book! [wrote Joel Benton in 1883]. The very pages in their precise form are pictured for us on indelible tablets. . . . Those who, in beginning to read, discovered that "She fed the old hen," "Ann can hem my cap," "Fire will burn wood and coal," "A tiger will kill and eat a man," and other significant facts, little thought that in all their after life nothing they might learn would ever seem so touching and significant.[115]

Not least among the qualities which endeared the old Blue-Back to many generations were the illustrations.[116] The many statements of those who long ago dreamed over the pictures bear testimony to that fact.

The first schoolbook I ever saw [wrote Chase Osborn, Governor of Michigan (1911–12)] was a Speller. It had a picture of a good dog

[112] Krapp, *The English Language in America* (1925), I, 339. Copyright Modern Language Association.

[113] Scudder, *Noah Webster* (1882), p. 72.

[114] Everett E. Thompson, "Noah Webster and Amherst College," *Amherst Graduates' Quarterly*, XXII (Aug., 1933), 291.

[115] *Magazine of American History*, X (1883), 299.

[116] Webster summed up the objections often made against the excessive use of pictures in texts and showed that he was somewhat in sympathy with them. It was objected that children waste their time, as well as soil and wear out the book

Tray getting a beating because he was caught in the company of bad dogs. "Evil communications corrupt good manners" was the lesson. On another page was a wood-cut of a boy up in an apple-tree and an old man pelting him with clods. The boy laughed and the old gentleman took stones and brought him down. The interpretation was "If sticks will not do, take clubs [stones]." That's where Roosevelt got his "big stick" phrase. He got many of his other maxims and aphorisms out of McGuffey's Third Reader, too.[117] That is one thing that made him and his precepts popular—they recalled things everybody had learned at school and believed. They had almost the standing of the Ten Commandments.[118]

"The Country Maid and her Milk-Pail," wrote Benton,[119] "seemed to me particularly pathetic. I always felt profoundly sorry for that milkmaid . . . The fable was different from those most familiar to us, by having the moral drawn very solemnly as a preface to the story." The moral, taken verbatim from Dodsley reads: "When men suffer their imagination to amuse them with the prospect of distant and uncertain improvements of their condition, they frequently sustain real losses, by their inattention to those affairs in which they are immediately concerned." Benton's reaction as a child to this moral confirms the contention of psychologists today that moral abstractions are meaningless to children. "This moral," he continues, "was not at all the one that would have occurred to me. The most obvious and valuable lesson, I used to think, was that it would be better to carry a pail of milk with your hands, instead of trying to balance it on your head."

Another engraving of Anderson's which has brought forth considerable comment was the frontispiece,[120] which is also described by Benton:

---

while looking at pictures. Pictures increase the expense of books without giving an equivalent advantage; they do as much harm as good and promote superficial learning. Finally, they "are not representative *of the life* of real objects, but *fictitious* representations formed by a painter or the engraver."—*A Collection of Papers* (1843), p. 310.

[117] "Meddlesome Matties," for example.

[118] Mark Sullivan, *Our Times* (1927), II, 207. C. Scribner's Sons.

[119] Joel Benton, "The Webster Spelling-Book," *American Magazine of History,* October, 1883, p. 299.

[120] See p. 63.

That wonderful picture of Minerva, the Goddess of Wisdom, with her lofty and dignified cap (I suppose it was she, though when a boy it bewildered me not a little), taking a young aspirant by the hand and pointing, with her right hand upraised, to the two temples of Knowledge and Fame in the distance, everybody will remember. It was a picture which I have pored over for hours on the school bench, wondering how those rocks and precipices could ever be surmounted which stood so gloomily in the way of the coveted journey.[121]

Webster Advocated the Alphabet Method throughout His Entire Career

IN 1782 Webster wrote John Canfield,[122] "The more I look into our language & the method of instruction practiced in this country, the more I am convinced of the necessity of improving one & correcting the other." In the Preface to his first speller (1783), the author said, "We find Englishmen practicing upon very erroneous maxims in politics and religion; and possibly we shall find upon careful examination, that their methods of education are equally erroneous and defective." Webster did not, however, introduce a new method of instruction in his *Institute*. The novelty of his "plan" consisted in the grouping of words in tables according to the law of association, the arrangement of words into a more natural division of syllables, and in using devices to aid in pronunciation.[123] The method of instruction around which the speller was compiled was the alphabet method —a method which had been used as far back as the history of education extends.[124] His system had much in common with that which was used by the English Edmund Coote in the sixteenth century [125] and recommended by Charles Hoole in 1659.[126] In 1843 Webster described his method of teaching spelling and

[121] This engraving is an adaptation of the frontispiece in R. J. Dodsley's *Preceptor* (1748), Vol. I.
[122] *Op. cit.*, Webster MSS.
[123] See p. 307.
[124] For a discussion of the history of the alphabet method see R. R. Reeder's *Historical Development of School Readers and Method in Teaching Reading* (1900), p. 61.
[125] *The English Schoolmaster* (1596).
[126] *A New Discovery of the Old Art of Teaching School* (reprint, 1912).

reading in "Modes of Teaching the English Language." [127] A comparison of the principles set forth in this article with those meagerly set forth in his first spellers reveals that he held practically the same ideas regarding method during his last years as those he held when he started his career. Since Webster has written very little on method, these remarks are quoted at length.

[I]   In learning the English language, the first thing is to make the pupil perfectly acquainted with the letters in the alphabet. While he is learning the shape and the name of each letter, he should learn to repeat the letters in the alphabetical order, and commit them to memory in this order, so as to be able to repeat them without the least hesitation. The reason is that every person through life has frequent occasion to use the letters in this order, in seeking words in a dictionary, in consulting indexes, in arranging documents, &C. Hence the extreme unpropriety of dividing the alphabet into sections, and arranging the letters in any other order than the alphabetical. Let a child form a habit of repeating letters of the alphabet in any other order than the alphabetical, and he will be liable to be embarrassed with it all his life. These observations are applicable to learning the days of the week in their order; as also the months of the year, and the books of the Old and New Testaments.

If it should be objected that the learning of the alphabet is difficult, let the importance of the practice be the answer; take more time; one great fault in teaching is going too fast, learning the first rudiments imperfectly, and thus retarding future progress.

The necessity of going very slow and being perfect "without book" before proceeding, a theory which Webster and other compilers of his age constantly reiterated, is a direct inheritance from the past—from methods used in teaching Latin grammar. The early English Latin master was instructed to "make him [the pupil] to rehearse so that until he hath perfectly that, which is behinde, he suffer him not to go forward . . ." [128] This method was later recommended by John Brinsley, who had a strong influence in matters educational during the seventeenth century. [129] "A child should never," Webster declared in 1783, "be put to a second lesson before he has perfectly learnt the first. . . ." Again,

[127] *A Collection of Papers on Political, Literary and Moral Subjects* (1843), p. 307.
[128] William Lily, *A Short Introduction to Grammar* (1709), "To the Reader."
[129] *Ludus literarius* (1612; 1917 ed. by E. T. Campagnac), pp. 51 ff.

in 1843, he expresses the opinion that "to do one thing at a time" is "the most important point perhaps in a system of education." [130]

[II]   From single letters, the pupil should proceed to combinations of two letters, and learn perfectly the pronunciation of each combination; then proceed to combinations of three letters; and this without much regard to the signification of words. The opinion that a pupil should never pronounce a word which he does not understand, is a great error; as it makes it necessary that a knowledge of spelling should proceed no faster than that of definition. A more absurd opinion, and one more directly opposed to the laws of the human mind, was never broached.

[III]   When this is accomplished, pupils should proceed to *words, monosyllables.*[131] If the words are what are called household words, as words in daily use, they probably understand their meaning, and if not, the teacher may explain them. This, however, is not very important, in this stage of instruction; as it is the spelling and pronunciation which they are learning.

In this stage of instruction are first seen the benefits of *classification* in elementary books. Words of like formation are to be pronounced alike. Similarity of words aids the memory. In this and in the following stage of instruction, the pupils should be taught in classes; and *every one* in the class should be directed to spell *every* word in the lesson, and then to pronounce every word. This repetition should be continued till *every child* can spell and pronounce correctly *every* word in the lesson without the smallest hesitation. Such repetition will fasten the true spelling and pronunciation upon the mind of every child; and this process occasionally repeated *in reviews* will accomplish the object.

[IV]   From monosyllables the pupil will proceed to dissyllables. In this stage, a knowledge of accent is to be added to that of spelling and the pronunciation of letters. The pupil is to be taught what accent is, and pronounce every word in the lesson with its proper

[130] *A Collection of Papers* (1843), p. 307.
"It was assumed that there was a necessary connection between naming the letters of a word and pronouncing the word. No other approach to the pronunciation of the printed symbol was imagined by the great majority of teachers. So universal was this opinion that it passed into a proverb: 'You must learn to spell before you can read.' "—Reeder, *op. cit.*, p. 63.
[131] This lesson was considered by the pupils as one of the important ones in the book. "High day when we advanced to table number 2, bag, big, bog."—A. M. Colton, *American Magazine of History*, XXIV (1890), 467.

accent. The whole class should be taught to repeat, pronounce, and spell every word in the lesson.[132]

In a proper classification of words those of like termination should be arranged in the same column. In many classes of words of like termination, the accent is uniformly on the same syllable; that is, at the same distance from the termination. Suppose the pupil is to spell words of three syllables ending in *ity;* as in *amity, dignity, lenity;* he is to be informed that all words with a similar ending have the accent on the last syllable but two, (the antepenult). When, by repeating and spelling a lesson of these words, he is made familiar with the pronunciation he may be put to words of more syllables, as in *ability, deformity, mutability, immutability, infallibility.* From practice in these classes, he will learn to accent and pronounce correctly every word in the language, having a like termination.

In like manner, the pupil will learn that all words ending in *tion* and *sion,* have the accent on the last syllable but one, (the penult;) that all words ending in *ology* and *ography,* have the accent on the last syllable but two, as in *doxology, orthography,* &C.

Webster's method, in teaching children to spell, then, was similar to that which had been used for centuries in that it followed the alphabet, syllable, and word route with little or no emphasis on content or meaning, and in that he insisted progress should be slow, each element being perfectly learned before the next step is undertaken. It was different from the earlier methods in that words were arranged in tables according to common elements, in such a way that the learner was able to generalize, an arrangement which educators today believe is advantageous in the learning process. It was different from the earlier methods in that the author did not include many of the long retired words found in earlier spellers; that is, he attempted to adapt the text to the capacities of the child. Lastly, it was different in that there was a more natural division of syllables, and numbers were used to indicate the quality of the vowels and the accented syllable.

In later editions, one gets a hint now and then that Webster was conscious of changing times and of new methods. For ex-

---

[132] The same idea was held in the 1783 speller. "All the words in the same column being sounded alike, when a child has the sound of the first, the others will naturally follow." Later, in the 1795 edition, he recommended that the table

ample, in the *Elementary Spelling Book* (1829) he says, "In the plan and execution of this work, I have had the advice and assistance of some of the most experienced instructors in New-York, to whom I would present my most grateful acknowledgements." On the second alphabet page of this edition, he takes a slight bow to the word method, which was then being advocated in some quarters, by saying, "The teacher may ask the pupil, which is A or a in Ape, and face? Which is B, or b in Boy, box, &C. taking one, two or three letters as a lesson." [133]

In this edition he acknowledged several other principles held by modern educators. He recommended that the reading lessons be used to substitute variety for the dull monotony of spelling . . . [134] The reading lessons will, he explained, "show the practical use of words in significant sentences, and thus enable the learner the better to understand them.[135] In spite of this declaration, which at least implies that words are meant to be used in discourse, he still clings to one of his old tenets, namely, that since the understanding can hardly keep pace with the memory, the children may well be employed in learning to spell and pronounce words whose signification is not within the reach of their capacities, believing that what they do not clearly understand at first, they will understand as their capacities are enlarged.[136] This was one belief for which advocates of progressive education criticized him frequently in later years.

Most of the Nineteenth-Century Criticisms of Spelling As It Was Taught Had to Do with the Alphabet Method, which the Popularity of Webster's Spellers Had Thoroughly Entrenched

IN THE preface to Part I of the *Institute,* Webster shows that he anticipated the critics who later attacked the book. He

---

be read sometimes across the page, "to make children attentive to the different ways of expressing the same sound."
[133] Page 16, Philadelphia edition.
[134] *Ibid.,* p. 7.
[135] *Ibid.*
[136] *Ibid.*

also shows his characteristic perseverance and his detachment
from the opinion of the world, which kept him on his course as
long as he believed in an undertaking:

The author feels the danger to which he exposes himself by this
publication: He foresees that some will find fault with it, because
they think it has merit; others, because they think it has none: Some
will condemn it from motives of prejudice, some from ignorance,
some perhaps from worse motives and not a few, who seldom look
further than the title page, will gravely enquire, with the harmless
Israelite of old, *whether any good thing can come out of Nazareth?* [137]

Although the speller had in it the promise of success from the
beginning,[138] it is said that "when first published it encountered
an opposition which few publications have sustained with success." [139] A number of anecdotes which illustrate this opposition
have come down to the present day. One story goes that Webster's speller had been introduced by a Yankee schoolmaster into
a school district in the Allegheny mountains of Pennsylvania,
where the heresies it contained began to spread among the
people, disturbing in particular a Scotch elder, who came riding
down the road shouting to the storekeeper at Four Corners as he
drew up to the door one morning:

"Have ye heard the news, mon? Do you ken what's gaen on? Here's
a book by a Yankee lad called Wobster, teaching the children clean
agenst the Christian religion!"
"Oh, how so? " asked the storekeeper.
"Why, ye ken ye canna sing the Psalms of David without having
salvation and such words in four syllables, *sal-va-ci-on,* and he's making the children say *salvashun.*" [140]

During Webster's day matters pertaining to philology and
orthography engendered an enmity similar to that enkindled by
religious differences. Benton relates that an old gentleman in
the neighborhood from which he wrote, who greatly disliked
Webster's changes in English orthography, on seeing a Webster

[137] *Grammatical Institute,* Part I (1783), p. 13.
[138] Scudder, *op. cit.,* p. 52.
[139] Ford, *Notes* (1912), II, 447.
[140] Ford, *Notes,* I, 58 f. For pronunciation of words ending in *tion, sion,* and
cion, see *Institute,* Part I (1783), p. 65.

spelling book in his little grandson's hands, took it speedily away from him, and tradition says it was never seen afterward.[141]

Generally speaking, not much criticism of Webster's speller appeared in the press during the early life of the text. The criticism of Webster, which finally appeared copiously in newspapers, magazines, and pamphlets, followed in the wake of his advocacy of language reform,[142] which became more apparent to the public through his dictionaries than it was in his less aggressive spelling books.

One of Webster's first critics made capital of the fact that Webster had taken much of his material for the speller from Dilworth's *Guide*. The critic used the signature "Dilworth's Ghost." The articles were written, it seems, "to deter the people of the state from the change" to Webster's speller.[143] "It was said," explained Webster, "and never denied, that the writer was a Mr. Hughes, an old teacher in New York before the revolution, father of Colonel (Udney) Hughes of the American Army, with whom I was afterwards acquainted." [144] Webster made several references to these attacks. In his diary for January 19, 1785, this entry appears: "Write another answer to the Ghost. I have exposed myself to malice, envy, criticism, & c. by my publication. I knew I should when I began and I am prepared for an attack on all sides . . ." [145]

Although it was not until the twenties and thirties of the nineteenth century that existing methods of instruction were generally criticized, as early as 1799, Samuel Knox showed that he was in advance of his age when he criticized the alphabet method then universally used in teaching children to spell and read. "Children," he declared, "will make much more progress by first teaching them to read, and after having read their lesson to

---

[141] Joel Benton, *op. cit.*, p. 299.

[142] See chap. viii.

[143] *American Journal of Education*, XVII (1868), 220.

[144] Ford, *Notes*, II, 447. Other references to the attack are a poem, *Philo dilworth*, perhaps by Barlow, published in the *Monitor*, March 1, 1785, and an article "Dilworth's Ghost," published in the *Monitor*, March 8, 1785.

[145] Ford, *Notes*, I, 124.

spell words out of it suited to their capacity, than by confining
their attention to long dry lists or arrangements of words and
syllables, however skilfully digested." [146] To assume that this
criticism of existing methods and that which followed during the
nineteenth century were aimed directly at Webster, would show
a failure to consider that other men had compiled spellers which
were being used. The facts, nevertheless, that Webster's spellers
were more widely used than those of any other compiler during
the first three quarters of the nineteenth century,[147] that many
compilers based their compilations on his work,[148] and that
through the popularity of his text the alphabet method became
strongly entrenched,[149] furnish valid ground for the conclusion
that practically all this criticism applied to his texts. Much of it
was of course aimed directly at them.

As early as 1800 Webster was attacked by the *Aurora,* a paper
which was a rival of his *Minerva,* from the active editorship of
which he had retired in 1798:

His spelling-book has done more injury in the common schools of
the country than the genius of ignorance herself could have conceived a hope of, by his ridiculous attempts to alter the *syllable*
division of words and to *new model* the spelling, by a capricious but
utterly incompetent attempt of his own weak conception.[150]

In 1827 and 1828 a series of articles appeared in the Albany
Argus. These were printed in pamphlet form in 1828 under the
title *A Critical Review of Noah Webster's Spelling Book,* "by
Examinator [Lyman Cobb]." Cobb gave what he believed the
characteristics of a speller worthy of introduction into the schools
should be. Next he showed that Webster's spelling book did not
measure up to this standard. The main charge that he made,
however, was that Webster's spellings and pronunciations in the

[146] *Essay on Education* (1799), p. 95.
[147] See pp. 88 ff.
[148] See pp. 84 ff.
[149] "So magical indeed has been the charm of popularity woven around it, that
all desire for or efforts to improvement seem to be paralyzed."—Lyman Cobb,
Critical Review (1827), p. 29.
[150] Allan Nevins, *American Press Opinion, Washington to Coolidge* (1928), p. 30.

various spellers and dictionaries were not consistent, a charge which was frequently made in later years during the "war of the dictionaries." This "critical review," it is apparent, was meant to be more of a boost for Cobb's texts than a criticism of Webster's spelling book. The advertisement advised that teachers, school committees or inspectors, clergymen, and the friends of elementary instruction compare Webster's spelling book with those of such authors as Perry, Marshall, Sears, Kelly, Cummings, Balles, "but more particularly with Cobb's, in which, it is believed, the *defects* are remedied."

Much of the controversy over method in teaching, which appeared in educational journals in great profusion, was a debate concerning the efficacy of the alphabet method with its accumulated appendages versus the word method and its proposed "fads and frills." But the educational periodicals did not appear until Webster's spellers and the many others, which, like his, were compiled with the alphabet method in mind, were thoroughly established in the schools of the country. The first educational magazine, the *Academician,* edited by A. and J. W. Picket, principals of the Manhattan School, New York, appeared in 1818, but it was short lived.[151] The *American Journal of Education,* edited by William Russell, began its career in 1826.[152] The first numbers of the *American Annals of Education and Instruction* were published in 1831;[153] of *The Common School Journal,* in 1839;[154] and of the *American Journal of Education,* in 1856.[155]

The organization of teachers' institutes, the publication of educational periodicals by such men as Henry Barnard and Horace Mann, and the establishment of institutions for the training of teachers, all in the twenties and the thirties of the nineteenth century, mark the beginnings of modern methods in

[151] Published from Feb. 7, 1818, to Jan. 29, 1820, semimonthly (irregular).
[152] Vols. I–V, Boston, 1826–30.
[153] William C. Woodbridge, editor, Vols. I–VIII, Boston, 1831–39.
[154] Horace Mann, editor, Vols. I–X; William B. Fowle, editor, Vols. XI–XIV, Boston, 1839–52.
[155] Henry Barnard, editor, Vols. I–XXXII, Hartford, Conn., 1856–81.

America. From the discussions in these magazines, usually in praise or denunciation of the methods then in vogue, we learn much about classroom procedure during the first three quarters of the nineteenth century. But it is impossible to accept all of this criticism at face value, for, since many of the articles were not signed, one is certain at times that much of the favorable comment was written by the authors, by their publishers, or by friends in order to boost sales; while on the other hand, articles containing adverse criticism of a book or method were often written by rival authors, rival publishers, or by enemies of the author.[156]

One untiring educator who worked in opposition to the alphabet method was Horace Mann. Because of his prominence and his detachment from commercial interests, his opinions are frequently quoted in this study rather than those of anonymous writers. While he was Secretary of the Board of Education in Massachusetts he visited, in 1843, the principal schools in England, Ireland, Germany, Holland, Belgium, and France. In the report which followed he stated, among other things, that "Reading was taught by the 'word method' instead of requiring the children first to learn the alphabet, then to combine letters in syllables, and finally to build up words from these elements, according to the usual American practice . . ."[157] But his report was not favorably received in America. The charge was made that his holding up the schools of the old world, especially those of Germany, as models for America to follow showed a most unpatriotic attitude. In Boston, the "Committee of thirty-one" attacked Mann's report, defending the alphabet method as well as other methods and practices in the schools of Massachusetts.[158] But there were many teachers, educators, and critics in America

[156] The *Academician* is a case in point. This magazine seems to have been published largely in support of *American School Class Books,* one of the early series of textbooks. It was "said to form a systematic gradation from the alphabet to Walker's Dictionary."—Reeder, *op. cit.,* p. 44. Lyman Cobb and other critics were evidently guilty of the same practice.

[157] Edwin E. Slosson, "The American Spirit in Education," *The Chronicles of America,* XXXIII (1921), 132. Copyright Yale University Press.

[158] *Ibid.*

who along with Horace Mann and Henry Barnard opposed the alphabet method.

Several writers have given accounts of what the early nineteenth century school with its torture of innocents was like under the alphabet method:

> And what a day that was when we stood on the hilltop of human greatness and grappled with our first reading lesson! "No man may put off the law of God; My joy is in his law all the day." See, that boy in his mighty wrestlings to spell out the words! Lips move vigorously; brow knit; book turned this way and that, to give room for the great idea to come in; his whole frame writhing and screwed down hard and tight to the supreme task. Perhaps he will fetch it, perhaps not. . . . But don't you give that small boy up. There is promise for him in such energy and bent as that.
>
> Then a succession of easy and familiar lessons. But come to the *fables* and the pictures. Here is richness.
>
> The preface we did not have to read. But the next half-dozen pages, "Analysis of Sounds," we in our school had to commit to memory and recite. This amazed us and still does. Just to think of a child eight or nine years old required to recite understandingly the opening sentence: "Language, in its more limited sense, is the expression of ideas by articulate sound." [159]

In championing the cause of the word method, Mann gave an account of the alphabet method in full operation:

> Let us examine a line with which we are all familiar—the initiatory sentence in Webster's old spelling-book:
> "No man may put off the law of God."
> The manner in which we were taught to read this was as follows: "En-o, No, emm-ai-en, man, emm-ai-wy, may, pee-you-tee, put, o-double eff, off, tee-aitch-ee, the, ell-ai-double you, law, o-eff, off, gee-o-dee, God." [160]

[159] A. M. Colton, "Our Old Webster Spelling-Book," *Magazine of American History*, XXIV (1890), 467.

[160] *The Common School Journal*, II (1840), 301. The custom of spelling words *syllabically*, some argued, was superior to that in which letters were merely named. "Take the word *example* . . . if spelled syllabically, the speller says, *e, x, ex, a, m, am, exam, p, l, e, ple, example* . . . To spell the words by syllables, instead of spelling by letters, tends to fix the true line between the syllables, in pronunciation. It tends also to give clearness and distinctness to the articulation of his voice, so that each syllable may come out by itself, in speaking, like a well struck note in music . . . Without this distinct enunciation of the syllables, the articu-

Writing in 1833, Warren Burton, who started to school when
he was three and a half years old, gives a striking picture of the
first years at school under the alphabet method:

My first business was to master the A B C, and no small achievement it was; for many a little learner waddles to school through the
summer, and wallows to the same through the winter, before he
accomplishes it, if he happens to be taught in the manner of former
times . . .

We will suppose it is the first day of the school. "Come and read,"
says the mistress to a flaxen headed creature of doubtful gender . . .
"Put your hands down by your side and make a bow." . . . The
alphabet page of the spelling book is presented and he is asked
"What's that?" But he cannot tell. He is but two years and a half
old, and has been sent to school to relieve his mother from trouble
rather than to learn.

Solomon Richardson has at length said A B C, for the first time
in his life. He has *read*, "That's a nice boy; make another bow, and
go to your seat" . . .

The little chit, at first so timid, and almost inaudible in enunciation, in a few days becomes accustomed to the place and the exercise;
and in obedience to the "Speak up loud, that's a good boy," he soon
pipes A-er, B-er, C-er, & C., with a far-ringing shrillness, that was
even with chanticleer himself.[161]

Solomon, according to this chronicler, went the greater part
of two summers before he knew all the letters by sight, or could
call them by name. Finally he was permitted to turn the page,
where he for several months recited nonsense syllables. At length
he ceased to be an Ab-ite as he progressed to whole words of one
syllable arranged in columns.

Much of the criticism of the alphabet method was aimed at
the first step advocated by Webster, namely, the learning of the
alphabet. A writer in an early issue of the *Connecticut Common
School Journal*[162] declared that the child would never meet a
more difficult and tiresome lesson in his whole course than those

---

lation seems glutinous and gummy . . . "—*Connecticut Common School Journal*,
II, 109.

[161] Warren Burton, *The District School as It Was* (1833, ed. by Clifton Johnson,
1897), p. 47.

[162] Vol. II (1839), 16.

lessons he meets in learning the alphabet—that since the names
of the letters are unmeaning and the sounds are arbitrary and
since the forms, with one or two exceptions, are not associated
with any object previously recognized, the exercise cannot produce any reaction but weariness and disgust. The writer found
comfort, however, in the fact that "men of attainment in literature, have not thought it beneath their character and standing
to endeavor at least to facilitate the passage across this 'bridge of
sighs.' " The last note was often sounded in the periodicals, and
references were frequently made to texts that had been compiled
according to modern methods, by such authors as Gallaudet,
Worcester, Bumstead, Keagy, and Peabody.[163]

Aside from the tediousness of learning the alphabet, the charge
was made that the process wasted much time and effort.

Children, who spend six months in learning the alphabet will, on
the playground, in a single day or moonlight evening, learn the
intricacies of a game of sport,—where to stand, when to run, what to
say, how to count, and what are the laws and ethics of the game;—
the whole requiring more intellectual effort than would suffice to
learn half a dozen alphabets. . . . And the reason is, that for one,
there is desire: while against the other, there is repugnance.[164]

The time, effort, and patience wasted on nonsense syllables,
the second step Webster advocated, was widely criticized, for,
wrote one critic, "we learn to spell only what we may write." [165]
Among those who criticized the method, the denunciation of
Horace Mann, the persistent advocator of the word method, is
outstanding.

Now let us examine the course ordinarily pursued in teaching
children to read, and see if it does not violate all ideas of ease and
consistency. A child is required to learn the names of twenty-six
letters, to repeat them day after day and month after month, giving
to each letter a single and uniform sound. He then is required to
follow up his repetition in tables of *ab, eb, ib, ob, ub,* & C.; then in
tables of *ba, be, bi, bo, bu,* & C.; then *bla,* with its conjuncts; then
bra, ska, qua; then *bram, flam,* & C. & C., until the infinite of non-

[163] See *Common School Journal,* IV (1842), 46 ff.; VI (1844), 353.
[164] Horace Mann, *Common School Journal,* I (1839), 325.
[165] *Common School Journal,* V (1844), 330 and 361.

sense is exhausted. After having repeated these letters and particles, thousands of times, where the same sound is uniformly given to the same letter or combination of letters, he is then taken into words where each of the principal letters, in the rapidity of its changes from one sound to another, out does ventriloquism;—where the first five vowels to which respectively he has been accustomed to give the same alphabetic sound, assume twenty-nine different sounds, so that, according to the doctrine of changes, it will happen only once in five or six times that he will be correct, if he sounds them as he was taught;—where the twenty-six letters, and the same combination of two or three of them, assume hundreds of different sounds, without any clew by which to follow them so they glide from one into another;—where letters are often dropped out of notice altogether; where *g* sometimes becomes *j*, and *x* becomes *gz*; where *th* changes every brea*th* we brea*the;* where *tion* and *sion* are *shun; cial, sial,* and *tial,* are *shal*, (not *shall*, which is different still); *ceous, cious,* and *tious,* are *shus; geous* and *gious* are *jus,* (not the Latin *jus* either); *sion* is *zhun; qu* is *kw; wh* is *hw; ph* is *f;* and *c* is uniformly concealed in *s,* or sacrificed as a victim to *k* or *z*.[166]

In the Second Annual Report of the Secretary of the Board of Education in the state of Massachusetts, Mann further denounced the alphabet method: [167]

The general practice is founded upon the notion that the learning of letters facilitates the correct combination of them into words. For this reason children are drilled into the alphabet until they pronounce the name of each letter at sight. But when the letters are combined into words, the sounds that belonged to the letters are forthwith discarded. The first time the letter *a* is found, even in the most familiar words,—as in *father, papa, mamma, apple, peach, walnut, hat, cap, bat, rat, slap, pan* & C., it no longer has the sound he was taught to give it, but one entirely different.

The extent to which pupils actually learned to spell was not, it was claimed, commensurate with the amount of time that was given to the subject. To the arrangement of words based on the law of association some critics traced the blame.

The teacher usually relies on reiterated *spelling from the columns of a spelling book or a dictionary.* . . . In both kinds of books mentioned, there is such a similarity and regular sequence in the words

[166] *Common School Journal,* IV, 14.
[167] *Ibid.,* p. 15.

of a lesson, that the spelling of one word is for the time a sufficient guide to that of a large number of others of similar sound or of similar etymology; and the leading word being once given, all the others are very fluently spelled, with very little attention on the part of the scholars. . . . In consequence of this method of going through a lesson in orthography, it is not uncommon to find a child quite unable to spell a word the moment you take it out of the column to which it belongs and give it out separately.

To obviate all these difficulties, the natural recourse is, *to take the spelling lesson out of the reading lessons;* prescribing the former from so many lines or paragraphs of the latter. . . .

Another error prevalent in the teaching of orthography, is, to depend entirely on *memory and oral recitation.* But it is one thing to be able to spell a word correctly when it is "put out" from a lesson, and quite another to retain it with such distinctness before the mind that the pupil never fails in her attempts to put down every letter of it on paper.[168]

Mann was among those who condemned the "uselessness and untowardness" of that arrangement of words which brings all the monosyllables together, at the beginning of the spelling book, to be followed by dissyllables, trisyllables, and polysyllables, in numerical order . . .[169] This arrangement had been used by both Webster and Perry. Another of Webster's points of departure, that is, the arrangement of words in tables according to the law of association, Mann commended very highly. "When reading has become easy and it is expedient to carry forward the orthography of the language faster than it is possible to comprehend the meaning of all its words, a spelling book," he advised, "constructed according to the law of association, should be put into the hands of the pupil." [170]

One of the features of Webster's "new system" was a "new and simple scheme or key for exhibiting the pronunciation," which, as has been noted, employed the numbers from one to eleven.[171] During the first half of the nineteenth century, many rival spelling books and dictionaries were published, and in these

[168] *American Journal of Education,* II (1827), 680.
[169] *Common School Journal,* IV (1842), 40.
[170] *Ibid.,* p. 47.
[171] See p. 307.

similar devices for indicating accent, quality, and quantity to vowel sounds, and so forth, were used. Later, various systems of diacritical marks and various combinations of systems were used. Webster's texts, published at close intervals during the century, show this shift from numbers to diacritical marks.

Commenting on the anomalies of the English language and the attendant difficulties for the pupil who studies spelling, Mann had this to say:

The dissonance of this Babel has been sadly aggravated because spelling-book and dictionary makers have adopted different modes for the notation of sounds. Some have used the Arabic figures to designate sounds as long, short, broad, acute, grave, & C.; while others employ such characters as the horizontal mark, the circum-flex, diacresis, cedilla, & C., so that, in order to learn the signs by which the same letters are to be translated into different sounds, we must begin by learning the different languages of the translators. This seems a gratuitous and wanton imposition of labor. Surely there might be an understanding among the leading orthoepists and lexicographers, so that the same signs might be uniformly used to indicate the same sounds; and so that, after a child has learned twenty-six capital, and twenty-six common, Roman letters, and twenty-six capital, and twenty-six common, Italic letters, together with double letters, diphthongs, and triphthongs he need not be obliged to learn a multitude of signs whereby the sound of each one of this multitude of letters is indicated. It is of less importance what is agreed upon than that there should be an agreement. It may be remarked, however, that as the Arabic figures have their specific uses and significations, in regard to number and quantity, there seems to be no reason for using them as the signs of different sounds, except it be that the learner may find a different meaning attached to them all, when he comes to arithmetic, and thus encounter the same gratuitous difficulty which embarrassed his acquisition of read-ing. If a pupil is taught that the figure 1 denotes the sound of *a,* as in *fame;* 2, the sound of *a,* as in *far;* 3, the sound of *a,* as in *fall;* and 4, the sound of *a,* as in *fat;* and, at the same time, should be studying numeration, he might very naturally infer that these letters had 1234 different sounds. What, then, shall we say of the mischievousness of using both modes indiscriminately, by the same compiler, as has been done in some modern spelling books.[172]

[172] *Common School Journal,* IV (1842), 11 ff.

Writing in 1927, Sullivan [173] reported that nearly all who sent him their recollections of their school days have shown pride and affectionate approval for the proficiency in spelling that the old schools developed. In this vein, Josephus Daniels wrote: "The pupils really learned how to spell. At recess they would try to stump each other with hard words so that spelling became a sort of recreation at playtime." Senator Fess sent in a similar testimony: "The result was a superior ability to spell, over the present day . . . The practical value in insuring correct spelling was immensely important in after life . . . "

These testimonials are from men who attended school during the 1880's and 1890's. According to their testimony the methods employed were the same employed earlier in the century. "The spelling-match was held every Friday afternoon," wrote James M. Cox. "During the winter months there was a competition between different schools . . . It's amazing when one stops to think of it, how the youngsters could spell then as compared to those of the present day . . . "

The testimony of these men is somewhat at variance with the claims set forth by critics in the educational periodicals during the second quarter of the century. "The ability to spell with uniform correctness," wrote Horace Mann, in the *Common School Journal,* "is a rare possession amongst our people . . . This almost universal illiteracy in regard to spelling, seems to me to have two sources;—one, the inherent difficulty of the language itself,—the other, the manner in which, and the instruments by which orthography is usually taught." [174]

Many plans were proposed in the journals to make the teaching of spelling more efficacious. Written spelling was recommended—written on the blackboard or on the slate. At times it was recommended that teachers adopt the improved method of teaching orthography by dictation, or that teachers teach pupils to spell by reading, just as one learns to spell French words in translating.[175]

[173] *Our Times* (1927), II, 131. C. Scribner's Sons.
[174] *Common School Journal,* IV (1842), 13.
[175] *Ibid.*

Although Webster occasionally indicated that he was at least aware of newer methods, and at times he feebly suggested their use in modified form, with the exception of numbers 3 and 4, the following recommendations [176] were revolutionary to the methods he had in mind when he compiled his spellers and, as we have seen, even when he published his *Collection of Papers on Political, Literary and Moral Subjects* [177] in 1843. They are also revolutionary to the methods, which, largely because of the popularity of Webster's spellers, persisted in the schools during the greater part of the nineteenth century.

1. Teaching children to read by means of words first, and letting them learn the names of the letters afterwards.

2. Avoiding all senseless fragments of words, and all nonsense columns.

3. Beginning with familiar, household words, the names of things, actions, processes and relations, with which children are familiar, and proceeding to the names of things less familiar.

4. Adapting instructions not only to the capacities but to the taste of children.[178]

Obviously, one of the greatest weaknesses of the alphabet method is the fact that it required children to be taught "as if the only faculty they possessed needing culture was memory—as if the only intellectual appetite God had given them was for facts and forms . . . [179] The whole process of learning to spell was purely mechanical, little effort ever being made to explain the meaning of the words of the lesson and none at all to use them in the construction of sentences." [180] Writing in the *Connecticut Common School Journal* a contributor says that it was full two years after he could "read in the Testament" that he learned to his joyful surprise that there are "stories in books." [181]

[176] *Common School Journal,* V (1843), 361.

[177] See pp. 92 ff.

[178] Although Webster claimed that the texts were "adapted to the capacity of children," in this respect he knew better than he sometimes did. There was, however, it must be admitted, something in the "Old Blue-Back" which caught and held the attention of children.

[179] James Pyle Wickersham, *A History of Education in Pennsylvania* (1886), p. 203.

[180] *Ibid.,* p. 204.

[181] Vol. XI (1864), 301.

The criticisms of educators protesting against the alphabet method were during the greater part of the nineteenth century voices crying in the wilderness. Although soon after the first quarter of the century books were beginning to be compiled by authors who advocated the word method,[182] it was not until after 1870 that this method made headway.[183] "The breaking away from this time honored system [alphabet method]," says Reeder, "was the signal for a veritable renaissance of method all along the line of the common-school curriculum. The more rapid mastery of word symbols by improved methods of teaching opened the door to interest as a factor in the child's school life and led to an enrichment of the elementary curriculum." [184]

Among the various influences that Webster's speller had on American life, the social influence is perhaps not the least. Because of the popularity of spelling, the spelling bee came not only to rival but to surpass the singing school and the horse race as a popular pastime.[185]

The spelling-bees, singing schools, and debating societies constituted what might be called the "extension department" of the country school. . . . The spelling-bee was not a mere drill to impress certain facts upon the plastic memory of youth. It was also one of the recreations of adult life, if recreation be the right word for what was taken so seriously by every one. The spectacle of a school trustee standing with a blue-backed Webster open in his hand while gray haired men and women, one row being captained by the schoolmaster and the rival team by the minister, spelled each other down is one that it would be hard to reproduce under a more centralized and less immediately popular form of school government.[186]

Eggleston's account in the *Hoosier Schoolmaster* [187] is not only

---

[182] Worcester's series of four books (1828), says Reeder, was "remarkable for its advanced position as to the method of beginning reading. It was the first American to advocate the word method."—*Op. cit.*, p. 45.

[183] *Ibid.*, p. 78.

[184] *Ibid.*, p. 68. "The word method was a great insight, and did more to relieve children from the torture of spelling-book and primer than any discovery of the century."—*Ibid.*, p. 79.

[185] George Philip Krapp, *The English Language in America* (1925), I, 339. Copyright by the Modern Language Association.

[186] Edwin E. Slosson, "The American Spirit in Education," *The Chronicles of America*, XXXIII (1921), 111. Copyright by Yale University Press.

[187] Edward Eggleston, *The Hoosier Schoolmaster* (1913, revised ed.), pp. 53 ff.

a faithful transcript of such events but is also a poignant commentary on the attitude taken toward spelling and on the
methods employed in teaching the spelling lesson.

It [the spelling-bee] is the only public literary exercise known in
Hoopole County. It takes the place of lyceum lecture and debating
club. . . . There is one branch diligently taught in a backwoods
school. The public mind seems impressed with the difficulties of
English orthography, and there is a solemn conviction that the
chief end of man is to learn to spell. "Know Webster's Elementary,
came down from Heaven," would be the backwoods version of the
Greek saying but that, unfortunately for the Greeks, their fame has
not reached so far. It often happens that the pupil does not know
the meaning of a single word in the lesson. This is of no consequence.
What do you want to know the meaning of a word for? Words were
made to be spelled, and men were probably created that they might
spell them. Hence the necessity for sending a pupil through the
spelling-book five times before you allow him to begin to read or
indeed to do anything else. Hence the necessity for those long spelling classes at the close of each forenoon and afternoon session of the
school, to stand at the head of which is the cherished ambition of
every scholar. Hence, too, the necessity for devoting the whole of the
afternoon session of each Friday to a "spelling-match." In fact, spelling is the "national game" in Hoopole County. Baseball and croquet
matches are as unknown as Olympian chariot races. Spelling and
shucking are the only competitions.

"The mute umpire of these matches was a book," writes Sullivan, "one of the most widely known ever printed in America.
'The Blue-Back Speller' or 'Webster's Blue-Back Speller,' was a
universal text-book in the schools, but was more than that, the
master-book on spelling everywhere . . . Every one was familiar
with its vivid blue covers and had a curious affection for it." [188]

Summary and Conclusions

WEBSTER published Part I of *A Grammatical Institute* at the
close of the Revolution in order to ease the burden of teacher and
pupil in the teaching and learning of reading and spelling and
in order to lessen the dependence of the United States of America

[188] Sullivan, *Our Times*, II, 125. C. Scribner's Sons.

on foreign supplies. He based the compilation on Dilworth's *New Guide* and Fenning's *Universal Spelling Book,* his point of departure being his arrangement of words according to the law of association, his more logical division of the words into syllables, and his marking of the vowels in the stressed syllables to indicate their quality and the place of accent. He also made it an informative book by including more encyclopedic material than former authors had included. Many of the words Webster listed were taken from Dilworth and Fenning, to which he added other practical words with which he had become acquainted. He disclaimed any help from dictionaries other than Dr. Johnson's, but acknowledged that he used them freely in his revisions of the work.

Soon after the publication of Part I Webster set about to revise and correct his text. Some of the outstanding editions that followed were the *American Spelling Book* (1786) and the *Elementary Spelling Book* (1829). Within four or five years after the publication of the latter, the book achieved substantially its final form, the form which was widely used and was affectionately referred to as the "Blue-Back Spelling Book" or "Webster's Old Spelling Book."

Although the work encountered some opposition at first, it had the marks of success from the beginning. The number of copies printed and used up to the eighties of the nineteenth century has been estimated at figures ranging from seventy-five to eighty million copies. Many criticisms of current methods in teaching spelling appeared in the educational periodicals of the nineteenth century. These had to do with the alphabet method, the arrangement of words according to the law of association, the lack of uniformity in texts, oral spelling, etc., all of which were appendages of Webster's spellers.

Webster compiled Part I with the alphabet method in mind, a method used in the schools of England and elsewhere as far back as the history of education extends. This method followed the alphabet, nonsense syllable, and word route. It was probably because of the popularity of Webster's speller that the alphabet method became so thoroughly entrenched that in spite of the protests of progressive educators it persisted during the greater part of the nineteenth century. For the same reason other compilers were drawn into the field and spelling came to occupy an unduly prominent place in the schools of America. The social life of the American people was consequently enriched. The spelling bee became a rival with other pastimes, such as the singing school, the school exhibition, the husking bee, the horse race, and so forth.

IV

GRAMMARS

I WILL *even venture to assert, that two-thirds of all the corruptions in our language have been introduced by* learned grammarians, *who, from a species of pedantry acquired in schools, and from a real ignorance of the original principles of the English tongue have been, for ages, attempting to correct what they have supposed,* vulgar errors, *but which are in fact established analogies.*[1]

It needs the club of Hercules, wielded by the arm of a giant, to destroy the hydra of educational prejudice. The club and the arm, I pretend not to possess, and my efforts may be fruitless; but it will ever be a satisfaction to reflect that I have discharged a duty demanded by a deep sense of the importance of truth. *It is not possible for me to think with indifference, that half a million of youth in our schools are daily toiling to learn that which is not true. It has been justly observed that ignorance is preferable to error.*[2]

EARLY in the eighteenth century a vigorous skepticism set in as to the necessity of a knowledge of Greek and Latin for the understanding of English grammar.[3] Latin speaking in the schools sank from the position of an avowed aim to that of a tradition.[4] Numerous English grammars were written in this century. Among those most important to this study were Brightland's *Grammar of the English Tongue* (1712), Dilworth's *New Guide* (1740), Harris's *Hermes* (1751), Johnson's *An English Grammar* (1755), Lowth's *A Short Introduction to English Grammar* (1758), *The British Grammar* (1762, author unknown), and Priestley's *Rudiments of English Grammar* (third ed., 1762). In spite of the fact that these early texts aimed to teach the English language, they were, in the main, based on the principles of Latin grammar in that parallels in English were in-

[1] Noah Webster, *Letter to Governors, Instructors and Trustees of the Universities, and Other Seminaries of Learning in the United States, on the Errors of English Grammars* (1798), p. 30.

[2] *Ibid., An American Dictionary of the English Language* (1828), advertisement to the grammar, n. p.

[3] Foster Watson, *Beginnings of the Teaching of Modern Subjects in England* (1909), p. 529.

[4] *Ibid.*, p. 530.

vented to correspond to every detail of Latin grammar [5] as found
in the compilations of Lily and Wallis.[6]

In a letter to Henry Barnard, dated 1840, Noah Webster stated
that "No English grammar was generally taught in common
schools when I was young, except that in Dilworth and that to no
good purpose." [7] This statement seems to be an accurate estimate
of the extent to which grammar was taught in the common
schools of America before the Revolution. It was taught, however, in many private schools.[8]

These early experiments in the private schools had prepared
the way so that "the period immediately after the Revolution
marks the well-nigh universal adoption of English into the
curricula of the American schools." [9] Insofar as prospectuses may
be relied upon to give an accurate account of school practices,
Webster's advertisement, dated "Sharon, April 16, 1782," shows
what his school offered:

> The little regard that is paid to the literary improvement of
> females, even among people of rank and fortune, and the general
> inattention to the grammatical purity and elegance of our native
> language, are faults in the education of youth that more gentlemen
> have taken pains to censure than correct. Any young gentlemen and
> ladies, who wish to acquaint themselves with the English language,
> vocal music, & C, may be waited on at particular hours for that pur-
> pose . . .[10]

Again, in a prospectus for his proposed Rhetorical School,
dated Hartford, December 30, 1783, he says:

> The Subscriber having devoted himself for a considerable time to
> the cultivation of the English Language, and having lately obtained
> the best standard of pronunciation hitherto published, in order to
> diffuse propriety and uniformity of speaking . . . proposes to open

[5] E. A. Cross, *Fundamentals in English* (1926), p. 257.

[6] John Wallis published his *Grammatica lingual Anglicanaes* (1653). Webster
says that Lowth and Johnson borrowed most of their rules from Wallis.—*Philosophical and Practical Grammar* (1807), p. 3.

[7] *American Journal of Education*, XIII (1863), 123.

[8] Rollo LaVerne Lyman, *English Grammar in American Schools before 1850*
(1921), p. 21.

[9] *Ibid.*, p. 70.

[10] Scudder, *Noah Webster* (1882), p. 10. Houghton Mifflin Company.

an Evening School in this town for instructing Gentlemen and Ladies
in the most elegant pronunciation, from the simple sounds that compose words to a just and graceful elocution.[11]

The universal interest that was taken in the vernacular after
the war is further shown by the fact that the various states passed
laws recommending instruction in the vernacular or making it
compulsory.[12] The number of textbooks compiled at this time
also indicates that the rise of instruction in the English language
was very rapid after the Revolution. Leonard[13] states that
"whereas fewer than fifty writings on grammar, rhetoric, criticism and linguistic theory have been listed for the first half of
the eighteenth century, and still fewer for all the period before
1600, the publications in the period 1750-1800 exceeded two
hundred titles."[14]

According to Lyman, it is doubtful whether many English
grammars found their way from England to the colonies before
1750.[15] Wickersham says it is unknown whether any more than
a few straggling copies of old English grammars ever found their
way from England to Pennsylvania.[16] We know, however, that
Dilworth's *Guide* was printed in Philadelphia in 1747,[17] undoubtedly in answer to a demand for this universally used text.
Among other English texts that were printed in Philadelphia
and may have been used to some extent were Lowth's[18] in 1775
and Sheridan's in 1783.[19] "But the first works generally taught
in the schools," says Wickersham, "were the Philadelphia editions of the grammars of Webster, Harrison, Murray and Comly,

[11] Ford, *Notes,* I, 64.

[12] Lyman, *op. cit.,* p. 72.

[13] S. A. Leonard, *The Doctrine of Correctness in English Usage, 1700–1800*
(1929), p. 12.

[14] For a list of early English grammars, see *American Journal of Education,*
XIII, XIV, XV; also William Harvey Wells, *A Grammar of the English Language*
(1848), pp. v–viii.

[15] *Op. cit.,* p. 22.

[16] James Pyle Wickersham, *A History of Education in Pennsylvania* (1886),
p. 202.

[17] Lyman, *op. cit.,* pp. 22 and 34.

[18] Some time before 1782 Joel Barlow had "ventured an impression" of Lowth
in Connecticut. Letter from Barlow to Webster, dated "Camp, August 31, 1782."—
Ford, *Notes,* I, 54.

[19] Wickersham, *op. cit.,* p. 202.

mainly the two last named." [20] This statement would perhaps apply to other states as well, although it might in the case of some states be an overstatement, since according to at least one authority Pennsylvania led in the teaching of the vernacular.[21]

Although Webster Deplored the Prevalent Slavish Imitation of Latin Texts and Methods, His Part II of A Grammatical Institute Followed the Traditional Pattern

IT HAS been affirmed that Noah Webster was the first American grammarian.[22] From a standpoint of authorship, however, Webster had been antedated by at least four other grammarians: Hugh Jones,[23] professor of mathematics at the College of William and Mary; William Samuel Johnson,[24] first president of King's College; Thomas Byerly,[25] a New York schoolmaster; and Abel Curtis.[26]

Although grammars by these authors antedate Webster's Part II, there is no record of second issues or new editions or any other indication that they were widely used or that they gave impetus to the tendency to teach the vernacular; furthermore there is nothing to show that they influenced Webster in his compilations or that he even knew of their existence. In one sense, then, in that he wrote the first grammar to attain anything like wide usage,[27] Webster is deserving of the priority frequently assigned to him as America's first grammarian.

[20] *Ibid.*
[21] According to Lyman, the New England colonies apparently "lagged behind the middle colonies, and somewhat behind the Southern, in bringing to the fore instruction in all secondary branches of English, especially grammar."—*Op. cit.,* p. 21. See also *ibid.,* p. 29.
[22] See Reeder's *Historical Development of School Readers* (1900), p. 30.
[23] *An Accidence to the English Tongue* (1724). Printed in London. A full description of the text, of which the only extant copy is said to be in the British Museum, is to be found in Meriwether's *Our Colonial Curriculum* (1907), pp. 152 ff.
[24] *An English Grammar* (1765). This was the first English grammar to be written and printed in America.—Evans, 10,025.
[25] *A Plain and Easy Introduction to English Grammar* (1773). Evans, 12,704.
[26] *A Compend of English Grammar* (1779).—Evans, 16,249.
[27] Lyman, *op. cit.,* p. 77.

In 1784, the year following the appearance of the spelling book,[28] Webster published his grammar, the title-page bearing the following descriptive title:

A Grammatical Institute of the English Language, comprising, an easy, concise, and systematic method of Education, Designed for the use of *English* Schools In *America.* In three Parts, Part II Containing a plain and comprehensive Grammar, grounded on the true principles and Idioms of the Language; with an analytical Dissertation, in which the various Uses of the Auxiliary Signs are unfolded and explained; And an Essay towards investigating the Rules of English Verse.[29]

Part II of a *Grammatical Institute* was not an original text, nor was it based on Dilworth's *Guide,* the text upon which Webster had leaned heavily in the compilation of the spelling book. In the Preface to Part II, Webster denounced the *Guide,* declaring that it was founded entirely upon principles of the Latin language, that it was "A mere Latin grammar very indifferently translated," and that "the only circumstance that renders it tolerably harmless, is that it [the grammar part] is very little used and still less understood."

Webster acknowledged Dr. Robert Lowth's *A Short Introduction to Grammar* (1758) as the source from which he drew. Although Lowth indicated in his Preface that he had been influenced by James Harris's *Hermes or a Philosophical Inquiry Concerning Universal Grammar,*[30] Webster refers to Lowth's

[28] In the Introduction to Part I (1783) Webster announced that the "second and third Parts are preparing for the Press, and will be published as soon as they are ready, unless an unfavourable reception of the first should prevent." He also explained that "No grammar is attached because it would be worn out before children would be ready to study it." *An Introduction to English Grammar* was an abridgment of Part II, which was appended to several of the editions of the speller, Part I. See *American Spelling Book* (1788).

[29] The book was uniform in size and appearance with Part I of the *Institute.* Pages 3 to 6 contain the prefatory remarks; pages 7 to 139 the contents as described on the title-page.

[30] "Harris's work . . . was influential in shaping most of the grammars earliest in America."—Lyman, *op. cit.,* p. 155.

grammar as an original performance which cannot be studied too much. Other grammars which had been based on Lowth's and which Webster quoted approvingly in his grammar were John Ash's *Grammatical Institute, or an Easy Introduction to Dr. Lowth's English Grammar* (first American reprint, 1774) and James Buchanan's *A Regular English Syntax* (first American reprint, 1780). In later editions Webster included "Critical Notes" [31] from Joseph Priestley's *The Rudiments of English Grammar* (third London edition, 1762). After Webster came under the spell of Horne Tooke in 1787, he modified parts of his grammar in accordance with the principles of that author.[32]

Of all the grammars compiled in the eighteenth century, Lowth's has undoubtedly exerted the strongest influence. "His text," says Wells, "has probably exerted more influence than any other treatise in forming the character of the numerous grammars that have since been used as schoolbooks in Great Britain and the United States.[33] Lowth's attitude toward the vernacular is very much like that of those who first advocated that it should be taught as an aid to Latin. "If children were first taught the common principles of grammar by some short and clear system of English Grammar," he declared in his Preface, "they would have some notion of what they were going about, when they should enter into Latin Grammar; and would hardly be engaged so many years, as they now are, in that most irksome and difficult part of literature, with so much labour of the memory and with so little assistance of the understanding." [34]

Although Webster criticized Dilworth for his "Latin grammar indifferently translated," he did not at first recognize that the same might have been said about Lowth's work. He points

[31] These, like notes from Lowth and other grammarians, "were concerned in whole or in part with solecisms, barbarisms, improprieties, and questions of precision in the use of English."

[32] The Horne Tooke influence is present in the Boston, 1790, edition.

[33] William Harvey Wells, *Common School Journal*, III, 230.

[34] *A Short Introduction to English Grammar* (1758), p. x.

out that until recently the English nation at large entertained
the idea that the English language was an irregular language, incapable of being reduced to a system of rules. And "even now,"
he continued, "many men of much classical learning warmly
contend that the only way of acquiring a grammatical knowledge
of the English Tongue, is first to learn a Latin Grammar." He
admits that Lowth errs in some respects, notably in his treatment of the passive voice[35] and the imperative mode.[36] Yet, he
says commendingly, Dr. Lowth was acquainted with the genius
of the language. Since, however, his book was designed for
private and domestic use rather than for use in the common
schools, the style and method are, he says, not suited to the capacities of youth.

Webster, like most of the Latin and English grammarians who
preceded him, looked upon grammar as the art of communicating thought,[37] thus confusing the nature of grammar with the
purpose of teaching it. It is true that in later editions of his
grammar[38] and in utterances made elsewhere,[39] he seemed to
look upon grammar as a science whose rules state the principles
of usage as exemplified by the best speakers and writers of the
English language, a science whose principles may be found by
an analysis of the whole into parts.[40] But, here again, we have

[35] Contrary to Lowth and Buchanan, Webster quotes Dr. Ash in support of his
theory that there is no passive voice. In the sentence, I am loved, *loved* is an
adjective or participle and no part of the verb. Part II (1784), p. 19.

[36] Webster took the stand that the second person only took the imperative mode
and not all three persons as some grammarians had contended. Part II (1784),
p. 37.

[37] In Part II (1784), p. 5, Webster says, "Grammar is the art of communicating
thoughts by words with propriety and dispatch."

[38] In *Rudiments of Grammar* (1790), p. 2, he says, "Rules are drawn from the
most general and approved practice, and serve to teach young students how far
their own practice in speaking agrees with the general practice." Again, in his
Improved Grammar (1831), p. 3, he says that grammar is "A system of general
principles, derived from the national distinction of words, deduced from the customary forms of speech in the nation using that language."

[39] For a further exposition of Webster's theory regarding the nature of grammar, see his *Letter to the Governors, Instructors, and Trustees of the Universities
and Other Seminaries of Learning in the United States, on the Errors of English
Grammars* (1798), p. 5.

[40] Lyman, *op. cit.*, p. 106.

an example of the variance that often existed between Webster's theories and his practice.

In the organization and general arrangement of the text we find on every hand the influence of the Latin grammars of the past. Webster, like Lowth and other English grammarians, used the divisions of the subject that had been used by the Latin grammarians: orthography, prosody, analogy or etymology, and syntax.[41] Since the first two divisions had been treated in Part I, the speller, in his grammar Webster dealt in the main with the last two, that is etymology and syntax.

Just as the compilers of primers and spellers started with the smallest parts, the A B C's, syllables, and words, in teaching children to spell and read, so both Lowth and Webster devote their first pages to definitions and discussions of letters, syllables, and words.[42] The parts of speech are then defined and their properties given.[43] Going on to the sentence, the next unit in this gradation, both authors give *A Praxis; or, Example of Grammatical Resolution.*[44] Other features of Webster's grammar were sections on ellipsis ("the elegant omission of a word or words in a sentence"), transposition, arrangement, redundancy, and punctuation.[45]

The extent to which Webster and other grammarians of his age were held in thralldom to the past is further shown by the

[41] These terms Webster defined as follows:
"Orthography teaches to spell and write words with proper letters.
"Prosody teaches pronunciation of words.
"Analogy or Etymology teaches the derivation and declension of words.
"Syntax teaches the proper arrangement of words in a sentence."—*Grammatical Institute,* Part II (1784), p. 7.
[42] Lowth (1775 ed.), pp. 1–10; Webster, pp. 7–9.
[43] Lowth, pp. 10–67; Webster, pp. 9–87.
Webster's efforts to define and explain the various combinations of auxiliary verbs was perhaps something of a contribution to the study of grammar. In his efforts, he reported, "I was obliged to struggle with a multitude of embarrassments almost insuperable . . . I was under a necessity of introducing a variety of distinctions and terms unknown to former Grammars, which may possibly offend those who are firmly attached to the rules and forms of antiquity."—*Institute,* Part II (1784), p. 5.
[44] Lowth, pp. 126–32; Webster, pp. 87–96.
[45] The discussion of punctuation was "abridged from Dr. Lowth."

fact that their texts were compiled around the age-old methods that had been employed in teaching the Latin grammar, namely, memorization, parsing, and correction of false syntax.

The emphasis placed on what was thought to be a fundamental principle of pedagogy, the complete mastery of the parts in their order, meant slavish memorization of rules and paradigms.[46] As a device to aid in memorizing Webster used the question and answer method, a very old method, having been used by Donatus and Lily and followed by such grammarians as Greenwood, Dilworth, Fisher, and Priestley in the eighteenth century. This method, however, never had wide vogue in America, as it was not used in such representative works as those of Bingham, Murray, and Brown.[47]

Parsing or grammatical resolution was the method par excellence which was used from the time of Lily until about 1900. In 1823 Goold Brown, who became the most ardent champion of parsing in America, published his *Grammar of Grammars,* which gave great stimulus to this method.[48] In the teaching of the English language "A constant process of dividing wholes into parts, even to the letters as a starting point," it was reasoned, "is the natural and logical method for teachers who will start their pupils rightly. As written and spoken language is accomplished by the putting together of parts, so the taking of them apart is the initial step of the learning process."[49] Then, too, "It is an exercise for all the powers of the mind, except the inventive faculty. Perception, judgment, reasoning, memory, and method are indispensable.[50]

The following comparative study indicates the manner in which both Lowth and Webster initiated the pupil into "the system of torture called parsing":

[46] Lyman, *op. cit.,* p. 113.
[47] *Ibid.,* p. 118.
[48] *The Institutes of English Grammar, Methodically Arranged, with Examples for Parsing, Questions for Examination, False Syntax for Correction, Exercises for Writing . . .*
[49] Lyman, *op. cit.,* p. 122.
[50] Brown, *op. cit.,* p. v.

A PRAXIS; OR, EXAMPLE OF
GRAMMATICAL RESOLUTION.[51]
I. In the fifteenth year of the
reign of Tiberius Caesar, Pontius
Pilate being governor of India,
the word of God came unto
John, the son of Zacharias, in the
wilderness.

.　.　.　.　.

In is a preposition; *the,* the
definite article; *fifteen,* an adjective; *year,* a substantive, or noun,
in the objective case, governed
by the preposition *in; of,* a preposition; *the reign,* a substantive,
objective case, etc.

AN EXERCISE [52]
The following examples will
teach children to distinguish the
parts of speech and enable them
to understand their connection
by agreement and government
according to the foregoing rules.

A woman who has merit, improved by a virtuous and refined
education, retains, in her decline, an influence over the men,
more flattering than even that of
beauty: she is the delight of her
friends, as formerly of her ad-
mirers.

.　.　.　.　.

A	Is the indefinite article.
woman	A common noun, in the singular number, and is the nominative word to the verb *retains.*
who	A relative pronoun, in the nominative case, sin- gular, referring to *wo- man,* its antecedent the nominative word to the verb *has* by rule 6, etc.

Another method, though not used as early in the teaching of
English as were the others mentioned, was the correction of false
syntax, perhaps introduced first by Fisher (1752) and the author
of the *British Grammar* (1760). Later it was used by Lowth,
Priestley, Murray, and Brown. Lowth, the avowed source of Webster's first text, was a firm believer of teaching "what is right . . .
by pointing out what is wrong," [53] and he gives many examples
of false syntax from the pages of English literature. In order to
show "The importance of our studying our language gram-

[51] Lowth, *op. cit.* (1775), pp. 126–32.
[52] Webster, *op. cit.* (1784), pp. 87–95.
[53] Lowth, *op. cit.,* p. viii.

matically," Webster also gave illustrations of "the obvious errors which are found in the sacred writings and in the works of our best authors." [54]

The following examples, some of which Webster took from Lowth, are representative of Webster's corrections:

ERRORS	CORRECTIONS
There is two or three of us.— Shakespeare	There are two or three of us.
Great pains has been taken.— Pope	Great pains have been taken.
Whoever the King favors.— Shakespeare	Whomever the King favors.
Who should I meet the other night.—*Spec.* 32	Whom should I meet the other night.
I fancy they are these kind.— Addison	I fancy they are this kind.
She not denies it.—Dryden	She denies it not.

In making the foregoing corrections, Webster obviously considered grammatical rules and what he considered the usage of his day was, or ought to be, rather than the idiom of the age in which the passages were written. He was of course following in the footprints of Lowth whose lists of errors by "standard authors" had aroused considerable interest. Of his offense, he seemed to be aware later. "The grammars of our language, now taught in our seminaries of learning," he wrote in 1806, "are rapidly banishing from books, some of its best established idioms." [55]

In correcting passages from the Scriptures, he anticipated his "picayune revision" of the Bible (1833), in which, says Scudder, "he attempted to square Elizabethan English to suit the regularity and uniformity of language which have been the dream of all schoolmasters." [56]

---

[54] *Op. cit.*, p. 96.
[55] *A Compendious Dictionary of the English Language* (1806), p. v.
[56] Scudder, *Noah Webster* (1882), p. 72. See pp. 295 f. of this study.

EXAMPLES FROM THE SCRIPTURES	CORRECTIONS BY WEBSTER
The number of the names together were about an hundred and twenty.—Acts I, 15	The number of the names together was about an hundred and twenty.
And there were stays on either side.—I Kings X, 19	And there were stays on each side.
Thine often infirmities.—I Tim. V, 23	"Quickest and frequent," the author explained, "would be employed with more propriety."

Under the caption "Other Improprieties" Webster anticipated the glossaries found in handbooks of current usage today. In this section he attempted to correct improper expressions as he corrected improper pronunciation of words in the speller.[57]

OTHER IMPROPRIETIES	CORRECTED
He is a great ways off.	He is at a great distance.
I had as goods go.	I may as well go.
What is wanting.	What is wanted.
Must needs.	Must necessarily, or of necessity.
I have got to go.	I must go.

The Grammatical Institute, Part II, passed through at least a score of editions and reprints between 1784 and 1804, the year the last issue was published.[58] Compared with Part I, the speller, the grammar was not a popular text. Webster's correspondence with his publishers shows that there was only a limited demand for Parts II and III. Writing to Webster in 1803 regarding the copyright for another term of years, Thomas and Andrews, Webster's Boston publishers, state that "The Selection [Part III] and Gram^r [Part II] are so little used and the small demand for them being on the decrease, that though we might wish to continue to print them, to have them accompany the Spell^g Books when wanted, we should not be willing to pay anything for them but

[57] See pp. 308f.
[58] This estimate is based on a check list made by the author of this study from the Webster grammars available in the leading libraries today.

should expect to have them be considered as included in the contract for the Spell^g Book." [59]

Another letter indicates that there was no more demand for Parts II and III in the Middle States than in New England. Writing a letter of inquiry regarding the rights of the spelling book for Pennsylvania, Delaware, and Maryland, Bonsal and Niles inquire "also of the right for the second and third parts of the institute; for these parts," they continue, "there has been as yet very little demand, indeed we may say none, but we think that by proper execution they might be made somewhat more in request than they are at present." [60]

In spite of this limited demand Part II "was the first American textbook on the subject to attain wide circulation . . . Webster's success appears to have attracted other American writers into the field at once, since at least 17 other works on grammar appeared before 1795," [61] the date when Lindley Murray published his *English Grammar, Adapted to the Different Classes of Learners,* another banner text, destined to take a place by the side of the "Old Blue-Back Speller."

Of the other American grammars which appeared between 1784 and 1795 and which numbered about a score, two were other texts written by Webster, *The Rudiments of English Grammar* (1790)[62] and an anonymous work usually assigned to Webster, *The Young Gentleman and Ladies Accidence,* published in 1792. Since these texts were shorter than the earlier Webster grammars, it is clear that he was in step with the current tendency to compile shorter and more concise grammars. Even

[59] Webster MSS. Letter dated "Boston, November 22, 1803," and sent to Webster at New Haven.

[60] Webster MSS. Letter dated "Wilmington, Delaware, November 28, 1803" and sent to Webster at Philadelphia, where he had gone to procure types for the revised Spelling Book.

[61] Lyman, *op. cit.,* p. 78.

[62] According to Evans (*op. cit.,* VIII, 105, 233) this text passed through six editions in the first two years. It was published first as Part II of *The Little Reader's Assistant* (1790); then at the request of the Hartford school authorities, was printed as a separate text. Barnard lists New Haven, 1791, and New York, 1811, editions.—*American Journal of Education,* XV, 569.

in the 1790 revision and subsequent editions of Part II, Webster shortened the grammar proper by putting much of the contents in an Appendix.[63]

Of the remaining grammars published in America before Murray's test appeared in 1795, only two offered anything like competition to Webster's text. These were Caleb Alexander's *A Grammatical System of the English Language* (1792) and Caleb Bingham's *The Young Ladies Accidence* (1785).[64] Bingham, who was Webster's most formidable competitor as a compiler of grammars before Murray entered the field, opened a private school for girls in Boston in 1784 and began what was undoubtedly the first pretentious effort to teach grammar in the Boston schools.[65] His text was an outgrowth of his instruction in this school. In 1789 he was employed to reorganize the Boston schools and his *Young Ladies Accidence* was adopted as the official text. It is an interesting comment on the budding rivalry which existed between compilers and publishers that the anonymous *Young Gentleman and Ladies Accidence* appeared in Boston soon after Bingham's text was adopted. Of the competition which existed between Webster and Bingham, the *Common School Journal* has this to say: "No two men ever exercised more influence over the schools of this country. . . . Webster's grammar was but little used compared with Bingham's; but his spelling book was far more extensively used. . . . The two authors divided the field between them." [66]

As has been shown, the popularity of other grammars began to wane after Murray published his *English Grammar* in 1795. Of its widespread use and longevity Sullivan writes: "Ranking with McGuffey's Readers and Noah Webster's speller in ubiquity and venerableness was Murray's *Grammar of the English Language*, first issued by Lindley Murray in 1795, regarded as the standard text-book on its subject throughout England and America for

[63] Thomas and Andrew's first edition, Boston, 1790.
[64] Lyman, *op. cit.*, pp. 78 f.
[65] *Ibid.*, p. 79, n. 36.
[66] Vol. XIII (1851), 218.

nearly a hundred years, and still studied in some American schools as late as the seventies." [67]

In none of the many fields of endeavor in which Webster participated did he show his uncertainty and inconsistency more clearly than in his compilation of grammars. In the preface to his 1787 revision of Part II of the *Institute*, he says, "With respect to some points, I acknowledge I have changed my opinion since the publication of the first edition. This change has been produced by a more laborious and critical investigation of the language, particularly in ancient authors; by comparing our translation of the Bible with the original; and by consulting the best English writers of the last and present century." [68] It is true that some of this shifting might be excused on the ground that usage changes. Since usage does not change as suddenly as his pronouncements would indicate, his acknowledgment that he had changed his mind seems the better explanation. A few examples will serve to illustrate:

As early as 1785, Webster states in Part II that *you* "is always plural and ought always to be joined to a plural verb, tho' it be applied to an individual." [69] In 1798, however, he says that the rule of grammarians is not correct. "When *you* refers to an individual it becomes singular," that the expression *you was* "is getting the better of old rules and probably will be established." [70] In the 1784 *Institute*, Part II, he condemned the use of the singular verb with the word *news*, as, "What is the news?" "This," he opined, "is certainly an impropriety however authorized by custom." [71] In the 1787 edition, we are told that "anomalous phrases creep into languages, in its infancy; and become established idioms, in its most refined state. On this principle we admit these expressions . . . *you are*, applied to an individual; *this news is favorable*, and many other expressions in our language." [72]

[67] Mark Sullivan, *Our Times* (1927), II, 133. C. Scribner's Sons.
[68] Page iii.
[69] Hartford ed., p. 15.
[70] *Letter to the Governors . . . on the Errors of English Grammars* (1798), p. 25.
[71] Hartford ed., p. 12.
[72] Hartford ed., p. iv.

In his attitude toward the subjunctive mode, he was notori-
ously unsteady and inconsistent; yet, says Leonard, his "change
of position on the entire matter of the subjunctive is the best
possible illustration of his honest attempt to record the facts of
usage." [73] In his Part II, 1784, he quotes Lowth verbatim: "The
subjunctive represents an action under some *condition* or *limitation* or else *doubtful;* and is always preceded by a verb or some
conjunction; such as "if," "though," "unless," "whether, &C." [74]
At this early date, however, he was conscious of the variance that
existed between the rule and actual usage. In a note he says, "It
seems to be now customary to use indicative to express a
doubt . . . We say, *if he is, if you are,* in cases of uncertainty,
and *you be, I be,* in declaratory phrases. This is, however, an
error and a real misfortune to the language, because it destroys a
distinction that is essential and ought to be preserved." [75]

In his various editions of Part II and in the *Dissertations*
(1789) [76] he expressed his doubts as to the extent to which usage
supports the rules of grammarians concerning the use of the subjunctive mode. Finally, in 1798, he came out boldly, maintaining
"that by the construction of our language, no subjunctive mode
is necessary—in most cases it is improper—and what is the strongest of all arguments, *it is not used in the spoken language,* which
is the only true foundation of grammar." [77]

*After Denouncing the Latinists, Webster Based His Gram-
mars on the Theories of Horne Tooke, Who Claimed
He Had Discovered the True Principles of the
Language through a Study of Anglo-Saxon*

WEBSTER'S tendency to shift from one position to another, to
set down his opinions before they were maturely formed, a tendency which he later recognized and criticized,[78] is further illus-

[73] S. A. Leonard, *The Doctrine of Correctness in English Usage, 1700–1800,*
(1929), p. 204.
[74] Page 23.
[75] *Ibid.,* p. 41.
[76] Pages 240 ff.
[77] *Letter to the Governors* (1798), p. 15.
[78] See p. 59.

trated by his denunciation of Lowth and his acceptance of the tenets of Horne Tooke. In 1787 Webster read Tooke's *Winged Words* or *The Diversions of Purley* (1786),[79] which "unfolded by a single flash of light, the whole theory of language, which had so long lain buried beneath the learned lumber of the Schools." [80]

"Purley" was Tooke's country estate in Surrey, where he had retired after having been imprisoned for a year and fined 200 pounds for having raised money by subscription for the relief of widows and orphans of American soldiers who had been killed at Lexington and Concord, a fact within itself that would have endeared Tooke to Webster. While here at Purley, Tooke and his friends diverted themselves by discussing many phases of language, among them being the nature of particles.[81] The *Diversions of Purley* is a transcript of these discussions.

After reading Tooke's work in 1787, Webster "entered upon an investigation of his principles for the purpose of obtaining full evidence of their correctness . . ." emerging "in full persuasion of mind or rather in absolute certainty, that his general theory is well founded." [82] After this date Webster no longer put his faith in grammarians and seldom lost an opportunity to denounce Lowth and the whole grammar tribe. "I have no hesitation," he wrote to Ramsay in 1807, "in affirming that the grammars now taught in our schools, *introduce more errors than they correct.* Neither Lowth nor Johnson understood the Saxon or Primitive English, without which no man can compile a real English Grammar." [83]

---

[79] This work is described by Leonard as "An attempt at comparative linguistics . . . a surprising mixture of fairly clear views of the nature and history of language and of completely absurd ideas."—*Op. cit.,* p. 26.

[80] Erasmus Darwin, *Zoonomia* (1794), sec. 39, p. 531. Quoted by Webster in *A Philosophical and Practical Grammar of the English Language* (1807), p. 10.

[81] For a discussion of Tooke's theories, see Webster's *Dissertations* (1789), pp. 186 ff.

[82] Webster, *Philosophical and Practical Grammar* (1807), p. 3.

[83] Webster, *A Letter to Dr. David Ramsay, Respecting the Errors in Johnson's Dictionary and Other Lexicons* (1807), p. 28.

To Tooke's remark that "Lowth has rejected much good English" Webster added that "he has criticized away more phrases of good English, than he has corrected bad." Continuing, he declared that Lowth "has not only mistaken the true construction of many phrases, but he has rejected others that have been used generally by the English nation from the earliest times, and by arbitrary rules, substituted phrases that have been rarely, or never used at all." [84]

After Webster had "explored the more remote sources of our language," that is, the Anglo-Saxon with Horne Tooke as a beacon light, he was convinced that his Part II "wanted material correction." [85] In consequence of this conviction, believing it to be "immoral to publish what appeared to be false rules and principles," he determined to suppress his grammar and did so.[86] The last issue of Part II appeared in 1804.

In 1807 Webster's *A Philosophical and Practical Grammar of the English Language* appeared. "For the outline of the system here offered," Webster wrote in the preface, "I am indebted to the *Diversions of Purley*." [87] Continuing, Webster says:

It is now an ascertained and a received fact that the indeclinable words, in our language (and probably in all others), are derived from declinable words, and were primitive significant as verbs, nouns, adjectives or participles. . . .[88] I have at length undertaken to construct a Grammar, upon what my own researches into the ancient English, or Saxon language, with various and extensive reading in modern books, have proved; to my full satisfaction, to be its only legitimate principles and established usages.

From a letter [89] written to Webster by Benjamin Stillman, dated "Edinburgh, 1805," and an enclosed letter from David

[84] *Dissertations* (1789), p. 287.
[85] Advertisement to "Philosophical and Practical Grammar," *American Dictionary* (1828), n. p.
[86] *Ibid.*
[87] Preface, p. 10.
[88] For example, "if" is radically the same word as "give" (Saxon, "gifan"); "unless," "lest," and "else" are derivatives from Saxon verb "lesan," meaning to dismiss . . .—*Dissertations* (1789), pp. 186 ff.
[89] Webster MSS.

Ogilvy, dated "London, 1805," we learn that Webster had sent
the manuscript of his *Philosophical and Practical Grammar of
the English Language* to Stillman, who had in turn submitted it
as an anonymous work to Ogilvy of London, who had agreed to
publish it. On reading the manuscript, however, Ogilvy was a
good deal startled with *the novelty of the plan* and for this reason
he passed it on to a "very eminent critic," whose name was very
laboriously and effectively blotted from the letter, for criticism.
The decision reached by the critic was that "the Author has not
sufficiently studied his own *new principles,* because in almost
every page there is a deviation from them . . ." The author was
advised "to maturely reconsider the work before it is put to
press." Finally, because of a series of complications, the copy was
returned with all due secrecy to Webster and was printed in
America in 1807.

The Philosophical and Practical Grammar was reissued in
1822 and an abridgment of it was prefixed to the *American Dictionary* in 1828. But in this edition Tooke was also relegated to
the ranks of Lowth and other corruptors of the English language.

To Horne Tooke [says Webster] are we indebted for the first explanation of certain indeclinable words, called conjunctions and
prepositions; and for this let him have all the merited praise. But
his researches were very limited, and he has fallen into most material
errors particularly in his second volume. I have made no use of his
writings, in this work.

An Improved Grammar of the English Language, which appeared in 1831, 1839, and 1843, was a revision of the *Philosophical and Practical Grammar* (1807). The number of editions
seems to indicate that this grammar was not widely used, that is,
compared to some of the banner texts of the age.

The question arises then, in what respect did Webster's 1807
grammar differ from his former works? First, much of his discussion in this work had to do with the nomenclature of grammatical terms.[90] The names now in use and the distribution of

[90] Lindley Murray, whose octavo edition of the English Grammar appeared the
following year (1808) and who, according to Webster, had examined and copied

the parts of speech "have the sanction of antiquity," he declared; "some of the classes of words still bearing the names assigned to them in the days of Aristotle; and I am no stranger to the power of custom." [91] The word "article," he explained, means a joint, and can be applied only to conjunctions. "An," "a," and "the" are not distinct parts of speech, but are adjectives.

The word "name," since it is a literal translation of Greek "onoma" and Latin "nomen," is preferable to "substantive," which is not sufficiently distinctive nor intelligible.

For the term "pronoun," which means "in the place of a noun," Webster proposed "substitute," for such words are often used in the place of sentences and adjectives.

Since the word "adjective" denotes something added, Webster substituted "attribute."

Since "verb" and "preposition" were the only words in the language that could possibly be used, they were retained, but they were considered very unsatisfactory, since the former lacked descriptive qualities and the latter was significant of position only.

Since "adverb" is significant of position only, Webster gave the "appellation of 'modifiers'" to this part of speech.

The word "conjunction" denotes "a joining" instead of what it is meant to signify, "a joiner." The term "connective" was adopted instead.

"In short," the author says by way of summary, "the science of grammar is nearly in the condition which chemistry stood, about thirty years ago. The terms employed, like *spiritus sylvestris,* the salt of Sylvius, the sugar of Saturn, the putty of tin, and the luna

---

from the latter's 1807 text, refers to, it would seem, Webster's changes in terminology: "An adherence to the established terms and arrangement, produce many advantages, and occasions no material inconvenience. It is easy to advance plausible objections against almost every definition, rule, and arrangement of grammar. But in most cases of this nature, it is certainly much better, to supply the defects and abridge superfluities, by occasional notes and observations, than by disorganizing, or altering, a system which has been long established and generally approved."—*An English Grammar,* p. 98.
[91] Preface, p. 5.

Cornea of the old Chemists serve only to show the obscurity of men's ideas on the subject and to bewilder the student." [92]

In the Preface to his abridgment of the 1807 grammar, published in the *American Dictionary* (1828), Webster continues this arraignment under the caption, "Some of the More Prominent Errors of the English Grammars." (1) Articles are not a distinct part of speech, but adjectives. (2) Words are arranged in a class to which they do not belong. Pronouns, such as, *that, if, though, unless, notwithstanding* are classified as conjunctions, "a most palpable mistake." (3) There is no correct and complete exhibition of the English verb in the British grammars known to the author. "The definite tenses [progressive tenses] . . . are wholly wanting . . ." [93] (4) The syntax of British grammars is extremely imperfect in that "There are many phrases which are perfectly well established and correct, which are not brought within the rules." They should be "brought within the rules" so that they can "be parsed or resolved by the student." (5) "There are several false rules of construction which mislead the learner; rules which are in direct opposition to the practice of the best writers." (6) "There are some phrases or modes of expression, frequently used by authors, which are not good English, and which it is the business of grammarians to correct."

The Early Criticism of the Subject of Grammar as Taught in the Schools Had to Do in the Main with the Texts and Methods Which Had Been Inherited from the Latin

GENERALLY speaking, any criticism of Webster's grammars and the methods employed in teaching the subject from his texts applies not only to him but also to his predecessors, and contemporaries, and in most cases, to his successors. His first texts, as we have seen, were in the main based on Lowth's grammar, which was written in slavish imitation of Latin texts. After 1807,

[92] Webster, *A Philosophical and Practical Grammar* (1807), pp. 5–9.

[93] In the 1807 grammar Webster gives twelve tense forms: indefinite tenses, that is, the present, past, future, perfect (present perfect), prior-past tense (past perfect), and the prior future (future perfect), along with the six definite tenses (same as the above using the progressive tense verb form).

his compilations were an exposition on Horne Tooke's theory of language, texts which were not widely used and which, it seems, did not exert a perceptible influence on the language, grammar compilation, or methods of instruction. In short, Webster belonged to that early period, which extended to the end of the first quarter of the nineteenth century, when "instruction in grammar in America . . . proceeded on the wrong basis—that of inflection; it began with the wrong unit—the word, and it followed entirely erroneous methods of study in proceeding from theory and rules to practice instead of reversing the process." [94]

As early as 1786, two years after Webster published his first grammar, Dr. Benjamin Rush protested against the practice of teaching grammar to young children. A grammar, he declared, "is to most boys under 12 years of age an unintelligible book. As well might we contend that a boy should be taught the names and number of the humors of the eye or the muscles of the tongue, in order to learn to see or to speak, as be taught the English language by means of grammar." As for the memorization of rules, he had this to say: "Sancho Panza in attempting to learn to read by chewing the four and twenty letters of the alphabet did not exhibit a greater absurdity than a boy of seven or eight years old does in committing grammar rules to memory in order to understand the English language." [95]

The editors of the *Academician* (1818) recommended memorization, with the reservation that the child should be taught the meaning of the rules. "No department of early education,"

[94] Lyman, *op. cit.*, p. 132. According to this author, the efforts to teach grammar in the American school fall within four more or less distinct periods: (1) before 1823, when English grammars imitated slavishly the Latin and the subject was looked upon as the art of speaking and writing correctly; (2) 1823–47, the parsing period, in which there was a conflict between old ideals and innovations fostered largely by the trend toward inductive study. During this period the grammars of Kirkham, Brown, Bullion, and Smith were very widely used; (3) 1847–73, the inductive period, in which grammar was conceived as the science of the sentence. The compilations of Wells and Green are characteristic of the period; (4) 1873–91, the rhetorical period, marked by the works of Swinton and White; (5) 1891–1920, the elimination or incidental study period in which formal grammar was gradually subordinated to its proper place as incidental to the study of composition and literature.—*Ibid.*, pp. 132–54.

[95] Wickersham, *History of Education in Pennsylvania* (1886), p. 234.

they declare, "gives more exercise to the memory, the judgment
and all the moral powers, than the science of grammar. But in the
course of instruction, we do not mean to substitute that jargon
of words, which is rattled off daily in most of our schools, for
grammatical knowledge . . . make him [the child] not only
commit the words to memory, but make him understand the
principles of the science, and apply them to miscellaneous reading. Make him read selections from Addison, Johnson, and
Pope, as a Latin scholar would read Caesar or Horace." [96]

Although during the second quarter of the nineteenth century
other methods were beginning to supplant the methods inherited
from the Latin, the comments in the journals indicate that memorization was a method still in use for many years. In the *Common School Journal* for 1842 we find this statement: "It is the
fault of most elementary works that they deal more with rules
than with principles and compel a reliance upon a quick memory
rather than upon independent thought . . ." [97] Commenting on
early methods, Wickersham says:

So much of Geography and Grammar as was taught in the early
schools was taught mainly by question and answer. The master read
the questions from the book, and the pupil gave the answer he had
committed to memory. Taught in this way, without maps, globes,
illustrations, pictures of life past or present, even Geography was a
dull study; much more dull must Grammar have been, presented
wholly in the form of abstract definitions and rules, uncombined
with practical exercises of any kind.[98]

Writing in 1833 [99] Warren Burton left a transcript of the manner in which he studied grammar. During his fifth summer in
school, at the age of seven and a half, he was put to work "to get
the parts of speech" in Bingham's *The Young Ladies Accidence*.
The next winter he journeyed "half way through the verb" in
Murray's abridgment. The next summer he began the book

[96] The *Academician,* I (1818), 193.
[97] Vol. V, 269.
[98] Wickersham, *History of Education in Pennsylvania* (1886), p. 206.
[99] *The District School as It Was* (1833), p. 34.

again and arrived at the end of the account of the parts of speech.
The winter after he went over the same ground again on through
the rules of syntax. The next summer he reviewed the whole
grammar, for the mistress thought it necessary to have "its most
practical parts firmly fixed in memory, before attempting the
higher exercises of study." During the third winter he began to
apply his supposed knowledge in the process of parsing or "passing" as it was called, first in simple prose and then in poetry,
Pope's *Essay on Man* being the parsing manual used.

Of this custom of using poetry to parse, "an unhappy denatur-
ing device for taking the poetry out of poems," Albert Mordell
writes: "We would be given selections from poems and told to
find the subject, which might be half a dozen lines away from the
predicate, with dependent clauses strung all around. Prose was
not used for parsing because the subject was before the predicate
where it belonged, and therefore provided no puzzle to sharpen
our wits—or confuse them. In the opening lines from 'Snow-
bound,' often used as an exercise,

   A chill no coat however stout . . . The coming of the
      snow-storm told,
how could I see that in parsing the object 'chill' belonged after
the verb 'told'?" [100]

During the first half of the nineteenth century educators questioned the correlation, as we say today, that existed between a
knowledge of formal grammar and one's ability to express one's
thoughts. In the *Common School Journal* [101] the editor points
out, "It may admit of question whether Washington, Franklin,
and others, whose writings are models of purity and ease, and
who never studied the Classical languages, ever saw an English
Grammar; and it would be easy to show that a large majority of
those who have studied grammar, since it became a common
school exercise, owe none of their celebrity to the lessons learned
at school."

[100] Mark Sullivan, *Our Times* (1927), II, 134. C. Scribner's Sons.
[101] Vol. XI (1849), 258.

Among the criticisms of grammar teaching during the nineteenth century was the claim that teachers, being "very favorable specimens of what the lessons in English grammar had hitherto accomplished," [102] did not understand the subject, nor had grammar enabled them to master the "art" of communicating thoughts. "We were educated," wrote W. B. Fowle, "at one of the best schools in one of the most celebrated towns in Massachusetts; but, although we studied English grammar seven years, and received a silver medal for our proficiency, we never wrote a sentence of English at school, and never did any thing which implied a suspicion on our part that grammar had anything to do with writing or conversation . . ." [103]

As an experiment, Fowle asked a group of teachers at an institute, numbering more than a hundred, to write on so trite a subject as *Happiness*. At the end of fifteen minutes, only two or three had written anything. Fifteen minutes more was given and this measure was repeated until an hour had elapsed, when only about a dozen had written anything. Half of the dozen papers were apologies for inability to write, and the other six had no merit. The teachers were then tried at English parsing and were found generally well acquainted with the exercise. "It was evident," Fowle concluded, "that they had been drilled in the analysis of common English sentences, but the composition of them had been neglected, or had been performed in connection with grammatical rules, and in such a technical manner as to stiffen rather than to facilitate the expression of thought and ideas. To remedy this defect, he announced, "we proposed to reverse the usual method, and teach the use of language before we attempt to teach what is technically called grammar." [104]

What, then, was the contribution which Noah Webster made to the teaching of grammar in the American schools? "A history of English grammar in the United States," wrote W. B. Fowle in

[102] *Common School Journal*, XI (1849), 258.
[103] *Ibid.*
[104] *Ibid.*

1850, "would afford some amusement if a rational mind could derive any amusement from perusing a record of abortive attempts to teach the correct use of language by every means but actual practice in the art of speaking and writing." [105] To this period of abortive attempts Webster belongs, first as a disciple of Lowth the Latinist and then of Tooke, who based his ill conceived theories on the Anglo-Saxon. Perhaps Webster's greatest influence, for good or ill, on the teaching of grammar was due to the fact that he published the first American grammar to attain anything like wide usage, thus drawing other compilers into the field, among them Lindley Murray. It is probable, too, that through his many protests concerning the Latin element in texts and in methods, Webster hastened the day when the teaching of grammar became more rational.

Since Lindley Murray's *English Grammar,* first published in 1795, was another banner text ranking with Webster's speller and McGuffey's readers in ubiquity and venerableness, the extent to which Webster's grammars influenced Murray's text is of interest to this study. In Murray's introduction to his Octavo edition in 1808 he acknowledges his indebtedness to Harris, Johnson, Lowth, Priestley, Beattie, Sheridan, Walker, Coote, Blair, and Campbell. "But," says Webster, "on examination, it appears that the greatest portion of the grammatical part is from Lowth." Commenting further, he says, that in his 1808 edition Murray gave Webster credit for one passage which he had chiefly taken from Webster's 1807 grammar. In later editions Murray acknowledges that a few positions and illustrations were selected from Webster's grammar. "Now the fact is," says Webster, "that the passages borrowed amount to thirty or more, and they are so incorporated into his work, that no person except myself would detect plagiarism . . ." [106]

[105] W. F. Fowle, *Common School Journal,* XII (1850), 5.
[106] This charge was made in the Introduction to Webster's abridged grammar prefixed to the *American Dictionary* in 1828, two years after Murray's death. A similar charge had been made, however, in Webster's letter to Pickering in 1817.

A comparison of Webster's grammar with Murray's 1808 edition does not indicate that Murray "borrowed" to the extent Webster says he did. That Murray's compilation was influenced by Webster's cannot be denied. The following comparative study shows how at least one section of Webster's grammar was adapted to Murray's use:

WEBSTER'S PHILOSOPHICAL
AND PRACTICAL GRAMMAR
(First edition, 1807)[107]

It is very common, when this verbal agrees with a number of words, or a whole clause, to omit the whole except the verbal; and in this use of *notwithstanding*, we have a striking proof of the value of abbreviations in language. For example: "Moses said, let no man leave of it till the morning, *notwithstanding*, they hearkened not unto Moses." Ex. 16, 20. Here *notwithstanding* stands without the clause to which it belongs; to complete the sense in words, it would be necessary to repeat the whole preceding clause or the substance of it. "Moses said, let no man leave of it until morning. *Notwithstanding this command of Moses,* or *notwithstanding Moses said that which has been recited,* they hearkened not unto Moses."

"Folly meets with success in this world, but it is true, *notwithstanding,* that it labors under disadvantages." *Porteus, Lecture* 13.

MURRAY'S ENGLISH GRAMMAR
(Octavo edition, 1808)[108]

It is very frequent, when the word *notwithstanding* agrees with a number of words, or with an entire clause, to omit the whole except this word; and in this use of *notwithstanding,* we have a striking proof of the value of abbreviations in language. For example: "Moses said, let no man leave of it till the morning; *notwithstanding,* they hearkened not unto him." Here *notwithstanding* appears without the clause to which it belongs; and to complete the sense in words, it would be necessary to repeat the whole preceding clause, or the substance of it.—"Moses said, let no man leave of it till the morning. *Notwithstanding this command of Moses,* or, *notwithstanding Moses said that which has been recited,* they hearkened not unto Moses—"Folly meets with success in this world; but it is true, *notwithstanding folly meets with success in the world,* that it labours under disadvantages."

[107] Pages 136f.
[108] Vol. I, 309.

It is also very common to use a substitute, *this, that, which,* or *what,* for the whole sentence; as, "Bodies which have no taste, and no power of affecting the skin, may, *notwithstanding this,* notwithstanding they have no taste, and no power to affect the skin, act upon organs which are more delicate."

It is not unusual to apply a pronoun, *this, that, which* or *what,* to represent nearly the whole of a sentence; as, "Bodies which have no taste, and no power of affecting the skin, may, notwithstanding *this,* act upon organs which are more delicate." Here *this* stands for, *"they have no taste, and no power to affect the skin."*

Whether or not Murray leaned heavily on Webster's compilation is perhaps of little importance. Both Murray and Webster belong to that period of "abortive attempts to teach the use of language by every means but actual practice in the art of speaking and writing." It is quite probable that the grammars of Webster and Murray and their contemporaries, cluttered as they were with the Latin influences of the past, retarded the development of the subject as a science, the rules of which are generalizations based on the facts of usage.

Commenting on Webster's place among his contemporaries, Leonard says that Webster's "effort at observation and record of the language was more thoroughgoing and more honest than that of most of his contemporaries." Lowth and Murray, this author says, were more dogmatically sure, though just as frequently wrong, as Webster, and for this reason Webster was less followed than they. "The eighteenth century schools, and almost as fully those of the following century, wanted assurance and authority." [109]

The following table, based on Leonard's "Topical Glossary of Dicta by Eighteenth Century Writers of English Usage," [110] shows graphically Webster's place among a few of his predecessors and contemporaries:

[109] S. A. Leonard, *The Doctrine of Correctness in English Usage, 1700–1800* (1929), p. 209.
[110] *Ibid.,* pp. 251–307.

	NOAH WEBSTER	DR. SAMUEL JOHNSON	JOSEPH PRIESTLEY	ROBERT LOWTH	LINDLEY MURRAY
Number of opinions given concerning usage	73	198	79	103	40
Opinions opposing usage..	33	49	50	59	18
Opinions sanctioning usage	40	149	29	44	22
Opinions that represent the fact and trend of the time	5	31	7	9	3
Opinions which show that writer misinterpreted the trend of usage.........	22	23	13	16	9
Proposals which probably never represented usage	3	8	5	12	3
Number of cases in which writer influenced a change	0	0	1	5	0

The backward state of English grammar in America during the first half of the nineteenth century is well summed up in the *Common School Journal:* [111]

Dr. Wallis, in speaking of the grammarians, says, "All of them, by forcing our English rules to conform to the Latin, have inculcated many useless rules about the conjugation, modes and tenses of verbs, which are entirely foreign to our language, and, therefore, rather increase its confusion and obscurity than aid in its illustration." Dr. Crombie says, "In exhibiting a paradigm of the conjugation of our verbs, many grammarians have implicitly and servilely copied the Latin grammar, transferring into our language the names both of tenses and modes, which have formally no existence in English. It appears to me that nothing but prejudice or affectation could have prompted our English grammarians, to desert the simple structure of their own language, and wantonly to perplex it with technical terms for things not existing in the language itself."

It is to be regretted that, when Dr. Webster had so fair a chance, to restore the true English grammar to the half million, now two millions of youth in our schools, and to establish rules that would

[111] Vol. XII (1850), 56.

have corrected many errors, and have laid a foundation for the sure and gradual reduction of many anomalies to analogy and order, he should not only have run off the English track, but have deviated farther from it than any of his predecessors.

Summary and Conclusions

PART II of a *Grammatical Institute* (1784) was based on Robert Lowth's *A Short Introduction to English Grammar* (1758), a work which exerted a great influence over the English grammars of the late eighteenth and early nineteenth centuries. Realizing that Part II, like its predecessors and contemporaries in the field of English grammars, was written in imitation of Latin grammars, Webster withdrew his work in 1804.

While under the spell of Horne Tooke, who based his pronouncements on his perfunctory researches in the field of Anglo-Saxon, Webster compiled his *Philosophical and Practical Grammar* (1807). This work had to do in the main with the nomenclature of grammatical terms.

Although Webster's grammars appeared in several editions and many reprints, they were in no sense of the word as popular as the spelling book. They belong to the period when unsuccessful attempts were made to teach the use of language by every method except that of actual practice.

Webster published the first American grammar to be at all widely used. It was probably the popularity of his text which drew other compilers into the field, thus giving the subject a more and more prominent place in the curriculum.

His grammars are filled with inconsistencies and inaccuracies. It would seem, however, that he made a sincere effort to observe and record the usage of his day. Although it does not appear that he added anything of permanent value to the content of the subject, his constant protest against the Latin influence on the contents of English Grammars and the methods used in teaching the subject may have hastened the day when the subject became more rational.

V

THE EARLY AMERICAN READER

I HAVE *endeavoured to make such a collection of essays as should form
the morals as well as improve the knowledge of youth . . . I have been
attentive to the political interests of America. I consider it as a capital
fault in all our schools, that the books generally used contain subjects
wholly uninteresting to youth, while the writings that marked the revolution, which are perhaps not inferior to the orations of Cicero and
Demosthenes, and which are calculated to impress interesting truths upon
young minds, lie neglected and forgotten.*[1]

IN 1785 Webster's *Grammatical Institute of the English Lan-
guage,* Part III, appeared. In the third edition, 1787, the text
was greatly enlarged and the title was changed to *An American
Selection of Lessons in Reading and Speaking, Calculated to Im-
prove the Minds and Refine the Taste of Youth*[2] *and Also to
Instruct Them in Geography,*[3] *History, and Politics of the
United States. To which is prefixed, Rules in Elocution, and
Directions for Expressing the Principal Passions of the Mind.
Being the Third Part of a Grammatical Institute, Greatly En-
larged.*

During the first period of American schoolbook production,
which immediately followed the Revolution, textbooks appeared
in great profusion and "authorship was characterized by erratic
efforts and random shots in many directions. Books were not
produced in nicely graded series; compilers were influenced
more by the public demand and the commercial success of their
undertakings than by the problems and theories of education . . .
The result was that many single and isolated primers, spellers,

[1] Webster, *An American Selection* (Boston, 1802), pp. v and vi.

[2] This is the edition upon which most of the remarks in this study, however,
not all, are based, since it was with its publication that the reader took the form
in which it remained in substance till the date of the last issue, 1816; that is, the
last issue but one. *Instructive and Entertaining Lessons for Youth,* 1835, was
substantially the same as *The American Selection.* See p. 146.

[3] Geography was a science in which Webster was much interested. At one time
he and Jedidiah Morse, America's first geographer, contemplated collaborating
on a gazetteer of the states. See Webster MSS.

and readers were published and used for a brief period within a limited area." [4] As soon as the new American nation got well under way, "Clergymen, pedagogues, and printers or publishers seem to have been most ready to try their hand at meeting democracy's educational needs, but any fairly intelligent citizen seemed to feel invited to join democracy's textbook free-for-all." [5] Among those making "erratic efforts and random shots" at compiling readers and primers of various sorts, Noah Webster was foremost, both as to time and extent. Unimportant as some of these may be in many respects, no survey of his contribution would be complete without a consideration of all of his texts.

Four years after Webster published his Part III, he brought out his first edition of the *New-England Primer* in 1789, amended and improved. Again, in 1801, he edited the same text, which, according to the subtitle, was "improved and adapted to the use of schools" and "designed as an introduction to the American spelling book." Webster attempted to secularize the *Primer* by omitting some of the religious selections and by compressing others. For the omissions he substituted moral material, including stories. But, since other editions did not follow, one may safely conclude that his secularized editions did not make a strong appeal.

The first of Webster's lesser original texts, in point of time, was a sort of omnibus text, published in 1790, *The Little Reader's Assistant; Containing: I. A Number of Stories Mostly Taken from the History of America, and Adorned with Cuts. II. Rudiments of English Grammar.*[6] *III. A Federal Catechism, Being a Short and Easy Explanation of the Constitution of the United States. IV. The Farmer's Catechism, Containing Plain Rules of Husbandry—and Calculated for the Use of Schools. V. General*

[4] Rudolph Rex Reeder, *The Historical Development of School Readers and Method in Teaching Reading* (1900), p. 41.

[5] Oscar Adolph Tingelstad, *The Religious Element in American School Readers up to 1830: A Bibliographical and Statistical Study* (1925), p. 245.

[6] During the same year (1790) *The Rudiments of English Grammar* was published separately as *An Introduction to the Second Part of the Grammatical Institute of the English Language.*

Principles of Government and Commerce. All Adapted to the Capacities of Children.

Several other Webster readers were published during Webster's lifetime. In 1831 appeared *The Elementary Primer, or First Lessons for Children, being an Introduction to the Elementary Spelling Book.* In 1835, *An American Selection* was slightly revised and published under the title of *Instructive and Entertaining Lessons for Youth; with Rules for Reading with Propriety Illustrated by Example: Designed for Use in Schools and Families.* The last reader to be compiled by Webster was the *Little Franklin,* published in 1836, "teaching children to read what they daily speak, and to learn what they ought to know."

Two other so-called Webster readers appeared after the death of the author. *The National Pictorial Primer,* published after 1844 (?), was "designed for the use of Schools and Families." This text seems to have been a sort of by-product of the *Pictorial Elementary Spelling Book* (1844 ?), as it was published by the same company and the hundred and fifty "fine engravings" with which the book was "embellished" are in the main those used in the *Pictorial Spelling Book.*[7] The second posthumous reader, *The Webster Elementary Reader,* designed to follow Webster's *Elementary Spelling Book,* was published in 1867, twenty-four years after Webster's death. There is nothing in these texts to indicate their authorship. It is doubtful whether they had any connection with Webster except in name, although they appeared under the aegis of the publishers of some of his other texts and may have been compiled or supervised by his son, William Greenleaf Webster, who was active in the publishing business and in editing Webster texts. As these texts did not appear in second editions, they obviously were not widely used.

Webster's Part III Meets Formidable Rivals

ALTHOUGH Webster's Part III of *A Grammatical Institute* was reprinted frequently during its life of about thirty years

[7] See pp. 80f.

(1785-1816),[8] and, as we have seen, several other readers and primers were compiled by the same author, yet if "evidence of an extensive sale of textbooks . . . is taken as reliable proof as to what constituted the subject matter of schoolroom activities,[9] we are forced to conclude that Webster's readers were not in wide use. They did not at any time have in them the promise of success which the speller had from the first; there was only a limited demand for Part III.[10]

Among the first rival texts to appear in the field were Joseph Dana's *A New American Selection of Lessons in Reading and Speaking* (1792); Caleb Bingham's readers; [11] and the *English Reader*,[12] published in America in 1799 by Lindley Murray, an expatriated American Quaker living in London. This was the banner reader in America during the first half of the nineteenth century. It was to that age, perhaps because of its pronounced religious flavor, what the *New England Primer* had been to the eighteenth century. It was the text before which hundreds of other readers that disputed its supremacy, including Webster's, fell, in spite of their vigorous Americanism. Other well-known competitors, some of which were exponents of special interests that found their way into the readers, were Abner Alden's texts; [13] George Chipman's *American Moralist* (1801); Daniel

---

[8] Although Tingelstad records sixty-three imprints in his check list of extant copies in fifty-nine of the leading American libraries, when one considers that the reader was usually published by the numerous publishers of the speller in the various states, the number of editions is not very large compared with that of the speller.

[9] Rollo Laverne Lyman, *English Grammar in American Schools before 1850* (1922), p. 8.

[10] See pp. 125 f.

[11] *The Child's Companion* (1792); *The American Preceptor* (1795, 2d ed.); *The Columbian Orator* (1797). Eighteen editions of this text were published in Boston before 1816, as well as many editions in other towns.

[12] First American edition (1799). Other Murray texts were *The Sequel to the English Reader* (1801: at least 23 issues followed); *The Introduction to the English Reader* (1805: at least 48 issues followed); and *An English Spelling Book* (1809, 6th American edition; at least 14 issues followed).

[13] *An Introduction to Spelling and Reading*, Vol. I (1797; five editions followed, latest being the 1819 ed.); Vol. II (1797; eleven editions followed); Vol. III (The Reader, 1802; five editions followed); Vol. IV (The Speaker, 1810).

Stanford's *The Art of Reading* (1800); and several texts by Daniel Adams.[14]

Webster Published Separate Texts for Subjects Formerly Found in Composite Texts

THE elementary texts used in the English and American schools up to Webster's day were of a composite nature. In publishing the three parts of *A Grammatical Institute of the English Language,* Webster's point of departure was his attempt to compile separate texts for the different subjects, instead of putting them together in one compend as did Coote, Dilworth, and Fenning. It is obvious that the contents of the five parts of Dilworth fall within the classifications used by Webster in his three books, namely, spelling, grammar, and reading.

Although books purporting to be grammars and spelling books had appeared before Webster published his texts, an analysis of their contents, especially of the latter, reveals that subjects as we understand them today were not clearly defined in the minds of the compilers. It was not, says Reeder, until after 1840 that beginning reading was separated from spelling as a school exercise.[15] With regard to the early spellers, Tingelstad says, "Very many of these books might have been called readers as well . . ." and "Almost without exception in the colonial period every school-book had something to say about spelling . . ." [16] Webster's Part I was at first almost entirely a spelling book; however, as has been shown, he later yielded to requests and in the 90's included fables and maxims. Any discussion of the early American reader will therefore of necessity include the "Old Blue-Back Speller."

Writing to Barnard in 1840, Webster said that insofar as he knew, no books for reading, other than Dilworth's *Guide,* the Psalter, the Testament, and the Bible, were used in America be-

---

[14] *The Understanding Reader* (1803); *The Agricultural Reader* (1824).
[15] *Op. cit.,* p. 49.
[16] *Op. cit.,* p. 136.

fore he published the third part of his *Institute*.[17] Webster's belief that his reader was the first to be used in the elementary schools of America seems to be founded on fact. It is even doubtful whether an elementary reader in the modern sense of the word existed in the English language before his compilation was published in 1785. There were, of course, composite texts and readers and speakers for academies and colleges.

The first school reader in the modern sense of the term, that is, giving interesting bits of information concerning the earth and nature, as well as selections of a didactic and religious character, was *Der Kinderfreund,* designed *die grosse lucke zwischen Fibel und Bibel auszufullen,* published in 1776 by Frederick Eberhard Rochow in Germany, where it was approved and used for nearly a hundred years by Protestants and Catholics alike. "The first reading-book corresponding to Rochow's *Kinderfreund* in American Schools, was Webster's Third Part Reader, published in 1785."[18] There is, however, nothing to indicate that Webster knew of Rochow's book. In fact it is more than likely that he did not know of its existence. Noah Webster was, then, the first American to "achieve" a reader. He did not, however, use the word "reader" in his titles. Lindley Murray seems to have been the first to use it to apply to a book of reading selections in his *English Reader* (1799).

Webster Contributed Little to the Development of the Graded Series

NUMEROUS primers had existed in England, from, it is thought, Saxon times,[19] until in 1651, when the Puritan Parliament passed a resolution "That all Primers formerly used in the time of Kingship in the Nation, be suppressed, and shall henceforth be no further used in any School, either Publique or

---

[17] *American Journal of Education,* XIII (1863), 123.
[18] Reeder, *op. cit.,* p. 19.
[19] Foster Watson, *English Grammar Schools to 1660* (1908), p. 32. The Macmillan Company.

Private, within the Commonwealth," [20] These primers, however, were unlike the modern primer in that they were very religious church books, the lay-folks service books, as well as books used by children. It became the custom to print the A B C's in the front of the primer, of which the catechism formed a large part, hence the term *A B C Primer,* or *Catechism.* These religious primers were the first books used by the colonists and were the early prototype of the *New England Primer,* which was destined to exert a great influence on American life during the eighteenth century.

It was not until about the turn of the century that the development of the modern primer began, and even then it had many of the earmarks of the Puritan A B C primer. Many of these primers were small books with paper covers, containing a rudely illustrated alphabet, a syllabarium, several pages of words for spelling, and sometimes a few reading lessons. Among these early primers were *The Columbian Primer* (1799), *The American Primer* (1803), Willard's *The Franklin Primer* (2d ed., 1802), *The Franklin Family Primer* (6th ed., 1806), Saunders's *An Easy First Book for Children* (1809), and Oram's *American Primer* (1816).

Readers of any sort for beginners were very few previous to 1825. About that date began, along with the development of the series idea, the publication of primers that were more like the present-day primers in that they were less religious and made a stronger appeal to the child's interests and needs than did the first primers. Among the most popular of those published were *The Child's First Book, or New Philadelphia Primer* (1824), Worcester's *A Primer of the English Language* (1828), Keagy's *The Pestalozzian Primer* (1827), *The American Primer* (1828), *The American Primary Class Book* (1830), and Bartlett's *The Clinton Primer* (1830), which was a first book in a series of readers. The development of the modern primer is of prime importance, since it was the first schoolbook actually to make an attempt to provide easy material of interest to the beginner.

[20] *Ibid.,* p. 34.

Even after the series idea was established it was the primer that was the exponent of childhood interests. As children were looked upon as miniature adults, both mentally and physically, compilers of readers held adult needs uppermost in their minds. This practice was but a continuation of the attitude held, for example, by the compiler and later editors of the *New England Primer,* which has been called the "Little Bible of New England" and in reality contained "strong meat" instead of the avowed "spiritual milk for babes." Among the subtitles of the early American primers and readers we find phrases which indicate that they were designed for families as well as for schools; for adults as well as for children.

After subjects within the composite text had been treated separately and the primer was in the early stages of its development, the arrangement of the graded series, that is, texts that were adapted to the capacities of children of different ages and degrees of development, was the logical step. Two- and three-book series began with the century. Usually there was a main book, an introduction, and a sequel.[21] In some cases a primer and a speller carried out the series idea. Among the series of American readers that appeared before 1830 were those compiled by A. and J. W. Picket (1818 ff.), by John Pierpont (1823 ff.), and by Samuel Putnam (1828 ff.).

After 1825, as more and more attention was paid to method in teaching children to read, to adaptation and subject matter, the series idea made rapid strides in its development. The first fully developed series of readers was compiled by Lyman Cobb (1830 ff.). Other series to be compiled in the thirties were those of M. R. Bartlett, Samuel Worcester, and S. G. Goodrich (Peter Parley Series). After 1840 readers were compiled almost entirely in series, the outstanding authors being Goodrich, Swan, and Tower, to be followed in the next decade (1850-60) by such compilers as McGuffey,[22] Sanders, Hillard, Parker, Watson, Town, and Halbrook.

[21] This was the plan used by Lindley Murray.
[22] McGuffey entered the field in 1836.

Although, as will be shown, the graded series owed something to Webster's early readers in that the materials used and the general tone of the former were similar to the latter, Webster contributed very little to the development of the series from a standpoint of adapting the materials to the different levels of capacity. His edition of the *New England Primer* (1801) was, for example, according to the subtitle, *Designed as an Introduction to the American Spelling Book,* but this book was more closely related to the medieval A B C primer than to the modern easy primer for beginners. It is true that at times his various texts were arranged in a series [23] and advertised as a complete system of instruction, yet the classification was obviously one of convenience rather than a carefully-thought-out system that would lead the child step by step in his development.

Webster Set the Pattern for the American Reader

SINCE Webster was a successful author of textbooks, other compilers lost no time in entering a field which was not beneath the efforts of this first and foremost textbook compiler and it was through this wide interest and experimentation that the graded series and other features of the modern reader developed. Above all, he set the pattern for the American school reader, the pattern which was followed in varying degrees, even in the graded series, throughout the greater part of the nineteenth century.

This pattern has been well described by Henry H. Vail: "The school readers are the proper and indispensable texts for teaching true patriotism, integrity, honest, industry, temperance, courage, politeness, and all other moral and intellectual virtues." [24] According to Kellogg, the ideals which early compilers of readers held and followed were four in number: I. To pro-

---

[23] For example, his *New England Primer* (1801) was an Introduction to the *American Spelling Book* (1786) and *The Little Reader's Assistant* (1790) was designed to fill the gap between the speller and the reader, *An American Selection* (1785). Here in a sense was a series of four books. Another Webster "series" was the *Elementary Primer* (1831), *The Elementary Spelling Book* (1829), and *The Teacher* (1836).

[24] *A History of the McGuffey Readers* (1911), p. 2.

mote the principles of morality and religion; II. To improve manners and deportment; III. To waken national feeling and cultivate a respect for government; IV. To teach the art of reading.[25] This classification seems to summarize in the main the ideals which determined the choice of selections in Webster's readers and in those of his contemporaries. To contend, however, that all the contents of the early readers fall within one of the four categories would be to ignore the facts in the case. "Early readers," says Tingelstad, "were made the depository of the thoughts and ambitions of the people, even to the extent of serving special interests," [26] such as agriculture,[27] animal life,[28] history, geography, arithmetic, oratory, and citizenship under the Constitution, each of which were served also by special readers.

Since a consideration of the four ideals, namely, those pertaining to religion and morality, patriotism, manners, and the

[25] A. E. Kellogg, "Contents of School Readers," *The Educational Review*, VIII, 337.

[26] *Op. cit.*, p. 250.

[27] Webster's "Farmer's Catechizm, Plain Rules of Husbandry . . . Calculated for the Use of Schools," found in *The Little Reader's Assistant* (1790), Part IV, is a good example. Besides giving questions and answers concerning kinds of soil, use of manure, crops, plowing, planting of trees, preserving butter, making cheese, and making and keeping cider, Webster indulges in a little indoctrination; for example,

"Question. What is the best business a man can do?
"Answer. Tilling the ground, or farming.
"Question. Why is farming the best business?
"Answer. Because it is the most necessary, the most helthy, the most innocent, and the most agreeable employment of men.

. . . .

"Question. Why is farming the most *innocent* employment?
"Answer. Because farmers have fewer temptations to be wicked than other men. They live much by themselves, so that they do not see so many bad examples as men in cities do. They have but little dealings with others, so that they have fewer opportunities to cheat than other classes of men. Besides, the flocks and herds which surround the farmer, the frolicks of the harmless lambs, the songs of the cheerful birds, and the face of nature's works, all present to the husbandman, examples of innocence, beauty, simplicity, and order, which ought to impress good sentiments on the mind, and lead the heart to God."

Other readers serving the interests of agriculture were Adams's *Agricultural Reader* (1824), and *The Farm Yard Journal* (1819).

[28] See Webster's "History of Animals," *Elements of Useful Knowledge* (1812), Vol. IV.

art of reading, and a consideration of the extent to which early compilers subscribed to them, is of no small importance in determining Webster's contribution to the early American school reader, they are made the basis of the discussion in the remainder of this chapter.

Religious and Moral Elements Were Pronounced in the Early American Reader

THE PRACTICE OF STRESSING RELIGION AND MORALITY IN THE AMERICAN SCHOOLS WAS INHERITED FROM THE PAST

THE predominance of provisions for instruction in religion and morality in the curriculum of the early American school was not of native origin, although America furnished a congenial environment for its continuance and growth. Throughout the Middle Ages, the outward organization and the supervision, as well as the general atmosphere of the European school, was in the main religious.

After the Reformation, the Protestant Church exercised its prerogative to instruct the young, just as vigorously as had the Catholic Church during the Middle Ages. Led by such ardent champions as Luther and Erasmus, the belief that people should be able to go directly to the fountainhead of all religious authority—the Bible itself—gained momentum and to this end the Holy Word was brought out of the Latin into the vernacular and the people taught to read.[29] It was furthermore held desirable that Protestants be instructed in order that they might hold their own in disputations with Catholics.[30] "Personal salvation, in a

[29] Rollo Laverne Lyman, *English Grammar in American Schools before 1850*, p. 16.

[30] The anti-popish aspect of the instruction given in the English schools after the Reformation is well illustrated by *The Protestant Tutor* (1707); published and sold in London by B. Harris and V. Harris, of whom the former was perhaps the author of the *New England Primer* (c. 1690). Part of its subtitle indicates its scope: "Discovering to them [youth and others] the Errors and Deceits of the Papists, and Grounding them in the True Protestant Religion." The *Protestant Tutor for Children* (Boston, 1685), which is said to be the direct forebear of the *New England Primer,* is also very anti-popish.

sense, depended, indirectly at least, on the power of reading, which thus became a necessity of education for religion's sake, and if we may add that some degree of power of interpretation was also necessary as a part of the demand for the exercise of private judgment, a trained educated mind was also, inferentially essential."[31]

So intent were the authorities that training in matters pertaining to conduct be given that the records referring to the government of the English schools of the fifteenth, sixteenth, and seventeenth centuries are replete with statutes concerning school prayers and religious observances,[32] church attendance,[33] religious instruction,[34] instruction in manners and morals,[35] and so forth. As in other practices, the early American schools followed the customs of the mother country.[36]

EARLIEST ENGLISH TEXTS AND PROMINENT EDUCATORS
STRESSED RELIGION AND MORALITY

An examination of a few of the most popular early English texts used in elementary and grammar schools shows the prominent place which religion and morality were given in the British schools. In 1557 Francis Seager's *The School of Vertue, and Booke of Good Nourture for Chyldren, and Youth to Learne Theyr Dutie By* appeared in verse.[37] Prayers to be said in the morning when getting up and in the evening when going to bed

---

[31] Watson, *The Old Grammar Schools* (1916), p. 71.

[32] Foster Watson, *The English Grammar Schools to 1660* (1908), pp. 38 ff. The Macmillan Company. In addition to the history of the early English Grammar School, this book is something of a source book of the materials upon which the history is based. Many statutes are given verbatim.

[33] *Ibid.*, pp. 45 ff.

[34] *Ibid.*, pp. 63 ff.

[35] *Ibid.*, pp. 98 ff.

[36] *The American Journal of Education, January,* 1877, pp. 107 ff.
See also Sanford Fleming's "Children and Puritanism; the Place of Children in the Life and Thought of the New England Churches, 1620–1847" (1933), p. 105; also E. P. Cubberley's *Public Education in the United States* (1919), p. 28.

[37] Reprinted by the Early English Text Society, The Babees Book, ed. F. J. Furnivall (1865), pp. 333–55.

are given along with the advice that the Lord's Prayer be said morning and evening.

Edmund Coote's *The English School Master* (1595) gives eighteen pages to the catechism, prayers, and psalms. This was a popular text, having passed through twenty-six editions before 1656. It was an early prototype of a succession of similar English texts in the eighteenth century, such as the compendiums brought out by Thomas Dyche (1709),[38] Daniel Fenning (1756),[39] Thomas Dilworth (1740),[40] and William Mavor (1801).[41]

In addition to these early English texts, the comments by men who wrote on education during the seventeenth century show that the religious and moral was held the most important part of a child's education. Brinsley urged that the very youngest should be required to bring some notes of the sermon, or else to be taught short sentences by the older scholars, such as "Without God we can doe nothing" and "All good gifts are from God."[42] Prompted by the doctrine of total depravity, Hezekiah Woodward declared that "We have filled our children's bones with sin. It is our engagement to do all we can to root that sin out, which we have been a means to root so fast in . . ."[43] John Milton held that "to repair the ruins of our first parents by regaining to know God aright, and out of that knowledge to love him, to imitate him, to be like him . . ." is the end of learning.[44] John Locke, who exerted a great influence on the schools in England and America, declared that "Heaven being our great business and interest, the knowledge which may direct us thither is certainly so too, so that this is without peradventure the

[38] *A Guide to the English Tongue, in Two Parts.* The forty-fifth edition was published in 1764.
[39] See p. 67.
[40] See pp. 116 and 161.
[41] *The New English Spelling Book.* "Passed through numerous editions."—*Dictionary of National Biography.* Vol. XIII, 108.
[42] *Ludus Literarius* (1612; edited by E. T. Campagnac, 1917), p. 255.
[43] Watson, *The English Grammar Schools to 1660* (1908), p. 114. The Macmillan Company.
[44] "On Education," addressed to Samuel Hartlib, *Old South Leaflets,* VIII, No. 188, p. 2.

study that ought to take the first and chiefest place in our thoughts . . ."[45]

In Charles Hoole's *A New Discovery of the Old Art of Teaching School* (1660), we learn that after parliament suppressed the A B C primer,[46] Hoole, a prominent English schoolmaster and translator of Comenius, substituted the Lord's Prayer, the Creed, and the Ten Commandments. He recommended that a child read over the psalms, thanksgivings, and prayers "till he have them pretty well by heart" and that the psalter, the "Psalmes in meeter" and the "Schoole of good manners" be read at least three times. As soon as the child can read "any whit readily" he should be encouraged, even hired, to read the Bible and commit passages to memory.[47]

This early tendency to stress conduct was supported by no less an authority than Comenius, who was one of the great influences in education during the seventeenth century. Although Comenius was much interested in promoting methods of teaching sciences and arts, his ultimate aim was to bring pupils to wisdom through the practice of morality and piety "by means of which we are exalted above all other creatures and drawn nigh to God himself."[48] "We may . . ." says Watson, "by summarizing Comenius's Method of Morals, accept the general position there stated as acceptable, educationally, by English, and indeed, European Puritanic Protestantism.[49] This influence was inherited by the colonists and exercised an influence on the compilers of the early spellers and readers. Some of the characteristics of Webster's texts, for example, might be used to illustrate Comenius's pronouncements, although there is no evidence to indicate that Webster was directly acquainted with the works of the great educator.

[45] *Some Thoughts Concerning Education* (1693; ed. by R. H. Quick, 1913), p. 196.
[46] See pp. 149 f.
[47] Watson, *The English Grammar Schools to 1660* (1908), p. 64.
[48] Watson, *The English Grammar Schools to 1660* (1908), p. 118. For Comenius's sixteen fundamental rules for shaping morals, see M. W. Keatinge's *Comenius* (1931), pp. 181–87.
[49] *The English Grammar Schools to 1660* (1908), p. 118. The Macmillan Company.

RELIGIOUS AND MORAL ELEMENTS WERE PRONOUNCED IN THE FIRST
TEXTS USED AND IN THE JUVENILES READ IN AMERICA

An examination of the early texts used in America before
Webster compiled his *Institutes* serves to give a further explanation of why he and other compilers emphasized religion
and morality in their texts. These early textbooks were few in
number. Before the publication of *The New England Primer* in
1690, New England schools had to depend on books imported
from England. Bibles were the universal reading texts, convenient because found in every home and logical because a
knowledge of religion was legally prescribed.[50] In short, the procedure described by John Locke—"the ordinary road of the
Horn Book, Primer, Psalter, Testament, and Bible"[51]—was the
common practice in America as in England.

In spite of the fact that the Puritan spirit was on the decline
after the Revolution, that unity in religious belief gave way to
diversity, that there were many indications of religious discord
as well as liberality and infidelity,[52] and that Webster was in step
with these tendencies, an examination of Webster's spellers and
readers reveals that these early texts which preceded his compilations, in regard to religion and morality, left their stamp on his
works as well as on those of his contemporaries and successors.

Perhaps the most influential of all was *The New England
Primer* (c. 1690), at times called "The Little Bible of New England" and the "Mirror of Puritanism." It began with the alphabet as did the hornbook and the A B C primer. It was a church
book, a very religious book, which showed the influence of an
earlier religious primer, *The Protestant Tutor for Children*
(1685).[53] It kept alive the religious flavor introduced earlier into

---

[50] Lyman, *op. cit.*, p. 19.
[51] John Locke, *Some Thoughts Concerning Education* (1693; ed. of 1913), p. 134.
[52] Rudolph Rex Reeder, *The Historical Development of the School Reader* (1900), p. 17.
[53] See note, p. 154.

colonial education by including hymns, prayers, and cate-chisms.[54]

In this primer, as in other books of the age intended for chil-dren, there were poems sounding warning of the inevitable end that must come to all and that "It is a great work to dye, and to dye well is a greater." The following lines are typical:

> I in the burying place may see
> Graves shorter there than I;
> From death's arrest no age is free,
> Young children too may die,
> My God, may such an awful sight
> Awakening be to me!
> O! that by early grace I might
> For death prepared be.

James Janeway's *A Token for Children* was an English Book which appeared during the middle of the seventeenth century, "Being an exact account of the conversion, holy and exemplary lives, and joyful deaths of several young children . . . To which is added a token for the children of New England or some ex-amples of children in whom the fear of God was remarkably budding before they died; in several parts of New England . . ."[55] Other "juveniles" were Wigglesworth's *The Day of Doom* (1662) and Cotton Mather's *Memorials of Early Piety Occurring in the Holy Life and Joyful Death of Mrs. Jerusha Oliver* (1711).

Another very popular book of the eighteenth century was the *History of the Holy Jesus* (16th ed., Boston, 1749), a metrical version of the New Testament. In Thomas White's *A Little Book for Little Children* the author recommends, not "ballads and foolish books," but the Bible, *The Practice of Piety, Call to the Unconverted, Almost Christian, Advice to Young Men, The Plain Man's Pathway to Heaven,* and the *Book of Martyrs.* Children were also advised to read often treatises of death, and hell, and judgment, and of the love and passion of Christ. Chil-dren go to sleep at church or during prayer, they were told, be-

[54] For a further discussion of the contents of *The New England Primer,* see Flem-ing's *Children and Puritanism* (1933), pp. 80–82, 105, 112, 113.
[55] The New England portion was written by Cotton Mather (1700).

cause the devil rocks the cradle. Those who play at church or on the Lord's Day have the devil for a playfellow, while those who go to bed without saying prayers have the devil for a bedfellow.[56]

Early in the seventeenth century the "old deluder" was abroad in the persons of chapmen and peddlers.

> I am informed [wrote Cotton Mather], that the minds and manners of many people about the Countrey are much corrupted by foolish Songs and Ballads, which the Hawkers and Peddlars carry into all parts of the Countrey. By way of antidote, I would procure poetical compositions full of Piety, and such as may have a Tendency to advance Truth and Goodness, to be published, and scattered into all Corners of the Land. These may be an extract of some, from the excellent Watt's Hymns.[57]

Judging from the number of extant copies of Isaac Watts's *Divine and Moral Songs,* one concludes that Mather's advice was taken. "To the present-day reader, many of the sentiments of Dr. Watts are so extraordinarily unchristian in spirit, and so unutterably smug in expression that their great popularity is one of the best guides to our understanding of the mental outlook of the time."[58] Some of his best-known lines, such as "Birds in their little nests agree," "Let dogs delight to bark and bite, for God has made them so," and "How doth the little busy bee," became familiar to the masses through the nineteenth-century readers.

Before the end of the eighteenth century, writers began to write books that appealed to the interests and understanding of children. As early as 1761 such books were published in America,[59] but the first really important man in children's literature was John Newbery (1713–67), who, realizing the importance of training and educating the childish taste from every point of view, employed such men of genius as Goldsmith and the Bewicks (whom Anderson, the engraver who illustrated

[56] Fleming, *Children and Puritanism* (1933), pp. 89 f. Copyright Yale University Press.
[57] *Diary of Cotton Mather 1709–1724* (1912), entry for Sept. 27, 1713, VIII, 242.
[58] A. S. W. Rosenbach, *Early American Children's Books* (1933), p. xxxv.
[59] Andrew Barclay published *Tom Thumbs Play Book* in Boston, 1761; Hugh Gaine an abridged *Robinson Crusoe* in New York, 1774.

Webster's speller, imitated). Among the juvenile books published by Newbery were *The History of Mistress Margery Two
Shoes, Mother Goose Melodies, The Royal Battledoor, Babes in
the Woods,* and *London Cries.*

In connection with this emphasis on religion and death, a
consideration of the juveniles written for and recommended to
colonial children helps to explain the contents of the readers of
the same age. Outstanding among these books was *Pilgrim's
Progress,* and abridgments, perhaps by Goldsmith, of outstanding novels of the day, such as *Tom Jones, Pamela,* and *Clarissa
Harlowe.* These books were imitated and pirated in America.
Among the publishers in America who published books for
children as distinct from grown-ups was Isaiah Thomas (1749–
1831), founder of the Antiquarian Society of Worcester, Massachusetts, who deliberately imitated Newbery's "Lilliputian
Library." [60]

There is nothing among the facts of Webster's life or in his
readers to indicate that he ever came under the spell of this
better class of literature during his childhood. It required half
a century, says Algernon Tassin, to convince parents that the
combination of amusement together with instruction, religious
or mundane, which ventured to show its head about the middle
of the eighteenth century, was not pernicious.[61]

Daniel Fenning's *Universal Spelling Book* [62] and Thomas Dilworth's *New Guide to the English Language* were two English
books that were very widely used in America and upon which,
as has been shown, Webster leaned in compiling Part I, the
speller, in 1783.[63] In these texts the religious and moral element
was pronounced.

[60] Rosenbach, *op. cit.,* pp. xli f.
[61] *Cambridge History of American Literature* (1907), II, 396. The Macmillan
Company.
[62] For the religious element in Fenning's book, which is closely blended with
selections teaching manners, see pp. 178 f.
[63] Part IV in Dilworth is made up of the following: pp. 125–30, Sentences in
Prose (short moral paragraphs); pp. 130–36, Sentences in Verse (short moral
stanzas); pp. 137–48, twelve crude cuts, each with a moral aphorism, such as
"Honesty is the best policy" and "A bird in the hand is worth two in the bush,"
and a fable with the moral or "The Interpretation" stated below.

THE RELIGIOUS AND MORAL ELEMENTS IN THE TEXTS WHICH
PRECEDED WEBSTER'S COMPILATIONS INFLUENCED
HIS SPELLERS AND READERS

"Noah Webster . . . had a singular faculty of being the first
in time in many departments of literary industry, and constantly
to have anticipated other people." [64] Then, too, his feet were
planted solidly on the earth in that he was able to appraise the
present with a fair degree of accuracy. The reading lessons in
the speller, for example, were carefully gauged to meet the requirements of an age in which religion and morality, in spite of
the wave of liberalism that followed the Revolution, were still
dominant factors.[65] The fact that slightly less than fifty per cent
of the reading lessons in the speller were highly religious and
moral in tone, approximately the percentage of such selections
in Murray's *English Reader,* may have contributed to the success
of the former as it did to the latter. It is interesting to note that
Webster's revisions of his speller take close cognizance of the
changing spirit of the times in its religious aspect. From 1783 to
1802 the percentage of religious content in the *American Spelling Book* was 33 per cent, and from 1802 to 1829, 47 per cent,
the same as in Murray's *English Reader;* but when the *American
Spelling Book* became the *Elementary Spelling Book* (1829), this
percentage was dropped to 10 per cent, which was also in har-

---

Part V is made up of: Particular Forms of Prayer; Public Prayers for the use
of Schools; In the evening; Private Prayers, a prayer for Wisdom and Knowledge to be said by a child going to school, or at any other Time; A morning
prayer for a child; An Evening Prayer for a Child; Grace before Meat; Grace
after Meat; Before going into Church; for a Child seating himself in the
church; and When Divine Service is Ended, pp. 149 ff.

[64] Scudder, *op. cit.,* p. 68.

[65] N. B. Smith calls the period 1776–1840, the period in which Webster was
active, the "period of patriotic-moralistic emphasis" in contradistinction to the
preceding period, 1620–1776, the "period of religious Purpose." It is true that
the tendency was toward the moral rather than religious, but the high percentage of religious contents in the most popular texts of the century, such as
Webster's "Old Blue-Back," Murray's *English Reader,* and even McGuffey's
readers during the last half of the century, shows that the religious was present
along with the moralistic and patriotic. See N. B. Smith's *American Reading
Instruction* (1934), pp. 36 ff.

mony with the tendency of the day and an anticipation of future developments.[66]

With respect to Part III of the *Grammatical Institute*, it would seem, however, that Webster, looking too far into the future and realizing that the religious selections would eventually have to give place to those of a mere moral nature, indulged his tendency to secularize his texts and overshot the mark, just as he did in his revisions of *The New England Primer*.[67] The failure of Webster's reader to achieve the success that attended his speller and Murray's reader was perhaps due to the fact that the percentage of its religious content was very low and for that reason it failed to gain the approval of teachers and parents,[68] for as William Godwin once pointed out to Charles Lamb, it is the children who read children's books when they read, but it is the elders who choose them.[69]

In Webster's spelling book, which, as we have seen, was in part a reader, there was a copious supply of short sentences, most of which were aphorisms relating to morality, religion, manners, and patriotism; others were informational or purely prudential in tone. These sentences did not appear, however, until in the early editions of the 1790's. In providing the aphorisms, Webster and others were merely following the advice of Comenius, who declared in his fourteenth rule that "precepts and rules of conduct must be given." The following selection of maxims is fairly representative of the kind of sentences used:

[66] Oscar Adolph Tingelstad, *The Religious Element in American School Readers up to 1830; a Bibliographical and Statistical Study* (1825), p. 201. This study is based on an examination of 3,544 readers and spellers. According to this author, the general curve of distribution of the religious content exhibits four noteworthy features:

a. A period of religious dominance up to 1775.
b. A sharp decline in religious contents, 1774–1792.
c. A first reaction from this decline, 1795–1812.
d. A second and stronger reaction, beginning about 1815, and declining after 1820, sharply after 1827.
[67] See p. 145.
[68] The percentage of religious content in Webster's Part III was 7 per cent. Tingelstad, *op. cit.*, p. 244.
[69] Rosenbach, *op. cit.*, p. xxvi.

PROVERBS, COUNCILS, AND MAXIMS IN WORDS OF ONE SYLLABLE [70]

Hot love is soon cold.
Look ere you leap.
Soon hot soon cold.
A good man is a wise man.
A good cow may have a bad calf.
As you brew so you must bake.
A bird that *can* sing and *will not* sing must be made to sing.
As you make your bed, so you must lie.
He that lies down with dogs must rise up with fleas.
The new broom sweeps clean.
Youth, like the spring, will soon be past.
The time will come when we must all be laid in the dust.
He is a fool that does not chuse the best boys when he goes to play;
    for bad boys will cheat and lie, and swear, and strive to make him
    as bad as themselves.
If you want to be good, wise and strong, read with care such books
    as have been made by wise and good men; think of what you read
    in your spare hours; be briske at play, but do not swear; and waste
    not too much of your time in bed.

In later editions sentences appealing to a wider interest appeared, such as:

To filch is to steal; we must not filch.
Good men obey the laws of God.
Careless girls misley their things.
God will destroy the wicked.
A good boy will try to spell and read well.
Never pester little boys.
The idle boy is a very lazy fellow.
A vain girl is fond of fine things.
God made the ear and he can hear.
We look with amazement on the evils of strong drink.
Washington was not a selfish man. He labored for the good of his
    country more than for himself.
An orator makes orations; and oratory is the art of public speaking.
A virago is a turbulent masculine woman. No one loves a virago.
You must be good or you cannot be happy.
We are sorry when a good man dies. Washington was a successful
    general.

[70] *The American Spelling Book* (Hartford, 1792), pp. 61–66.

It is a solemn thing to die and appear before God.
Teachers should try to implant good ideas in the minds of their
  pupils.
If sinners entice thee, consent thou not, but withdraw from their
  company.
The chewing of tobacco is a useless custom.
It is every man's duty to bequeath to his children a rich inheritance
  of pious precepts.
The most refined education does not embellish the human character
  like piety.
Large bush whiskers require a good deal of nursing and trimming.[71]

Although, as has been shown, Webster did not approve of the
use of the Bible as a reading text in the schools,[72] in the first
edition of Part I (1783) he followed the example of Dilworth and
Fenning by including several excerpts from the Psalms. There
were also dialogues in which church attendance, obedience to
parents, cursing, swearing, and tattling were discussed. These,
along with the simple stories, were calculated, the author explained, "Not only to entertain; but to inspire the minds of
youth, with an abhorrence of vice, indolence and meanness; and
with a love of virtue, industry and good manners." [73] He also
included his version of Fenning's highly moral *Story of Tommy
and Harry,* a story of the Alger type which anticipated Day's
Sanford and Merton. In a footnote he gives his idea of a style
"fitted to the capacity of youth." The style, he explains, should
be so simple that the child will understand what he reads, and
be so pure that neither he nor his language will become corrupted. He says nothing, however, about interesting the child.
The practice of giving stories of ghosts and witches to children
he calls highly criminal, because such stories frighten children
to such a degree that they remain cowards to their death.[74]

Other highly moral and religious selections that appeared in
some of the various editions of the speller were: "The Four

[71] These maxims were taken from the *Elementary Spelling Book* (New York,
1843).
[72] See p. 53.
[73] Part I (1783), p. 12.
[74] Part I (1783), p. 112.

Seasons," "Death the Destroyer," [75] "Three Little Boys and the Three Cakes," "The History of Thrifty and Unthrifty," and so forth. Other lessons were curious blends of moral lessons with arithmetic, such as two paragraphs on the five states of human life followed by one paragraph on linear measure and one on liquid measure, in one lesson. "The Description of a Bad Boy" and "The Description of a Good Boy" make it clear that good children are obedient to parents and teachers. They have all the virtues, such as rising early, saying prayers, washing themselves clean, and loving their books. One feature which appeared in many of the editions was the moral catechism, with "Lessons for Saturday," "Of Humility," "Of Mercy," "Of Peace Makers," "Of Purity of Heart," "Of Anger," "Of Revenge," "Of Justice," "Of Generosity," "Of Gratitude," "Of Truth," "Of Charity and Giving Alms," "Of Avarice," "Of Frugality and Economy," "Of Industry," and "Of Cheerfulness." This catechism sounds almost the entire gamut of morality and religion.[76]

Webster's reader, as well as his spelling book, continued the tradition of using moral and religious selections, although, as we have seen, emphasis was decidedly on the moral in the reader. In Part III, about fourteen pages were given to "Select Sentences calculated to form the morals of youth, from the best authors." [77] The following sentences are typical:

There is an heroic innocence, as well as an heroic courage.

There is but one way of fortifying the soul against all gloomy presages and terrors of the mind, and that is, by securing to ourselves the friendship and protection of that Being who disposes of events and governs futurity.

A contented mind, and a good conscience, will make man happy in all conditions. He knows not how to *fear,* who *dares to die.*

Prosperity *gains* friends, and adversity *tries* them.

[75] Although Webster's texts show a distinct departure from the emphasis that was placed on death in *The New England Primer* and the juveniles, yet he occasionally refers to death in his select sentences. In "Death the Destroyer" he concludes,

All that is made, must be destroyed;
All that is born, must die.

[76] See *American Spelling Book* (Boston, 1788), pp. 145–53.

[77] These were taken verbatim from Enfield's *Speaker.* See pp. 194 f.

Several stories, whose subtitles indicate their content, were given: "The Cobbler and His Son,[78] illustrating the force of habit, which renders labor agreeable"; "Honesty Rewarded, a story about Perrin and Lucetta, an industrious and virtuous pair, who were made happy by their strict honesty"; "*The Character of a Young Lady*"; [79] "*Agathocles and Calista,* an example of the felicity derived from pure affection between the sexes"; "*Story of La Roche,* an interesting example of a genuine sorrow for the death of a near friend, of sincere piety, devotion, and filial obedience"; and "*Story of Sir Edward and Louisa,*[80] a tale in which true kindness was rewarded with ingratitude and the injury was repaired by a generous act."

ALTHOUGH THE TEACHING OF "MORAL SCIENCE" WAS GENERALLY APPROVED BY EDUCATORS IN THE NINETEENTH CENTURY, THE PRACTICE HAD ITS CRITICS

The beliefs held by Webster and other men of his age concerning moral and religious training are very explicitly stated in *Elements of Useful Knowledge.*[81]

By reading frequently and repeatedly, passages containing just rules and principles, even above the comprehension of young minds, the pupils will learn many of them by heart, and bear the impressions into future life; by which means, when their understandings are matured, they will be enabled to direct, to useful purposes, the principles with which they had stored their minds in school.

The quoting of a few subtitles and prefatory remarks from several of the many readers that appeared in the wake of Webster's texts serves to illustrate the religious and moral element as

[78] Taken from *Scott's Lessons in Elocution* (1779).

[79] *Ibid.*

[80] Taken from the *Mirror*. "The Story of La Roche" was an adaptation of Henry McKenzie's story in numbers 42, 43, and 44. "Sir Edward and Louisa," was taken from McKenzie's "Story of Louisa Venoni," found in numbers 108 and 109. The *Mirror* was a four-page biweekly periodical, published by its "associated authors," members of the bar, in Edinburgh. The first of the 110 issues was published January 23, 1779, and the last, May 27, 1780. Among the contributions were stories and essays, the latter being of the nature of those found in the *Tatler* and *Spectator*.

[81] Preface, Part II (4th ed., 1809).

found in later readers, rather than indicate the extent to which it was present. The great extent to which such materials were used in readers and spellers of the nineteenth century can be realized only after an examination has been made of the texts in American libraries that are rich in Americana.[82]

The title-page of the *Columbian Reading Book or Historical Preceptor* (1799) has, for example, this note: "A Collection of authentic Historic Anecdotes, Characters, etc., etc., calculated to incite in young minds a love of virtue, from its intrinsic beauty, and hatred of vice from its disgusting deformity." In the *Franklin Primer* (1805), the title-page announces "a new and useful selection of moral lessons adorned with a great variety of cuts calculated to strike a lasting impression on the tender minds of children." In addition to spelling, this book contained moral and religious lessons and pictures of Bible scenes.

In the *Child's Instructor* (1808) there is a constant reiteration of the idea that "it is profitable both spiritually and materially to be good," which is the keynote of prudential wisdom found in such selections as Franklin's "The Way to Wealth" and "Advice to Young Tradesmen," both of which Webster had included in Part III. In Picket's *Juvenile Mentor* (1818) we find that one of the objects was to imbue the minds of children "with sentiments of virtue, morals, and religion." The sentence, "The selections contain many salutary precepts and instructive examples, for a life of piety and morality, of activity and usefulness," found in the Preface of Leavitt's *Easy Lessons in Reading* (1823), is quite characteristic of prefatory statements. In Strong's *Fourth Class Book* (1827) appeared "Little Charles," a poem which seems to be the acme of everything which this emphasis on piety brought

[82] When Tingelstad collected data for his study (see n. 66, p. 163) he visited fifty-nine American libraries. Of this number eight collections consisted of more than one hundred American spellers and readers, none of which were published later than 1830. The eight libraries containing more than a hundred copies were: American Antiquarian Society (Worcester, Mass.), 783 copies; Harvard College Library, 406; Watkinson Library (Hartford, Conn.), 327; Private Library of G. A. Plimpton (New York City), 233; Boston Public Library, 217; Library of Congress, 136; New York Public Library and New York State Library, 126 each.

forth. We are told it was greatly admired (by parents and teachers), and it was a favorite on the exhibition program:

LITTLE CHARLES

Well, Charles is highly pleased today,
I gave him leave to go and play
Upon the green, with bat and ball;
And when he heard his playmate call,
Away he sprang across the plain,
To join the little merry train.
But here he comes—why, what means this?
I wonder what has gone amiss,—
Why, Charles, how came you back so soon?
I know it, sir, and I intended
To play till every game was ended;
But, to say the truth, I could not bear
To hear those little fellows swear—
They cursed so bold and fearlessly
That the cold chills ran over me—
For I was filled with awful dread
That some of them would drop down dead—
And so I turned and came away,
For, Pa, I was afraid to stay!

Murray's *English Reader* (1799), as we have seen, had a high percentage of selections with religious and moral content. Considering the curve of religious content and the nature of Murray's books, Tingelstad concludes "that this English quaker became the nineteenth-century exponent of the religious tradition of *The New England Primer,* and that his ability to satisfy this religious need better than any of his competitors is the real reason for his supremacy in the field of American education for a third of a century." [83]

The McGuffey readers, which were even more popular during the second half of the century than Murray's readers were during the first half, especially in the Middle West, followed the Webster pattern in that distinct emphasis was placed on conduct. Speaking of the activities of Noah Webster, S. G. Goodrich, and

[83] *Op. cit.,* p. 243.

John Pierpont in the field of textbook production in New England and those of McGuffey in the Middle West, Sullivan says that "this distinction between the New England dynasty and the McGuffey one is more geographical than spiritual." [84] A few extracts from prefaces will indicate the moral stand McGuffey took:

For the copious extracts made from the Sacred Scriptures, he [the author] makes no apology. Indeed, upon a review of the work, he is not sure but an apology may be due for his not having still more liberally transferred to his pages the chaste simplicity, the thrilling pathos, the living descriptions, and the matchless sublimity of the sacred writings.[85]

Again he says:

In the selection of articles for Reading Exercises, great care has been taken to present variety of style and subject, to attract by interest of matter, to elevate by purity and delicacy of sentiment, and especially to furnish the mind with valuable information and to influence the heart by sound moral and religious instruction.[86]

Perhaps in this last quotation lies the main explanation which accounts for the success of McGuffey's readers and the failure of Webster's. "McGuffey's Readers," says Kellogg, "seem to have combined most successfully the literary and ethical elements as these stood developed at the middle of the present century." [87] Of course the paucity of American literature at the time Webster compiled his readers and the antagonism felt toward all things English precluded the possibility of Webster to include much that was not commonplace.

Articles in the educational periodicals of the nineteenth century indicate that educators in general were in sympathy with this moral education. At the State Convention of County Superintendents held at Albany, New York, in July, 1843, Francis Dwight reported for the Committee on Christian Morals,[88] offer-

[84] Sullivan, *Our Times* (1927), II, 18. C. Scribner's Sons.
[85] *Eclectic Third Reader* (1848), Preface.
[86] *New Sixth Eclectic Reader: Exercises in Rhetorical Reading, with Introductory Rules and Examples* (1857), Preface.
[87] A. E. Kellogg, "The Contents of School Readers," *Educational Review*, November, 1894, p. 338.
[88] *District School Journal*, IV (1843), 52.

ing a resolution that the practice of having children repeat sentences, the ones he proposed or similar ones, be recommended by the convention to the favorable consideration of the trustees, employers and teachers of our common schools throughout the State. The sentences he proposed follow:

> I must not be angry.
> I must be pleasant and kind to all.
> I must obey my parents.
> God will not hold him guiltless who takes his name in vain.
> God always sees me.
> I should depart from evil and learn to do good.

The beliefs of the nineteenth century concerning character education were further set forth in the discussion of Mr. Dwight's motion by the Reverend Mr. Jacob Abbott,[89] who said that the safeguard of the country and its institutions is dependent upon the character which the next generation will bear. He also spoke of the effect which this moral training has in advancing intellectual powers and referred to the excellence of Wayland's *Moral Science*[90] as a schoolbook, describing the effect which such a work had upon the minds and conduct of the pupils of the schools in which it was used and expressing the hope that the book would have universal circulation. Dwight's resolution was unanimously adopted.

Another means used to inculcate morality and religion was the study of biography. "The proper study of mankind is man" was turned from the pages of Pope to a common adage. In 1830 Webster published a collection of sixty-five biographies of men, beginning with Homer and extending down to Washington. In the main these short biographies are a statement of fact, or rather what was thought to be fact, bolstered by a certain amount of exhortation, and could not have been inspiring to children.[91] "The biography of great and good men," wrote one contributor to the *Common School Journal*, "is one of the most efficient of all in-

[89] Author of *The Teacher; or Moral Influences Employed in Instruction of Young* (1833); also such juveniles as the Rollo, Lucy, Jonas, and Franconia books.
[90] Francis Wayland, *Elements of Moral Science* (1835).
[91] *Biography for the Use of Schools.*

fluences in forming the character of children . . . It ought to be remembered, that, in all the objects and operations of nature, and in the lives of genuine men, we converse with God, and with the course of his providence at *first hand*, and not with mock-shows, and counterfeits, and hearsays." [92]

If Locke is right [he continued] in saying "that nobody is made anything by hearing of rules and laying them up in the memory," and if the teacher is anxious to convert dead rules into living principles, remembering that the mind is not a storehouse to be filled, but a spirit born of God, to be trained for usefulness and happiness, this miserable rote system will soon be abandoned, and methods calculated to attain these ends be introduced into these nurseries of a people.[93]

There were those, in the minority it seems, who questioned the value of the moral instruction given to children at that tender age when the mind is "wax to receive and marble to retain." Writing in the *District School Journal* in March, 1844,[94] one critic quoted Plutarch, who said, "It is our fashion to discuss and to doubt whether virtuous habits and upright living are things which can be taught," and, this writer continues, "it would seem to have remained a matter of doubt to the present day, from the general want of 'fit methods' in our schools."

Although Webster was undoubtedly very sincere in his purpose when he included the aphorisms and moral fables and most people accepted his offering without question, there is a record of at least one attempt to burlesque this feature of his works. In

[92] Vol. II (1840), 147 ff.

[93] This conclusion is not unlike that reached by Hartshorne: "A scientific morality cannot be transmitted . . . Only through genuine moral experience can this new morality develop . . . A dynamic morality does not consist of a set of precepts or even of a set of habits. It cannot be achieved by study, by imitation, by inspiration, or by fragmentary occasions of freedom and minute experiments in limited self direction. Morality which is more than conventional respectability results from the realities of one's personal relations . . . relations to other persons—his teacher, his principal, the janitor, his fellow pupil and playmates, his parents, the agents of state, and representatives of the economic life of the community. It is what he does with, for, and to these persons that constitutes his educative experience."—Hugh Hartshorne, *Character in Human Relations* (1932), p. 6. C. Scribner's Sons.

[94] Vol. IV (1844), 182.

the play, *The Deed of Gift*,[95] Mrs. Barton, a would-be blue stocking of Boston, frequently quoted Parts I and III. "Though not himself held up to ridicule," says Krapp, "Webster shares to some extent in the absurdity of Mrs. Barton." [96] In the half dozen references to Webster, his remarks on "articulation" [97] are especially treated with levity, the following lines being typical: "It is highly proper for us to speak according to Webster,—who, in his third part, says that—*artickelation*—." And then the aphorisms, as set forth in the lines: "For as it is elegantly expressed in Webster's first part, 'As you brew, so you must bake,' and 'As you make your bed, so you must lie.'" Also the lines in which Webster was held up by the flighty Mrs. Barton as the acme of erudition: "My stars! What a great man for his size and age. He must have studied Webster to some purpose—and my dress in such a pickle."

The passing of this emphasis on religion and morality in the public schools of America has been deplored by people of an older generation, who, viewing the practice in retrospect, have pronounced it good. "It remains a question," says Wickersham, "whether our ways of conducting moral and religious education are better than the ways of our forefathers." [98]

There are those who regret the present-day lack of early religious and moral training because it, they believe, supplied the youth with standards.

Human nature instinctively looks about for common standards, gropes for them, seeks them in custom or civil authority, leadership, or religion . . . The unsettlement of standards, the uncertainty about moral anchorages, the weakening of authorative criterions of ethics and taste, were the unhappiest of the consequences that attended the decline of religion that came during the nineteen-twenties, in the schools and elsewhere.[99]

[95] Samuel Woodworth, *The Deed of Gift* (1822).
[96] George Philip Krapp, *The English Language in America* (1925), II, 337.
[97] For Webster's remarks on articulation, see p. 195.
[98] James Pyle Wickersham, *A History of Education in Pennsylvania* (1886), p. 206.
[99] Sullivan, *Our Times* (1927), II, 92. C. Scribner's Sons.

Henry H. Vail wrote as follows:

I cannot but wish the teachers had made us bound the states less, and solve fewer puzzles in "position" and the "cube root" and made us commit to memory the whole series of the McGuffey Eclectic Readers . . . In these books we were indeed led by a schoolmaster from beautiful maxims for children up to the best thoughts of a long line of sages, and poets, and naturalists.[100]

In the Preface to his *Elements of Useful Knowledge,* Webster points out that he has frequently taken occasion to deduce moral and pious reflections from the subjects treated—to lead the mind into a contemplation of the necessity and certainty of the existence of a Creator, of infinite power, wisdom, and goodness. "This mode of employing natural philosophy in the service of religion and piety," he declared, "has been practiced by the ablest authors and best men in all ages . . ." [101] This declaration is an accurate statement of the attitude many compilers of texts held in the nineteenth century. "As education broadened, with the addition (in about the following order) of arithmetic, grammar, geography, and history, the religious tradition and the moral was carried on in all the text-books in which it could be included appropriately." [102]

Not everyone, however, who was exposed to the "system," placed as high a value on the training as did those whose testimonials have been cited. Gene Stratton Porter, who, having had from her youth something of a scientific turn of mind, rebelled against the teach-a-moral-at-any-price attitude of the McGuffey readers, which ignored the facts in the case. On the first day of school, Miss Porter recounts in her autobiographical work, *Laddie,* she spelled through the ubiquitous line by Watts, "Birds in their nest agree." The teacher then came forth with this sermon:

Classes, attention! Our Youngest Pupil has just completed her first sentence. This sentence contains a Thought. A Thought that suggests a great moral lesson for each of us. "Birrrds—in their little nests—agreeee." There is a lesson in this for all of us. We are here in

[100] *A History of the McGuffey Readers* (1911), p. 12.
[101] Vol. II (1809, 4th ed.), Preface.
[102] Sullivan, *op. cit.,* p. 88.

the schoolroom like little birds in their nests. Now how charming it would be if all of us would follow the example of the birds, and at work, and in our play, agreeee—be kind, loving, and considerate of each other. Let us all remember always this wonderful truth: "Birrrds —in their little nests—agreeee."

Miss Porter continued,

In three steps I laid hold of her apron . . . "Ho but they don't . . . They fight like anything! Every day they make the feathers fly."

In a backward stroke Miss Amelia's fingers, big and bony, struck my cheek a blow that nearly upset me. A red wave crossed her face, and her eyes snapped . . .

"I don't see why you slap me!" I cried. "It's the truth! Lots of times old birds pull out bunches of feathers fighting and young ones in the nest bite each other until they squeal."

Miss Amelia caught my shoulders and shook me . . .

"Take your seat!" she cried, "you're a rude, untrained child!"

"They do fight," I insisted, as I held my head high and walked to my desk.[103]

Lessons in Manners Were Included in the Early American School Reader

THE PRACTICE OF TEACHING MANNERS IN THE EARLY AMERICAN SCHOOLS WAS NOT INDIGENOUS

GENERALLY speaking, the teaching of manners and morals went hand-in-hand in the European schools, with perhaps the greater emphasis on manners, until during the middle of Elizabeth's reign, when morals became closely allied to religion and through the Puritanic influence were eventually absorbed into religion.[104]

Just as the stressing of religion had its origin in the early church schools, so the tendency to teach manners goes directly back to the education of nobles and gentlemen. In medieval times young gentlemen were sent to the homes of noblemen and even to the courts of kings, where they were taught the elements

[103] Gene Stratton Porter, *Laddie* (1913), pp. 126f. Copyright by Doubleday, Doran & Company, Inc.

[104] Foster Watson, *The English Grammar Schools to 1660* (1908), p. 108. The Macmillan Company.

of proper conduct. Sir Thomas More, for example, was brought up in Cardinal Morton's household and Roger Ascham in the house of Sir Anthony Wingfield.[105] This method of training young English nobles has been traced as far back as Anglo-Saxon times.[106] The teaching of manners was not an independent movement in England, but in a large part a result of her contact with France, who in turn had been influenced by Italy, whose long series of courtesy books culminated in the *Cortigiano* of Baldassori Castiglione in 1553. This work, which Doctor Johnson says is "the best book that was ever written on good breeding," was translated into English by Sir Thomas Hoby in 1588 and published under the title *Courtier*. It was widely used in England.

A number of treatises and pamphlets on conduct appeared in the fifteenth and sixteenth centuries, soon after the invention of printing. They provided "the antithesis to monkish or literary education." [107] They "were written to fit the young gentlemen for this world, not for the next; and for the active life of this world rather than for the contemplative." [108] Their ideal was anticipated in Chaucer's squire.[109] These "Bookes of courtesy" have been grouped and published by the Early English Text Society under the titles *The Babees Book* (1868) [110] and *Queene Elizabeth's Achademy* (1869).[111] They were not schoolbooks except in the sense that they were used in households of nobles where young gentlemen were being taught.

[105] F. J. Furnivall, *The Babees Book* (1868), pp. ix and xx.
[106] *Ibid.*, p. vi.
[107] *Cambridge History of English Literature* (1930), XI, 366. The Macmillan Company.
[108] *Ibid.*
[109] *Ibid.*
[110] Edited by Frederick James Furnivall. In this compilation more than fifty poems, treatises, and books are printed, some of which are French and Latin poems on manners and Latin graces for meals. Among the longer and better known of the treatises are Hugh Rhodes' *The Boke of Nurture, or Schoole of Good Manners* . . . (1577); John Russell's *The Boke of Nurture Followyng Englondis gise* . . . ; and F. Seager's *The School of Vertue, and Booke of Good Nourture for Chyldren and Youth to Learne Their Dutie By* (1557).
[111] Edited by F. J. Furnivall. Part II contains W. M. Rossetti's *Italian Books of Courtesy.*

We learn, however, that the manner books found their way into the English grammar schools of the sixteenth and seventeenth centuries through the recommendation of such schoolmasters as Brinsley [112] and Hoole.[113] Other treatises on manners which were used in the schools were Cato's *Disticha de moribus* [114] and La Flèche's *Bienséance de la conversation entre les hommes* (1595), which was translated into Latin in 1617 and into English by Francis Hawkins in 1646. It was from this source that Washington drew his *Rules of Behaviour.*[115]

In Coote's *English Schoolmaster* (1596), admonitions regarding manners and etiquette were given to elementary school boys. It is not known to what extent Coote's text was used in America, but Meriwether is of the opinion that it "was pretty well known to some of the teachers, with its numerous stanzas forming practically a school code. Certainly the duty to God and parents and to all that were considered superior was properly emphasized." [116]

Another manner book was Lily's Latin Grammar, the *Brevissima institutio.*[117] It contained the *"Carmen de moribus,"* which is an epitome of manners in eighty-six Latin verses, and which, it is said, was as well known in England as any lines of the classics.[118] When we consider how well Lily's grammar was known and what an influence it wielded over textbooks and methods of instruction even after the Latin had been replaced by the vernacular, we realize the important place it had in the practice of teaching manners in the schools.

[112] *Ludus literarius* (1612; ed. of 1917 by E. T. Campagnac), p. 261.
[113] *A New Discovery of the Old Art of Teaching School* (1660; ed. of 1912 by T. Mark), pp. 52 and 63.
[114] Many of the short precepts found in early primers and spellers show the influence of Cato's "Common Collection of Distichs," such as "Be neat; Salute freely, Pray to God, Love thy parents; Play with a hoop; Learn to read; Never lie." See W. J. Chase's *The Distichs of Cato* (1922), pp. 13 and 15.
[115] Monroe, *Cyclopedia of Education* (1911), III, 20. These rules were fifty-seven in number. See Jared Sparks, *Life of Washington* (1843), p. 513.
[116] *Our Colonial Curriculum 1607–1776* (1907), p. 27.
[117] *A Short Introduction to Grammar* (1709), n. p.
[118] Watson, *English Grammar Schools to 1660*, 1908, p. 107.

The similarity between Lily's "order of duties for the day" and that which later English and American texts prescribed is striking. The boy was told to wash his face and hands clean, to comb his hair, see to it that his clothes are clean. He was not to loiter on the way to school, was to salute his master on arriving and to sit where he was told to sit. His conduct was not to follow such bad patterns of manners as to imitate those who spend their time in trifles, or those boys who worry their friends in any way, or who reproach others with their parentage. He was admonished to put noise, contention, scoffing, lies, thefts, loud laughter, and fighting far behind him.

WEBSTER CONTINUED THE PRACTICE OF INCLUDING LESSONS IN MANNERS

Since *The New England Primer* and Dilworth's *Guide* were highly contemplative of the life to come, manners were not stressed in either. Some of the other texts that were used in the early American school, however, contain lessons on conduct. In George Fox's *Instructions for Right Spelling* (1702), which was used extensively in Pennsylvania, table manners are treated in detail:

Spit not, cough not, nor blow thy nose at the table if it may be avoided; but if there be necessity, do it aside, and without much noise.—Lean not thy elbows on the table, or on the back of the chair.— Stuff not thy mouth so as to fill thy cheeks, be content with smaller mouthsful.—Smell not of thy meat—nor put it to thy nose; turn it not the other side upward to view it upon thy plate.—Gnaw not bones at the table but clean them with thy knife (unless they be very small ones) and hold them not with a whole hand, but with two fingers.— Drink not nor speak with anything in thy mouth.

Perhaps none of Webster's reading lessons, excluding of course the fables, are better known than the part he took from Fenning's *Universal Spelling Book,* which are a blend of religion, morals, and manners. Fenning's sentences show the influence of Cato's distichs. The use that Webster made of Fenning's lessons is illustrated by the following:

FENNING [119]

Be a good Child.
Love and fear God.
Mind your Book.
Love your School.
Strive to learn.
Tell no Tales.
Call no Names.

Do not lie nor swear.
Do not cheat nor steal
Play not with bad Boys.
Serve God, and trust in him.
Use no ill Words at Play.
Pray to God to bless you.
Take not God's Name in vain.

WEBSTER [120]

Be a good child; mind your
book; love your school, and
strive to learn.

Tell no tales; call no ill names;
you must not lie, nor swear, nor
cheat, nor steal.

Play not with bad boys; use no
ill words at play; spend your time
well; live in peace, and shun all
strife. This is the way to make
God love you, and to save your
soul from the pains of hell.

That these earlier texts left their mark on Webster's speller,
Part I (1783), is further shown by his dialogues, maxims, and
stories. In the dialogues he followed the advice of Comenius who
stated in his eighth rule in the *Great Didactic* that "There should
be rules for conversation. These should be practised by daily
intercourse with tutors, school fellows, parents and servants."
Under the caption, "Familiar Phrases and easy Dialogues for
young beginners," Webster teaches manners to the children of
the yeomanry, such as, for example, the amenities that should
pass between people when meeting:

> Sir, your most humble servant
> I have the pleasure to be yours.
> I hope you are very well.
> I am very well, Sir, I thank you.
> How do they do at your house?
> They are all well . . .

Another dialogue did service by commenting on conduct on
the way to school. Webster also utilized the opportunity to comment casually on the practice of too much scraping and bowing
when "making one's manners," which was much in vogue by
those who aped foreign manners.

[119] *Universal Spelling Book* (1787), pp. 14 ff. First edition, 1756.
[120] *A Grammatical Institute of the English Language, Part I* (1783), pp. 102 ff.

How came you so late to school?

I stopped to pull off my hat to a gentleman.

How long did that hinder you?

A considerable time.

Pray, Sir, how do you make your manners?

I parade myself with my face to the person, take off my hat with both hands, make several bows and scrape with my right foot.

I do not wonder you are late at school; for surely you met several persons, it must employ most of your school-hours.

It takes some time, indeed; but we must do as we are taught.

But I was taught a shorter way to be mannerly—I was directed not to stop, but to pass on and take off my hat with the hand that is opposite to the person I meet, without turning my head or scraping the ground with my foot.

Well if you are taught the best way to pay your respects to people, I am happy. But I think that you are faulty in another particular. You run and bawl along the streets, like a madman, without any regard to decency.

I am apt to be a little noisy sometimes; and this is the case with all boys who are in high spirits.

It is very well at proper times and places; but in passing along the road it is very rude and indecent.

I hope we shall both take pains to correct our faults.[121]

Among the select sentences and moral aphorisms, scattered througout the speller, such sentences as the following appeared:

Children should answer questions politely.

Keep your mouth clean and save your teeth.

Good manners are always becoming; ill manners are evidence of low breeding.

The saucy stubborn child displeases his parents.[122]

In some of the editions table manners were given, as, for example:

James, hold your spoon in your right hand; and if you use a knife and fork, hold the knife in your right hand. Do not eat fast; hungry boys are apt to eat fast, like the pigs. Never waste your bread; bread is gained by the sweat of the brow. Your father plants or sows corn; corn grows in the fields . . .[123]

[121] Page 111.

[122] These sentences were selected from the *Elementary Spelling Book* (1829), Phila. ed.

[123] *American Spelling Book* (1816, Utica, N. Y.), p. 77.

In part III, the reader, admonitions concerning conduct are given under "Rules of Behavior, taken mostly from Chesterfield":

Never hold any body by the button or the hand, in order to be heard through your story; for if the people are not willing to hear you, you had much better hold your *tongue* than hold them.

Frequent good company—copy their manners—imitate their virtues and accomplishments.

Never whisper in company . . .

Good breeding does not consist in low bows, and formal ceremony; but in any easy, civil, and respectful behavior.

Be very attentive to neatness. The hands, nails, and teeth should be kept clean. A dirty mouth is not only disagreeable as it occasions an offensive breath, but almost infallibly causes decay, and loss of teeth.

Never put your fingers in your nose or ears—it is a nasty, vulgar rudeness, and an affront to company.

Frequent and loud laughter is the characteristic of folly and ill manners—it is the manner in which silly people express their joy at silly things.[124]

A number of readers and spellers that appeared in the late eighteenth and early nineteenth centuries included lessons in which manners were stressed. But this training did not continue to be a part of the reading texts as did some of the other elements, such as morality, religion, patriotism and the "art of reading." It is true, manners continued to be stressed, but they were taught more incidentally,[125] as they were often incorporated in the rules of the school, along with the penalty for each infraction.[126]

Special texts soon appeared emphasizing manners. Among them were such readers as William Miln's *The Well-Bred*

[124] In view of the fact that Chesterfield's maxims concerning behavior are of course a summation of European standards of conduct, which along with other European standards had been eschewed by America and an effort was being made to develop men and women of a distinctly American type, one wonders why Webster quoted Chesterfield.

In *The Contrast* (see pp. 185 f.) it is made clear that the foppish ways of Mr. Dimple are due to a too-steady diet of Chesterfield, while the homespun virtues of Colonel Manly are due to his American ideals and training.

[125] "Whatever may be said of their own conduct, an old-time schoolmaster, especially one of foreign birth, would not tolerate bad manners in his pupils."—Wickersham, *A History of Education in Pennsylvania* (1886), p. 206.

[126] Edgar Wallace Knight, *Education in the United States* (1934), pp. 450 f.

Scholar (2d ed., 1797) and *The School of Good Manners* (1813). During the nineteenth century appeared numerous books of etiquette, such as *The American Chesterfield, or, way to wealth, honour, and distinction; being selections from the letters of Lord Chesterfield to his son; and extracts from other eminent authors, on the subject of politeness; with alterations and additions, suited to the youth of the United States* (1828); and *Advice to a Young Gentleman, on Entering Society* (1839).

Judging from the number of French, English, and Italian etiquette books which were printed during the first half of the nineteenth century, some of which were translated into English and which are still extant in American libraries, one concludes that the foreign influence on American manners during that period must have been tremendous and that Webster's protests against aping foreign ways were based on fact. During the last half of the century, however, many American books on the subject were printed.

*Among the Textbooks the Reader Was the Chief
Depository of the Patriotic Sentiment
That Followed the Revolution*

THE STRONG FEELING OF AMERICANISM AFFECTED
THE ARTS IN AMERICA

ONE can get an idea of the strength of the national feeling which had rapidly grown up in the liberated colonies by glancing at almost any books taken at random from the publications of the period following the Revolutionary War. "Belief in the grand future of the United States is the keynote of everything done and said.[127] All things American are to be grand—our terri-

[127] Of this tendency Frances Trollope wrote in 1832: "On the subject of national glory, I presume I got more than my share of buffeting . . . It is amusing to observe how soothing the idea seems, that they are more modern, more advanced than England. Our classic literature, our princely dignities, our noble institutions, are all bygone relics of the dark ages."—*Domestic Manners of the Americans* (1832). See Nevins' *American Social History* (1923), p. 179. In *Martin Chuzzlewit*

tory, population, products, wealth, science, art,—but especially
our political institutions and literature [128] . . . and over and above
all a belief in, and concern for, materialistic progress, there were
enthusiastic anticipations of achievements in all the moral and
intellectual fields of national greatness." [129]

Anticipating this post-war Americanism Philip Freneau had
written, in 1771, in a manner common to his day and days to
follow:

> I see, I see
> Freedom's established reign; cities, and men,
> Numerous as sands upon the ocean shore,
> And empires rising where the sun descends:—
> The *Ohio* soon shall glide by many a town
> Of note; and where the Mississippi stream,
> By forests shaded, now runs weeping on,
> Nations shall grow, and states not less in fame
> Than Greece and Rome of old! We too shall boast
> Our Scipio's, Solon's, Cato's, sages, chiefs
> That in the lap of time yet dormant lie,
> Waiting the joyous hour of life and light . . .[130]

The first half century after 1776 was "a period whose key the
social historian finds in the determination to achieve social independence in the same sense that the founders of the nation had
won political independence. This audacious effort was in many
cases premature, and its results sometimes grotesque, but it was

---

(1843–44) Dickens satirized the "tall talk" which Mrs. Trollope reported she had
found everywhere.

[128] Of American literature following the Revolutionary war, Bliss Perry has this
to say: "It is idle to look in the writings of the Revolutionary period for the literature of beauty, for a quiet harmonious unfolding of the deeper secrets of life. It
was a time of action rather than reflection, of the turning of many separate currents into one headlong stream . . . But our Revolution, in truth, never had an
adequate poet. The prose-men, such as Jefferson, rose nearer the height of the
great argument than did the men of rhyme . . . There was patriotic verse in
extraordinary profusion, but its literary value is slight, and it reveals few moods
of the American mind that are not more perfectly conveyed through oratory, the
pamphlet, and the political essay . . ."—"The American Spirit in Literature,"
The Chronicles of America, XXXIV (1918), 66 ff. Copyright by Yale University
Press.

[129] R. O. Williams, *Our Dictionaries* (1890), p. 30.

[130] Philip Freneau, "The Rising Glory of America," in *Poems of Freneau*, ed.
Haydon Clark (1829), p. 13.

a necessary preparation of the national mind for the clear pure notes of Emerson, and certain of its accomplishments were of enduring importance."[131] Among these accomplishments were achievements in the fields of religion, law, and governments. As a contribution to the fine arts, Charles Wilson Peale painted fourteen pictures of Washington, and Gilbert Stuart executed nearly forty of the same subject. The Hudson River School of Landscapists preserved on canvas glimpses of American scenery. The old English tradition of architecture was rejected and in its stead a mode more fitting the stern republican virtues of the new nation, the architecture of classical Rome, was adopted. In music, three of our greatest national hymns were produced: "Hail, Columbia," "The Star-Spangled Banner," and "America." In education great strides were taken in establishing common schools. The first state universities were founded and a national university was projected, favored by such men as Washington and succeeding presidents.[132]

This "audacious effort" to achieve social as well as political independence is well illustrated by the activities of a contemporary and friend of Webster's, Dr. Samuel Latham Mitchill, who, in his efforts to attain 100 per cent Americanism, wrote a series of minor poems for the nursery. Among these poems was the revision of "Four-and-Twenty Blackbirds," the old version of which, he explained, abounds with errors; consequently the infantile mind is led astray by the acquisition of such verses. His revised version reads,

When the pie was open,
The birds they were songless;
Was not that a pretty dish,
To set before Congress.

I thus correct, he explained, the error that might be imbibed in infancy of the musical functions of cooked birds; and while I discard the King of Great Britain, with whom we have nothing to do,

[131] A. M. Schlesinger, "American History and American Literary History" in Norman Foerster's *Reinterpretation of American Literature* (1928), pp. 164 f. Harcourt, Brace and Company.
[132] Ibid., pp. 165 f.

I give them some knowledge of our general government, by specifying our Congress.[133]

Several changes in the *New England Primer* show this universal chauvinistic attitude. In some of the post-Revolutionary-War editions of the primer the descriptive rhyme for the letter W, "Whales in the sea God's voice obey" was changed to "By Washington great deeds are done." This change, Francis,[134] at least, suspected, was made by the ardent Mitchill. The *New England Primer* of 1776 also bears the imprint of this Americanism-at-any-price attitude. In editions before that date, the frontispiece had been a portrait of the ruling English sovereign, George III. But after the colonies had revolted, it was reasoned, a representative of democracy should occupy this prominent place; consequently the printer merely relabeled the portrait of George III, "John Hancock." In the 1777 edition, however, the portrait as well as the name of Hancock appeared.

The American writings following the Revolution repeatedly sounded the note that America must be free from Britain in all respects—literary as well as political. "For America in her infancy to adopt the present maxims of the Old World," declared Webster, "would be to stamp the wrinkle of decrepit old age upon the bloom of youth, and to plant the seed of decay in a vigorous constitution."[135] Although *The North American Review* and other American periodicals persistently urged the need of a national literature, they insisted, also, and just as persistently, that a more thorough knowledge of European literature was highly desirable. This was the thesis of William Ellery Channing's *A National Literature*, written in 1823.[136]

A very good summary of young America's literary aspirations is given in the prologue to "The Contrast,"[137] the first American play to be "regularly" produced in America. The prologue

---

[133] Charles Wakefield Francis, "Remembrances of Samuel Latham Mitchill," Stedman and Hutchinson, *Library of American Literature* (1888–90), V, 190.
[134] *Ibid.*
[135] Webster, "Part III," Preface.
[136] *Old South Leaflets* (1903), VI, No. 141.
[137] Written by Royall Tyler (1757–1826), and performed in 1787 at the theater in John Street, New York.

is "in Rebuke of the Prevailing Anglomania." Since it is so
thoroughly in keeping with the subjects Webster discussed,
especially in his *Collection of Essays and Fugitiv Pieces*,[138] it is
quoted at length:

> Exult each patriot heart!—this night is shewn
> A piece, which we may fairly call our own;
> Where the proud titles of "My Lord!
>   Your Grace!"
> To humble Mr. and plain Sir give place.
> Our Author pictures not from foreign climes
> The fashions, or the follies of the times;
> But has confined the subject of his work
> To the gay scenes—the circles of New York.
> On native themes his Muse displays her pow'rs;
> If ours the faults, the virtues too are ours.
> Why should our thoughts to distant countries roam,
> When each refinement may be found at home?

WEBSTER'S TEXTS WERE INFORMED BY A
STALWART AMERICANISM

To the trend of the times, Noah Webster was thoroughly
awake. He was "undoubtedly wise in his generation beyond all
understanding, a deep student of men and often a real
prophet." [139] He was "the greatest intellectual force in the American literary culture of the era; and far from being the dry-as-
dust pedant that he is usually pictured, he was a robust national-
ist whose influence on the form and spirit of American letters
has been as great as his illustrious namesake on the spirit of
American government." [140]

An examination of the publications that followed the Revolution shows that the words "American" and "Columbia," in
keeping with the quickened patriotic fervor of the age, were fre-

[138] See pp. 43 f.
[139] Wilber Webster Judd, "Noah Webster," *Connecticut Magazine,* n. d., n. p.
Book of pamphlets on education in Teachers College Library.
[140] Schlesinger, "American History and American Literary History," in Foerster's
Reinterpretation of American Literature (1928), p. 167.

quently used in titles. In 1788, Part I of the *Institute* became *The American Spelling Book;* in 1787, Part III, *An American Selection.* In 1788, Webster christened his venture in journalism *The American Magazine* and many years later, in 1828, *An American Dictionary of the English Language* was the title chosen for his *magnum opus.*

A perusal of the Table of Contents of Part III (1787) will show that of the sixty-odd selections of varying lengths, more than a score are American patriotic selections. Among them were such favorites as Freneau's "On General Washington," "General Washington's Farewell Orders to the Army," Warren's "Oration on the Boston Massacre," Hancock's oration on the same subject, and "The Declaration of Independence." In Webster's *The Little Reader's Assistant* (1790) most of the reading lessons are of a historical nature. Many of the selections relate adventures with the Indians, which must have come closer to arousing the interest of children than anything that had appeared in readers up to that time. Then in the "Federal Catechizm," part of the same reader, he explained three kinds of constitutional government, showing that a representative democracy or republic is the best form. He also explained the three powers of the United States government, the houses of Congress, and qualifications for voting.

On the title-page of *An American Selection of Lessons in Reading and Speaking* (1787) was the motto, taken from Mirabeau: "Begin with the Infant in his cradle; let the first word he lisps be Washington." This motto along with a part of the long subtitle, "Calculated to Instruct Them in Geography, History, Politics of the United States," shows that Webster was in sympathy with his age and was attempting to help develop the national consciousness through the medium of the public schools. In his Preface he points out that the selections used in the colleges and academies, however judicious, are not calculated for American schools; that the essays respect distant nations or ages, or contain only general ideas of morality. He says that "a love of our country and an acquaintance with its true state are indispensable and should be acquired early in life." This is the theme that he expanded later in his *Essays and Fugitiv Pieces*.[141]

Of the pieces here selected [he explains] some are from British writers of eminence—some are fugitive American publications—some are taken from the manuscripts of my friends—and a few are my own compositions. . . . I have not been inattentive to the political interests of America. Several of those masterly addresses of Congress written at the commencement of the late revolution contain such noble, just, and independent sentiments of liberty and patriotism that I cannot help wishing to transfuse them into the breasts of the rising generation.

This substitution of American for British selections marks the beginning of the struggle between such compilers as Webster, Bingham, Pierpont, and Cobb, who, on one hand, strove to kindle patriotism and to give an impetus to the production and appreciation of American "literature," which at that time scarcely existed, and on the other hand, those, principally Murray in his *English Reader,* who favored English literature.

This struggle was not confined to the selections in school readers. In fact the zeal which prompted many to extol the virtues of American literature amounted to almost a boycott of English literature. This chauvinistic spirit is well illustrated by Webster's pride in using excerpts from American authors to illustrate the definitions in his *American Dictionary* as late as 1828.[142] In this work he cites Franklin, Washington, Adams, Jay, and other American writers as authorities, on the same page with Boyle, Hooker, Milton, Dryden, and other English writers, declaring that Franklin and Washington "present as pure models of genuine English as Addison or Swift" and mentioning other American writers whose style is "equaled only by that of the best British authors, and surpassed by that of no English compositions of similar kind."

[141] *Collection of Essays and Fugitiv Pieces* (1790).
[142] See p. 234.

OTHER COMPILERS OF READERS INCLUDED
PATRIOTIC SELECTIONS

The introduction of text-books which were neither imported from English publishing houses nor written in close imitation of trans-Atlantic models [declares Slosson] became a potent factor in Americanizing the school. Of these the works of Noah Webster were perhaps the most widely influential in molding the ideas of the first generation of children born under the flag of the Republic. . . . There had been not a few text-book writers in the colonies but none had ventured so boldly upon innovation nor emphasized the patriotic motive so constantly.[143]

We find that many authors who compiled textbooks during the nineteenth century followed Webster's example in choosing American selections. Some subtitles and prefatory remarks from a few of the many readers that followed in the wake of Webster's texts will illustrate the patriotic bias of the selections.

In the Preface to Bingham's *American Preceptor* (1795), one of the foremost of American competitors of Webster's texts, the author admits having given a preference to the "productions of American genius," but he shows a liberality in that he has "extracted from approved writers of different ages and countries."

In his Preface to *The First Class Book of American Literature* (1826), consisting principally of selections in the departments of history, biography, prose fiction, travels, the drama, popular eloquence, and poetry, John Frost points out that the selections are taken from the "best writers of our own country." Lyman Cobb, another competitor with whom Webster had to reckon during his last days, imitated the latter in that his *North American Reader* (4th ed., 1836) contained "a great variety of pieces in prose and poetry, from the very highest esteemed American and English writers. . . . Also the Declaration of Independence; the Constitution of the U. S.; Political definitions."

[143] Slosson, "The American Spirit in Education," *The Chronicles of America,* XXXIII (1921), 117. Copyright Yale University Press.

As late as 1827, we find the *American Journal of Education* [144] publishing John Pierpont's Preface to *"The National Reader,* a Selection of Exercises in Reading and Speaking, designed to fill the same place in the schools of the United States, that is held in those of Great Britain, by the Compilations of Murray, Scott, Enfield, Mylins, Thompson, Ewing and others." This Preface is such an accurate epitome of declarations made by Webster in his essays (1788) and prefaces and by other compilers who followed him that it is given in full:

Notwithstanding the number and variety of reading-books, of all complexions, forms and characters, with which the country is supplied, and more than sufficiently supplied, no one, who is conversant with the subject, will deny that a *good* compilation for the use of common schools, has been wanted. The truth is, we have depended too much and too long on Great Britain, for elementary works in the different branches of education. We do not object to a British School-book, because it is British, but we object to it because it is not, and, from the nature of things, cannot be adapted to the circumstances of a country, a state of society, political institutions, and a condition of education for which it was never intended.

It is a recommendation to the "National Reader," that contributions are so freely drawn from the statesmen and scholars and poets of America,—from Jefferson, Patrick Henry, Webster, Everett, Irving, Bryant, Percival, and many others, whose genius and learning do honor to their country. It may be regretted by some, that a still larger proportion of the compilation has not been borrowed from American Authors. There is no dearth of matter; and it is desirable, that children should early become familiar with the names of the gifted and the eloquent of their own country.

.   .   .   .

This country has political institutions of its own;—institutions which the men of each successive generation must uphold. But this they cannot do, unless they are early made to understand and value them. It has a history of its own, of which it need not be ashamed;— fathers, and heroes, and sages, of its own, whose deeds and praises are worthy of being said or sung by even the "mighty masters of the lay,"—and with whose deeds and praises, by being made familiar in our childhood, we shall be not the less qualified to act well our part, as citizens of a republic. Our country, both physically and morally,

[144] Vol. II, 1827, p. 620.

has a character of its own. Should not something of that character be learned by its children while at school? Its mountains, and prairies, and lakes, and rivers, and cataracts,—its shores and hilltops, that were early made sacred by the dangers, and sacrifices, and deaths of the devout and daring—it does seem as if these were worthy of being held up as objects of interest, to the young eyes that, from year to year, are opening upon them, and worthy of being linked, with all their sacred associations, to the young affections, which, sooner or later, *must* be bound to them, or they must cease to be—what they now are—the inheritance and abode of free people.

The readers mentioned in the foregoing paragraphs were, with the possible exception of those compiled by Bingham, of minor importance when compared with such popular texts as Webster's "Old Blue-Back," Murray's *English Reader,* and Mc-Guffey's *Eclectic Readers.* Murray's texts did not emphasize patriotism, since the author lived in England and his sympathies were more English than American. McGuffey's texts were compiled during the middle of the century when the spread-eagle doctrine was on the wane.

As we have seen, it was through the reader that history made its way into the curricula of American schools. Undoubtedly, it was to this early violent championship of the American cause that a certain complacent patriotism, which foreigners were quick to observe and which men of the present age write about in retrospect, was due. In the letters of Sullivan's correspondents, men who went to school after the middle of the nineteenth century, we find the following statements:

It seems to me that the United States History and other books that told us about our country gave us the impression that it had been founded and led by men of virtue and wisdom—and that no other country could compare with ours in liberty, enlightenment, or progress. I am mighty sure there was no "internationalism" taught in those old books. We have much taught in the schools nowadays [1927] in the way of patriotism, but it seems to me, as I look back, that patriotism was just our native atmosphere then; whereas now we have to use a ventilator fan to force it.[145]

[145] B. L. Eddy in Sullivan's *Our Times* (1927), II, 60. C. Scribner's Sons.

I think considerable attention might be given to American history. How much of it was "trumpet and drum" history? How biased and distorted was it, on the Revolution, the "bloody" British, the Civil War, etc.? [146]

There was much more of patriotism fifty years ago than now. At least it was talked more. We were strongly American. No other country could compare with the U. S. A.[147]

Sullivan concludes his discussion of patriotism and the American reader with the assertion that the treatment of the British in American schoolbooks accounted for the sympathy America had for the Boers in 1899, for the Irish in their struggle against the British, and for the general anti-British strain in American thought and feeling, a good example of which was Mayor William H. Thompson's denunciation of King George in 1927, not George the Third but the Fifth.[148]

The Early American Reader Stressed the "Art of Reading"

THE TIME FOR THE INTRODUCTION OF THE ELOCUTIONARY READER WAS RIPE IN AMERICA

THE stress which was placed on the "art" of reading and speaking is another example of America's borrowing from Europe. In England "The pride of each school of repute in the seventeenth century was the thoroughness with which the boys could speak and write Latin. One of the supreme tests, therefore, was the ability to compose and deliver orations." [149] When, in the eighteenth century, emphasis shifted from Latin to the vernacular, the practice of giving orations was retained and, as has been shown, orations and disputations occupied a prominent position in the early American colleges.[150]

[146] Niles Carpenter, Sullivan, *ibid.*, p. 59.
[147] E. E. Smith, *ibid.*, p. 60.
[148] *Ibid.*, p. 61.
[149] Foster Watson, *English Grammar Schools to 1660* (1908), p. 460. The Macmillan Company.
[150] Slosson, "The American Spirit in Education," *The Chronicles of America,* XXXIII (1921), 50. Copyright Yale University Press.

The time for the introduction of the elocutionary reader into the elementary schools of America was especially propitious. People had been under the spell of such English orators as Pitt, Fox, and Burke, and the patriotic utterances of such Americans as Patrick Henry and James Otis. As has been shown, Revolutionary literature in America, insofar as it existed, was confined almost entirely to the pamphlet and the oration.[151] Literature and speech making were, in the minds of the people, one and the same thing. The time was ripe for the appearance of the elocutionary reader in America. Webster supplied the need.

Why the art of speaking was stressed in the post-Revolutionary schools of America, backed by public sentiment, presents something of an enigma, unless one considers conditions. The two most highly respected professions in America were law and the ministry, and these involved courtroom forensics and pulpit eloquence. Then the United States Congress, the state legislatures, and the numerous town and city councils provided ample opportunity for the use of public address. Political campaigns were frequent and to the attractive political orator was attached some of the glamor which the stars of the stage and movies came to have later.[152]

WEBSTER'S READER EMPHASIZED THE
"ART OF READING"

Children of Webster's day learned to read from the pages of his spelling book or in some cases from a primer before the reader was studied. The ideas concerning "the art of reading" which Webster and other compilers held and set forth in their readers were such as we would now call elocutionary. Part III of the *Institute* had as its subtitle "An American Selection in Reading and Speaking... To Which Is Prefixed Rules in Elocution, and Directions for Expressing the Principal Passions of the Mind."

[151] See p. 183.
[152] Sullivan, *Our Times* (1927), II, pp. 95 f. C. Scribner's Sons.

In the Preface, the author states that it was his design "to furnish schools with a variety of exercises for Reading and Speaking. Colleges and Academies," he continues, "are already supplied with many excellent collections for this purpose; among which, the *Art of Speaking*,[153] Enfield's *Speaker*, Enfield's *Exercises*,[154] the *Preceptor*,[155] the *Young Gentleman and Lady's Monitor*[156] and *Scott's Lessons*[157] are used with great reputation." These are the professional and semiprofessional speakers of English authorship upon which Webster based his reader, meant to be used in the elementary schools of America. It was these English speakers that furnished the pattern which Webster attempted to adapt to the needs of the children of the "yeomanry of America." In this adaptation, he substituted American patriotic selections for those extolling the "Glory that was Greece, and the grandeur that was Rome." Most of these selections were chosen, it would seem, because, in addition to the aforementioned considerations, they lent themselves to declamation and to the expression of the "passions."

Following the table of contents in Webster's *An American Selection*, four rules for reading and speaking are given:

1. Let your articulation be clear and distinct.
2. Observe the stops, and mark the proper pauses, but make no pause where the sense requires none.
3. Pay the strictest attention to accent, emphasis, and cadence.
4. Let the sentiment you express be accompanied with proper tones, looks and gestures.

Each of the four rules is discussed briefly. They are largely a condensation and revamping of the eight rules given in Enfield's *Speaker* (1774) and would be accepted today in the main as a

[153] James Burgh, *The Art of Speaking* (1768), n. p., England; 4th ed. Phila., 1775.
[154] Wm. Enfield, *The Speaker; or, Miscellaneous Pieces, Selected from the Best of English Writers* (1774), London; *Exercises* (1780), London.
[155] Robert Dodsley, *The Preceptor* (1748), 2 vols., London.
[156] John Hamilton Moore, *The Young Gentleman and Lady's Monitor, or the Teachers Assistant* (4th ed., 1787), London.
[157] William Scott, *Lessons in Elocution* (1799), Edinburgh.

compendium of good sense as related to the art of speaking. The following comparative table illustrates the use Webster made of the material in Enfield's *Speaker*:

Enfield's *Speaker*	Webster's *Part III*
A good articulation consists in giving a clear and full utterance to the several simple and complex sounds.	A good articulation consists in giving every letter and syllable its proper pronunciation of sounds.
Accompany the emotions and passions which your words express by Correspondent Tones, Looks and Gestures.	Let the sentiments you express be accompanied with proper tones, looks, and gestures.

In a concluding paragraph Webster sums up the rules by saying: "The whole art of reading and speaking—all the rules of eloquence may be comprised in the concise direction: *Let a reader or speaker express every word as if the sentiment were his own.*[158] Concerning the pauses to be observed at the signs of the comma, semicolon, colon, and the period, he refers the reader to Part I, where the length of the pause is fixed as having in relation to these marks of punctuation the proportion of one, two, four, and six syllables, respectively.

Following the four rules, "General Directions for expressing certain Passions or Sentiments" are given. The rules, or "System of Passions" as they were frequently referred to by contemporaries, were taken from Burgh's *The Art of Speaking* (1768).[159] The proper expression or "looks" for the whole gamut of emotions is given—mirth or laughter, melancholy, fear, shame, remorse, courage, boasting, pride, authority, commanding, inviting, hope, love, wonder, curiosity, anger, peevishness, malice, envy, aversion, jealousy, contempt, modesty, or humility. The following comparative table of directions illustrates the manner in which Webster simplified and condensed Burgh's system:

[158] *An American Selection* (1787), p. 16.
[159] Burgh's system was very elaborate, including rules for the expression of seventy-five "passions." Webster selected twenty-two of these.

Burgh's *The Art of Speaking* [160]

Mirth, or *laughter, opens* the *mouth* still *more* toward the ears; *crisps* the *nose; lessens* the *aperture* of the *eyes,* and sometimes fills them with tears; shakes and *convulses* the whole *frame;* giving considerable pain, which occasions *holding* the sides.

Webster's *An American Selection* [161]

Mirth or *Laughter* opens the mouth, crisps the nose, lessens the aperture of the eyes, and shakes the whole frame.

Perplexity . . . Suddenly the whole *body* is vehemently *agitated.* The person *walks* about *busily, stops* abruptly. Then he *talks* to himself, or makes *grimaces.*

Perplexity . . . Then suddenly the whole body is agitated, the person walks about busily, stops abruptly, talks to himself, etc.

Following the "General Directions for Expressing Certain Passions or Sentiments" Webster gave twenty-two excerpts from literature as illustrations. These are taken from Freneau, Rowe, Shakespeare, Otway, Pope, Home, Lee, and others. The excerpt given for the expression of grief, with "proper tones, looks, and gestures," was one of Gloucester's speeches from *King Lear:*

> All dark and comfortless!
> Where are these various objects, that but now
> Employ'd my busy eyes? Where those eyes?
> Dead are their piercing rays, that lately shot
> Ov'r flow'ry vales to distant sunny hills,
> And dream with joy the vast horizon in!

Perplexity was illustrated by lines from *Richard II:*

> If I know how to order these affairs,
> Disorderly thus thrust into my hands,
> Never believe me. All is uneven
> And every thing is left at six and seven.

Viewed from several angles these excerpts are interesting. In the first place, most of them were taken from plays, a form of

[160] 1782 ed., pp. 20 ff.
[161] 1787 ed., p. 16.

literature Webster frequently condemned. Then, too, they were scarcely "adapted to the capacity of children." It is interesting to note that since this book was the first American reader, it marks the introduction of Shakespeare into American school-books.

Following the illustrations, fourteen pages of maxims and poetry are given, taken verbatim from Enfield's *Speaker,* in some of which the emphatic words are indicated. For example:

It is much better to *reprove,* than to be angry *secretly.*
To *err* is human; to *forgive, divine.*
Pitch upon that course of life which is the most *excellent;* and habit will render it most *delightful.*[162]

The remainder of the book (333 duodecimo pages) is given over to the selections upon which the author depended for an awakening of national feeling, the promotion of the principles of morality and religion, the improvement of manners and deportment, and the cultivation of the art of speaking. Among the selections Webster included dialogues. Of the value of such selections he has this to say: "It is found by experience that Dialogues as bearing a near resemblance to the common talk of children, are the best calculated to prevent or break ill habits of reading, and to teach them an easy unaffected pronunciation. This will account for the number included in this collection."

In the Preface the author stated that schoolbooks generally treat subjects that are uninteresting to children, the inference being that his text was different in this respect. In choosing his selections, Webster perhaps knew better than he did in Part III. Since the dialogues were scenes taken from Shakespeare, Sheridan, Rowe, and other dramatists, they were much beyond the understanding and appreciation of children. The selections in general are tempered as to religious tones, yet the moral element is emphasized and the religious implication is frequently present. Since many of the selections were of an abstract nature, Webster's reader could not have had a strong appeal to children.

---

[162] This is a feature of Webster's reader which was widely used by other compilers, notably Murray and McGuffey.

Webster seems to have been aware of this shortcoming. In the subtitle of *The Little Reader's Assistant* (1790), meant to be used between Part I and Part III as a sort of introduction to the latter, this phrase appears, "All adapted to the capacity of children." In the advertisement placed in this text, the author says further:

It is said, with much truth, that most of the books published, are written on subjects and in a stile above the capacities of beginners. The following stories are selected and thrown into an intelligible form, to remove in part the common complaint, and assist young beginners in reading. It is hoped these few stories will not be useless, but serve as a step by which children will rise with more ease to the American Selection, or other books used in schools.

MOST OF THE READERS CONTINUED TO STRESS ELOCUTION DURING THE GREATER PART OF THE NINETEENTH CENTURY

To enter into a thorough discussion of the numerous elocutionary readers which followed in the wake of Webster's Part III, would take us far afield; to record a list of such texts would be to present an exhaustive catalogue of practically all the readers, and their number was legion, that appeared during the last decade of the eighteenth century and the greater part of the nineteenth.[163]

To claim also that all the compilers of reading books of Webster's age and later leaned directly on his compilations would be to make an assertion not supported by facts. Since, however, Webster was the first to compile an American reader, and since most of the compilers who followed him used his pattern and many of the details of their readers are similar to those in his, it would seem that his influence on the readers of the nineteenth century was considerable.

A few of the texts that show Webster's influence are described by way of illustration. Among the first readers which followed Webster's texts and which emphasized instruction in the "art of

[163] For a list of the texts used in America between 1804 and 1832, see *Annals of Education*, II (1832), 371.

speaking and reading" were *The American Preceptor* (1794) and *The Columbian Orator* (1797), compiled by Caleb Bingham. Then, there were the better known works of Lindley Murray, the most formidable competitor Webster met in the field of textbook compilation. The titles of these texts indicate their scope: *The English Reader . . . Designed to Assist Young Persons to Read with Propriety and Effect . . . with a Few Preliminary Observations on the Principles of Good Reading"* [164] (first published in America at Phildelphia in 1799) and *Introduction to the English Reader . . . Calculated to Improve the Younger Classes of Learners in Reading . . . with Rules and Observations for Assisting Children to Read with Propriety."* [165]

A few titles and comments from available McGuffey texts will show that these most popular readers included much material of the kind Webster introduced in his first reader for elementary schools. In the *Newly Revised Eclectic Third Reader . . . with Rules for Reading; and Exercises in Articulation, Defining . . .* (1848) fourteen pages are given to "Stops Used in Reading and Writing" and to articulation. In the short moral sentences, the kind Webster introduced into the reader, the emphatic words are italicized. In the *Eclectic Fourth Reader,* published the same year, twenty-five pages are given to "Directions for Reading." In McGuffey's *New Sixth Eclectic Reader; Exercises in Rhetorical Reading, with Introductory Rules and Examples* (1857), forty-five pages are given to the principles of Elocution, and the selections are arranged so as to lend themselves to rhetorical reading.

DECLAMATIONS AND EXHIBITIONS WERE EMPHASIZED IN
THE NINETEENTH-CENTURY SCHOOLS

Hand-in-hand with the reading went speaking or declamation, for speaking was considered "of the utmost consequence in this

[164] Title taken from the Philadelphia, 1816, edition. Twelve pages are given to the "Observations," many of which, the author states, were taken from the writings of Dr. Blair and from the Encyclopaedia Britannica. Webster openly accused Murray of plagiarizing his works, especially his grammars. See p. 139.

[165] Title taken from the New York, 1811, edition. Ten pages are given to the "Rules and Observations."

country, as any boy might be called to a seat in the legislature, perhaps, in the course of things." [166] To equip youth for this public duty which would at the same time give them an opportunity to "stand out," schools gave formal training at least once a week in declamation. In the earlier days, the readers were relied upon chiefly for the selections, but in the 1880's and 1890's, when there was a tendency to expand the number of textbooks for specific subjects, books designed exclusively for elocution were compiled.[167]

Another custom which the introduction of the elocutionary reader with its dialogues and "pieces" for declamation initiated was the practice of frequently giving "exhibitions" at the schoolhouse—a practice which gradually filtered down from the college and the academy, first to the village and then to the district schools. These occasions offered an opportunity for the pupils to practice "the art of speaking" before their parents and friends. In a selection entitled "Modern Education, A Dialogue between a Preceptor of an Academy and Parent of an Offered Pupil," published in Bingham's *Columbian Orator* (1797), a serious dialogue, which has the earmarks of propaganda, we learn that exhibitions, at least in the mind of this preceptor, were held too frequently in some schools, and that children were being transformed into "monkeys instead of men."

As declamation was a welcome relief from the dull routine of school, pupils entered into the matter with all their souls. "What a rummaging of books, pamphlets, and newspapers now took place to find pieces to speak!" says Burton. "The *American Preceptor*, the *Columbian Orator*, the *Art of Reading, Scott's Elocution, Webster's Third Part* and I know not how many other ancients, were taken down from their dusty retirement at home, for the sake of the specimens of eloquence they afforded." [168]

According to this author, those pieces were deemed best by them, grandsons of the Revolutionists, which most abounded in

[166] Burton, *The District School* (1850), p. 66.
[167] Sullivan, *Our Times* (1927), II, 95. C. Scribner's Sons.
[168] Warren Burton, *The District School as It Was* (1850, revised ed.), pp. 66 f.

"those glorious words, Freedom, Liberty, Independence, and other spirit-kindling names and phrases . . ." Another much prized quality was "high-flown language, and especially words that were long and sonorous, such as would roll thunderingly from the tongue." Dramatics were also introduced by presenting the extracts from plays, which, as has been noted, Webster and other compilers included in their readers. There was also much swinging of arms, shaking of fists, and waving of palms. "The whole school, with the exception of the very least perhaps, were engaged, indeed absorbed, in this novel branch of education . . ." [169]

THE ELOCUTIONARY READER WAS WIDELY CRITICIZED

As has been noted, the practice of emphasizing the art of speaking existed during the greater part of the nineteenth century as did the alphabet method in learning to read, in spite of the fact that both methods had their critics. As early as 1795 Scott pointed out in his *Lessons in Elocution* that Burgh's "system of passions," parts of which Webster "adapted" to the needs of public schools, however useful to people of riper years it might be, "is too delicate and complicated to be taught in schools."

In 1816 Daniel Adams published the *Understanding Reader: or, Knowledge before Oratory* (8th ed.). This book is of interest, as it was one of the first to emphasize content—to suggest that a vivid impression should precede a forceful expression. On the title-page he says his "method is wholly different from anything of the kind ever before published." This quotation from Franklin also appears: "Our boys often read as parrots speak, knowing little or nothing of the meaning." Adams advocated a constant use of the dictionary, claiming that because of this practice the minds of the pupils will be excited to inquiry, acquaintance with language will be enlarged, readiness and facility of expressing

[169] For a further account of exhibitions see Florence E. D. Muzzy, "A New England Childhood," *Connecticut Magazine*, XI (1905), 518–30; also *American Journal of Education*, XIII (1863), 127.

ideas will be acquired, and pupils be given confidence in themselves and their own understanding.

In Strong's *Common Reader* (1819), the dissatisfaction with
texts and methods is again expressed. He points out that,

The authors of readers have consulted their own taste rather than
the capacities of children; and the selections, where they do not
degenerate into childish vulgarity, are of too high a cast for the comprehension of the youthful mind, many of them are the purest and
most elegant compositions in the English language; and however
useful they may be in confirming habits of emphasis, pronunciation
&C. they seem nevertheless, better calculated for such as have
learned than for those who are *learning* to read.

Following in the footsteps of Adams, Strong states that his
"object is to furnish a pleasant and profitable exercise for children while pursuing their lessons in reading; and also, to enable
them to have a better understanding of the subjects which they
peruse as well as of language in general." In spite of these declarations, his book has much in common with Webster's Part III.
Three pages of rules for reading are followed by short paragraphs consisting of moral, religious, and scriptural selections.

The criticisms of those opposed to the system are well summed
up in Pierpont's *The American First-Class Book* (1854):

I have observed, however, that that part of school-books which consists of Brief Treatises upon Rhetoric, Rules for Reading, and
Essays on Elocution, is, almost uniformly, little worn,—an evidence
that it is little used,—in other words, that it is of little use . . . The
truth probably is, that reading, like conversation, is learned from
example rather than by rule. . . . It seems to me that the readiest,
indeed the only good way, to teach children to read well, is, to give
them to the charge of instructors who are themselves good readers.

It was not until the educational periodicals began to appear
during the latter part of the first quarter of the nineteenth century that the elocutionary reader and methods then practiced in
the teaching of reading were attacked with full force. The criticism was made that the drawling, hesitating, stammering manner
or nasal twanging tone, which, according to the contributions in
the periodicals, was very prevalent in the schools, was due to

lack of comprehension. Because of methods employed, the child read: "T-h-i-s, -i-s, -a, -n-i-c-e,- f-a-n," or "This — is — a — nice — fan." [170]

This condition, according to the testimony of Wickersham, was quite usual.

The beginners in reading were accustomed to spell nearly all the words as they went along before pronouncing them, thus forming habits that rendered it almost impossible for them ever to become good readers. No attention was paid to the definitions of words or to the meaning of sentences. Nothing whatever was required of young learners but correct pronunciation and some attention to arbitrary pauses at the several marks of punctuation. Force, inflection, expression, and in most cases, sense, were wholly ignored. To read well was in a general way to read fast, without being compelled to stop to spell any of the words.[171]

Most of the criticisms, however, were not concerned so much with the methods of teaching as with the texts themselves. "It seems to have been the object of the compilers of readers, it was pointed out, to cull the most profound passages contained in a language, in which the highest efforts at learning, talent, and genius have been embalmed. Certainly from no ancient, probably from no other modern language," the criticism continued, "could such a selection of literary excellence be made, as some of the texts exhibit—demonstrated arguments on the most abstruse and recondite subjects, tasking the practical logicians, and appreciable only to them; brilliant passages of parliamentary debates, whose force would be irresistible, providing only that one were familiar with all the contemporary institutions and events; scenes from dramas, beautiful if understood, but unintelligible without an acquaintance with heathen mythology; wit, poetry, eloquence, whose shafts to the vision of educated minds are quick and refulgent as lightning but giving to the ignorant only an empty rumbling of words; everything, in truth, may be found in the pages of the readers, everything which is worthy

[170] District School Journal, VI (1845), 152.
[171] James Pyle Wickersham, A History of Education in Pennsylvania (1886), p. 205.

the highest admiration of the learned but which is wholly unintelligible to children." [172]

The foregoing is a fair sampling of the copious criticisms which attended the use of the elocutionary reader in the nineteenth century. Other conditions which were criticized, but which were the fault of existing methods and conditions rather than the texts used, were that reading lessons were too long, that too much was attempted with the result that nothing was well done, and that the heterogeneity of texts in use was responsible for much of the bad reading. Several lists of suggestions are to be found in the journals. These are interesting as well as significant, in that they tell much about methods in use and the newer methods that were coming in. One contributor declared that a better name than "reading," under existing conditions, would be "stultification." In his list of suggestions, which, he believed, would arouse interest if followed, there is much that would be accepted as sound today:

1. More emphasis should be placed on meaning.
2. Competitive reading exercises should be held. "Let them be *active* in the exercise, not *passive*."
3. Pupils should give the thought of the selection in their own words.
4. Pupils should be required to analyze paragraphs and sentences.
5. Pupils should be encouraged to converse on some topic suggested by the reading lesson.
6. Pupils should criticise one another's manner of reading.
7. Teacher should read with or for pupils.
8. Class might try reading together.
9. Individuals should read alone.
10. Teacher should ask questions.
11. Pupils should make their own reading lessons and read them to the teacher, for they will understand what they have written.[173]

Summary and Conclusions

WEBSTER'S reader, Part III of *A Grammatical Institute of the English Language* (1785), later called *An American Selection of*

[172] Horace Mann, *Common School Journal,* I (1839), 335.
[173] *District School Journal,* IX, 39.

Lessons in Reading and Speaking (1787), is usually conceded to be the first reader compiled in America. Soon after the compilation of this reader, other authors, notably Lindley Murray, published texts with which Webster's reader did not successfully compete.

Among Webster's other efforts in the field of reading was the publication of two secularized revisions of *The New England Primer,* in 1789 and 1801, *The Little Reader's Assistant* (1790), *The Elementary Primer* (1831), and *The Little Franklin* (1836) and two posthumous works which probably belong to the author in name only.

Although Webster's books were frequently advertised as a complete system of education, they were not arranged in series form as the term is understood today. Webster took, however, the first step in the development of the series in that he did not write a composite text, but wrote separate texts for the study of spelling, reading, and grammar.

The ideals held by Webster, ideals concerning religion and morality, manners, patriotism, and the art of reading and speaking, set the pattern for readers compiled during the greater part of the nineteenth century. The readers had, however, other features which do not fall within these classifications.

RELIGION AND MORALITY

The practice of stressing religion was inherited from the Middle Ages. The earliest English texts and prominent educators stressed the importance of training in conduct. The first texts used in American schools and the early American juveniles laid stress on the teaching of religion and morality.

Although the religious and moral atmosphere which followed in the wake of the Revolution seems pronounced to present-day students, yet the religious and moral elements were tempered considerably by the wave of liberalism which was in the post-Revolutionary air. The failure of Webster's readers to achieve the popularity enjoyed by Webster's speller and Murray's reader, was due, some have thought, to the fact that they stressed the moral to the exclusion of the religious. It is true that the efficacy of this moral and religious training was questioned in the nineteenth-century periodicals, but the prevailing sentiment favored it and such instruction continued to be given during the greater part of the century.

MANNERS

Just as the teaching of religion and morality had its origin in the religious training which dominated the Middles Ages, so the practice of teaching manners and deportment originated among the nobility in medieval times, during the age of chivalry. The custom found its way into the grammar schools and was sanctioned by such seventeenth-century educators as Brinsley, Hoole, and Mulcaster. Webster followed the custom of his predecessors, such as Coote, Fenning, and Fox, by including dialogues, maxims, fables, and stories that would tend, he thought, to improve manners. Perhaps this phase of Webster's reader exerted less influence on the nineteenth-century texts than did the other phases of his pattern. Manners soon came to be taught incidentally rather than through the reading lesson. During the nineteenth century many separate texts and books appeared, stressing manners and etiquette.

PATRIOTISM

After the Revolution, the strong nationalistic sentiment affected all aspects of American life. Education, government, law, poetry, painting, music, all were influenced by the chauvinistic belief that America was a land flowing with milk and honey, populated by a chosen people who were destined to set an example before a world which had grown decrepit because of its thralldom to the inertia of the past. From a cultural, economic, and social standpoint, America was to be as free from Europe and the past as she was politically independent.

Webster was in sympathy with this sentiment. His readers contained many American selections, rather than those emphasizing the glories of the past and present European civilizations. Appended to his *An American Selection* was a short American history; to *The Little Reader's Assistant,* a Federal catechism, both intended to acquaint the youths of the day with the history and government of their country and to inspire loyalty to America. This tendency to stress patriotism was followed by other compilers of Webster's day and was continued during the greater part of the nineteenth century.

THE ART OF READING

Webster's reader emphasized the "art of reading and speaking." This tendency was not without precedent as grammar-school students had been required for centuries to compose and deliver Latin orations. Furthermore, during the Revolution American youths were under the spell of such orators as Otis and Henry. Then, too, the two main professions to which boys aspired were the ministry and law. The United States Congress, the state legislatures, and local councils, to which, youths were told, anyone might be called, added further incentive to the study of reading and speaking.

Webster's readers were based on English speakers and readers that had been used in colleges and academies. Patriotic American selections were substituted for those extolling the virtues of foreign nations, and pieces that would lend themselves to the expression of the "passions" were selected. Although Webster criticized other compilers for including selections that were beyond the capacities of children, most of his orations, dialogues, and stories were either too difficult for children or entirely uninteresting to them.

The periodicals of the nineteenth century criticized the elocutionary reader in that it placed emphasis on expression rather than impression. During the greater part of the century, other compilers, foremost among them Murray and McGuffey, included copious directions for correct speaking and selections which, it was thought, lent themselves to public address. This emphasis on speaking probably gave impetus to the school exhibition, which rivaled the spelling bee in popularity.

VI

DICTIONARIES

From all the observations I have been able to make, I am convinced the dictionaries and grammars which have been used in our seminaries of learning, for the last forty or fifty years, are so incorrect and imperfect, that they have introduced or sanctioned more errors than they amended: in other words, had the people of England and of these States been left to learn the pronunciation and construction of their vernacular language solely by tradition, and the reading of good authors, the language would have been spoken and written with more purity than it would have been and now is by those who have learned to adjust their language by the rules which dictionaries and grammars prescribe.[1]

WRITING in 1900, Murray declared that a large number of English persons habitually speak of "the Dictionary," just as they do of "the Bible," or "the Prayer-Book," or "the Psalms," and if pressed as to the authorship of these works would certainly say that "the Psalms" were composed by David, and "the Dictionary" by Dr. Johnson.[2] In America, wrote Scudder (1881), the name "Webster" has become to many a most impersonal term, and we may almost expect in a few generations to find the word "Webster" defined in some revised edition of the unabridged as the colloquial word for a dictionary.[3]

The English dictionary is a growth that has slowly developed through the ages. Each of many workers had added his stone or stones, some larger than others, "to the lexicographical cairn which had already risen to goodly proportions when Johnson made to it his own splendid contribution. . . . Its beginnings lie far back in times almost prehistoric. And these beginnings themselves, although the English Dictionary of today is lineally developed from them, were neither Dictionaries nor even English." [4]

[1] *American Dictionary* (1828), Advertisement, n. p.

[2] James A. H. Murray, *The Evolution of English Lexicography* (1900), p. 6. The Clarendon Press.

[3] *Noah Webster* (1882), p. 275. Houghton Mifflin Company.

[4] Murray, *The Evolution of English Lexicography* (1900), p. 7. The Clarendon Press.

The dictionary as we know it today is of comparatively recent origin. Its direct forbears were the glosses,[5] which were popular in England during the seventh and eighth centuries but which were perhaps of much earlier origin,[6] and the vocabularies,[7] at first Latin-English but later English-Latin. These early glossaries and vocabularies were useful to teachers and pupils as dictionaries. Moreover, they are to us "curious records of the history of education. . . . It is certainly not uninteresting to trace the various efforts which were made, at all periods of the middle ages, to simplify and render popular the forms of elementary instruction, and the several modifications which these forms underwent . . ."[8]

At this early stage of development some of the characteristics of the modern dictionary came into being. In one of the earliest extant glosses, the *Leiden,* no attempt was made to arrange the words in alphabetical order or according to subject headings. In the *Epinal glossarium,* however, the words are arranged alphabetically, the initial letter only being considered. In the alphabetical arrangement of the words in the *Corpus glossarium*[9] the two initial letters were considered. These glosses contained, as did the first dictionaries to be compiled, only the harder words.[10]

[5] These were made by monks, who wrote interlinear or marginal explanations of the difficult words in the Latin manuscripts they read, very much in the manner employed by students of foreign languages today. At an early age these explanations or glosses were written in easy or colloquial Latin, but later, as the vernacular was accepted more and more, they were given in English. In the eighth century, *glosses collectae* were often made from the glossed manuscripts in the monasteries.—M. M. Mathews, *A Survey of English Dictionaries* (1933), p. 8. The Clarendon Press.

[6] The earliest gloss now extant is the *Homeric Lexicon* or *Homeric Words,* made during the reign of Augustus by Apollonius, an Alexandrine grammarian, said to be the oldest Greek lexicographer.—Emery Littlefield, *Early Schools and School Books of New England* (1904), p. 306.

[7] These were classified lists of words, usually compiled by schoolmasters. These lists of vocables, with their meanings in the vulgar tongue, constituted the vocabularies memorized by the pupils. As the glosses and vocabularies fulfilled similar offices they were often combined.—Murray, *op. cit.,* p. 10.

[8] Thomas Wright, *Anglo-Saxon and Old English Vocabularies* (1884), I, v.

[9] Edited by W. M. Lindsay, 1921, pp. 1–187.

[10] See Griggs and Sweet, *The Epinal Glossary* (1883), p. vi.

For more than three hundred years after the conquest English lexicography stood still. In a collection of the early glosses and vocabularies made by Thomas Wright in 1857 and enlarged by R. P. Wulcker in 1884, only two minor vocabularies are given for the period 1066–1400. But at the beginning of the fifteenth century, after the vernacular had been used by such writers as Langland, Wyclif, Gower, Chaucer, and many others, after it had been sanctioned by Parliament and the courts of law, lexicographical interest burst forth with new vigor.[11]

Wright and Wulcker have printed six vocabularies of the fifteenth century. Among the English vocabularies made in explanation of Latin terms was the *Medulla grammatice,* compiled in the middle of the fifteenth century. In 1500 it was enlarged and published under the title *Ortus vocabulorum,* said to be the first Latin-English dictionary to be printed in England.[12]

The interest which was beginning to manifest itself in the use of the vernacular left its mark on the vocabularies of the fifteenth century just as it had on the literary works, the textbooks, and the instruction in the schools.[13] The first vocabularies had used the Latin-Latin or Latin-English arrangement, as the main concern was the explanation of Latin terms. As early as 1440, however, we see a shift in emphasis taking place. In that year Golfridus Grammaticus compiled an English-Latin vocabulary, which was printed in 1499 under the title *Promptorius parvulorum sive clericorum* (Children's Storeroom or Repository). The popularity of this vocabulary, which contained about ten thousand words, is attested by the fact that it had passed through eight editions by 1528. Another vocabulary, similar to the *Promptorium,* was the *Catholicon Anglicum,*[14] compiled in 1483, an independent work named after Johannes de Balbis's *Catholicon* or *Summa,* the celebrated Latin dictionary of the Middle Ages made in 1286.

[11] Murray, *op. cit.,* p. 14.
[12] S. A. Steger, *American Dictionaries* (1913), p. 5.
[13] See pp. 114 f.
[14] Printed by Early English Text Society in 1881.

The *Pictorial Vocabulary,* another fifteenth-century work, was illustrated with rude pen-and-ink drawings of many of the articles described.[15] These illustrations, appearing at this early date, remind us once again, "how little of novelty there is in most of the plans for simplifying school teaching in more modern times, for in these medieval treatises we meet with the prototypes of almost every scheme that has been proposed, from the more recent Hamiltonian system to the *Orbis sensualium pictus* of Comenius, which made so much noise by its novelty of plan in the earlier part of the seventeenth century." [16]

We see then that by the end of the fifteenth century the vocabularies were no longer designed as aids only to Latin-speaking, Latin-reading students, but as aids to English-speaking students studying Latin; however, whether the object was to explain the Latin words, as it was in the earlier glosses and vocabularies, or to translate English words into Latin, as in some of the later vocabularies, Latin was an essential element in the vocabularies and dictionaries to the end of the sixteenth century. During this century, which was under the spell of the renascence of ancient learning, many Latin-English and English-Latin vocabularies and dictionaries were compiled and published. The history of the sixteenth-century dictionary is significant in that more of the characteristics found in dictionaries of later periods were developed during that time.

The First English Dictionaries Appeared in the Sixteenth Century

IN THAT most of the compilers of dictionaries during the sixteenth century leaned heavily on Elyot's work, just as compilers of later periods borrowed extensively from Johnson and Webster, perhaps the most important compilation of the sixteenth century was *The Dictionary of Syr Thomas Elyot,* a Latin-English dictionary published in 1538. It is said to be the first work in

[15] Wright, *op. cit.,* pp. 747–813.
[16] *Ibid.,* p. xi.

English to take the name "dictionary." [17] Following the method used in some of the earlier glosses and vocabularies, Elyot arranged the words alphabetically. This arrangement was not followed, however, in the second dictionary of importance to appear in the century, *A Short Dictionary for Young Beginners* (1554), by J. Withals, who reverted to the subject arrangement, which had been used in the earlier glossaries.

Richard Huloet's *Abecadarium* (1552) has been called the first English dictionary.

[This work] was the first in which the meanings of English words were explained in English but in addition thereto Latin synonyms and definitions in French were included.[18]

In compiling his dictionary, Huloet, like most of the compilers of the sixteenth century, leaned heavily on Elyot, the Johnson of his age. Twenty years later (1572) John Higgens, schoolmaster and editor, enlarged Huloet's *Abecadarium*. In his method Higgens anticipated the method used by lexicographers at a much later date. In his introduction he wrote,

For ye better attayning to the knowledge of words, I went not to the common Dictionaries only, but also to the Authors themselues . . . and finallye I wrote not in the whole Booke one quyre, without perusing and conference of many authors.

After publishing enlarged editions of Elyot's dictionary in 1548, 1552, and 1559, Thomas Cooper brought out his *Thesaurus linguae Romanae and Britannicae* in 1565. This work was based on Elyot's dictionary and a thesaurus by Robert Stephens, a French lexicographer. Cooper's *Thesaurus* was the basis of later Latin-English dictionaries, and "traces of it may still be discovered in the Latin-English dictionaries of to-day." [19]

[17] The early vocabularies and dictionaries had many names, often quaint and striking, such as *Nominale, Vocabulorum, Promptorium, Catholicon, Alvearie, Abecadarium, Bibliotheca,* and *Thesaurus.* "It would have been impossible to predict in the year 1538, when Sir Thomas Elyot published his 'dictionary,' that this name would supplant all the others, and even take the place of the older and better descended word *vocabulorum.*"—Murray, *op. cit.,* p. 18. Oxford University Press.

[18] "The Development of the Dictionary," *New Age,* 1909, p. 385.

[19] Murray, *op. cit.,* p. 20.

Another dictionary of the century, ranking in importance with Huloet's *Abecadarium*, was Baret's *Alvearie, or Triple Dictionary in English, Latin, and French* (1573). In a later edition Greek synonyms and definitions were added to some of the Latin words.

During this stage of Latin-English and English-Latin dictionary compilation in the sixteenth century, dictionaries of English along with another modern language were being compiled. These dictionaries, like those in which the Latin element was pronounced, were meant to assist students to learn foreign languages rather than to help them understand their native tongue. Palsgrave's English-French dictionary appeared in 1530; Salesbury's Welsh-English, in 1547; Percival's Spanish-English, in 1591; Florio's Italian-English, in 1598; Cosgrave's French-English, in 1611; and Minsheu's polyglot dictionary of eleven languages, in 1617, said to be the first to introduce etymology of words and to cite authors' names and passages from their works in the treatment of some of the words, and the first book to be published by subscription in England.[20]

Early in the sixteenth century, the purists, apprehensive lest the wide renascence borrowings, the "ink-horn" terms taken from other languages, should cause England to keep "her house bankrupt." An effort was made to restore archaic words to use. The works of Chaucer, Trevisa, and others, were gone over in a search for old words. In the sixteenth century so many difficult words appeared, many of them archaic, that glosses were made for some of the works, among them being "E. K.'s" gloss for Spenser's *Shepherdes Calendar*, in 1579.[21] By the end of the century, however, a general need was felt for a dictionary which would give the meaning and spelling of these many learned words taken from the Latin, Greek, Hebrew, Arabic, and other languages. "The first attempt to supply it, marks, on the whole, the most important point in the evolution of the modern English Dictionary."[22] With a few exceptions,[23] for more than a

---

[20] Mathews, *English Dictionaries* (1933), pp. 10f., 23. Oxford University Press.
[21] *Ibid.*, p. 17.
[22] Murray, *op. cit.*, p. 27.
[23] *A New English Dictionary* (1702) by "J. K." had for its subtitle "a compleat

century compilers of dictionaries placed emphasis not on the most-used words in the English language but on the hard words that had found their way into English speech from other languages.

The Real Beginnings of English Lexicography Are to Be Found in the Seventeenth Century

BEFORE the beginning of the seventeenth century the glosses, vocabularies, and dictionaries were used as an aid in the learning of foreign languages, principally the Latin. Early in the seventeenth century compilers began to have as their main concern the elucidation of English words to English-speaking people. For this reason the dictionaries of the seventeenth and early eighteenth centuries have been called the "incunabula of English lexicography."

Since space forbids a full discussion of the round dozen of seventeenth-century compilers and their works, comments will be limited to certain characteristics upon which later compilers built.[24] Among these compilations, Cawdrey's *Table Alphabetical of Hard Words* is significant, as Cawdrey worked in virgin soil in preparing an English dictionary explaining English words, most of them borrowings from other languages, in English to English people.

As has been shown, in Minsheu's polyglot dictionary, the *Ductor in linguas* (1617), the etymology of some of the words was given. Blount also made a crude effort at etymology in his *Glossographia* (1656) by giving the source word, as did Phillips,

---

collection of the most proper and significant words, commonly used in the language."

[24] To this group belongs: Robert Cawdrey, *Table Alphabetical* (1604); Dr. John Bullokar, *English Expositor* (1616); Henry Cockeram, *The English Dictionary* (1623); Thomas Blount, *Glossographia* (1656); Edward Phillips, *New World of Words* (1658); John Ray, *A Collection of English Words Not Generally Used* (1664); Dr. Stephen Skinner, *Etymologican linguae Anglicanae* (1671); Eliza Coles, *English Dictionary* (1677); Edward Crocker, *English Dictionary* (1704); J. K. (John Kersey ?), *A New English Dictionary* (1702); (anonymous) *Glossographia Anglicana nova* (1707); and John Kersey, *Dictionarium Anglo-Britannicum* (1708).

who was accused by Blount of plagiarism in the former's *New World of Words* (1658). From a standpoint of etymology, however, Skinner's *Etymologican linguae Anglicanae* was the most important work of the century. The use of illustrations from the works of authors, a distinctive characteristic of later dictionaries, was anticipated during the seventeenth century by both Minsheu and Blount, while pictorial illustrations of terms having to do with heraldry were introduced in the anonymous *Glossographia Anglicana nova* (1707).

The use of encyclopedic material, which later became a distinctive characteristic of textbooks and dictionaries, especially those compiled in America, was introduced by Dr. John Bullokar in his *English Expositor: Teaching the Interpretation of the Hardest Words Used in Our Language* (1616) and by Henry Cockeram, the first compiler to use the title *The English Dictionary* (1623).

During the Eighteenth Century Several Strides Were Taken in the Development of the Modern Dictionary

MORE than a dozen dictionaries, which at the time of their publication were more or less important, appeared in the eighteenth century.[25] Of these, however, only three are of prime interest to this study, namely, Bailey's (1721), Johnson's (1755), and Walker's (1791). As opposed to the dictionaries of the seventeenth century, which aimed to include only the more difficult terms, the dictionaries of the eighteenth century strove to be

[25] The outstanding eighteenth-century dictionaries are as follows: Nathan Bailey's *Universal Etymological English Dictionary* (1721); Thomas Dyche and William Pardon's *A New General English Dictionary* (2d ed., 1725); Francis Junius's *Etymologicum Anglicanum* (1742); John Wesley's *The Complete Dictionary* (1753); Dr. Samuel Johnson's *The English Dictionary* (1755); John Entick's *The Spelling Dictionary* (1764); Frederick Barlow's *A Complete English Dictionary* (1772); Dr. William Kenrick's *A New Dictionary* (1773); Rev. James Barclay's *Complete and Universal English Dictionary* (1774); William Perry's *The Royal Standard English Dictionary* (1775); John Ash's *New and Complete Dictionary of the English Language* (1775); Thomas Sheridan's *A General Dictionary of the English Language* (1780); John Walker's *A Critical Pronouncing Dictionary*

more comprehensive, emphasizing the more useful words. It was in these compilations that dictionaries began to take the form in which they are found today.

Following the crude efforts of Minsheu, Blount, Phillips, and Skinner, Nathan Bailey, the most important English lexicographer before Johnson, placed emphasis on etymology. Junius's work, which has been called the "first systematic and comprehensive work on the analogies of our tongue," [26] along with a later edition of Bailey's compilation,[27] was of great assistance to Dr. Johnson in the compilation of his dictionary. In the field of etymology Johnson went little beyond his predecessors, relying as he did largely on the early attempts of Skinner and Junius.[28]

The custom of illustrating the use of words by quoting authors, anticipated by Minsheu and Blount in the seventeenth century, received impetus in Bailey's work, which may have suggested to Johnson that he include quotations from standard writers to illustrate the various meanings of words. In that a full treatment of the different senses of the words was given along with more lucid definition, fully illustrated in their different significations by examples from the best writers, Johnson's work excelled that of his predecessors.

It was during the eighteenth century that the first efforts were made to indicate the pronunciation of words. Bailey, the fountainhead from which most eighteenth-century efforts in the field of lexicography flowed,[29] made the first attempt at syllabification. He, followed by Johnson, also marked the accented syllables. Pronunciation was indicated by a system of numbers, similar to that used by Webster in his spelling book (1783), first by William

---

(1791); and Stephen Jones's *A General Pronouncing and Explanatory Dictionary of the English Language* (1798).

[26] Mathews, *op. cit.*, p. 24.

[27] *Dictionarium Britannicum*, 1730 and 1736. It was an interleaved edition of this compilation that Johnson used as the basis of his dictionary.

[28] Thomas Babington Macaulay, *Life of Samuel Johnson* (1905), p. 80.

[29] In addition to the other "firsts," Bailey's was the first English dictionary to be illustrated by woodcuts.—Littlefield, *op. cit.*, p. 311.

Kenrick in his dictionary (1773), by William Perry (1775),[30] and by John Walker (1791). Thomas Sheridan used a phonetic respelling of words, assisted by numbers, to indicate pronunciation. It was only in the field of orthoëpy that other compilers of the eighteenth century excelled Dr. Johnson, the acknowledged lexicographical dictator of his age.

America Entered the Field of Dictionary Making at the Close of the Eighteenth Century

FROM the foregoing, we see the steps by which the science of English lexicography developed in England and its state at the end of the eighteenth century when America entered the field. The first American dictionaries were school dictionaries. In fact there has always been a close relation between dictionary making and schoolroom procedure, the former resulting as an effort to meet the exigencies arising from the latter. In the first place, the glosses and vocabularies were prepared as an aid to pupils and teachers. Many of the title-pages and prefaces of the earliest dictionaries, which were usually compiled by ministers and schoolmasters, state that the compilations were intended for schools.

The year 1798 marks the beginning of dictionary making in America. That year, Samuel Johnson, Jr., son of the first president of Columbia University and the first man to write and publish a grammar in America, published *A School Dictionary*. In the Preface the author sets forth some of the salient features of compilation—features that have continued to be characteristic of school dictionaries until the present day. Although the author "selected useful words that are easily and generally understood by children," he did not, of course, at that early age, make a scientific inquiry of what the useful words were. The words, 4,150 in number, were selected from "preceding authors of established reputation." The avowed "true meaning" of a word was of course the definition in the original boiled down, in many

[30] Perry's *The Synonymus, Etymological, and Pronouncing English Dictionary,* a much larger work, appeared in 1805.

cases, so that it was meaningless to children. As was often reasoned in the compilation of works for children, the child, a
miniature adult, should have a small book, a miniature adult
book, as in this case, brought "into the compass of a sizable
cheap book."

In keeping with the current tendency to attempt to indicate
the pronunciation, Johnson devoted two pages to an explanation
of the symbols that indicate vowel sounds and pronunciation.
His system is very simple and crude,[31] as indeed was that of all
the early compilers. Of it he says in the Preface: "The different
sounds of the vowels are not so accurately pointed out in the
following work as they are in the *Grammatical Institute* by the
ingenious Mr. Webster . . ."[32]

In 1800 Johnson collaborated with John Elliott, pastor of the
church in East Guilford, Connecticut, in compiling *A Selected
Pronouncing and Accented Dictionary*. A second edition was
published the same year. This dictionary was little more than an
enlargement of Johnson's 1798 work.[33] The authors explain in
the Preface that the favorable reception which the school dictionary met has induced them to undertake the compilation on
an enlarged plan.

The education of youth [they declare] in a free republic is a matter
of the highest importance. The increasing attention which has been
paid to this interesting subject in our country, for several years past,
affords just grounds of congratulation, and joy, among the friends
of order, virtue, and religion.

[31] The words were divided into syllables. The long vowels in the accented
syllables were marked with the grave accent (e.g., a bàse), the short with an acute
accent (e.g., áb be). Such diacritical marks as the dieresis and circumflex were used
to a limited extent. Silent letters were italicized and in some cases words were respelled to indicate the pronunciation.

[32] That Webster was at an early age looked upon by his contemporaries as
something of an authority is evidenced by the fact that Johnson and Elliott sent
him their manuscript to read, before they published their dictionary in 1800.
Among the testimonies appearing in that work is this communication: "I have
no time to examine every sheet of your manuscript, but have read many sheets
in different parts of it; your general plan and execution I approve of and can
sincerely wish you success in your labors . . . Noah Webster, Jun."

[33] Pages 7-11 in the first 1800 edition are devoted to an Introduction of Grammar; pp. 11-13, to Latin grammar. In the second 1800 edition, the English grammar occupies pp. 7-17. No Latin grammar given.

Many dictionaries then in use, however, they maintain, lack delicacy and chastity of language.

Many words, there found are highly offensive to the modest ear, and cannot be read without a blush. To inspire youth with sentiments of modesty, and delicacy is one of the principal objects of early instruction; and this object is totally defeated by the indiscriminate use of vulgar, and indecent words.

The authors pointed to this compilation with pride and satisfaction for having contributed their mite "in attempting to disseminate the seeds of literature" and in "being first in an undertaking of this kind." [34] Steger's evaluation of Johnson's 1798 dictionary applies as well to the Johnson and Elliott compilation. It "shows no innovation and no improvements on previous English works. It is nothing more than a synopsis, a compendium of existing words, minus a number of their merits, lacking in individuality and following the beaten path of lexicography . . ." As a pioneer, however, this author declares that Johnson "should receive due recognition for a well-conceived and carefully executed school dictionary." [35]

Webster Published His First Dictionary in 1806

TO NOAH WEBSTER as a child, so tradition has it, words had a peculiar interest infrequently found among children.[36] As we have seen, he began as a youth out of college to publish spelling books, grammars, and readers. It is true that he made excursions into politics and general literature during the latter part of the eighteenth century, but it is likely that he discovered by successive trials that lexicography was the pursuit that belonged to him more than any other. Toward the end of the century his studies gravitated more and more toward lexicography "and the habits of mind which had been confirmed in his various pursuits were precisely such as would serve best the purpose

[34] Caleb Alexander published the *Columbian Dictionary* the same year (1800). "All of these dictionaries," says Mathews, "were small, and possess little interest beyond that which is inevitably attached to 'firsts' of anything."—*Op. cit.*, p. 43.
[35] S. A. Steger, *American Dictionaries* (1913), p. 23.
[36] Increase N. Tarbox, *Congregational Quarterly*, VII, Pt. I, p. 1.

DICTIONARIES 221

which he was gradually forming." [37] Although he had a tenacious memory, his experience as a journalist had taught him how idle and unsafe it is for a public writer to rely on mere recollection. Early in life he formed the habit of arranging all his acquired knowledge in the most exact order. He preserved documents with the utmost care.

"All that he had ever written, all that had been written against him, every thing that he met with in newspapers or periodicals which seemed likely to be of use at any future period, was carefully laid aside in its appropriate place, and was ready at a moment's warning." [38] The large collection of Webster's manuscripts in the New York Public Library lends credence to this statement. As his personal copies of texts and other books show, he was a great marker of books.

[He had] a particular mark by which he denoted, in every work he read, all the new words, or new senses of words, which came under his observation. He filled the margin of his books with notes and comments containing corrections of errors, a comparison of dates, or references to corresponding passages in other words, until his whole library became a kind of *Index Rerum,* to which he could refer at once for every thing he had read.[39]

Regarding the genesis of his first dictionary, Webster gave this account in 1828: [40] "In the year 1783, just at the close of the revolution, I published an elementary book for facilitating the acquisition of our vernacular tongue, and for correcting a vicious pronunciation, which prevailed extensively among the common people of this country." Soon after the publication of that work, the Reverend Mr. Goodrich of Durham, one of the trustees of Yale, suggested that Webster compile a dictionary, which should complete a system for the instruction of the citizens of this country in the language. Because he was not qualified by research nor had the means of support, he thought the plan impracticable. Later, being induced by friends and above all by the want of

[37] Scudder, *Noah Webster* (1882), p. 215.
[38] Chauncey A. Goodrich, "Memoir of the Author," *American Dictionary* (1848), XIX.
[39] *Ibid.*
[40] Introduction to *An American Dictionary,* n. p.

such a book while reading modern books of science, he set about
to compile a dictionary at the beginning of the nineteenth century. In 1806 appeared *A Compendious Dictionary of the English Language*. Webster's title-page to this dictionary shows that
he departed from the work of a dictionary proper by including
encyclopedic material,[41] such as "Tables of Moneys," "Tables of
Weights and Measures," the "Division of Time among the Jews,
Greeks, and Romans," a "List of Post-Offices in the United
States," the "Number of Inhabitants in the United States, with
the Amount of Exports, New and Interesting Chronological
Tables of Remarkable Events and Discoveries,[42] A Chronological Table of the Invention and Introduction of Arts and Im-
provements, and a Chronological Table of the Most Remarkable
Events, in or Respecting America, Intended for the Outline of
American History."

The Preface to the 1806 dictionary is an important document
in the history of lexicography as its twenty pages in small type
contain nearly all the views concerning language reform which
Webster held at one time or another and some of which he put
into practice in this work or other publications. This dictionary,
the author admits, was not an original work, but was an "enlargement and improvement" of John Entick's *New Spelling Dictionary*, 1764, a work, Webster believed, whose selection of words,
orthography, pronunciation, and definitions undoubtedly justify
this preference. To Entick's words Webster claimed to "have
added *about five thousand* others, which have been mostly collected from the best writers, during a course of several years and
defining correctly every word in a copious language,"[43] making
a total of about thirty-seven thousand words in the compilation.

[41] This feature has been a special characteristic of American dictionaries,
though it is not distinctly of American origin. During the late eighteenth and
early nineteenth centuries, people were poor and books were scarce. Webster, like
other compilers of his age, attempted to give people as much as he could within
the confines of one volume.

[42] This table was an enlargement of a similar table used by Entick in his *New
Spelling Dictionary*. The first events entered are "The Creation of the world and
Adam and Eve," 4004 B.C., and the birth of Cain, 4003 B.C.; the last, the conflict
of Nelson and Villeneuve and Gravina, Oct. 21, 1805.

[43] *Compendious Dictionary* (1806), Preface, p. xix.

In the Preface to this dictionary Webster began to exercise, in word and deed, his antipathy for Dr. Johnson. He admitted, however, that "Of the numerous dictionaries of the English Language which are used in the United States, Bailey's and Johnson's are those which are considered as containing the most original materials; and Johnson's in particular is the fund from which modern compilers have selected the substance of their works." He contends further that Sheridan, Walker, Perry, Entick, Jones, Ash, and others leaned heavily on Johnson, offering as proof the fact that they stumbled into the blunder made by Johnson in defining "misnomer," "obligee," and other words.

A comparison of the context of Webster's dictionary with that of Johnson and Elliott, Entick, and Dr. Johnson shows the truth of Webster's contention. Entick based his work on Dr. Johnson; Johnson and Elliott and Webster based theirs on Entick. The following comparative table shows this similarity; also the various (and inadequate) means used by these compilers to indicate pronunciation.

Johnson's *Dictionary of the English Language* (1755)	Entick's *New Spelling Dictionary* (1805 Edition)
To ABA′NDON, 1. To give up, resign, quit. 2. To desert. 3. To forsake, generally with a tendency to an ill sense.	Aban′don, v. a. to forsake, desert, give up, quit.
To ABASE, To cast down, to depress, to bring low, almost always in a figurative and personal sense.	Abáse, v. a. to bring low, humble, cast down, hate.
	Abásh, v. a. to put to blush, confound, perplex.
To ABA′TE, 1. To lessen, to diminish. 2. To reject, or depress the mind.	Abáte, v. to decrease, lessen, diminish, lower, sink.

ABBA,
A Syriac word, which signifies father.

A'BBOT,
The chief of a convent, or fellowship of canons.

Ab'ba, s.
a father, a scriptural name for father.

Ab'bot, s.
the head of or over a society of monks.

Elliott and Johnson's *A Selected Pronouncing and Accented Dictionary* (1800)

Webster's *Compendious Dictionary of the English Language* (1806)

A bán don, v. t. to forsake, give up, quit.

Aban'don, v. t. to forsake wholly, desert, quit.

A bàse, v. t. to bring low, humble, cast down.

Abáse, v. t. to bring low, humble, cast down.

A básh, v. t. to put to the blush, confound.

Abash', v. t. to put to the blush, confound, perplex.

A bàte, v. t. to decrease, lessen, diminish.

Abáte, v. to decrease, lessen, pull down, fail as a writ; remit as a tax (con.).

áb ba, n. a scriptural word for father.

Ab'ba, n. father, a scriptural word for father.

âb bot, n. the head of a society of monks.

Ab' bot, n. the head of a society of monks.

In his Preface [44] Webster explained his innovation in the arrangement of the alphabet:

In the alphabetical arrangement of words, I have separated the letters J and I, and V and U, placing first in order the primitive characters I & U. More than a century has elapsed, since J and V have been used as characters with powers distinct from I and U; and no man who ever consulted a lexicon, can have been insensible to the inconvenience and perplexity which are created by an intermixture of words beginning with different letters. Yet one compiler after another proceeds in the customary mode, and apparently for no reason, but because it is easier to transcribe than reform.[45]

The following year, 1807, appeared Webster's second dictionary, *A Dictionary of the English Language Compiled for the Use of Common Schools in the United States.* In the Preface, much in the manner of Johnson and Elliott, Webster speaks of the improvements that have been made in the education of youth

[44] Page xxi.
[45] Elliott and Johnson had used the I J and U V arrangement.

during the past thirty years, "particularly in common schools, in which are taught the branches of learning necessary for the yoemanry of the country." Failing to recognize the compilations of Elliott and Johnson, he says the list of books necessary in a system of instruction, has hitherto been incomplete, as the English pocket dictionaries are all imperfect. They contain obscene and vulgar terms, obsolete words, and definitions not true to American usage of terms. These texts are also very deficient in that they do not mark the accent or make a distinction between long and short vowels. "It is believed," said the author, "that an abridgement of that work [*Compendious Dictionary*, 1806], containing all the words which common people have occasion to use, and sold at a less price, will be well received by the great body of farmers and mechanics in the United States. Every family and every child in school has occasion for such a Dictionary." The work is very similar to the 1806 dictionary. Some words, however, were deleted, and the pronunciation and spelling were changed in some cases.

Webster's third dictionary, which was a new edition of his 1807 "Common School Dictionary," appeared in 1817. There is nothing to indicate that these common-school dictionaries met a wide demand. On the contrary, the fact that new editions did not appear indicates that they were not widely used. After 1807 Webster's activities were concentrated on his *magnus opus, The American Dictionary,* which appeared in 1828. After that date, Webster published other dictionaries "for Primary Schools," some of which were abridged from the *American Dictionary,* but many school dictionaries were compiled or edited by Webster's son, William G. Webster. The numerous editions of these indicates that during the middle of the nineteenth century there was a wide demand for the small school dictionary.

The American Dictionary (1828) Was the First of a Long Succession of Webster Unabridged Dictionaries

AFTER the publication of the *Compendious Dictionary* in 1806, Webster, according to his intention announced in the

Preface of that work, began to lay his plans for a larger compilation. In February he sent copies of his compendium to the presidents of colleges in the northern states, along with letters announcing that he contemplated making a revision of the 1806 edition, should it be used by the "literary gentlemen" and the colleges to an extent which would warrant the compilation of "the great work." [46]

The following year, 1807, Webster made further efforts to make his venture more secure. In February of that year he addressed a circular "To the Friends of Literature in the United States," [47] sending copies to men in various towns and asking them to give the circulars extensive circulation. In these he explained the sad state of philology, the extent to which he had worked in the field, and his plans for the future. Because of the expense involved in research and in the support of a "numerous family," Webster solicited help, declaring that there were two modes by which friends might be of assistance: by contributing money and by extending the use of the books which he had published for the use of schools.

In August of the same year he sent out another circular "To Friends of Literature in the United States," [48] announcing that the expenses attending the compilation and publication of the work exceeded his resources and that without pecuniary aid the work would have to be abandoned or imperfectly executed. Below the circular there was space for the signatures of subscribers. Those subscribing ten dollars were entitled to a copy of the dictionary, "on fine paper and in elegant binding."

There is nothing to indicate that the public responded at all liberally.[49] The editions of the *Compendious Dictionary* and its

---

[46] A copy of this letter is pasted in Webster's personal copy of the *Compendious Dictionary*, in the New York Public Library.

[47] Webster MSS, New York Public Library.

[48] Webster MSS, New Haven Colony Historical Society.

[49] According to Ford more than one thousand dollars was contributed to aid Webster in the "prosecution" of his dictionary. These contributions ranged from $50 to $200. *Notes*, II, 493. Fowler relates that Webster's Preface to the *American Dictionary* contained "certain statements . . . in respect to the opposition . . .

abridgment, the "School Dictionary," were limited to three over a period of eleven years. Writing to Dr. Ramsay in 1809, Webster says he has let the public know of his design, but so far he has had no reason to think he will receive help. He concludes by saying the task is Herculean, but it is of far less consequence to him than to his country.[50]

Webster's original plan, he explains in the Preface to the 1828 edition of *The American Dictionary,* did not extend to an investigation of the origin and progress of the English language, much less that of other languages, but aimed to correct the English dictionaries and supply words in which they were deficient. But after finishing two letters, he changed his plan, since he found himself embarrassed at every step for want of a knowledge of the origin of words, which Johnson, Bailey, Junius, Skinner, and others did not supply. The next ten years were spent in comparing radical words and in forming a synopsis of the principal words in twenty languages, arranged in classes, under their primary elements or letters.[51] "All the words of the several great races of men," he explained, "both in Asia and Europe, which are vernacular in their several languages, and unequivocally the same, are of equal antiquity, as they must have been derived from the common Chaldee stock which existed before the dispersion."[52] On this premise Webster formulated what he called a new view of language, that is, he believed that in cases where usage or analogy do not determine a correct form, it can be discovered by tracing the word to its ultimate source—the Chaldee.

After completing this synopsis, Webster corrected the part formerly written through letters A and B and started on the other letters. In spite of all discouraging circumstances, he continued to work alone, without substantial financial aid or en-

---

the ridicule he had experienced in the prosecution of his enterprise." It was with reluctance that he yielded to his friends, who persuaded him to omit these remarks. *Printed but not published* (n. d.), p. 1.

[50] *Letter to Dr. David Ramsay . . . respecting the Errors in Johnson's Dictionary and Other Lexicons* (1807), p. 27.

[51] This synopsis has not been published. See Webster MSS.

[52] *American Dictionary* (1828), Introduction, n. p.

couragement from home or abroad. Although there were textbooks to be written, textbooks to be revised, critics to be answered, and dozens of other projects that took their toll from his energy and time, the work went forward. Rising, as was his custom, about half an hour before sunrise in order to make "use of all the light of that luminary," year after year found him at his task. "I was often so much excited by the discoveries I made," he reported, "that my pulse, whose ordinary action is scarcely 60 beats to the minute, was accelerated to 80 or 85." [53]

In 1812 Webster moved his family from New Haven to Amherst, where the lower living expenses would permit him to pursue his lexicographical pursuits. While there he devoted time to many activities. Among other things, he helped found Amherst College and attended the Massachusetts state legislature.[54]

Since the dictionary was nearly completed, the income from the spelling book was increasing year by year, and the expense of his less "numerous family" was lower than in former years, Webster decided to move back to New Haven in 1822. This location placed his family nearer the two married daughters, who lived at Hartford and New Haven, and in a position where he could communicate with them during his sojourn abroad which he was then contemplating.

In order to obtain some books and other assistance he could not get in America, Webster went abroad in 1824, first to France and then to England.[55] He wished also to study the general state of philology in England, to hear the English pronunciation, and, if possible, to bring about some agreement or coincidence of opinion with regard to unsettled points in pronunciation and grammatical construction.[56]

According to his own account, Webster finished his dictionary in true Gibbonian manner:

[53] Mathews, *English Dictionaries* (1933), p. 40. The Clarendon Press.
[54] See Everett E. Thompson, "Noah Webster and Amherst College," *Amherst Graduates' Quarterly*, XXII (1933), 289–99.
[55] See Webster correspondence, June, 1824–June, 1825. Webster MSS; Ford, *Notes*, 199–293.
[56] Ford, *Notes*, II, 292.

I finished writing my Dictionary in January, 1825, at my lodgings in Cambridge, England. When I had come to the last word, I was seized with a trembling which made it somewhat difficult to hold my pen steady for writing. The cause seems to have been the thought that I might not then live to finish the work, or the thought that I was so near the end of my labors. But I summoned strength to finish the last word, & then walking about the room a few minutes I recovered.[57]

Webster had intended to publish his work in England, and "one of the principal booksellers, who examined the MS," told him the work would maintain its ground in that country. But the publishers were all embarked in other enterprises and would not bring into the market a book which would enter into competition with Johnson and others.[58]

In 1828 Webster's *American Dictionary of the English Language* was published in New Haven.[59] To it was prefaced an "Introductory Dissertation on the Origin, History, and Connection of the Languages of Western Asia and Europe" and a "Concise Grammar of the English Language."[60] The frontispiece was a "counterfeit representation" of Webster, painted by S. F. B. Morse and engraved by A. B. Durand.[61]

This Dictionary [Webster declared in the Preface], like all others of the kind, must be left in some degree imperfect; for what individual is competent to trace to their source, and define in all their various applications, popular, scientific, and technical, sixty or seventy thousand words. It satisfied my mind that I have done all that my health, my talents, and my pecuniary means would enable me to accomplish. I present it to my fellow citizens, not with frigid indifference, but with my ardent wishes for their improvement and happiness; and for continued increase of the wealth, the learning, the moral and religious elevation of character, and the glory of my country.

[57] *Ibid.*
[58] Letter from Webster to James Madison, dated "New Haven, March 17, 1826."— Webster MSS; Ford, *Notes,* II, 294.
[59] The dictionary was printed in two octavo volumes. Twenty-five hundred copies were printed, which were to be sold at $25 each. In 1832, three thousand copies were printed in London for the English trade.
[60] See p. 132.
[61] See frontispiece to this work. See Ford, *Notes,* II, 198, for circumstances under which portrait was painted.

In the "Advertisement" appearing in this dictionary, Webster compares its contents with that of the English dictionaries which he set out to correct and improve. Walker's dictionary (1791), he says, has been found by actual count to contain in round numbers, thirty-eight thousand words, and those of Johnson, Sheridan, Jones, and Perry have not far from the same number. The American edition of Todd's Johnson contains fifty-eight thousand. In the *American Dictionary*, the author claims, the number of words was increased to seventy thousand. The words used in augmenting the vocabulary were, the author enumerates, (1) words of common use; (2) participles of verbs; (3) terms of frequent occurrence in historical works; (4) legal terms; and (5) terms in the arts and sciences.

In 1829 the *American Dictionary* appeared in abridged form. This abridgment was made by Joseph Emerson Worcester, who had made an abridgment of Dr. Johnson's dictionary in 1828 and who was destined to be Webster's most formidable opponent in the "war of the dictionaries," which was then already beginning to smolder. Two features which were added to this edition and which show the increasing tendency to indicate pronunciation in works of this sort were Worcester's synopsis of words differently pronounced by different orthoëpists and Walker's key to the pronunciation of Greek, Latin, and scriptural proper names. This dictionary Webster sold to his son-in-law, Chauncey Allen Goodrich.[62] It was eminently successful. Numerous issues and editions were published before the middle of the century. In fact it was the only one of Webster's dictionaries to meet success during his lifetime.

The *American Dictionary* was too large and too expensive a work to find a popular demand. A second edition was not published until 1841. In this work Webster was assisted by his son William G. Webster, who later, after his father's death, was active in editing Webster dictionaries and other texts. The 1841 dictionary is little more than an expansion of the 1828 edition.

[62] See C. W. Fowler's, *Printed but Not Published* (n. d.), p. 8; also Webster's will.—Webster MSS.

Several thousand words, including words and phrases from foreign languages, were added. These were not inserted in the main part of the dictionary in their alphabetical order, but were placed at the end of the second volume. The definitions were practically those that had appeared in the former work, excepting those having to do with scientific terms, which were corrected by Professor William Tully of the New Haven Medical College. The spelling and pronunciation were very much the same as in the 1828 work, although more attention was given to the division of words into syllables and in some cases words were respelled in order to indicate the pronunciation. Worcester's "Synopsis of Words, Differently Pronounced by Different Orthoëpists," was included. The etymologies and illustrations were substantially those found in the earlier work. Webster and his son were making a revision of this work when the former died in 1843.[63]

This revision was also in two volumes and was to sell for $15. It lay, however, like Robinson Crusoe's boat, stranded, too big to be launched. After Webster's death in 1843, the G. & C. Merriam Company bought the unsold 1841 edition and the publishing right of the dictionary and spelling books. The company leased the speller and abridgments to other publishing houses and devoted its entire energy to the publication of the large dictionary. An effort was made to compile a serviceable dictionary that would meet the public demand. The days of the one-man dictionary were at an end. The publishers employed Professor Chauncey A. Goodrich, Webster's son-in-law, to re-edit the book. He was assisted by Yale specialists in the fields of science, law, theology, literature, and art.[64] No radical changes were made in the dictionary. The "eccentric" spellings which had not been changed by Webster himself were dropped. To the work Goodrich added his memoir of Webster from "materials . . . obtained from Dr. Webster himself, about ten years before his death."[65] An important revision was the enlarged edition with pictorial

[63] See Webster's personal copy of 1841 ed. in the New York Public Library.
[64] See Preface to *American Dictionary* (1847), pp. vi f.
[65] The biography appeared in the "National Portrait Gallery of Distinguished Americans" (1835), II, n. p.

illustrations [66] and a table of synonyms which appeared in 1859. This work was a formidable competitor of Worcester's dictionary.

During the remainder of the nineteenth century, to say nothing of the twentieth, there were few years that did not see a Webster dictionary of some sort published. So numerous were the editions and reprints, so varied the time and place of publication, that the bibliography has been the despair of biographers. One is tempted to join with Scudder, who says, "I can hardly expect my readers to follow me patiently through a close examination of the successive editions of Webster's large dictionary, and I have no such high opinion of my own patience as to suppose that I should continue on the road after my reader had dropped behind." [67] Add to this task the attempt to follow the destinies of the many abridged editions and the task becomes colossal.

During its life of more than a hundred years, four complete revisions have been made of Webster's large dictionary, in 1864, 1890, 1909, and 1934. In 1864 the *New Illustrated Royal* quarto unabridged edition of Webster's *American Dictionary* was published under the editorship of Noah Porter. The days of the one-man dictionary, as this work shows, had been left far behind. Among the thirty contributors to this work was the German philologist C. A. F. Mahn, who corrected and supplied the etymologies. The vocabulary in this work was estimated to be 114,000 words. Important revisions of this edition were the 1879 and the 1884 issues. The former contained a pronouncing biographical dictionary and the latter a pronouncing gazetteer.

In 1890, the second completely revised edition came out. In this edition the title was changed to the *International Dictionary*. Again Noah Porter was the editor and more than 175,000 words were entered. In the 1900 issue of this edition a supplement of new words appeared. In 1909 the date of the third complete revision, the title was changed to *The New International*. The work was under the direction of Dr. William Harris, assisted by

[66] The illustrations occupy a separate section, pp. 83–163.
[67] Scudder, *Noah Webster* (1882), p. 244.

F. Sturgis Allen and more than sixty office editors and specialists in various fields. The vocabulary in this work was increased to 400,000 words. The fourth and last edition, *Webster's New International Dictionary of the English Language* (2d ed., 1934), is a complete revision which was made under the editorship of William Allan Neilson, assisted by more than 250 editorial workers. The vocabulary contains more than 600,000 words. This monumental work with all the effort that went into its making is a far cry from the one-man dictionary published by Noah Webster in 1828. Yet his is the solid foundation upon which this great work rests. When one delves beneath superficial exteriors it is surprising how much of the first work really remains.

Of the five main functions of the dictionary, that is, to give spellings, indicate pronunciations, define words, and give etymologies and illustrations,[68] our concern in this chapter is with the last three, since the first two are considered at length in the chapter on language reform. Above all, Webster excelled in his definitions. "Webster," says Murray, "was a great man, a born definer of words; he was fired with the idea that America ought to have a dictionary of its own form of English, independent of British usage, and he produced a work of great originality and value. Unfortunately, like many other clever men, he had the notion that derivations can be elaborated from one's own consciousness as well as definitons, and he included in his work so-called 'etymologies' of this sort." [69]

This estimate with regard to his definitions is in general agreement with the bulk of criticism made by other scholars. Webster himself considered his definitions, along with the copious vocabulary, the great and substantial merit of the work.[70] Referring to variations in meanings of words, he declared that "between thirty and forty thousand definitions are contained in this work,

[68] For extent to which these features were present in the works of *Webster and his predecessors*, see Appendix IV, p. 312.

[69] Murray, *Evolution of English Lexicography* (1900), p. 43. The Clarendon Press.

[70] Preface to *American Dictionary*, 1828, n. p.

which are not known to exist in any other." [71] Generally speaking, the language in his definitions is plainer than that used by the high-gaited Johnson, whose definitions, Webster contended, were often mere explanations. He held the ideal that the primitive meaning of a word should be given first and the later meanings should be arranged in historic and chronological order, but he often deviated from that order. Definitions are illustrated by extracts from English and American authors, although at times only the name of the author is given and the extract is omitted.[72]

Of all the lines of endeavor that go into the making of a dictionary, Webster's efforts in the field of etymology were perhaps the most extended and surely of the least value.

It was an idle pedantry [says Scudder], which made him marshal an imposing array of words from Oriental languages; he was on the right track when he sought for a common ground upon which Indo-European languages could meet, but he lacked that essential knowledge of grammatical forms, without which knowledge of the vocabulary is liable to be misleading.[73]

"The fundamental weakness of Webster's work in etymology lay in his reliance upon external likenesses and the limitation of his knowledge to mere vocabularies." [74] As an example of Webster's penchant for seeing affinities, the word "Diana," suggested to him the Celtic word *dan* or *dian,* meaning swift, eager, strong, and he immediately saw an affinity. In the case of "Minerva," he explained, the first syllable contains the element of *manus,* hand, and of "mind." The last syllable corresponds to German *arbeit,* Dutch *arbeid*—labor, work. Minerva, he explained, was the goddess of wisdom and arts. "The sense of μενος would give one of her characteristics and *manus* the other; but which is the true word, I do not know." [75] Webster's etymologies are usually very brief and for many words they were not given.

[71] *Loc. cit.*

[72] See Advertisement, n. p. For further discussion of Webster's illustrations, see p. 188.

[73] *Noah Webster* (1882), p. 250.

[74] Mathews, *op. cit.,* p. 42.

[75] *American Dictionary* (1828), Introduction, n. p.

Most of his etymologies, then, were incorrect, but it is usually agreed that more of his were correct than were those of the lexicographers who had preceded him.[76] In later editions Webster's etymologies have been "cleared out en mass" and "the last edition of Webster, the *International* is perhaps the best of one-volume dictionaries.".[77] Wolff deplores the fact that Webster apparently had not come into contact with the "literati," who would have enabled him to correct his work by means of the comparative method which had been elaborated in Germany. "It was not until 1833 that Gessner Harrison received his material upon it from George Long; not until 1839 that Salisbury brought it to Yale, where Webster might have had a chance to hear of it." [78]

Webster's Dictionary Has Been Used Widely in the Schools and Has Influenced Lexicography in Both England and America

ON THE title-page to *An American Dictionary* (1828), Webster quotes from the *Rambler:* "He that wishes to be counted among the benefactors of posterity must add, by his own toil, to the acquisition of his ancestors." What then was Webster's achievement in the field of dictionary making—how did he influence other compilers and instruction in the schools? In the late forties and early fifties of the nineteenth century, a number of state legislatures appropriated funds for libraries in the country and village schools. One of the books widely adopted and placed in these libraries was the 1847 edition of Webster's unabridged *American Dictionary.*[79] In Massachusetts, in spite of the fact that

[76] Mathews, *op. cit.*, p. 42.
[77] Murray, *Evolution of English Lexicographers* (1900), p. 44. The Clarendon Press.
[78] Samuel Lee Wolff, "Scholars," *Cambridge History of American Literature* (1931), IV, 477. The Macmillan Company.
[79] The price of this edition was $6. The Merriam Company made a special price of $4 to states buying in large quantities. For the procedure by which the dictionary was adopted in New York State, see *New York Senate Documents,* III, Nos. 65–97.

each district was given the privilege of choosing the kind of dictionary it wanted and the fact that a strong feeling existed in favor of Worcester's dictionary,[80] 3,132 copies of Webster and 112 copies of Worcester were chosen. Likewise, New York State bought between nine and ten thousand copies of Webster's.[81] Records show that other states soon followed suit;[82] thus "Webster-on-a-bridge Dictionary," as its opponents facetiously referred to it, became established, and the numerous editions and issues that have since been published bear testimony of the extent to which it has been used.

From various sources we are able to piece together the manner in which the dictionary was used in the early days of the republic. The truth of the matter probably is that it was used as a reference book very much as it is today, but again many "random shots and erratic efforts" were made in an effort to put it to its best use.

In Webster's Part II (1783) he advised that children use "Entick's or Perry's pocket Dictionary, which distinguishes the parts of speech," as an aid in parsing.[83] In the use of the dictionary great stress was again placed on memory. Commenting on defective methods of teaching reading, spelling, and defining, "a Teacher" says that "the common mode of teaching the definition of words is also very objectionable; the pupil is obliged to commit to memory the definitions of a certain number of isolated and unconnected words in a dictionary; this is a mere exertion of the memory and that is a tedious, and often a most fruitless labor . . ."[84]

In the opinion of this writer and most educators of the day it is important that the faculties of the mind be exercised. "By

[80] Loc. cit.
[81] "Worcester's Dictionary Not a Standard Authority" (March, 1854), in Noah Webster, a bound volume of pamphlets in Yale University Library. These pamphlets were in the main published by the rival publishers of Webster and Worcester dictionaries, during the "War of the Dictionaries." Other authorities indicate that these figures are approximately correct.
[82] District School Journal of the State of New York, XII (Feb., 1852), 160.
[83] Page 87.
[84] American Journal of Education, I (1826), 318.

learning the definitions," it was pointed out, "the minds of the scholars are exercised, and the knowledge of language increased." In a review of Aaron Ely's *A School Dictionary of Selected Words according to the Orthography of Webster* . . . (1830), it is stated that the principal object of the work is to present to the pupils a *selection* of words to be committed to memory. The reviewer, however, expresses some doubt as to the expediency of teaching definitions in that way, a method extensively practiced, but grants that Ely's selection must greatly promote the object aimed at.[85]

In answer to the question "How can the dictionary be used in a school to the best advantage?" Noah Porter, who was editor of the 1864 edition of *An American Dictionary,* and who was of course solicitous that the sales of this dictionary be increased, recommended that Webster's large dictionary should lie upon the teacher's desk, "ready to answer any question that is forced upon its notice about spelling, pronunciation, derivation, and meaning of hard words which come up in the recitation." One of the smaller dictionaries should be in the hands of every scholar, he recommends further.[86]

Some teachers, he reports, "require of their classes in spelling to give the definition of a few words in every lesson. Some require very young children, as soon as they are old enough to write, to write out definitions in a copy book and to learn these definitions by heart. The young scholar finds the *definition* to be nearly if not quite as unintelligible as the word itself, and both are often words, words, and hard words too, *dictionary words* as they are

[85] *American Journal of Education,* New Series, I (1830), 472.
[86] In 1852 Webster's spelling book and dictionaries were advertised as "forming a complete series and affording a National Standard, thus securing uniformity of orthography and Pronunciation for the millions that are to constitute this vast republic." The series consisted of these titles:

Elementary Spelling Book	10 cents
Primary School Dictionary	45 cents
High School Dictionary	83 cents
Academic Dictionary	$1.25
Webster's University Dictionary, University Edition	$1.75
Webster's Quarto Dictionary, The American Dictionary	$6.00

District School Journal of State of New York, XII (1852), vi.

sometimes expressively termed." This method he finds objectionable because a mature mind is required to take an interest in the dictionary and special efforts are needed to make study pleasant and profitable.

To this end he made several suggestions. Believing, as do educators today, that a word separated from its connection, or rows of words looked up in a dictionary from the columns of a spelling book can never excite an interest, he says that the dictionary should teach scholars how to use words as they occur in sentences. One or two words a day should be studied. The pupil should write as many sentences using the word as there are definitions, sometimes with and sometimes without preparation. "If scholars reflect on the words which they use," he reasons, "they must learn to think." Then, too, he concludes, pupils should study the history of words from the dictionary, supplemented by the teacher's knowledge, which he may gain from Trench.[87]

In the many references to the uses to which the dictionary was or could be put, much is made of its use as a reference book. In Massachusetts, it was reported, wherever the dictionary "was enthroned in a district or village schoolhouse, not only the pupils and teacher, but the parents and citizens appealed to it to settle questions in orthoëpy and definitions, and thus it contributed to educate the entire community." [88]

In 1872, while Webster's grandson Gordon Lester Ford was business manager of the *New York Tribune,* a business arrangement was entered into between the *Tribune* and the Merriam Company whereby Webster's dictionary was offered as a premium to subscribers. This arrangement resulted in the placing of the dictionary in many farm and village homes. It did much to make the name of Webster a household word and the dictionary a household necessity.[89]

The appearance of Webster's *An American Dictionary* and the success that ensued later in the century is an example of success

[87] *Connecticut Common School Journal*, II (1854), 215.
[88] *New York Senate Documents*, III, Nos. 65–97.
[89] Ford, *Notes*, II, 396.

being reached by what seems inadequate means when the times are favorable.[90] The ineffectiveness of English lexicography after Johnson left a broad opportunity for American enthusiasm, talent, and industry. "In the seventy years following the first publication of Johnson's dictionary nothing had appeared which embodied a general improvement of that work . . . Webster's *American Dictionary* had so much in it that was original that it might properly be regarded as a new dictionary. . . ."[91] Webster's and Worcester's dictionaries "became a sort of mine for British lexicography to exploit—the more valuable, because their defintions of the words belonging to the arts and sciences were to a large extent the definitions of eminent experts."[92]

This supremacy, however, did not pass unchallenged. Writing in the *Quarterly Review*,[93] William Gifford declared that his expectations of the *American Dictionary*, which had been aroused by the praise that had been showered on the work, particularly by Americans, had in a great measure been disappointed. He admitted that the author had shown great industry and that he had added many words and corrected many errors, especially in terms relating to modern science. But his attempt to give derivations and primary meaning of words, he insisted, was throughout conducted on perverse and erroneous principles and must be considered a failure. "There is everywhere," he declared, "a great parade of erudition and a great lack of real knowledge; in short we do not recollect ever to have witnessed in the same compass a greater number of crudities and errors or more pains taken to so little purpose."

There were, however, those in England who recognized the merit of the work. "That the *best* dictionary of our language which has yet appeared should have been written by an American, is not to the credit of the Father land," declared the Reverend Angel James.[94] In 1847 John Craig pointed out that

[90] R. O. Williams, *Our Dictionaries* (1890), p. 31.
[91] *Ibid.*
[92] *Ibid.*
[93] Vol. LIV (1835), 304–5.
[94] *New York Senate Documents*, 1851, III, Nos. 65–97.

Webster's was the first English dictionary possessing at once etymological, technical, and pronouncing features.[95] Craig's comments show that the New England schoolmaster was coming into recognition among the English lexicographers and that the Johnsonian tradition of supremacy was being questioned. Although Craig criticized Webster's treatment of pronunciation, he admitted that insofar as his own work might be worthy of approbation, much of the merit was due to the elaborate researches of that distinguished philologist. In 1850 John Ogilvie wrote in the Preface to his dictionary, "Webster's dictionary, which forms the basis of the present work, is acknowledged both in this country and in America to be not only superior to either of the two former [Johnson and Richardson] but to every other dictionary hitherto published." In addition to the definitions and etymologies, Ogilvie included encyclopedic information concerned with science, art, and literature, "so that the charge usually preferred against English dictionaries, namely, that they furnish but *dry sort of reading,* will not apply to this dictionary." [96]

An examination of the many lesser dictionaries now in use or of the card catalogue of a large library reveals a surprisingly large number of dictionaries that claim to be based on Webster's. Among the dictionaries catalogued under "Webster" in the Library of Congress we find a whole bevy of "Webster's," qualified by such adjectives as "diamond," "excelsior," "supreme," "common-sense," "little gem," "monarch," "reliable," "sterling," "universal," "royal," "vest pocket," and so forth. Among the better-known dictionaries which have been based directly or indirectly, wholly or in part, on Webster are such works as Collier's, Winston's, Laird and Lee's, and such larger works as *The Imperial*[97] and *The Century* dictionaries.[98] The best-known of the Webster abridgments which are of legitimate

[95] John Craig, *A New Universal Etymological, Technological, and Pronouncing Dictionary* (2d ed., 1852), p. vii.
[96] John Ogilvie, *The Imperial Dictionary* (1853), I, ii.
[97] *Ibid.,* I, v.
[98] See Copyright Notice, *Century Dictionary* (1913).

apostolic succession include Merriam's *Secondary-School Dictionary* and Webster's *Collegiate Dictionary*.

Summary and Conclusions

BEFORE Webster published his first dictionary in 1806, many of the features of the modern dictionary had already been developed through the glosses and vocabularies, the Latin-English and the English-Latin dictionaries, and finally the English dictionaries of the sixteenth, seventeenth, and eighteenth cenuries. Webster had been preceded in America by such compilers as Elliott, Johnson, and Alexander. In 1807, Webster's 1806 dictionary was condensed and published as a school dictionary. A second edition was published in 1817.

Webster spent twenty years at incessant toil and privation while he compiled his *An American Dictionary*, which he published in 1828. During this time he supported his family on the royalties from his spelling book.

Of the five principal lines of endeavor that go to make up a dictionary, those having to do with orthography, pronunciation, definition, etymology, and illustration, Webster excelled in definition. His protracted efforts in the field of etymology were perhaps of the least value.

Excepting the abridgment of *An American Dictionary* made by Worcester in 1829 and sold to Goodrich, none of Webster's dictionaries were popular or profitable during his lifetime. Two circumstances which were instrumental in bringing about a wider use of later editions were the state adoptions of the dictionary for use in the common schools (c. 1850) and the giving of the work as a premium with the *New York Tribune* (c. 1872). The capital and the business acumen employed by the G. & C. Merriam Company, who bought the rights in 1843, were also of great importance in extending the work to a wider public.

In early days the dictionary was probably used very much as it is today, as a reference book in connection with the spelling, reading, and grammar lessons. As it contained encyclopedic material and as books were scarce in the community, it was consulted by the adults of the district. Many erratic efforts were made, however, to devise plans whereby the book could be put to its best use in the schools.

The publication of Webster's and Worcester's dictionaries caused leadership in lexicography to pass from England to the United States. During a period of more than thirty years, the two compilers and their publishers, their friends and enemies, engaged in the "war of the dictionaries." As the conflict involved the question of language reform, a subject preserved for later chapters, a great interest was taken in the English language, and for this reason the day was no doubt hastened when English was to be given a more prominent place in the school curriculum.

VII

LANGUAGE REFORM

To DIFFUSE an uniformity and purity of language in America, to destroy the provincial prejudices that originate in the trifling differences of dialect and produce reciprocal ridicule, to promote the interest of literature and the harmony of the United States, is the most earnest wish of the author, and it is his highest ambition to deserve the approbation and encouragement of his countrymen.[1]

WEBSTER'S activities directed toward language reform in America included the fields of grammar[2] and literature,[3] as well as those of pronunciation and spelling. It was, however, only in the fields of pronunciation and spelling that his efforts, as well as the criticism which ensued, reached a sizable magnitude.

So numerous were Webster's pronouncements on the subject of general linguistics and so many and varied were the editions of his spellers and dictionaries that it is difficult to bring a discussion of his activities in behalf of language reform within the confines of one chapter. There is little he said and did that lends itself to a brief discussion.[4] The subject of language reform obviously belongs in the field of linguistic study rather than in that of education; yet it was largely in his textbooks and his dictionaries that he waged a war against the language as spoken and written. Time after time he showed in his writings that he looked to the schools for aid in the bringing about of his proposed reforms.

In the Preface of his 1783 speller, he declared that "nothing but the establishment of schools and some uniformity in the use of books can annihilate differences in speaking," and that "the want of some standard in schools has occasioned a great variety of dialects in Great Britain and of course in America." In the

[1] *The American Spelling Book* (1787), p. viii.
[2] See chap. IV.
[3] See chap. V.
[4] M. M. Mathews, *Beginnings of American English* (1931), p. 44. University of Chicago Press.

preface to his first school dictionary (1807)[5] he stated that "It is very desirable that a uniform orthography may prevail among the citizens of the United States. This can never be the case, while they use a variety of English books, which do not agree in spelling and pronunciation."

Webster Considered the Anomalies of the Language a Bar to the Learning and Use of English

AN EXPOSITION of all the contradictions, complexities, and tortuosities in the formation of our language [declared Horace Mann in 1842], can never be given by any finite mind. It is one immense shuffle and prevarication . . . it is almost true, that what rules there are, are exceptions, and that the anomalies tend toward a law, not from one.

Commenting on the numerous sounds of the letters, he explained further:

In almost every line we read, these letters reappear several times; but however short their exit from the stage, they reenter in a changed dress. Proteus is held a proverb of changeableness, but compared with these he was no turncoat, but a staid, uniform personage. . . .
"Though the tough cough and hiccough plough me through,
   O'er life's dark lough, I still my way pursue.[6]

"English is the most bewept of tongues," says Ayres. "From the days of Caxton its uncertain syntax, its perplexing variety of forms, its exotic and luxuriant vocabulary have brought distress to most of those who have taken thought of it."[7] "English spelling is not only the despair of millions of adults as well as children," comments J. R. Aiken, "but in many of its aspects our orthography has come actually to constitute a bar to the easy use of English."[8] In her recent study, Dr. Aiken has listed 46

[5] *A Dictionary of the English Language; Compiled for the Use of Common Schools in the United States* (1807), p. iv. See pp. 224 f.

[6] *Common School Journal*, IV (1842), 9 ff.

[7] Harry Morgan Ayres, *Cambridge History of American Literature* (1931), IV, 554. The Macmillan Company.

[8] Janet Ranken Aiken, *English Present and Past* (1930), p. 191. The Ronald Press Company, Publishers.

English sounds which have a total of at least 456 spellings, an average of approximately ten spellings for each sound.[9]

If, then, the state of the English language is of so much concern to philologists today when "modern spelling appears regular and orderly" compared to that of earlier times and when the "writing and spelling of English have long been fixed,"[10] its vagaries must have been the despair of early philologists like Webster who worked alone without the aid of the science of philology as it is developed today to guide them.

As early as A. D. 1200, the author of *Ormulum,* realizing the chaotic condition of the language, invented a system of phonetic spelling.[11] From that day to the present time it has been the concern of scores of people that the English language be reduced to order and regularity.[12] That progress in the attempt to regularize spelling was made in the seventeenth century is well illustrated by Shakespeare's Folios in that the spelling in the 1664 and 1685 works is more regular than in those of 1623 and 1632. During the eighteenth century, especially after the publication of Johnson's dictionary in 1755, there were laid down many hard and fast rules which still survive.[13]

The language spoken and written by the Puritans and Pilgrims presented numerous examples of anomaly in spelling and pronunciation. To make matters worse, they altered and expanded their common stock of words in order to meet the needs of their new life. They had no thought of amending or improving or reforming the language. The vegetable and animal life, for example, presented features that were in some respects novel to the new comers.[14] Although there were educated ministers in

[9] *Ibid.,* pp. 202 ff.

[10] Mathews, *Survey of English Dictionaries* (1933), p. 42. The Clarendon Press.

[11] *Encyclopaedia Britannica* (1911), XX, 293 f.

[12] For a discussion of English reformers before Webster's day, such as Cheke, Smith, Hart, Wilkins, etc., see Richard G. White's *Every Day English* (1880), p. 152; of American nineteenth century reformers, see George Philip Krapp's *The English Language in America* (1925), I, 330.

[13] Henry Louis Mencken, *The American Language* (1921), p. 228. Alfred A. Knopf, Inc.

[14] Mathews, *The Beginnings of American English* (1931), p. 4. The University of Chicago Press.

the early colonies, most of the people were from humbler walks of life, people who had not had the formal school training which fitted them for the religious and governmental duties incumbent upon the members of the communities that were established.[15] Consequently the records are replete with phonetic spellings which added to the general confusion of the English tongue.[16]

Of the barbarous state of the English language Webster was keenly aware when he compiled his first speller at the age of twenty-three:

> The sounds of our letters are more capricious and irregular than those of any alphabet with which we are acquainted. Several of our vowels have four or five different sounds, and the same sounds are often expressed by five, six or seven different characters. The case is much the same with our consonants; and these different sounds have no marks of distinction. How would a child or a foreigner learn the different sounds of *o* in these words, *rove, move, dove,* or of *oo* in *poor, door?* Or that *a, ai, ei,* and *e,* have precisely the same sound in these words, *bare, laid, vein, there?* Yet these and fifty other irregularities have passed unnoticed by authors of Spelling Books and Dictionaries. They study the language enough to find the difficulties of it—they tell us that it is to be learnt only by the ear—they lament the disorder and dismiss it without a remedy.
>
> The consequence is, that few attempts have been made to reduce our language to rules, and expurge the corruptions that ignorance and caprice, unguided by any standard, must necessarily introduce. It is but a short time since we have had a grammar of our own tongue, formed upon the true principles of its Saxon original: And those who have given us the most perfect systems, have confined themselves chiefly to the two last branches of grammar, analogy and syntax. In the two first, Orthography and Prosody, that is the spelling and pronunciation of words, we have no guide, or none but such as lead into innumerable errors. The want of some standard in schools has occasioned a great variety of dialects in Great Britain, and of course, in America. Every county in England, every state in America and almost every town in each State, has some peculiarities in pronunciation which are equally erroneous and disagreeable to its neighbors.

[15] *Loc. cit.,* p. 4.

[16] See *ibid.,* p. 5, for list of spellings taken from early New Haven records.

National Sentiment Demanded that America Be Free from England Culturally as Well as Politically

AT THE close of the war, differences between America and England were sharply accentuated, each country laying claim to superiority. Among the differences to be noted was that which existed in the language spoken in the two countries. In consequence a hue and cry was raised which was out of all proportion to the slight difference which actually existed.[17]

Of the spirit of his time and of the newborn nation, Webster stands to a unique degree as a symbol.[18] The growing consciousness of Americanism was more rampant in him than in any of his contemporaries.[19] In the Preface to his 1783 spelling book, he announced, "The author wishes to promote the honour and prosperity of the confederated republics of America and cheerfully throws his mite into the common treasure of patriotic exertion." Electrified by the patriotic fervor of his age and the belief in the grand future of America, Webster declared that

This country must in some future time be as distinguished by the superiority of her literary improvements as she is already by the liberality of her civil and ecclesiastical constitutions. Europe is grown old in folly, corruption and tyranny—in that country laws are perverted, manners are licentious, literature is declining and human nature is debased.[20]

Deploring the fact that "in many parts of America, people at present attempt to copy the English phrases and pronunciation," [21] he pointed out that

Great Britain, whose children we are, and whose language we speak, should no longer by our standard . . .[22] [since the] English themselves have no standard of pronunciation, nor can they ever have one

---

[17] Mathews, *Beginnings of American English* (1931), p. 10. The University of Chicago Press.

[18] C. E. M. Winslow, "The Epidemiology of Noah Webster, *Transactions of the Connecticut Academy of Arts and Sciences*, XXXII (1934), 35.

[19] Scudder, *Noah Webster* (1882), pp. 46 f. Houghton Mifflin Company.

[20] *Grammatical Institute*, Part I (1783), 14.

[21] *Dissertations on the English Language* (1789), p. 22.

[22] *Ibid.*, p. 31.

---

on the plan I propose. The authors, who have attempted to give us a standard, make the Court and stage in London the sole criterion of propriety in speaking. An attempt to establish a standard on this foundation is both unjust and idle. It is unjust, because it is abridging a nation of its rights.[23]

After the Revolutionary War there was much discussion as to whether the colonies could or even should be held together. "We must, indeed, all hang together," declared Franklin in Independence Hall, or "most assuredly we shall all hang separately." Webster looked upon a uniform language as a tie that would further political and social harmony.[24] Should the confederation become disrupted, even then a uniform speech among the parts would be to the advantage of all concerned.[25]

Not being familiar with the laws of linguistic change, Webster believed that English in America might be mechanically reduced to a fixed standard as immutable as he supposed to have been the case with Arabic, Greek, and Latin.[26]

At the time Webster wrote his *Dissertations* in 1789, he had held the erroneous belief that "when a language has arrived at a certain stage of improvement, it must be stationary or become retrograde"; [27] that like a plant it has its periods of growth, flowering, fruition and then decay. He believed that this period of linguistic perfection began in England with the reign of Queen Elizabeth, came to full flower in the reign of Queen Anne, and ended with that of George II, and he deplored the fact that the language had not been "fixed" before later men, such as Garrick, Johnson, Gibbon, and their imitators, had a chance to corrupt it.

It is interesting to note that in Webster's opinion

The best models of purity and elegance, are the works of Sir William Temple, Dr. Middleton, Lord Bolingbroke, Mr. Addison,

[23] *Loc. cit.*, p. 24.
[24] *Ibid.*, p. 20.
[25] *Ibid.*, p. 30.
[26] "Reply to Dilworth's Ghost," *Connecticut Journal*, December 15, 1784.
[27] *Dissertations on the English Language* (1789), p. 30. Webster cites Condillac, *Origin of Human Knowledge*, Part II, as the source of his authority.

and Dean Swift. But a little inferior to these, are the writings of Mr. Pope, Sir Richard Steele, Dr. Arbuthnot, with some of their contemporaries.[28]

On examining the language and comparing the practice of speaking among the yeomanry of this country with the style of Shakespeare and Addison [he declared], I am constrained to declare that the people of America, in particular the English descendants, speak the most *pure English* now known in the world.[29]

This, then, Elizabethan and Augustan English, but particularly the latter, which was to be found in its purest form in America, uncorrupted by European influences nor weakened by its own decrepitude, was to be the uniform American speech, which, it was reasoned, should be fixed before decay set in.

Webster did not stand alone in advocating a reform of the English language. According to several authorities, some enthusiastic patriots after the Revolution went to the excess of advocating "the abrogation of English in 'these states' and the invention and adoption of a new language . . ."[30] This story, which has the earmarks of the apocryphal, has several versions. The Gifford version is that "One person indeed had recommended the adoption of the Hebrew, as being ready made to their hands, and considering the Americans, no doubt, as the 'chosen people' of the new world."[31] According to the Bristed version, a legislator seriously proposed that the young republic should complete its independence by adopting a different language from that of the mother country, "the Greek for instance," which proposition was summarily extinguished by a suggestion of a fellow representative that "it would be more convenient for us to keep the language as it was, and *make the English speak*

[28] *Ibid.*, pp. 30 ff. "I consider Dr. Franklin and Dr. Witherspoon as the two best writers in America. The words they use, and their arrangement, appear to flow spontaneously from their manner of thinking . . . the two American writers have bestowed their labor upon ideas, and the English historians [Gibbon and Gillies] upon *words.*"—*Dissertations*, p. 33.

[29] *Dissertations*, p. 288.

[30] *Cambridge History of American Literature* (1927), I, vi. The Macmillan Company.

[31] *The Quarterly Review*, X (January, 1814), 528.

Greek." [32] Whether this story is true or not, it is in keeping with the temper of the times. Webster, however, at no time expressed a desire to abandon the English language, but desired to foster the language as it was spoken in America, arguing, as shall be shown, that the English in America was purer than that spoken in England.

Other records and facts serve to illustrate the temper of the time with regard to language reform. In 1774, an American, writing in the *Royal American Magazine* says,

The English language has been greatly improved in Britain within a century, but its highest perfection with every other branch of human knowledge is perhaps reserved for the land of light and freedom. As the people through this extensive country will speak English, their advantages for polishing their language will be great, and vastly superior to what the people of England ever enjoyed . . .[33]

This writer urged that a society for perfecting the English language should be formed.

Along with the agitation for an American university [34] was much talk of an American academy, which, like the *Academie française* and the *Academia della crusca,* would have as its object the purification of the language.

On September 5, 1780, John Adams addressed a letter to Congress advising the establishment of an "American Academy for refining, improving, and ascertaining the English language." [35] That Webster entertained hopes that such an academy would be established is shown by a letter written to his publishers:

Should my health continue, this work [*An American Dictionary*], the fruit of twenty years labor will be offered to the public. Whether it will be an improvement on the best English dictionaries, whether it will be subjected to the revision of an Academy of literary men and by them approved as a standard work; or whether the labor of

[32] Charles Astor Bristed, "The English Language in America," *Cambridge Essays* (1855), p. 75.

[33] January, 1774, pp. 6f.

[34] See Slosson, "The American Spirit in Education," *The Chronicles of America,* XXXIII (1921), 94 ff. Copyright by Yale University Press.

[35] Charles Francis Adams, *The Works of John Adams* (1852), VII, 249.

a large portion of my life and an expenditure of $30,000 of my private property are to be thrown away—I do not presume to decide.[36]

The extent to which the establishment of an American language was held by some prominent men to be of importance is well illustrated by Samuel L. Mitchill's attempt to supply a generic name for the United States. Without such a name, he wrote Webster, "we cannot be completely national, nor properly express national feelings, concerns, relations of any kind." To supply this need he proposed the adoption of the radical word, "Fredon," along with its derivatives, "Fredonia," "Fredonian," "Frede," and "Fredish." Mitchill asked Webster's co-operation in giving the word publicity, adding that "By means of the elementary books which you edit and own, much might be done in diffusing it among the people."[37] The word, however, did not appear in Webster's texts.

Thomas Jefferson, who as a rule was not sympathetic toward the many activities of the "pedagogue" Webster, has this to say of the American language: "The new circumstances under which we are placed, call for new words, new phrases, and for the transfer of old words to new objects. An American dialect will therefore be formed."[38] Jefferson was one of the first in this country to advocate the study of Anglo-Saxon.[39] It was through his influence that this language was introduced in the University of Virginia in 1818.

From an early period of my studies [he wrote], indeed, I have been sensible of the importance of making it a part of the regular education of our youth.[40] He held that the study of Anglo-Saxon would "recruit and renovate the vigor of the English language, too much impaired by the neglect of its ancient constitution and dialects."[41]

[36] Webster MSS. Letter to Hudson and Co., dated "Amherst, September 22, 1820."

[37] Webster MSS, letter dated "New York, April 23, 1803." See Joseph Jones's "Hail Fredonia," *American Speech*, IX (1934), 12.

[38] Letter to John Waldo, dated "Monticello, August 16, 1813." Albert Ellery Bergh's *Writings of Thomas Jefferson* (1904), XIII, 340.

[39] *Ibid.*, "Introductory Note," XVIII, 360.

[40] *Ibid.*, Postscript (1825) to *Essays on Anglo-Saxon* (1798), p. 385.

[41] *Ibid.*, p. 391.

Beginning with the publication of the 1806 dictionary, Webster, from time to time, with varying degrees of consistency, retracted some of his former statements concerning "standard" speech and a "fixed" state of the language. In the Preface to this work, he declared that the more he reflected upon the subject of agreement on a standard speech, the more he was convinced that a living language admits of no fixed state nor of any certain standard of pronunciation by which even the learned in general will consent to be governed.[42]

Thus the English, like every living language, is in a state of progression, as rapid now as at any former period; even more rapid, than before the great Dr. Johnson "flattered himself that he might fix the language and put a stop to alterations"—an idea as chimerical as that of Sheridan and Walker who have attempted to make the mouthing enunciation of the stage, a fixed standard of national pronunciation.[43]

Generally speaking, then, after the publication of the *Compendious Dictionary* (1806), when Webster became interested more and more in questions of philology, the almost angry championship of the spread-eagle doctrine and Federal English indulged in former years was on the wane. Allowances must be made of course for an occasional outburst, as in his letter to Pickering in 1817 on the subject of Americanisms. By 1807 he looked upon differences between the American and English speech no longer as a political and cultural necessity to be fostered, but as a natural development. "It is a fact," he stated, "that two nations proceeding from the same ancestors cannot long preserve a perfect sameness of language." [44]

In 1824, when his dictionary was nearing completion, he went to Europe, first to France and then to England. While at Cambridge, England, Webster wrote the Reverend Samuel Lee:[45]

[42] Pages x and xi.
[43] *Ibid.,* p. xix.
[44] *A Dictionary of the English Language for the Use of Common Schools* (1807), p. iii.
[45] Letter dated "Decr. 20th, 1824." A copy was sent to Oxford but no answer was received.

The English language is the language of the United States; and it is desirable that as far as the people have the same things and the same ideas, the words to express them should be the same . . . It is therefore important that its principles should be adjusted and uniformity of spelling and pronunciation established and preserved as far as the nature of a living language will permit.

He pointed out, however, that there were many points in which "respectable men" are not agreed and suggested that a delegation of gentlemen from Oxford and Cambridge meet with him in an effort to adjust points of difference in the practice of the two countries, at which time he would lay before them some thoughts on a plan for correcting the evils of our irregular orthography without the use of any new letters. When his *American Dictionary* was published in 1828, after he had returned from England, he reported that "although the body of the language is the same [in America] as in England and it is desirable to perpetuate that sameness, yet some difference must exist . . ." [46]

This cooling of nationalistic fervor reached a new low point in Webster's letter presenting a copy of the 1841 edition of the *American Dictionary* to Queen Victoria. The dictionary may, he stated, "furnish evidence that the genuine descendants of English ancestors born on the west of the Atlantic, have not forgotten either the land or the language of their fathers." In his letter to Andrew Stevenson, who sent the dictionary to Lord Melbourne, who in turn presented the book to Her Majesty, Webster said, "Our common language is one of the ties that bind the two nations together; & I hope the work I have executed will manifest to the British nation that the Americans are not willing to suffer it to degenerate on this side of the Atlantic." [47]

After Webster's death, the Merriam Company sent the Queen a copy of the 1847 edition. In the elaborate presentation letter, the dictionary was called the "product of science and the arts, from the republic which is proud to call England her mother country . . . May these countries, which are united by common

[46] *American Dictionary* (1828), Introduction.
[47] Webster's MSS, Miscellaneous Papers. Letter dated "June 22, 1841."

language, be also one in the common purpose to make this language the bearer and symbol of Civilization, the Science, the Freedom, and the Christianity which they shall together diffuse throughout the earth." [48]

Reform Schemes Were Presented by Franklin and Others

ALTHOUGH, as we have seen, linguistic reform, prompted by a realization of the barbaric state of the language and by patriotic fervor, was in the post-Revolutionary air, "it is very likely that Webster's first impulse to reform our spelling was given by Dr. Franklin," [49] a man with whom Webster by natural temperament had much in common. When Webster visited Philadelphia in 1786 he gave his lecture on language. Franklin at once recognized in the youth a champion [50] for a scheme of language reform which he had vainly cherished and which, because of his advanced age, he would not be able to carry through to success. He explained to Webster his scheme for a new alphabet and a reformed mode of spelling. Because of the many sounds in the English language, Franklin realized that an alphabet which would represent all the sounds with regularity and precision would be of infinite value to those who speak and write the language. As early as 1768 he had elaborated his project and had type struck for six new symbols, which were to be used with the original Roman letters of the alphabet in a "new and independent way." [51]

Although young Webster knew of the fruitless attempts that had been made in England to reform the language,[52] he was

[48] Webster MSS, Yale University. Letter of presentation directed to Her Majesty, Queen Victoria.

[49] *Old South Leaflets*, VIII, 400.

[50] Writing to Webster in 1789, Franklin thanked him for a copy of *Dissertations on the English Language*, which Webster had dedicated to him. He also adds, "I cannot but applaud your zeal for preserving the Purity of our Language, both in its Expression and Pronunciation, and in correcting the popular errors several of our states are continually falling into with respect to both."

[51] John Biglow, *Franklin's Works*, IV, 198–209.

[52] See *Dissertations*, p. 394.

interested at once in Franklin's theories. He believed that
former attempts had "failed through some defect in the
plans proposed, or for reasons that do not exist in this country.[53] In the correspondence which ensued, "the young man
showed himself so ardent a disciple of the old as to win for
himself a certain place as the doctor's residuary legatee in
ideas." [54]

In 1786, Webster wrote to Franklin, [55] "Enclosed is a plan for
the purpose of reducing the orthography of the language to perfect regularity, with as few new characters and alterations of the
old ones as possible," requesting that should this or another plan
be adopted "your Excellency would lay it before Congress for
their critical consideration." This request illustrates the naïve
faith that people in the early years of the Republic had in Congress and the laws it enacted. "General Washington," continued
Webster, "has expressed the warmest wishes for the success of my
undertaking to refine the language and could he be acquainted
with the new alphabet proposed, would undoubtedly commence
its advocate."

In answer to this letter, Franklin replied that he had so much
to say on the subject that he wished to see and confer with Webster as further correspondence would mean an expenditure of
much time and money. "Our ideas," wrote Franklin, "are so
nearly similar that I make no doubt of our easily agreeing on a
Plan, and you may depend on the best Support I may be able to
give you as a part of your Institute." [56]

In the autumn of 1786 Webster went to Philadelphia, where,
as we have seen, he remained a year, during part of which time he
taught mathematics and English in the Episcopal Academy.
There is no special record which indicates what, if any, steps
were taken to carry out the doctor's project. Franklin died in
1790. Speaking of Franklin's proposed reform the same year,
Webster says:

[53] Letter from Webster to Franklin, dated "May 24, 1786."—Ford, *Notes*, II, 455.
[54] Horace Scudder, *Noah Webster* (1882), p. 191.
[55] Ford, *Notes*, II, 455.
[56] Ford, *Notes*, II, 257.

This indefatigable gentleman, amidst all his other employments, public and private, has compiled a Dictionary [57] on his scheme of a Reform, and procured types to be cast for printing it. He thinks himself too old to pursue the plan; but has honored me with the offer of the manuscript and types, and expressed a strong desire that I should undertake the task. Whether this project, so deeply interesting to this country, will ever be effected; or whether it will be defeated by indolence and prejudice, remains for my countryman to determine.[58]

Webster apparently made no definite attempt to reform the alphabet. He was, above all, a practical compiler—an editor of school textbooks. In Part I, *A Grammatical Institute,* the spelling was conventional and had this scheme for reformed spelling been successfully launched it would have rendered his textbooks obsolete,[59] a consideration, we are told, which stands in the way of a reformed alphabet today.[60]

In the Preface to his *Compendious Dictionary of the English Language,* 1806, Webster comments further on Franklin's plan:

I declined accepting his offer, on a full conviction of the utter impracticability, as well as unutility of the scheme. The orthography of our language might be rendered sufficiently regular, without a single new character by means of a few trifling alterations of the present characters and retrenching a few superfluous letters, the most of which are corruptions of the original words.

Again, in the *American Dictionary* (1828) similar views are stated:

"The mode of ascertaining the proper pronunciation of words by marks, points and trifling alteration of the present characters, seemed to be the only one which can be reduced to practice." "This was the characteristic contribution of the Webster dictionaries to the popular understanding of phonetics in America," says Krapp, "and remains

[57] Excepting the Table of the Reformed Alphabet and two six-line stanzas, and a letter written to Miss S——— of Kensington, England, and a reply from Miss S——— (see Biglowe, IV, iv, 198–209) all written in the reformed alphabet, we have no record today of Franklin's scheme.

[58] *Old South Leaflets,* VIII, 396.

[59] Krapp, *The English Language in America* (1925), I, 335. Modern Language Association.

[60] Aiken, *English Present and Past* (1930), p. 205. Ronald Press Company, Publishers.

today the chief obstacle in the way of securing a treatment of the subject in elementary books which is based on scientific principles." [61]

Between the years 1787 and 1789, while Webster was considering language reform with Franklin, he wrote a number of essays on moral, historical, political, and literary subjects, which he published in his *American Magazine* and other periodicals. In 1790, the year following the publication of the *Dissertations,* he published these essays under the title *A Collection of Essays and Fugitiv Writings.* In about a third of these essays, Webster introduced "a considerable change of spelling" by "way of experiment." An excerpt from the Preface will serve to illustrate:

Most of thoze peeces, which hav appeered before in periodicals, papers and Magazeens, were published with fictitious signatures; for I very erly discuvered that altho the name of an old and respectable karacter givs credit and consequence to hiz ritings, yet the name of a yung man iz often prejudicial to hiz performances. By conceeling my name, the opinions of men hav been prezerved from an undu bias arizing from personal prejudices, the faults of the ritings hav been detected, and their merits in public estimation ascertained.[62]

In spite of the fact that Webster's defenders explained that the spelling was an experiment, that his other writings were written with conventional spelling, and that the queer spellings represented a sort of phonographic system of orthography, introduced to gratify his aged friend, Franklin, who was then quite infirm, a system of orthography which they had mutually elaborated four years before,[63] this experiment served as a boomerang which frequently returned in later years to plague Webster and his adherents.

There were, however, those who were in sympathy with this system of spelling. During the same year that the *Essays* appeared, Daniel George wrote him an encouraging letter. "Go on, Sir," he wrote, "and make a thoro reform in our orthography, the irregularity of which, must give every American pain." At

[61] *Op. cit.,* I, 333.
[62] *Essays* (1790), p. ix.
[63] Y—E, *Webster's Orthography, a Reply to Dr. Noah Webster's Calumniators* (1857), p. 10.

the close of the letter he writes out the first paragraph of the Preface in Webster's *Essays* showing that he would go to even greater excesses than did Webster: "Dhe folloing Kollekshan Konsistz of Essayz and fugitiv pessiz, ritten at varius timez, on diferent Okkazhonz, az wil appeer by dhare datez and subjektz." [64]

In 1793 William Thornton, a Scotchman, published *Cadmus, or a Treatise on the Elements of Written Language*.[65] In this work he proposed a phonetic alphabet of thirty characters more radical than Franklin's. Addressing the "Citizens of North America," he declared, "You have corrected the dangerous doctrines of European powers, correct now the languages you have imported, for the oppressed of various nations knock at your gates and desire to be received as your brethren . . ." [66] *Di Amərikən languidj uil dəs bi az distint az də gəvərnmənt, fri from əəl foliz ov əntilosofikəl farən . . .*[67]

In 1808 Neef commendingly referred to Thornton's "rational way" of representing the language in writing and of the recognition he received by the Philosophical Society; but he deplored the fact that "learned wiseacres laughed at it, derided and ridiculed its author, and those who applauded an undertaking so necessary . . ." Continuing, he addressed the people of America,

Sole and only sovereigns of a free nation on this globe, with you it rests, on you it depends . . . to discard those nonsensical remains of an ignorant and barbarous antiquity . . . stretch forth your hands in your might, abolish the scourge and rack, and torture of harmless childhood. Give the world one great and useful lesson more, and let the instruction of infancy be conducted with the same wisdom that directs your government. Bid your legislators take up the all-important subject. Bid them chuse a few select but capable men; not those who are by privilege denominated learned, but men of sense, who understand your language.[68]

[64] Webster's unpublished MSS; letter dated "Portland, September 27, 1790."
[65] A Prize Dissertation, which was honored with the Magellanic Gold Medal, by the American Philosophical Society, January, 1793.
[66] *Cadmus* (1793), p. vii.
[67] *Ibid.*, p. vi.
[68] Joseph Neef, *Sketch of a Plan and Method of Education* (1808), p. 56.

Webster Proposed a Definite Plan
for Reform in 1789

ACCORDING to tradition, Webster began early in life to advocate a reform of the English language. Living in the home of Governor Smith while he taught at Sharon in 1781, he and the Governor, who was a purist of the old school, "fell afoul over such points as *musick and favour* (two of the trilogy in his cardinal reforms, the other being *theatre*), etc., on which thus early young Webster showed great depravity." [69]

Realizing that the psychological time for reform was at hand, Webster declared in 1789 that "men are prepared to receive improvements, which would be rejected by nations whose habits have not been shaken by similar events . . . Let us then seize the present moment, and establish a *national language,* as well as a national government." [70]

Webster first set forth a definite plan in "An Essay on the Necessity, Advantages and Practicability of Reforming the Mode of Spelling and of Rendering the Orthography of Words Correspondent to the Pronunciation." [71] The principal alterations which he deemed necessary to render English orthography sufficiently regular and easy were three in number:

I. "The omission of all superfluous silent letters; as *a* in *bread.* Thus *bread, head, give, breast, built, meant, realm, friend,* would be spelt *bred, hed, giv, brest, bilt, ment, relm, frend.*" [72]

II. "A substitution of a character that has a certain definite sound for one that is more vague and indeterminate." *Greef* should be substituted for "grief"; *kee* for "key"; *beleev* for "believe"; *laf* for "laugh"; *plow* for "plough"; *draft* for "draught,"

[69] Wilber Webster Judd, "Noah Webster," *Connecticut Magazine,* n. d., n. p. Book of pamphlets on education in Teachers College Library, Columbia University.

[70] *Dissertations* (1789), p. 394.

[71] *Ibid.* Most of the spellings proposed by Webster had been advocated by previous reformers. See Y–E., pp. 11 ff., and *Atlantic Monthly,* May, 1860, p. 632.

[72] It is interesting to note that none of these spellings found their way into Webster's dictionaries. Other similar words and their analogies were, however, given, such as *thred, fether, insted, bredth, welth, bild, thum, crum, mold, yest,* and so forth.

and so forth. "Character," "chorus," "cholic," and "architecture" should be written *karacter, korus, kolic, arkitecture.* "Machine," "chaise," "chevalier" should be written *masheen, shaze, shevaleer;* and "pique," "tour," "oblique" should be written *peek, toor, obleek.*[73]

III. A trifling alteration in a character or the addition of a point would distinguish different sounds, without the substitution of a new character. Thus a small stroke across *th* would distinguish one of its two sounds and a point over a vowel such as *à, ó,* or *ī,* might answer all the purposes of different letters. The two letters for the diphthong *ow* might be united with a small stroke or the letters united on one piece of metal.

The advantages to be derived from the proposed alterations, Webster claimed, are "numerous, great, and permanent." (1) The simplicity of the orthography would facilitate the learning of language, especially for children and foreigners.[74] (2) This plan would render the pronunciation of the language as uniform as in the spelling books; consequently all persons, of every rank, would speak with some degree of precision and uniformity, thus removing prejudice, and conciliating mutual affection and respect. (3) It would be a saving since it would reduce the number of letters to such an extent that one page in eighteen would be saved. (4) "A capital advantage of this reform," continued Webster, "would be, that it would make a difference between the English orthography and the American." This alteration would encourage the publication of books in the United States and would make it more or less necessary that the books be printed here. (5) Besides, over and above all these reasons, the *national language* which would result, would prove a bond of *national unity.* "Every engine should be employed to render the people of this country national . . ."

[73] With the exception of *plow, toor, and draft,* these spellings did not find their way into the dictionaries. Some words that are analogous to these did, however, appear: *frenzy, grotesk, groop, mask, bark* (for "barque"), *bolt* (for "boult"), and so forth.

[74] "These irregularities now operate against the propagation of the Christian religion."—*Letters to a Young Gentleman Beginning His Education* (1823), p. 39.

Following the exposition of his plan, Webster answered objections that he anticipated.

1. "This reform of the alphabet would oblige people to relearn the language . . ." To this objection he replied that the alterations he proposed are so few and so simple that an hour's attention would enable any person to read the new orthography with facility. The aged could read the new orthography, but would write the old.

2. "This reformation would injure the language by obscuring etymology." In a few instances, Webster admitted, etymologies might be obscured. On the other hand, it would restore the etymology of many. "The true meaning of words," he declared, "is that which a nation in general annex to them. Etymology therefore is of no use but to the learned, and for them it will still be preserved, so far as it is now understood, in dictionaries and other books that treat of this particular subject."

3. "The distinction between words of different meanings and similar sound would be destroyed." That distinction, he answered in the words of Franklin, is already destroyed in pronunciation. The word "knew" is not mistaken for "new," "peace" for "piece," "pray" for "prey" nor "flour" for "flower." The construction renders the distinction easy and intelligible, the moment the words of the sentence are heard. Then, too, he pointed out, there are many words in the language with the same orthography, such as "wind," "hail," "rear," and "lot." These have several distinct meanings, yet the spellings produce no sensible inconvenience.

4. "It is idle to conform the orthography of words to pronunciation, because the latter is continually changing." This was Dr. Johnson's contention. Webster declared that "if the pronunciation must vary, from age to age (and some trifling changes of language will always be taking place), common sense would dictate a correspondent change of spelling." This principle is illustrated by such words as *wol, ydilnesse,* and *eyen,* which are now spelled, according to the pronunciation, "well," "idleness," and "eyes." "On this principle of *fixing the orthography* while the

pronunciation is changing any spoken language must, in time, lose all relation to the *written language;* that is, the sounds of words would have no affinity with the letters that compose them . . . How much more rational is the opinion of Dr. Franklin," he concluded, "who says 'the orthography of our language began to be fixed too, soon.'"

Many of the reforms that Webster advocated in the *Dissertations* were abandoned before he published his first dictionary in 1806.[75] In this work, however, he took "independent Yankee ground." He set forth his views at length in the Preface and introduced many reforms in the vocabulary. The principles which guided him, according to his own avowal on numerous occasions, were "general practice" or "universal usage," "analogy" and "uniformity," and "etymology."

GENERAL PRACTICE OR UNIVERSAL USAGE

"The mode pursued in Great Britain of deciding questionable points by the practice of modern writers," Webster declared, "is liable to a serious objection, that it furnishes no standard of right and wrong. Authorities equally respectable for different modes of spelling may be cited without end, leaving the inquirer unsatisfied and the real truth undiscovered."[76] This condition of course did exist. In several of his dictionaries Webster published long lists of words showing the extent to which lexicographers differed in orthography and orthoëpy.[77] He found no difficulty in finding authority for usage in case he had a decided preference for a certain spelling or pronunciation. Since he was not aware of the nature of phonetic change[78] or refused to recognize its legitimacy, examples of usage could frequently be found in Chaucer, the eighteenth-century writers, or even among his American contemporaries. Thus, he reasoned, since

[75] H. L. Mencken, *The American Language* (1919), p. 251. Alfred A. Knopf, Inc.
[76] Noah Webster, *A Dictionary of the English Language* (1807), p. v.
[77] See *Compendious Dictionary* (1806), *American Dictionary* (1829); *ibid.*, 1841.
[78] J. H. Neumann, *American Pronunciation According to Noah Webster* (1925), p. 115.

Chaucer rhymed "lefe" with "defe," we have "almost conclusive evidence" that Chaucer pronounced the word *deef* and not *def;* [79] since Skelton rhymed "wound" and "ground," we have "presumptive proof" that the diphthong *ou* and not *oo* was sounded in "wound." [80]

ANALOGY AND UNIFORMITY

"Webster had taught himself some Anglo-Saxon, and, however imperfectly acquainted with it, had acquired a true and sensible feeling for the historical method and for the weight of analogy in deciding points where usage is doubtful." [81] He did not, however, understand the varied forces that occasionally neutralize what he thought to be an analogical pronunciation [82] or spelling. "Uniformity in the classes of words," he affirmed, "is the most convenient principle in the structure of the language and whatever arbitrary rules the learned may frame, the greatest part of men, will be governed by habits of uniformity." [83] For this reason we ought to write "defense," "pretense," "offense," "recompense" with an *s* instead of a *c,* since this spelling would be uniform with the derivatives, "defensive," "offensive," "pretension," "recompensing," and so forth.[84] Generally, Webster held every addition to the anomalies of the language to be a corruption and every elimination of them an improvement.

ETYMOLOGY

In deciding doubtful questions of usage where analogy failed to determine the correct form, Webster attempted to trace out the radical word and primitive spelling to ascertain the correct orthography. By this method he hoped to settle controversies and purify the language from many corruptions "introduced by

---

[79] *Dissertations* (1789), p. 26.
[80] *Ibid.,* p. 33.
[81] *Cambridge History of American Literature* (1931), IV, 475.
[82] J. H. Neumann, *American Pronunciation According to Noah Webster* (1925), p. 118.
[83] *A Compendious Dictionary of the English Language* (1806), p. ix.
[84] *A Series of Books for Systematic Instruction* (1831), p. 11.

ignorance or negligence under the Norman princes." [85] In his etymological spellings, as well as in those introduced on the basis of analogy, he generally guarded his reforms by consulting the usage of such authorities as "Newton, Camden, Thuyd, Davenant, Pope, Thomson, Gregory, Edwards, and a host of other writers." [86]

In comparison with modern philologists Webster of course was not equipped for the work he set out to do. But in consideration of the facts that the science of philology was in its infancy, that he was working alone away from centers of linguistic study, with scanty material at hand, his work was not hopelessly wrong nor entirely trivial.[87]

Disregarding centuries of usage and often basing his conclusions on surface likenesses [88] he introduced a number of etymological spellings, such as *ieland and iland* (from Sax. *ealand*), *wimen* (Sax. *wifman*), *chimist* (Fr. *chimie*), *hainous* (Fr. *haineux*), *melasses* (It. *melassa*), *nightmar* (*night* and Sax. *mara*), *bridegoom* (Sax. *brydguma*), *furlow* (D. *verlof*), *parsnep* and *turnep* (Sax. *naepe*), and so forth. When Webster's "queer" spellings were later removed from his dictionaries, the etymological spellings were the first to go.

Webster Introduced His Plan to Reform Spelling in the Spelling Book and Dictionaries

THE reformed spellings in Webster's spelling books which call for comment are not numerous.[89] In his first speller in 1783 he lamented the inclination of "pedants" to alter the spelling of words by omitting the superfluous letters and to follow new fashions in pronunciation. Those who drop the *u* in such words as "favour" and "honour," words that he later included in his trilogy of cardinal reforms, are informed that they are dropping

[85] Webster, *A Dictionary of the English Language* (1807), p. v.
[86] Letter from Webster to Thomas Dawes, dated "New Haven, August 5, 1809." *Monthly Anthology and Boston Review*, VII (1809), 208.
[87] Neumann, *op. cit.*, p. 115.   [88] See p. 234.
[89] Krapp, *The English Language in America* (1925), I, 338.

the wrong letter, that the words are pronounced *onur, favur* and that they may with the same propriety drop the *u* in "pious," "virtuous," and so forth. The *e* in "judgment," he explains, is the most important letter in the word, it being that alone which softens the *j*. "Into these and many other absurdities," he charges, "are people led by a rage of singularity. Our language is indeed pronounced very differently from her spelling; this is an inconvenience we regret, but cannot remedy." [90]

In fact, in some respects his spelling books are ultra-conservative. They contain a number of old spellings, outmoded even in Webster's day, which he perhaps copied from Dilworth, since they are the same in Dilworth's speller, contrary to Webster's dictionaries and those of Johnson and Walker, and "have been thus *contradictory* and *erroneously* spelled in Webster's old spelling book for more than forty years . . ." [91] Among words of this sort were *ancle, boult, chase, cholic, faggot, hindrance, offence, sallad, serjeant, shew,* and *vise.* In the 1829 revision most of these spellings were modernized but some of them were retained, among others *boult, cholic,* and *shew.*

Some of the reformed spellings, however, found their way into the speller. Most words in his trilogy of cardinal reforms, that is, words belonging to the "honor," "magic," and "theater" groups, are spelled according to his principle of economy. Among the few rationalized spellings one finds in the 1803 issue of the spelling book are *chesnut tree, enrol, musketoe, opake, sley* (for "sleigh"), and *turky.*

In the spelling of American place names Webster exercised a free hand in the spelling books. "The facility with which the English within the last century have adopted French words, without accommodating them to the genius of their language," he pointed out, "is as disreputable to the taste of the nation, as it has been injurious to the language." [92] He continued by showing that the Romans, the French, and the Spanish gave their borrow-

[90] *Grammatical Institute,* Part I (1783), p. 10.
[91] Lyman Cobb, *Critical Review* (1831), p. 47.
[92] *Elements of Useful Knowledge* (4th ed., 1809), II, Preface.

ings native spellings and terminations.[93] "How does an unlettered American," he asks, "know the pronunciation of the names *Ouisconsin* or *Oubasch* in French dress?" [94] Perhaps his greatest departure from the traditional spelling used by American authors had to do with the orthography of Indian names. In almost all instances his spellings are those which have become familiar in present use.[95]

Generally speaking, it was not until the publication of the *Compendious Dictionary*, in 1806, that Webster's reforms were introduced to any great extent. In the 1807 and 1817 school editions the reformed spellings began to disappear. In the *American Dictionary* (1828) many of them were omitted; others in the 1841 dictionary, the last to be published during Webster's lifetime. There are exceptions, however, as some reforms were also introduced in the 1807, 1817, and 1828 dictionaries. Among the queer spellings remaining in the dictionary when Webster died in 1843 were *oker, cag, grotesk, hainous, porpess, tung, chimist* and *neger*. These were removed in the 1847 and 1865 revisions.

The following list of words are representative of the main classes of words which at one time or another were involved in Webster's scheme to reform English spelling in America. These words have been gleaned from the battleground of the "War of the Dictionaries," that is, from the many articles, pamphlets, letters, prefaces, and so forth, that followed the publication of Webster's spelling books and dictionaries, especially the *American Dictionary* of 1828, when Lyman Cobb and Joseph Emerson Worcester entered the field. No attempt has been made to present a complete list of words that were "tinckered with" or to follow the fortunes of each word through the various editions of the dictionaries. The purpose is (1) to illustrate the main classes of words reformed; (2) to indicate the principle upon which the reform was based; (3) to indicate in a general way the extent

---

[93] *Loc. cit.*

[94] *Ibid.*

[95] Krapp, *English Language in America* (1925), I, 337. Modern Language Association.

to which the proposed reform endured; and (4) to show how the critics reacted.

1. In spelling "honor," "candor," "error," "favor," "odor," and similar words, Webster omitted the *u*. Although he protested against the simplified spelling of these words in his spelling book in 1783,[96] he introduced it in later editions, and it was given in the dictionaries with a fair degree of consistency. Those who objected to this spelling based their objections on the authority of Dr. Johnson, who had taken a stand for the *our* endings, which he used rather inconsistently, with the result that usage was unsettled.[97] In using this spelling, Webster's claim that he had the authority of English precedent as well as the tendency of the public mind is well supported by the fact that Bailey, Dyche, and other English lexicographers before Johnson were divided and uncertain as to the usage, and in America, Johnson and Elliott, Webster's immediate predecessors in the field of lexicography, were far from consistent in the spelling of words in the *or* class.[98] The etymology of these words was also given as a reason for the simplification. "I do not write *honour, candour, errour,*" he declared, "because they are neither French nor Latin. If we follow the French, the orthography ought to be *honeur, candeur, erreur;* if the Latin, as we ought, because they are Latin words, then we ought to write *honor,* &c, and this is now the best and most common usage." [99] Webster apparently did not know that the great bulk of words of ultimate Latin origin reached the language through the intermediary of the Norman French, but thought they came into English through a direct union of Anglo-Saxon and the Latin of the Romish clergy after the revival of letters and the invention of printing;[100] nor does he seem to have known of the *u* sound that existed in the native Anglo-Saxon.[101] In addition to these reasons, reform was undertaken in the inter-

[96] See p. 264.
[97] Steger, *American Dictionaries* (1913), p. 45.
[98] See lists of *or* words in Steger's *American Dictionaries* (1913), p. 35.
[99] Letter to Dawes, *Monthly Anthology,* VII (1809), 208.
[100] *Elementary Spelling Book* (1830), p. 18.
[101] Neumann, *American Pronunciation* (1925), p. 117.

ests of uniformity—to obviate "the inconvenience of writing *u*
in *labour* and omitting it in *laborious; u* in *vigour* and not in
invigorate; u in *inferiour,* and not in *inferiority.* These irregularities are perplexing to the learner." [102] Again the charge of inconsistency is made. *"Serious, curious, furious, famous,* etc., etc.,
have also the *u,"* Gould pointed out, "and they came to us as
Webster might say, 'from the Latin through the French.' Why
did Webster spare the *u* in them?" [103]

2. In writing such words as "meter," "theater," "luster,"
"center," "caliber," Webster changed the *re* spellings to *er* after
the analogy of "chamber," "number," "cider," and other words
from the French which had been reduced to English spelling.
This change was based on the principle of analogy and uniformity, at the expense of the principle of etymology upon which
Webster had insisted in other cases; for example, *theatron,*
Greek; *theatron,* Latin; *theatre,* French; *teatro,* Spanish and
Portuguese, and so forth.[104] Then, too, as the critics were quick to
point out, the *er* spellings introduced a discrepancy between the
spellings of the primitives and the derivatives, the principle of
uniformity upon which Webster based some of his reforms:
"theater" requires "theatrical"; "luster," "lustrous"; "center,"
"central." [105] This spelling was introduced in the early editions
of the *American Spelling Book* and the dictionaries, but was
very inconsistently followed. For this change he was criticized
for unsettling a long-established usage.[106]

---

[102] Noah Webster, *Series of Books for Systematic Instruction* (1831). Book of
pamphlets entitled *Noah Webster* (Yale University).
[103] Edward Sherman Gould, *Good English or Popular Errors in Language* (1867),
p. 160.
[104] *Ibid.,* p. 161.
[105] *Ibid.,* p. 162.
[106] *DeBow's Review,* XXVIII (1860), 561. In support of this spelling Webster
quotes from Selden, Hooker, Camden, Bryant, Dryden, Pope, the Bible, Milton,
Beattie, Newton, and other writers.—*Series* . . . (1831), pp. 11 and 12. "Pope and
Dryden sometimes wrote *centre, sceptre;* but like Milton they wrote *centered,*
sceptered, avoiding, inconsistently enough, the awkward spelling *centred,*
sceptred, which we now see in books, but which ought not to be suffered to dis-
figure the language."—*Series* . . . (1831), p. 12.

3. "Cubic," "music," "public," "rhetoric," and similar words of Greek and Latin origin and others formed in analogy with them were spelled without the *k* in order to make the primitives conform to the derivatives, "cubical," "musical," "publication," "rhetorical," and so forth, exceptions being participles which require *k* before *e* or *i* as "traffick," "frolick," "trafficking," "frolicking." [107] In words of different origin which have always been written with *k* and which have no derivatives, such as "fetlock," "hemlock," and "wedlock," the *k* was retained. Monosyllables also were excepted, such as "sick," "lock," and "flock," for, Webster explained, "most of them have derivative verbs and participles, as *sicken, locked, flocking.*" [108]

4. In changing the spelling of three *ense* words, "offense," "defense," and "pretense," Webster exercised the principle of uniformity and analogy by bringing the trilogy into the fold of other words in this class, such as "expense," "recompense," and so forth, whose spelling had been changed by usage. Then, too, a further reason given for making the change was the etymology of the first two words, "offense" and "defense." It was reasoned furthermore that the *s* spelling would make the spelling of the primitives more uniform with that of the derivatives, such as "defensive," "offensive," and "pretension." [109] To the conformity argument Gould replied that the derivatives "pretentious" and "pretentiousness" did not contain *s*. As to Webster's rule that etymology controls the spelling of the primitive word, which in turn controls the spelling of its derivatives, a rule which Webster frequently reversed, Gould pointed out further that the word "sentence," coming from *sententia,* should be spelled "sentents." [110]

5. The derivatives "appareled," "canceled," "dueling," "traveled," and so forth, were spelled with the single consonant,

[107] Webster, *Series of Books for Systematic Instruction in the English Language* (1831), p. 10.
[108] *Ibid.,* p. 11.
[109] *Series of Books . . .* (1831), p. 11.
[110] Gould, *Good English* (1867), p. 148.

the rule being that when a verb of two or more syllables ends in a single unaccented consonant, preceded by a single vowel, the final consonant is not doubled in the derivatives. "This rule, always admitted to be just, has been violated, probably from mere negligence; or partly from the omission of the participles from the English dictionaries. Keeping in mind the principle of analogy and uniformity, Webster declared "There is certainly no more propriety in doubling the last consonant in these words than in *limiting, pardoning, delivering,* and others, in which the last consonant is never doubled." [111] In Webster's first texts these consonants were doubled after the manner of English spelling. But in the 1828 dictionary and the dictionaries which followed, the rule stated above was followed.

6. In the interest of uniformity final consonants in such words as "appall," "befall," "enthrall" were doubled, since they are doubled in the derivatives. Besides, it was explained, it is a general rule that *a* before *ll* has its broad sound ("mall" and "shall" being excepted), and if *l* is dropped in *befal, miscal,* and so forth, the orthography leads to a false pronunciation.[112] Likewise, to prevent the inconvenience of exceptions, such words as "foretell," "distill," "fulfill," as well as such monosyllabic words as "dull," "full," and "skill," were spelled with *ll* in order to be uniform with their derivatives. Again Webster's inconsistency exposed him to the flail of the critics. Why, they asked, do we write "enroll" and "enrollment," when "control" and "controlment" are left unchanged? [113]

7. The orthography of "instructor," "suitor," "survivor," "visitor," and similar words, "used by all authors before Johnson's time and still used by many," [114] was restored. Webster pointed out that Johnson was not consistent in using the *er* spellings, by citing the *Rambler, Rasselas,* and the dictionary.

[111] *Series of Books* . . . (1831), p. 11.
[112] *Series of Books* . . . p. 11.
[113] Gould, *op. cit.,* p. 156.
[114] *Series of Books* . . . p. 11.

Besides, uniformity between primitives and derivatives requires the *or* ending, e.g., "visitor," "visitorial."

8. In the 1806 dictionary Webster omitted the final silent vowel in such words as *ax, determin, envelop, famin, libertin,* and *medicin* on the ground that it was not needed to indicate the length of the preceding vowel.[115] For some of the words in this class the *e* form was also recorded and others that seemed to belong to the class were written only with the *e*. Generally speaking, this spelling began to disappear with the publication of the school dictionaries of 1807 and 1817, and in practically all cases it had disappeared in the 1828 dictionary, although such spellings as *opposit* and *steril* are given in the duodecimo volume of 1829.

9. Words from the French, such as *bailif, mastif, plaintif,* and *pontif* were spelled with the single *f* on the basis of the single *f* in the French and the fact that the derivatives, such as "pontifical" and "pontificate" are spelled with one *f*. Webster criticized Johnson's inconsistency, in that he used the *ff* ending, except in the word *bailif*. Webster in turn exposed himself to a similar charge by writing "distaff." "As most of the monosyllables in *ff*, as *cuff, muff, miff, stiff,* are used as verbs and have derivatives, *cuffed, muffed, puffing, stiffen,* &c., they must retain *ff*; and for the sake of uniformity, other monosyllables may well be written in the same manner." [116]

10. Verbs, such as "generalize," "legalize," and "moralize," formed from the termination of Greek and Latin *izo,* and other verbs formed in like analogy were spelled with the *ize* termination, meaning "to make." Verbs from the French *priser,* such as "surprise," "devise," "merchandise," and so forth, retain the *s* of the original. In Webster's first publications the two spellings

---

[115] When discussing the tendency to prolong the sound of *i* in the termination *ive*, Webster said, "The final *e* must be considered as the cause of this vulgar dialect. It is wished that some bold genius would dare to be right and spell this class of words without *e, motiv.*"—*Dissertations,* p. 104.

[116] Webster, *Series of Books* (1831), p. 11.

were used indiscriminately, but in the later works this rule is followed with a fair degree of consistency.[117]

Webster Attempts to Reform Pronunciation

"THE pronunciation of our language," Webster declared in his 1783 speller, "tho the most important and difficult part of grammar, is left to parents and nurses—to ignorance and caprice—to custom, accident or nothing—nay to something worse, to coxcombs, who have a large share in directing the *polite taste* of pronunciation, which of course is as vicious as that of any other class of people. And while this is the case, every person will claim a right to pronounce most agreeable to his own fancy, and the language will be exposed to perpetual fluctuation." [118] Webster's statement is supported by the account given by Captain Marryat, who visited America in 1837:

The upper classes of the Americans do not, however, speak or pronounce English according to our standard; they appear to have no exact rule to guide them, probably from a want of any intimate knowledge of Greek or Latin. You seldom hear a derivation from the Greek pronounced correctly, the accent being generally laid upon the wrong syllable. In fact, every one appears to be independent, and pronounces just as he pleases.[119]

The variance in pronunciation revealed by an examination of early spelling books tends to substantiate the contention that there was no standard and shows beyond a doubt that there were no fine distinctions made in pronunciation. Under Fox's examples of "English words, which are alike in sound, yet unlike in their significations," [120] we find the following:

Ask the Carpenter for his *Ax;* If he leave not *coughing,* he will soon be in his *Coffin;* He spent so much on *Barley* that he went but *barely;* A *Bath* to *bathe* in; The *Bile* brake, the pot did *boil;* A *Kennel* for Dogs, sweep the *Channel* [121] clean; Bucks and *Does;* let

[117] *Series of Books* (1831), p. 11.
[118] *Grammatical Institute,* Part I (1783), p. 5.
[119] Captain Frederick Marryat, *Diary in America with Remarks on Institutions* (1839), II, 31.
[120] George Fox, *Instruction for Right-Spelling* (1702), pp. 71–82.
[121] *Canal* in 1769 edition.

him take but one *Dose;* He *shoots* 3 arrows; He has 3 *sutes* of apparel, and 3 *suits* in Law; It is *neither* thee nor I can lift the *nether* millstone. Thousands and *millions; Musk melons.*

Dilworth gives *air, Heir,* and *Are* in a similar list [122] and Webster gives *Bow* (to bend), *Bow* (to shoot with), *Bough,* and *Beau* as words having the same pronunciation.[123]

But this condition existed in England as well as in America, although perhaps not to such a great extent. In Webster's 1806 dictionary, he showed that there were many "contradictions between the most respected standard authors" and gave examples to prove his point:

SHERIDAN	WALKER	JONES
Ab'bey, abby	Ab'bee	Ab'by
Abbrévyate	Abbréveeate	Abbre'vyate
Abdom'inal	Abdom'enal	Abdom'inal
Bentsh	Bensh	Bentsh
Habitual	Habichual	Habitual
Shooperb	Superb	Superb
Chooter	Tutor	Tutor

In the abridgment of Webster's *American Dictionary* (1829) [124] Worcester included his synopsis of eight hundred words showing that they were pronounced differently by Webster, Sheridan, Walker, Perry, Jones, Fulton and Knight, and Jameson. Webster included this synopsis in his 1841 work and it appeared in some of the succeeding editions. In fact, such a synopsis is one of the features of the 1934 *Webster's New International Dictionary.*[125]

One difficulty encountered in trying to determine the pronunciation advocated by lexicographers of Webster's age is the absence of a phonetic transcript indicating exactly the pronunciation intended. It is true that from Bailey to Johnson the place of the stress accent had been marked, but "no attempt had been made to show how such a group of letters, for example, as

---

[122] *A New Guide* (1772), p 68.
[123] *American Spelling Book* (1787), p. 105.
[124] See p. 295.
[125] Introduction, pp. 59–73.

colonel or *enough* or *phthisical,* was actually pronounced . . .
This feature so obviously important in a language, of which
spelling had ceased to be phonetic," was supplied by Kenrick,
Perry, and Sheridan in their compilations of 1773, 1775, and
1780, respectively.[126] But that these systems were woefully inadequate, an examination of any of these texts will show. In
fact it was not until the last quarter of the nineteenth century
that progress was made in the development of language keys.[127]

Although Webster employed several aids to indicate pronunciation,[128] on the whole he did very little to record the pronunciation of words, saying that some of the finer points in
pronunciation could not be put down on paper.

From a careful attention to this subject [he declared], I am persuaded
that all such notations are useless, and many of them mischievous,
as they lead to a wrong pronunciation. In no case can the true pronunciation of words in a language be accurately and completely
expressed on paper; it can be caught only by the ear and by practice.
No attempt has ever been made to mark the pronunciation.[129]

Because of these conditions, then, philologists have been
handicapped in their attempts to determine what early American
pronunciation was like.[130] "It is mainly by indirect evidence that
we are at all able to reconstruct Webster's sounds." [131]

Added to the lack of phonetic markings are the usual Websterian inconsistencies, the shifting from one position to another.
Part of this was undoubtedly due to the fact that usage then as
now was divided, and that it changes from time to time. But it
is not probable that these reasons were entirely responsible for
his shiftings. Because of the chaotic condition of the language

---

[126] James A. Murray, *The Evolution of English Lexicography* (1900), p. 42. The
Clarendon Press.
[127] James Geddes, "Dictionaries in English and Foreign Languages," *Library
Journal,* LIV (1929), 843.
[128] See pp. 98 ff.
[129] *American Dictionary* (1828), Preface, n. p.
[130] Mathews, *The Beginnings of American English* (1931), p. 11. The University
of Chicago Press.
[131] Neumann, *American Pronunciation According to Noah Webster* (1924),
p. 118.

and his lack of training in philology, confusion perhaps played a great part.[132]

As has been shown, Webster, in some of his earier spellers, included footnotes, which gave warnings against the use of certain improprieties in pronunciation.[133] As we have seen, he traveled widely in the eighties in behalf of the copyright laws. He observed the speech in the various sections and lectured on language in the principal towns he visited. Later his observations and conclusions were published in his *Dissertations* (1789). He was aware that American speech differed from English speech, and that the speech in different sections of the country differed. These differences he ascribed to the nature of the government and the distribution of property.[134] "People of large fortunes, who pride themselves on family distinction," he explained, "possess a certain boldness, dignity, and independence in their manner, which give a corresponding air to their mode of speaking. Those who are accustomed to command slaves, form a habit of expressing themselves with the tone of authority and decision."

In New England, where there are few slaves and servants, less family distinctions than in any other part of America, the people are accustomed to address each other with that diffidence, or attention to the opinions of others, which marks a state of quality. Instead of commanding, they advise; instead of saying, *you must,* they ask with an air of doubtfulness, *is it not best?* or give their opinions with an indecisive tone; *you had better, I believe.* Not possessing that pride and consciousness of superiority which attend birth and fortune, their intercourse with each other is all conducted on the idea of equality, which gives a singular tone to their language and complexion to their manners.[135]

Such are the causes of the local peculiarities in pronunciation which prevail among the country people in New England, and which to foreigners are the objects of ridicule. The great error in their manner of speaking proceeds immediately from not opening the mouth sufficiently. Hence words are drawled out in a careless, lazy

[132] *Ibid.,* pp. 118 f.
[133] See pp. 74 f. of this study; also Appendix II.
[134] *Dissertations* (1789), p. 106.
[135] *Dissertations* (1789), pp. 106 ff.

manner, or the sound finds a passage through the nose . . . Nothing
can be so disagreeable as that drawling, whining cant that distinguishes a certain class of people; and too much pains cannot be taken
to reform the practice. Great efforts should be made by teachers of
schools to make their pupils open the teeth, and give a full clear
sound to every syllable.[136]

Much as Webster was opposed to this American characteristic,
he shows in a later publication that such speech is not without
precedent in England.

Let the English remove the beam from their own eye, before they
attempt to pull the mote from ours; and before they laugh at our
vulgar *keow, geown, neow,* let them discard their polite *keind,* and
geuide; a fault precisely similar in origin, and equally a perversion
of genuine English pronunciation.[137]

The author condemns the practice of imitating British stage
pronunciations, showing that stage English is as barbarous as the
keow and *neow* of the eastern people. The southern people
are criticized in turn for omitting the sound of *r* in such words
as "ware" and "there"; the middle states for pronouncing "off,"
"soft," "drop," and "crop" with the *a* (as in cat) sound and for
pronouncing "once" and "twice" with a final *t.* He then dis-
cusses a number of words, whose pronunciation he had observed
in his travels about the country.

Acceptable (Admirable, disputable, comparable): Accent on last
   syllable but two. This is the practice of the people at large.—*Dissertations,* p. 138.
Advertisement (Chastisement): In analogy with the radical words
   from which they are derived, they should be accented on the
   last syllable but one.—*Dis.,* p. 137.
Because: Becaze is frequent in New England, but is vulgar.—*Dis.,*
   p. 388.
Caught: Cotched is frequent but very barbarous.—*Dis.,* p. 111.
Chaise: Condemns *sha.* Singular is *shaze* and plural *shazes.*—*Dis.,*
   p. 118.
Croud: Skrouge and *skroud* sometimes "heard among people who
   should be ashamed of the least vulgarism."—*Dis.,* p. 111.
Deaf: English say *def;* American, *deef.*—*Dis.,* p. 128.

[136] *Ibid.,* p. 108.
[137] Webster, *Letter to the Honorable John Pickering* . . . (1817), p. 59.

Deceit (Conceit, receipt): Pronounced *desate, consate, resate* by eastern people. Pronounced *deceeve, conceeve, receet* in England and in the middle and southern states.—*Dis.,* p. 114.

Dictionary: Usually pronounced *disconary.* Standard writers require *dicshunary,* or *dicshonary.*—*Dis.,* p. 117.

Either (Neither): generally pronounced *ither, nither* by eastern people. "All standard authors give *ei* the *ee* sound as do people in middle and southern states.—*Dis.,* p. 114.

Fierce (pierce, tierce): Pronounced *feerce, peerce, teerce* in middle and southern states. Not so pronounced on English stage. Should be *ferce, perce, terce.*—*Dis.,* p. 125.

Fetch: Often pronounced *fotch* in several states, "but not among the better class of people."—*Dis.,* p. 111.

Heard: Pronounced *heerd* in America, but in the fashionable world since the Revolution the English pronunciation, *herd* or *hurd* are in vogue.—*Dis.,* p. 126.

Help: Holpe heard rarely except in Virginia.—*Dis.,* p. 111.

Immediate (Comedian, commodious, tragedian): Di frequently pronounced *j,* "a palpable corruption."—*Dis.,* p. 143.

Leap: Pronounced *leep* in America; *lep* in England.—*Dis.,* p. 126.

Leisure: Sometimes pronounced *leesure,* and sometimes *lezhure.* Should be pronounced *leasure* in analogy with *pleasure* and *measure.*—*Dis.,* p. 116.

Might: Mought is heard in most of the states, but not frequently except in a few towns.—*Dis.,* p. 111.

Oblige: Oblige and *obleege* are both used by standard writers.—*Dis.,* p. 117.

Raisin: Reesin very prevalent in several American towns and is recommended by a few standard authors. Derivation, analogy and general custom decide in favor of a long *a, raisin.*—*Dis.,* p. 116.

Rome: Pronounced both *rome* and *room* in America. Long *o* preferable.—*Dis.,* p. 119.

Sacrifice: a in first syllable should be "long."—*Dis.,* p. 123.

Tyranny: y should be given the sound of "long" *i.*—*Dis.,* p. 123.

Veal (vessel): Often pronounced *weal* and *wessel* in both England and America. Most prevalent in Boston and Philadelphia.—*Dis.,* p. 112.

Zealous: Vowel in first syllable should have the "long" *e* sound.—*Dis.,* p. 123.

The improprieties to which Webster objected in the spelling book and *Dissertations* were not the pronunciations used by the educated people.[138] But neither were many of the other words which Webster's critics branded Americanisms and which he declared were good old English words, now obsolete in England, but still used in America.[139] Many of the pronunciations to which he objected were a part of the seemingly miraculous cargo carried by the Mayflower.[140] They were deep rooted in the soil of the eighteenth century and can be found recommended in grammars of the eighteenth century.[141]

That they were widely used in Webster's day there can be no doubt. "Cooper has Noah Webster's own *creatur', ventur', f'erce.*"[142] Ellis is of the opinion that the use of these pronunciations in such humorous works as *Major Downing's Letters, The Clockmaker, Artemus Ward,* and the *Heathen Chinee* indicates a widely-known pronunciation. Otherwise the whole humor of their adoption would be lost. He believes that the remarks of Webster and others concerning Americanisms would best be supplemented by a selection of phonetic orthographies from the works of known humorists.[143]

Whether or not the speech that Webster advocated was the speech generally used in America has been disputed. In a letter written in 1787 to Webster's publishers by Sam Magan, vice provost of the University of Pennsylvania, and John Andrews, principal of the Academy of the Protestant Episcopal Church in Philadelphia, it was pointed out "that in some instances the author, confiding in his own sense of propriety, has ventured to depart from that pronunciation which has been generally received."[144]

More recent commentators have attempted to determine the source of Webster's proposed American language. Basing his conclusions on the facts that "Webster's contemporaries and critics frequently alluded to the fact that his pronunciation was

[138] A. J. Ellis, *An Early English Pronunciation* (1869–89), IV, 1,224.
[139] See pp. 284 ff.
[140] Harry M. Ayres, *Cambridge History of American Literature* (1931), IV, 559.
[141] *Ibid.*, p. 563.
[142] *Ibid.*
[143] *Op. cit.,* IV, 1,224.
[144] *American Spelling Book* (1790), p. viii.

local to New England . . ." and that Webster himself repeatedly affirmed that at the time he composed the first speller he had no access to the works of British orthoëpists other than the pocket dictionary of Entick and the essays of Lowth and Sheridan, Neumann concludes that the pronunciation advocated by Noah Webster of the speller of 1783 may be regarded as trustworthy evidence on New England speech in the last quarter of the eighteenth century.[145]

Krapp says it was the speech of the American people, "neither rustics nor peasants on the one hand, nor aristocrats on the other, corrupted by the false refinement of stage and court," that Webster would make the basis for his new American English, especially the speech of New England as the region where education and literary culture were most highly developed.

But [Krapp continues] Webster was not intent upon advocating a local New England standard as the general model for American English. . . . The standard of British English having been rejected, both for patriotic reasons and also because it was too remote to be applied . . . there remained only the choice between the speech of one geographical or social community, to be elevated above all the rest, and the speech of no community at all, that is, a manipulated generalization of speech habits which should cover the nation as a whole.

This same author points out that Webster knew that national speech must be to some extent theoretical and unreal and that his advocacy of it was somewhat contrary to his acknowledged principle that it is the duty of the student "to find out what language *is,* and not how it might have been made." [146] "He compromised with this general principle, however," concludes Krapp, "because a certain amount of artificial manipulation seemed necessary before the language could arrive at that ultimate uniformity short of which a democratic society cannot rest." [147]

[145] J. H. Neumann, *American Pronunciation According to Noah Webster* (1924), p. 1.
[146] *Dissertations,* p. ix.
[147] George Philip Krapp, *The English Language in America* (1925), I, 10ff. Modern Language Association.

Mencken is inclined to take an opposite view. Regarding Webster as America's first professional scholar, "there was," he says,

always something sequestered and almost medieval about him. Therefore the American language that he described and argued for was seldom the actual tongue of the folks about him, but often a sort of volapük made up of one part faulty reporting and nine parts academic theorizing.[148]

Again, this author says that Webster was far more a reformer of the American dialect than a student of it.

He introduced radical changes into its spelling and pronunciation, but he showed little understanding of its direction and genius. One always sees in him, indeed, the teacher rather than the scientific inquirer; the ardor of his desire to expound and instruct was only matched by his infinite capacity for observing inaccurately and his profound ignorance of elementary philological principles.[149]

Webster's Reforms Were Widely Criticized

THAT Webster was a conservative reformer whose reforms were in the main sensible, critics of today are agreed.[150]

My proposed corrections are few [Webster insisted], and my orthography differs from that of the English, not more than the English differ from each other. The truth is a reformation of orthography might be made with few changes, and upon a plan so simple as not to require an hour's attention to be perfectly master of it; and it might be introduced in a tenth part of the time required to render general the practice of reckoning money by dollars and cents.[151]

Yet the reviewers at once attacked his 1806 dictionary, accusing him of innovation and of listing localisms, vulgarisms, Americanisms, and other isms.[152]

[148] Mencken, The American Language (1919), p. 6. Alfred A. Knopf, Inc.
[149] Ibid.
[150] Krapp, op. cit., I, 343.
[151] Letter to Dawes, Monthly Anthology and Boston Review, VII (1809), 211.
[152] See, for example, James Savage's review of Webster's Compendious Dictionary in the Monthly Anthology and Boston Review, VI (1809), 246; also the Journal of the Proceedings of the Anthology Society (1910), pp. 71, 81, 93, 94, 120, 121, 193, 207, 266; also letter to Webster from John Quincy Adams, dated "Quincy 5. November 1806."—Ford, Notes, II, 9.

The nature of these criticisms and the response Webster made
to them is well shown by three letters Webster wrote, one to Dr.
David Ramsay,[153] who as member of Congress had favored Webster's proposed language reforms,[154] a second to his brother-in-
law, the Honorable Thomas Dawes,[155] and a third to John
Pickering, son of Webster's old friend, Timothy Pickering.
Although Webster was the possessor of a very thick skin and
an unusually tough mind, these letters, especially the one to
Dawes, show that he both winced and cried aloud at these attacks of the reviewers.

"If men choose to be perplexed with difficulties in language,"
he wrote Dawes, "I will not contend with them, by endeavoring
to remove such difficulties against their will." [156] To this resolution was probably due the fact that he abandoned many of the
reforms in his later dictionaries.

Perhaps the spark that set off this bomb of criticism was the
belligerent attitude toward Johnson which Webster took in his
1806 dictionary. In answer to Ramsay's warning that prejudices against any American attempts to improve Dr. Johnson
were very strong in Charleston, Webster admitted that "similar
prejudices have been manifested in some parts of the northern
states." He then proceeded to criticize Johnson at length, making
the following points: (1) Johnson's dictionary contains about
two thousand words that are not in the language, words that
were Anglicized by first compilers and have been included by
most compilers ever since. (2) Quotations chosen to illustrate
authors are frequently from authors who had no taste or knowledge of English. (3) Vulgar and cant words were included, such
as those used by Shakespeare and Butler. (4) The definitions
want just discrimination and show unpardonable negligence.
(5) There is lack of discrimination in defining words nearly

[153] *A Letter to Dr. David Ramsay of Charleston (S. C.) Respecting the Errors in
Johnson's Dictionary and Other Lexicographers* (1807). Reviewed in *Monthly
Anthology,* IV (1807), 670–75.
[154] Ford, *Notes,* I, 153.
[155] *Monthly Anthology and Boston Review,* VII (1809), 208 ff.
[156] *Monthly Anthology,* VII (1809), 211.

synonymous. (6) Johnson's etymologies were incorrect. Webster also criticized Johnson's grammar and history of the language [157] on the ground that the author did not have a sufficient knowledge of Anglo-Saxon and historical detail.

Webster was not content to tinker with spellings and pronunciations. He showed in his 1806 dictionary that he meant to do something about the words which have and do not have a legitimate place in the English language. "I have rejected also a great number of words introduced by a species of pedantry very common a century ago, such as *adjugate, abstrude, balbucinate.* Of this species, and other words not legitimate, between two and three thousand will be rejected." [158] On the other hand, Webster pointed out that he had

enriched the vocabulary with such words as *absorbable, accompaniment, acidulous, achromatic, adhesiveness, adjutancy, admissibility, advisory, amendable, animalize, aneurismal, antithetical, appellor, appreciate, appreciation, arborescent, arborization, ascertainable, bailee, bailment, indorser, indorsee, prescriptive, imprescriptible, statement, insubordination, expenditure, subsidize,* and other elegant and scientific terms, now used by the best writers in Great Britain and America. The number of these is not exactly known; but of the terms now well authorized, Johnson's dictionary is deficient in five or six thousand words, or about a seventh part of the English vocabulary.[159]

To the accusation that he had introduced "Americanisms" and "vulgarisms" into his 1806 dictionary, Webster replied by saying it was one of the most extraordinary charges which his opposers had ventured to suggest. He admitted that he had introduced a few words not used perhaps in Great Britain or not in a like sense, such as "customable" (authority of law of Massachusetts); "doomage" (authority of Dr. Belknap and laws of New Hampshire); "fourfold," as a verb (authority of laws of Connecticut and a century of usage); "decedent" for "deceased" (authority of laws of New Jersey and Pennsylvania); and a few others, prob-

[157] These were prefixed to Johnson's dictionary.
[158] Letter to Dawes, *op. cit.,* p. 211.
[159] *Ibid.*

ably not twenty, noting them, however, as "local." Since these
words exist, how, he asked, are such words to be understood,
without the aid of a dictionary? Johnson admitted "hog," a
sheep, and "tup," a ram, upon the basis of local usage and he
inserted many other similar words. Webster also admitted that
he had included one or two cant words, such as "caucus"; but
what, he inquired, are Johnson's "fishefy," "jackalent," "jiggum-
bob," and "foutre"! "Instead of *increasing* the list of vulgar
terms, I have *reduced* it, by expunging *two-thirds* of *such words*
inserted by Johnson! . . . There is not a vocabulary of the English language extant, so free from *local, vulgar,* and *obscene*
words as mine!"

In 1816 John Pickering, a Massachusetts lawyer, published
*A Vocabulary or Collection of Words and Phrases Which Had
Been Supposed to Be Peculiar to the United States of America.*
The collection contained about five hundred words, of which
a large number were taken from Webster's dictionary. To the
vocabulary was prefixed "An Essay on the Present State of the
English Language in the United States." In this Essay Pickering
states that "in this country as in England, we have thirsty reformers and presumptuous sciolists who would unsettle the
whole of our admirable language, for the purpose of making it
conform to their whimsical notions of propriety." To this remark Webster took exception in his letter to Pickering.[160]
"Sciolists we may have in multitudes," he admitted; "but who
are the men who would unsettle the whole language? Can you
name the men or any of them either in this country or in England? Surely the finger of scorn ought to be pointed at the men
who are base enough to wish, and selfish enough to attempt, to
unsettle a whole language."

This letter is an important document because it marks the
beginning of a controversy that has been going on ever since,
that is, the respective merits of American English and English

[160] *Letter to the Honorable John Pickering on the Subject of His Vocabulary; or
Collection of Words and Phrases Supposed to Be Peculiar to the United States*
(1817).

English. In Webster's letter he reverts to the independent Yankee ground he had occupied earlier in his career as champion of Federal English and the spread-eagle doctrine.

I deprecate the effects of blind acquiescence in the opinion of men [he declared] and in the passive reception of everything that comes from a foreign press.—My mind revolts at the reverence for foreign authors, which stifles inquiry, restrains investigation, benums the vigor of the intellectual faculties, subdues and debases the mind. I regret to see the young Hercules of genius in America chained to the cradle.

Webster informed Pickering that the so-called "Americanisms" in his list were of three kinds, all of which had a legitimate place in the American language: (1) new words; (2) old words acknowledged to be legitimate, to which new significations have been annexed; and (3) local words, including obsolete words, that is, words obsolete in England, but in use in America.

1. *New words.*—Webster expressed his doubt "whether ten words can be found among men of reputable character in the United States, which are not authorized by English usage, either general or local . . ." He declared, however, that "new words will be formed and used without a license from Englishmen." Following his vitriolic attack in the introduction, Webster discussed one hundred and seventy-five of Pickering's words. Among the words whose legitimacy was questioned were "congressional," "departmental," "applicant," "lengthy," "demoralize," and "presidential." "Presidential," he explained to Pickering, "is an American word which springs from a new application of the term President and which in my opinion ought not to be condemned."

2. *Old words with new meanings.*—As early as 1807, Webster said,

From the diversity of objects in different climates; from differences in government and modes in life; from continual improvements in arts which give existence to different artificial objects in different nations; from accidental changes which no efforts can restrain, or from other physical and moral causes which can neither be controlled nor defined; new terms will be added to a living language, with new applications of old terms; while some dialectical variations in oral utterance will inevitably vary the spoken language of remote nations.

Again, in his letter to Pickering, he says: "New objects, new ideas, and association in ideas, compel us either to invent new terms, or to use English words in a new sense . . . "

Among the English visitors who visited America and who recognized the so-called Americanisms as old English words was Captain Basil Hall. At first he was inclined to disagree with Webster's assertion that there were not fifty words which were used in America and not in England, but upon subsequent inquiry he came to the conclusion "that, with very few exceptions, all these apparent novelties are merely old English words brought over to America by the early settlers, being current at home when they set out on their pilgrimage, and here they remained ever since." [161]

Captain Frederick Marryat came to a similar conclusion after his visit to America.

When the people of England [he explained] emigrated to the United States, they came from every county in England, and each county brought its provincialisms with it. These were admitted into the general stock; and were since all collected and bound up by one Mr. Webster. With the exception of a few words coined for local uses (such as *snags* and *sawyers,* on the Mississippi) I do not recollect a word which I have not traced to be either a provincialism of some English county, or else to be obsolete English. There are a few from the Dutch, such as *stoup,* for the porch of a door, etc.[162]

In his letter to Pickering as elsewhere, Webster was quick to come to the defense of American writers, suggesting that the American millennium of authorship was beginning to dawn. Referring to the tendency to convert nouns into verbs,

A practice which has furnished critics, on both sides of the Atlantic, with many bones to gnaw [he declared] nothing excites more rage among the nibbling gentry, than to find *test* or *advocate* used as verbs. "Test," says one of them, in the Anthology, "is a verb only in writers of an inferior rank, who disregard all the land-marks of

[161] Captain Basil Hall, *Travels in North America, in the Years 1827 and 1828* (1829), I, 319 ff.
[162] Marryat, *A Diary in America* (1830), II, 31.

language." Then Washington, Marshall, Hamilton, Adams, Walsh, and almost every other writer of any reputation in America, is doomed to an "inferior rank."

He goes on to show, furthermore, that it has been a common practice to make verbs from nouns—a practice sanctioned by the best writers in England.

You observe, Sir [he continues], under the words *locate* and *location*, in your vocabulary, that the verb, and one of the significations I have given to the latter word, in my Dictionary, are not in English Dictionaries. No, Sir; and that was one reason why I compiled mine. How can the English locate lands, when they have no lands to locate!

Captain Marryat reported that

Many English words are used in a very different sense from that which we attach to them; for instance: a *clever* person in America means an amiable good-tempered person, and the Americans make the distinction by saying, I mean English clever. Our clever is represented by the word smart.

Among the words listed by the Captain were the following: "suspicion" and "opinion" (as verbs); "some" (for "somewhat"); "how" (for "what"); "reckon," "calculate," "guess" (for "suppose"); and "right away" (for "at once").[163]

3. *Local words including obsolete.*—As has been shown, many of the so-called new words, or pure Americanisms about which the critics talked were in reality English provincialisms and words that were obsolete in England. To the criticism that Webster had included localisms and obsolete terms in his dictionary, he replied:

Let it be observed, by the way, that so far as a difference between the language of Englishmen and Americans, consists in our use of words obsolete in the higher circles in Great Britain, the change is not in *our* practice, but in that of Englishmen. The fault, if any, is theirs, when they declaim with vehemence against innovations, let them not censure our adherence to old words and phrases—manifesting a disposition not to innovate . . . There are many instances in which we retain the genuine use of words, and the genuine pronunciation, which they have corrupted . . .

[163] Marryat, *A Diary in America* (1839), II, 33 ff.

Among the words objected to as being obsolete was "avails." Webster declared in his letter to Pickering that it was a well-formed word, like "proceeds," and although it may be antiquated in England, he saw no reason why Americans should be censured for using it. "Will any gentleman," he asks, "invent a process for antiquating a word in America, at the same time it is antiquated in England?" To Pickering's comment that "tarry" sounds as strange to an Englishman as "wist" or "wot" would to an American, Webster said he supposed Pickering meant in conversation as he presumed Englishmen still read the Bible.

It is a word [he affirmed] far preferable to *stay* or *stop*—indeed *stop* will not always answer as its substitute. It will hardly do to say, "I stopped at my friend's house all the week." If the English will blame us for retaining the use of the best words in the language, we cannot help it. They ought however to be so civil as either to respect our practice or devise some mode to render words obsolete in both countries at the same time.

The War of the Dictionaries Followed the Publication of the American Dictionary in 1828

ALTHOUGH the criticism that followed the publication of Webster's dictionaries in 1806, 1807, and 1817 was copious, there was yet more to come. In 1827 and 1828, a series of articles by Lyman Cobb, an author of spelling books and other texts, appeared in the *Albany Argus,* attacking Webster's orthography and orthoëpy, showing that the spellers and dictionaries were not consistent.[164]

These attacks mark the beginning of what later developed into the "War of the Dictionaries." "Since the famous Battle of the Books in St. James Library, no literary controversy has been more sharply waged than that between the adherents of the rival Dictionaries of Doctors Worcester and Webster."[165] In 1828 Webster published his great work, *An American Dictionary.*

---

[164] This series was published in 1828 under the title *A Critical Review of Noah Webster's Spelling Book,* by "Examinator."

[165] *Atlantic Monthly,* V (1860), 631.

The following year, 1829, Webster employed Joseph Emerson
Worcester, who had edited Johnson's dictionary in 1828, to prepare an abridgment of the *American Dictionary*.[166] Also in 1829
Webster's *American Spelling Book* was revised and published
under the title, *The Elementary Spelling Book*. When in 1830
Worcester brought out his *Comprehensive Pronouncing and Explanatory Dictionary*, Webster immediately prepared a list of
words and asked Worcester where he got them if not from his
1828 dictionary. Dr. Worcester replied by showing that most of
the words were to be found in previous English dictionaries,
but added that he freely acknowledged as Dr. Webster's exclusive property such words as *"Ammony, Bridegoom, Canail,
Ieland, Naivty, Nightmar, Prosopopy,"* and others, declaring
that it had been his intention scrupulously to avoid them. "You
coined them, or stamped them anew, to enrich the language . . ." [167] Among other words about which the contest raged
was Webster's pronunciation of "deaf" (deef) and his spelling
of "honor." In case of the latter word, Worcester was forced to
give ground as this spelling appeared later in his works.

    In 1831 Cobb attacked Webster again in his *Critical Review
of the Orthography of Dr. Webster's Series of Books for Sys-*

[166] In the Preface of this abridgment, Webster states that Worcester "has strictly
adhered to the general principles laid down for his direction by the author" and
that "cases of doubt . . . and such changes and modifications . . . as seemed
desirable . . . were referred to Webster's son-in-law, Professor Goodrich." In an
article by another son-in-law, Professor Fowler, *Printed but not Published*, the
charge was made that Worcester and Goodrich had not followed Webster's principles and that many of the inconsistencies in Webster's works about which
critics complained were due to the changes made in this edition and copied in
subsequent issues. Webster sold this abridgment to Goodrich, according to
Fowler, because he would have nothing to do with such a work. Webster did not
include Goodrich and his wife in his will (see unpublished Webster MSS, in the
New York Public Library), since the dictionary, which Goodrich had bought at
a low price, proved to be very profitable. There is some truth in Fowler's contention. An examination of the table showing the different spellings (p. 230) reveals the fact that many of the spellings given in the abridgment are changed
to the conventional, or the conventional spelling is given along with the reformed
spelling. It is also interesting to note that in Webster's duodecimo dictionary,
A Dictionary of the English Language, brought out the same year, most spellings
conform to those in the *American Dictionary*.

[167] "Among the Dictionaries," *Eclectic Magazine*, XCVII (1881), 246.

tematic Instruction of the English Language,[168] giving a long list of words in which the discrepancies that existed between Webster's spellings in the old and new spelling books and the various editions of his dictionaries were made apparent. The fight was on. Worcester's dictionaries of 1846, 1855, and 1860, his dictionary published in England under Webster's name "because of Webster's high reputation there," as well as the many various editions of Webster's dictionaries which appeared frequently, renewed the fray from year to year. Even the Webster dictionaries that appeared after the death of the author in 1843 fanned the fire of controversy to white heat.

It was during the middle of the century, especially after 1860, when the last edition of Worcester's "pugnacious dictionaries" came out, that the Merriam Brothers encountered their severest competition and were stimulated to make the publication of Webster's dictionary a successful enterprise. It is said that one of the Merriams added this appropriate postscript to his evening prayers, "Thank God for Worcester." [169] After 1860, hostilities between the two camps gradually ceased, but during the remainder of the century there was much discussion concerning relative merits of the works of the two authors.

Language reform was not the real issue at stake in the "War of the Dictionaries," although it did provide most of the ammunition used by the two camps. "Apart from the irrelevant personalities, the controversy is reducible to one between a retiring and conservative scholar, willing to record the actualities of usage, and a brisk business man and linguistic reformer.[170] After Webster's death, the war continued, supported by "immense capital and a large stock of energy" which, according to the Schele de Vere, was applied to the propagation of Webster's

[168] This contained a review of Webster's Quarto (1828), Octavo (1829, ed. of 1831), Duodecimo (1829) dictionaries, and his *American* and *Elementary* spelling books.

[169] "The 100th Anniversary of the G. & C. Merriam Company," *The High School Teacher*, VII (1931), 395.

[170] Harry Morgan Ayres, *Cambridge History of American Literature* (1931), IV, 478. The Macmillan Company.

"new and arbitrarily imposed orthography." [171] "Trade rivalries," says Krapp, "soon became very keen and the resultant confusion was more a confusion of the market than spelling itself." [172] One has only to consult the records of the state legislatures during the middle of the century in order to learn of the general scuffle that ensued when legislatures were adopting dictionaries for use in the public schools.[173]

When the war was at its height in the fifties, although Webster had been in his grave since 1843 and most of his advocated reforms had been abandoned, scores of pamphlets were printed by the adherents of the rival factions, giving testimonials, anti-testimonials, advertisements, amounts of sales, narratives, lists of words showing inconsistencies or exhibiting "borrowings," and so forth. Webster was accused of being a determined reformer, who, through his inconsistencies had sadly corrupted the language. "By comparing the words with each other," one pamphleteer wrote, "as found in his first Spelling Book, his Dictionaries of 1806, of 1817, of 1828, of 1840, and in his New Spelling Book, the reader would be led to infer that he actually labored to see how inconsistent he could be with himself." [174]

One of the most aggressive of the Webster opponents was Edward Sherman Gould, who indulged in personal invective, saying "Webster's career was a mistake because it was based on false assumptions. He assumed that the language needed reforming and that he was able to reform it . . . He mistook the duties of a lexicographer, whose province is to record and not to *legislate;* to say what language is, and not what it should be." [175] Gould published a similar invective in a long article in the *Democratic Review* in March, 1856. According to this author, the article so precisely hit the literary opinion that it was copied into several of the papers of New York, Boston, and Philadelphia. William

[171] *Studies in English* (1866), p. 64–65.
[172] Krapp, *op. cit.,* I, 346.
[173] See pp. 235 f.
[174] *A Reply to Messrs. G. & C. Merriam Attack . . .* (1854).
[175] Letter from Gould to the Hon. James W. Beekman, chairman of Committee on Literature in the New York Senate. *New York Senate Documents,* III, Nos. 65–97.

Cullen Bryant, editor of the *New York Evening Post,* copied it
at length in his columns, remarking that "We do not remember
to have seen elsewhere such full justice done to Noah Webster's
system of orthography, under which the English language has
been undergoing a process of corruption for the last quarter of a
century." Bryant furthermore expressed his willingness to contribute toward the expense of having Gould's essay read twice a
year in every schoolhouse in the United States "until every trace
of Websterian spelling disappears from the land." [176] Bryant also
lamented the fact that Webster's system of orthography was
adopted and propagated by the largest publishing house (Merriam's); through the columns of the most widely circulated
monthly magazines (*Harper's*), and through the ablest and most
widely circulated newspaper in the United States (*The New
York Tribune,* edited by Horace Greeley).[177]

Although most of the serious authors of the first part of the
nineteenth century, such as Irving, Bancroft, and Bryant, ignored the new spellings, they were quickly adopted by the newspapers;[178] and the spellings advocated by Webster were in the
main followed by all other compilers of spelling books in America, who, as has been shown, were very numerous.[179]

Webster Was in Sympathy with Nineteenth-Century Tendency to Euphemize

ONE question that has confronted compilers of dictionaries has
been the extent to which vulgar and obscene words should be included. Although, generally speaking, the dictionaries of the
seventeenth century gave a more prominent place to the more
difficult, learned words, most of them borrowings from other

---

[176] Gould, *Webster's Orthography* (n. d.), p. 6.

[177] *Ibid.* From Boston, where Worcester's dictionary was esteemed higher than
Webster's, Holmes wrote of Greeley and New York, "Where *their own printers
teach them how to spell.*" Gould, *op. cit.,* p. 6. In Chapter I of the *Poet at the
Breakfast Table* (1872), Holmes refers to the popularity in Boston of Worcester's
dictionary, "on which as is well known the literary men are by statute allowed to
be sworn in place of the Bible."

[178] Mencken, *op. cit.* (1919), p. 253.

[179] Krapp, *op. cit.* (1925), I, 346.

languages, vulgar terms were included in John Bullokar's *English Expositor* (1616), in which "the vulgar words are prefixed in an alphabetical order before the others as a ready direction for the finding of them out," and in Stephen Skinner's *Etymologican linguae Anglicanae* (1671) both vulgar and obscene terms were listed.

Since the tendency in the eighteenth century was to include the common words that were in everyday use, several compilers included the "low" words of the language. Nathaniel Bailey's *Universal Etymological Dictionary* (1721) contained obscene terms, taken, it would seem, from the *Etymologican linguae Anglicanae*. Although toward the end of the century dictionaries were compiled more and more for the use of schools and an effort was made to guard the youth against all indelicacies of speech, we find low terms in compilations by John Ash [180] and Francis Grose.[181]

The first American dictionaries, compiled by Elliott and Johnson, and Alexander, were school dictionaries. These compilers pointed with pride to the fact that their works contained "no low or indecent word." In Webster's dictionaries, which began to appear in 1806, obscene terms were omitted, and the Webster tradition has been continued to the present day.

Although it is usually affirmed that in Johnson's *English Dictionary* (1755), the "sturdy moralist" was unusually meticulous in omitting obscene terms,[182] in spite of the fact that his work was based on Bailey's, Webster attacked Johnson's dictionary, saying it contained "more of the lowest of all vulgar words than any other now extant, Ash excepted." [183] In his letter to Ramsay (1807) he continued his attack on Johnson for illustrating his definitions with passages from Shakespeare and Butler:

Vulgar manners and characters must be represented by vulgar language; the writer of plays must accommodate his language to his audience; the rabble in the galleries are entitled to their share of

[180] *The New and Complete Dictionary of the English Language* (1775).
[181] *A Classical Dictionary of the Vulgar Tongue* (1785).
[182] Read, "Obscenity Symbol," *American Speech,* IX (1934), 270f.
[183] *Compendious Dictionary* (1806), Preface.

amusement; and a part of every play must be composed of obscenity and vulgar ribaldry. In this manner, the lowest language and the coarsest manners are exhibited before a promiscuous audience, and derive some importance from the reputation of the writer and of the actors. From plays *they* pass into other books—yes, into standard authorities; and national language, as well as morals, are corrupted and debased by the influence of the stage.[184]

One reason why so much concern was shown over the kind of word that should be placed between the covers of a dictionary was the fact that people of Webster's age were very moral conscious. This high religious and moral seriousness, carried to the extent of priggishness, was of course a survival of the Puritan spirit, inherited along with other elements of a somewhat complex Puritan conscience, intensified by the rigors of pioneer life in America. A growing tendency to cover up or gloss over the facts of life by the use of euphemisms reached its height in the thirties of the nineteenth century.[185] During the first half of the century many plain words associated with facts that it was thought desirable to conceal if possible were changed to words having what was thought to be a less offensive and suggestive connotation. "Legs" became "limbs" or "benders" [186] (joints or trotters in the case of chicken); [187] a "chair" became a "seat"; a "female," a "woman"; "breasts," "bosom"; and a "wife," a "lady." Girls were "betrayed" rather than "seduced." The names of such articles of clothing as shirt or corset were not uttered aloud.[188]

English travelers who visited American shores were quick to point out that there was much prudery in America. Among those who commented on this aspect of the American scene was Cap-

---

[184] Webster, *Letter Written to Dr. David Ramsay, Respecting the Errors in Johnson's Dictionary and in Those of Other Lexicographers* (1807).

[185] Eric Partridge, *Words, Word, Words* (1933), pp. 97 ff.

[186] Allan Walker Read, "An Obscenity Symbol," *American Speech*, IX (December, 1934), 265.

[187] *Ibid.*, "Webster's Euphemisms," *Dialect Notes*, VI (July, 1934), 385.

[188] H. L. Mencken, *American Language* (1919), p. 126. Alfred Knopf, Inc.

Commenting on the use of the word "limb" as used in "Little Victories" in *McGuffey's Fifth Reader*, Sullivan has this to say: "No polite little boy would have spoken of his leg in that generation, the baddest boy would not have been equal to the diabolical audacity of standing in front of a mixed company of boys

2

94 LANGUAGE REFORM

tain Frederick Marryat. His account of the lady who hurt her
"limb" at Niagara Falls,[189] of his visit to the female seminary
where the four "limbs" of the piano were chastely encased in
trousers with lace frills around the bottom,[190] and of his visit at
the home of Governor Everett of Boston, where he saw a cast of
Apollo Belvidere, which in compliance with general opinion was
hung with drapery,[191] tends to lend credence to the statements
made by the English. The Americans wish, Marryat reported,
"in everything, to improve upon the old country, as they call us,
and affect to be excessively refined in their language and
ideas." [192]

When Frances Trollope visited America in 1827-31, she
charged the Americans with having a prudish attitude toward
literature. In her account of a conversation with a serious literary gentleman, she illustrates her point:

But I persevered, and named "The Rape of the Lock" as evincing
some little talent, and being in a tone that might still hope for
admittance in the drawing-room; but, on the mention of this poem,
the serious gentleman became almost as strongly agitated as when he
talked of Don Juan; and I was unfeignedly at a loss to comprehend
the nature of his feelings, till he uttered, with an indignant shake of
the handkerchief, "The very title!"

. . . .

"And Shakespeare?"

"Shakespeare, Madam, is obscene, and, thank God, *We* are sufficiently advanced to have found it out! If we must have the abomi-
nation of stage plays, let them at least be marked by the refinement of
the age in which we live." [193]

Webster was thoroughly in sympathy with this nineteenth-
century tendency to euphemize. "In my many months of resi-

-----

and girls, and using the word 'leg.' A thunderbolt would have been expected from
heaven, and if that source were inattentive, the teacher would have supplied
one."—Mark Sullivan, *Our Times* (1929), II, 38. C. Scribner's Sons.
[189] *A Diary in America* (1839), II, 44.
[190] *Ibid.*, p. 45.
[191] *Ibid.*, p. 44.
[192] *Ibid.*, p. 43.
[193] Mrs. Frances Milton Trollope, *Domestic Manners of the Americans* (1832),
I, 126 ff.

dence with him," wrote Mrs. Ford, "I never saw him roused to anger but once, and that was when a dubious and rather indelicate word was mentioned before him." [194] From a letter written to Webster by his brother-in-law Dawes in 1823, we learn that Webster was planning to publish an edition of noted English poems which he had carefully expurgated. As this work did not appear, he perhaps gave up the plan because Dawes advised him that David Hale was publishing an "immense edition" of a similar work.[195]

His penchant for expurgating and euphemizing was later turned to another field. When he published his edition of the Bible in 1833,[196] he explained in the Preface that

In no respect does the present version of the scriptures require amendments than in the use of many words and phrases which cannot now be uttered, especially in promiscuous company, without violation to decency . . . and it is well known that some parents do not permit their children to read the scriptures without prescribing the chapters . . . Further, many words and phrases so offensive, especially to females, as to create a reluctance in young persons to attend Bible classes and schools, in which they are required to read passages which cannot be repeated without a blush; and containing words which, on other occasions, a child could not utter without a rebuke. The effect is, to divert the mind from the *matter* to the *language* of the scripture, and thus in a degree, frustrate the purpose of giving instruction.[197]

In his revision, Webster substituted euphemisms for expressions he found offensive, such as "womb," "dung," "fornification," "whore," "stink," "suck," and "spew," but the revision was by no means thorough. In addition to these changes, he changed obsolete terms to more modern words: "Kine" to "cows," "even" to "evening," "meat" to "food," "mad" to "insane," "usury" to

[194] *Notes*, II, 379.
[195] Dawes wrote to Webster: "I should like to have the poets weeded . . . Some of their best poems have veins of black in their whitest marble."—Ford, *Notes*, II, 191.
[196] *The Holy Bible, Containing the Old and New Testaments, in the Common Version. With Amendments of the Language* (1833).
[197] That other people of Webster's day were of the opinion that the Bible contained language "too foul to be uttered in decent society" is shown in the *Knickerbocker Magazine*, VII (1836), 349.

"interest," and "trow" to "suppose." He furthermore changed the language by substituting "who" for "which" when persons were referred to and "its" for "his" in the neuter gender and changed "shall" and "will" according to his ideas of propriety.

"Most of Webster's improvements," says Warfel, "were adopted by the authors of the revised version, and it is probable that Webster's work, though slow to gain a footing, helped to make the success of the later work possible." [198] Webster's revision of the Bible, this same author thinks, was his crowning achievement. "His school-books were designed for the instruction of the young; his dictionaries regulated so far as books can, the spellings and meanings of words; the Bible gave American scripture for daily reading correctly translated into their own language." [199]

With regard to the place of vulgar words in the language and the use lexicographers should make of them, Webster again showed his inconsistency, as well as his honesty of conviction, in his attempt to get at the root of matters pertaining to linguistics. His prefatory remarks in the 1841 dictionary show that he came to look upon these terms more in the light that some of his predecessors had viewed them and as modern philologists are prone to look upon them, although the linguistic sense of the moderns is not always strong enough to enable them to dissociate themselves from the warped outlook of the age.[200]

It is to be remembered that, in general, vulgar words are the oldest and best authorized words in language; and their use is as necessary to the classes of people who use them, as elegant words are to the statesman and the poet. It may be added, that such words are often particularly useful to the lexicographer, in furnishing him with the primary sense, which is nowhere to be found but in *popular use*. In this work I have not gone quite so far as Johnson has done, in admitting vulgar words. Some of them are too low to deserve notice.[201]

[198] Harry R. Warfel, "The Centenary of Noah Webster's Bible," *The New England Quarterly*, VII (Sept., 1934), 581.
[199] *Ibid.*
[200] Read, "Obscenity Symbol," *American Speech*, IX (1934), 264.
[201] *American Dictionary* (1841), p. lxix.

*The Successes and Failures of Webster's Reforms Were
Due in a Measure to the Schools*

WRITING to Pickering in 1817, Webster declared, "I have contributed in a small degree, to the instruction of at least four million of the rising generation; and it is not unreasonable to expect that a few seeds of improvement planted by my hand, may germinate and grow and ripen into valuable fruit, when my remains shall be mingled with the dust." [202] Probably no one would deny that this prophecy has been fulfilled.

Webster's proposed language reform affected what was taught rather than methods in teaching.

It was one of Webster's merits . . . [says Krapp] that both by his publications and by ceaseless lecturing, advertising and sometimes wirepulling, he succeeded in arousing a great popular interest in spelling and in language in America, an interest so great that dictionary making became a profitable publisher's undertaking. The battle of the dictionaries which followed the publication of Webster's quarto of 1828 reflects therefore not only popular interest, but also to a very considerable extent the commercial rivalries of opposing publishing houses. [203]

Since Webster's texts were so widely used in the instruction of American youth, the extent to which his reform succeeded or failed is undoubtedly due in great measure to the schools. The effects that his attempts at reform had on the American language are therefore of interest to this study. They are at least three in number: (1) the uniformity of the language in America is due to a very great extent to the great interest that Webster's activities and textbooks aroused in language; (2) because of the great interest in language, especially in spelling, Americans became spelling conscious; (3) it is probably due to Webster's efforts that spelling in America and to a certain extent in England became more simple.

1. The widespread interest in spelling and language which the popularity of Webster's texts and those of his contempo-

[202] *Op. cit.*, p. 60.
[203] Krapp, *op. cit.*, I, 346.

raries, who were probably to a great extent drawn into the field because of Webster's success, was responsible for a uniformity of speech which has often been remarked by both natives and foreigners.[204] "But for the use of his books by schools in every part of the country the nation might have been divided by dialects and there would have been not one American language but a dozen." [205]

In "Webster the Schoolmaster of Our Republic," a much quoted article taken from *Glances at the Metropolis,* this estimate was given later in the century:

There has never been a great nation with a universal language without dialects. The Yorkshireman can not talk with a man from Cornwall. The peasant of the Ligurian Apennines, drives his goats home at evening, over hills that look down on six provinces, none of whose dialects he can speak. Here, five thousand miles change not the sound of a word. Around every fireside, and from every tribune, in every field of labor, and every factory of toil, is heard the same tongue. We owe it to Webster.[206]

2. Although Webster argued for a spelling that would follow the pronunciation, there is a tendency, especially in America, for pronunciation to follow the spelling.[207] "The spelling book has exerted a powerful influence in America where so many speakers have learned their language in school and looked to it as a more compelling authority than the sometimes uncertain tradition of homes." [208] The notion that all letters of a word are entitled to a certain amount of respect, reinforced by the native slowness of utterance, is responsible for the retention of unstressed vowels in "tapestry," "medicine," "venison" and has produced a secondary stress in such words as "secretary" and "extraordinary." This belief that all letters should be pronounced led Americans to reject the eighteenth-century refine-

[204] Marryat, *op. cit.,* II, 30.
[205] E. E. Slosson, "The American Spirit in Education," *The Chronicles of America,* XXXIII (1921), 118. Copyright by Yale University Press.
[206] *Elementary Spelling Book* (1857), Advertisement.
[207] Aiken, *English Present and Past* (1930), p. 205. The Ronald Press Company, Publishers.
[208] Ayres, *Cambridge History of American Literature* (1931), IV, 562. The Macmillan Company.

ment of "dropping the *g*" in such words as "going" and "seeing," and has led to the retention of the *h* in "hotel" and "hostler" and the pronouncing of the *r* final and before consonants, in spite of the frankly expressed disgust of their own countrymen in the East and South.[209] For the same reason there is a tendency to pronounce the silent *b* in "subtle" and the *t* in "often." Because the English pronunciation of such words as "clerk," "sergeant," and "derby" is at variance with the spelling, these words are usually pronounced according to the spelling in America.[210] This tendency to use spelling pronunciations is further illustrated by our pronunciation of place names, such as "Greenwich," "Thames," "Edinburgh," and "Berkeley." [211]

Just as the number of words which Webster attempted to reform was very small, so the number of those whose spelling was changed, according to Krapp, is trifling, "compared with the whole body of spellings common to British and American English." [212] Granting that Webster's spelling books and dictionaries undoubtedly exerted some influence in determining the form American spelling was to take, this author says that "the main result of Webster's radical proposals has been to leave a vague traditional feeling on the part of some Englishmen that American spelling is extreme and grotesque." [213]

Admitting that Webster was forced to give occasional ground and often held out in vain, Mencken says,

Webster lived to see the majority of reforms adopted by his countrymen. He left the *or* triumphant over the ending *our,* he shook the security of the ending *re,* he rid American spelling of a great many doubled consonants, he established the *s* in words of the *defense* group and gave currency to many characteristic American spellings, notably *jail, wagon, plow, mold,* and *ax.*[214]

This view is shared by Mathews, who says that the Websterian tradition in spelling has been sufficiently strong to cause notice-

[209] *Loc. cit.*
[210] See p. 72.
[211] John S. Kenyon, *American Pronunciation* (1930), pp. 136 f.
[212] Krapp, *op. cit.,* I, 348.
[213] *Ibid.,* 335.
[214] *The American Language* (1919), p. 252. Alfred A. Knopf, Inc.

able differences to exist at the present time between English and American spelling. In the United States we spell a considerable number of words in a manner slightly different from that preferred in British use.[215] Our orthography is more consistent. We no longer write, for example, *proveable* along with *approval* or *bedawb* by the side of *daub.*" [216]

These simplified spellings have founded a general tendency whereby new words and particularly loan-words are simplified and naturalized much more quickly in America than in England.[217] Commenting on simplification of the *our* words in America, Ayres says that British men of letters could be cited who have employed the same simplifications . . . Britons themselves are quite as likely to spell "cider" and "pajamas" in the fashion employed in America as they are to write "cyder" and "pyjamas." [218] Among the spellings which came out in the *Concise Oxford Dictionary* in 1914, and which show that the purists had surrendered in a wholesale manner, were "ax," "alarm," "tire," "asphalt," "program," "toilet," "balk," "wagon," "vial," "inquire," "pygmy," and "czar." [219]

Summary and Conclusions

THERE were two main reasons why Webster and others at the end of the eighteenth century and beginning of the nineteenth century advocated language reform: (1) A recognition of the fact that the English language is an anomalous language, difficult for children and foreigners to learn; (2) A desire prompted by the nationalistic sentiment of the day to be free from England in all things, free from literary as well as political dependence on the mother country. Webster's interest in language reform was given further impetus by his association with Franklin, a man with whom he had much in common.

[215] *Beginnings of American English* (1931), p. 52. University of Chicago Press.
[216] *Ibid., Survey of English Dictionaries* (1933), p. 43. The Clarendon Press.
[217] Mencken, *The American Language* (1919), p. 252. Alfred A. Knopf, Inc.
[218] *Cambridge History of American Literature* (1931), IV, 562.
[219] Mencken, *The American Language* (1923), p. 243. Alfred A. Knopf, Inc.

His plan of reform included the omission of silent letters, the substitution of letters with a definite sound for those that are vague and indeterminate, and the use of signs to distinguish different sounds. His guiding principles were *usage, analogy,* and *etymology.* In the main, his ideas concerning reform in spelling affected his spelling books very little. Some of his ideas were abandoned and others were modified. Many of them, however, were put into practice in his 1806 dictionary. Generally speaking, the reforms began to disappear in the 1807 and 1817 school dictionaries. They were removed in wholesale lots in the 1828 dictionary; others, in the 1841, 1848, and 1865 editions. After Webster's death, in 1843, the majority of the few remaining queer spellings were regularized. In some cases both the conventional and reformed spellings were given in the dictionaries, the conventional occupying first place.

Since Webster's spelling books and dictionaries did not employ an adequate system of marks to indicate his pronunciation with any degree of accuracy, among his most significant efforts in the field of pronunciation were the warnings against improprieties given in the footnotes of his first spellers and the discussion of pronunciation in his *Dissertations.* Whether or not the pronunciations that Webster advocated were representative of American speech has been debated. The consensus of opinion seems to be that it was fairly representative, with a distinct leaning toward New England speech.

Immediately after the publication of the 1806 dictionary Webster was attacked by the critics for his denunciation of Dr. Johnson, for his innovations, and for the localisms, Americanisms, vulgarisms, and other *isms* he had listed. To this charge he pleaded *not guilty,* insisting that most of these were good old English words that the English had discarded in favor of newer terms. In making this claim he had the sanction of some authorities in both England and America. After the publication of the 1828 dictionary the "War of the Dictionaries" began. This was largely a contest between the rival publishers of Webster's and Worcester's dictionaries. It had little to do with language reform, although the views and pronouncements of both compilers, many of which had already been repudiated, were used for ammunition.

Webster was in sympathy with the early nineteenth-century tendency to euphemize. He contemplated an expurgated edition of the English poets and did publish a revised version of the Bible in which many of the words which appeared to him and his age as vulgar and obscene terms were changed to words with a less offensive connotation.

In that Webster's books, theories, and pronouncements produced a wide interest in the English language, especially during and following the "War of the Dictionaries," he was undoubtedly instrumental in promoting the prominent place that English was to occupy later in the curricula of the American schools. It is probably due to this universal interest in language that the speech in America is uniform to a marked degree. Furthermore, the deliberate manner in which Americans pronounce their words is perhaps caused by the fact that they are spelling conscious. It is undoubtedly due to Webster's efforts in behalf of language reform that American spelling is in general more simple than English spelling.

GENERAL SUMMARY AND CONCLUSIONS

GENERALLY speaking, Noah Webster was not a great original thinker. When making a cursory survey of his life and works, one is likely to ascribe "firsts" to him which further study does not support. One of his greatest assets was his ability to appraise the past and present, to anticipate future needs, and to adapt the material at hand, be it books or ideas, to the requirements of the present and the future. His indomitable courage, his energy and perseverance were the forces which enabled him to carry his many undertakings through to completion.

His texts were not original works. His first speller was based on somewhat similar English works by Dilworth and Fenning. His first grammar was based on Lowth's compilation and his second on the theories of Horne Tooke. The pattern for his reader was taken from the English speakers and readers used in academies and colleges. His dictionaries were compiled on the broad foundation laid by English lexicographers. His school dictionaries followed the pattern used by such American compilers as Elliott, Johnson, and Alexander. In all these works, however, he showed originality in that he did not follow his models slavishly, but took independent Yankee ground, adapting the material freely and adding to it so as to meet the needs of the new-born republic. He was, however, the first to compile a short American history which was in part a geography. This he appended to his reader. Other school histories followed.

Perhaps the greatest of the forces that gave impetus to Webster's many activities was his patriotic fervor, his chauvinistic support of the spread-eagle doctrine. Again he was the child of his age. His *Sketches of American Policy*, which recommended that a constitution be adopted to take the place of the articles of confederation, gave utterance to an opinion that was generally held among thinkers of his age. The ideas he held concerning education in America, that is, that the approach should be scientific, that youths should be indoctrinated in those things which were held to be peculiarly American, and that education should be pragmatic, were shared by many of his contemporaries. These theories were not put into practice, however, until a later age. It is likely that his efforts in behalf of American education were seeds sown which bore fruit in the following century, when the public-school system developed.

To existing methods of instruction Webster added very little. In fact, as he himself owned, he had occupied his time supplying what should be taught and had given little thought to methods of instruction. His speller, which was to be used as a beginning book in teaching children to spell and read, was compiled with the alphabet method in mind. In spite of the efforts of Horace Mann and other progressive educators who recommended the word method, Webster still clung to the alphabet method in 1843, the year of his death. It was probably because of the popularity of his speller that the alphabet method gained such a strong foothold that it endured during the greater part of the nineteenth century and has not entirely disappeared even today. In fact, according to some authorities, it was not until more modern methods were introduced by which children could learn to read with greater ease that primary and elementary education was enriched by the introduction of other subjects into the curricula.

Webster's ideas concerning reading as taught to and studied by the older pupils were what we would today call "elocutionary." Emphasis was placed on the "expression of the passions" rather than on an understanding of the thought set forth on the printed page. This method was taken by Webster, apparently without question, from the methods used in English and American colleges and academies. Emphasis on the alphabet method and the "art of reading," along with the fact that selections were not adapted to the capacity of the child, placed a real barrier between the pupil and the learning process.

Although Webster protested vigorously against the prevailing methods used in the teaching of grammar, yet his grammars, like those of his contemporaries, show that he was in thralldom to the Latin methods of the past. It is possible, however, that his constant denunciation of current methods hastened the day when the teaching of grammar became more rational, when instruction gave cognizance to inductive methods, and actual practice in expression was employed.

Time after time Webster stated that he looked to the schools for aid in bringing about the uniformity of language which he deemed essential to the healthy political life of the Republic. Because of Webster's many activities, the intrinsic value of his texts and dictionaries, and the aggressive business methods which were employed to increase the sale of his texts, a great interest was aroused in the study of language and the day was hastened when the study of English occupied a prominent position in the curricula of American schools. Webster's extreme reforms were not introduced in his speller, but the reforms that were introduced in this work were generally those that have been adopted. It is probably due to Webster's efforts to reform the language that the English language in America is more uniform than it is in England or than is the language spoken by the people living in various sections of any other large country. Perhaps for the same reason, pronunciation in America tends to follow spelling, and spelling is generally more simple in this country than in England.

One of the criticisms frequently made of Webster was that he was inconsistent, that he shifted from one position to another. This tendency is especially noticeable in his grammars and in the language reforms he proposed. To this charge, he was the first to own his guilt. "I have," he said, "in the course of my life, been often obliged to change my opinion." But his changes of opinion were usually based on conviction rather than a fear of the opinions of the critics. Authorities are generally agreed that his sincerity was beyond question and that most of his shiftings were due to his honest effort to observe and record actual usage.

Many of the opinions of his youth, he himself admitted, were visionary and deceptive. Then, too, because of his activity in very many fields and because of human frailty, it is undoubtedly true that confusion played a part in his inconsistencies.

Webster perhaps made his greatest contribution to education in America through his publication of textbooks and through his successful efforts in behalf of copyright laws, rather than through the theorizing and pronouncements in his essays and dissertations. His success as a compiler and the financial remuneration which the copyright laws assured successful authors drew other compilers into the field. In fact, so numerous were the early nineteenth-century texts that according to the educational periodicals of the day their heterogeneity proved a hindrance rather than a help. But among these numerous texts stood the banner text of all times and places, the *Old Blue-Back Spelling Book*, which "taught millions to read but not one to sin." Webster, the pioneer in many fields of endeavor on the American intellectual frontier, taught the masses to spell and read. He was truly the Schoolmaster of the Republic.

APPENDIX I

PRONUNCIATION [1]

Index or Key

Long.				Short aw.		
1	1	1		5	5	5
a	name,	late.		a	what,	was.
e or ee	here,	feet.		o	not,	from.
i	time,	find.			*Oo proper.*	
o	note,	fort.		6	6	6
u or ew	tune,	new.		o or oo	move,	room.
y	dry,	defy.			*Oo Short.*	
	Short.			7	7	7
2	2	2		oo	book,	flood.
a	man,	hat.		u	bush,	full.
e	men,	let.			*Short u.*	
i	pit,	pin.		9	9	9
u	tun,	but.		i	sir,	bird.
y	glory,	Egypt.		o	come,	love.
	Broad a or aw			e	her.	
3	3	3			*Long a a.*	
a	bald,	tall.		10	10	10
o	cost,	sought.		e	there,	vein.
aw	law.				*Long e.*	
	Flat a.			11	11	11
4	4	4		i	fatigue,	pique.
a	ask,	part.		oi, oy	}diphthong; voice, joy.	
				ou, ow	}diphthong; loud, now.	

EXPLANATION OF THE INDEX

A figure stands as the invariable representative of a certain sound. The figure 1 represents the long sound of the letters, *a, e, i, o, u,* or *ew,* and *y;* number 2, the short sound of the same characters; number 3, marks the sound of broad *a,* as in *hall;* number 4, represents the sound of *a,* in *father;* number 5, represents the short sound of broad *a,* as in *not, what;* number 6, represents the sound of *o* in *move,* commonly expressed by *oo;* number 7, represents the short sound of *oo* in *root, bush;* number 9, represents the sound of *u* short, made by *e, i,* and *o* as in *her, bird, come,* pronounced *hur, burd, cum;* number 10, represents the first sound of *a* made by *e,* as in *their, vein,* pronounced *thare, vane;* number 11, represents the French sound of *i,* which is the same as *e* long.

[1] *American Spelling Book* (1795), p. 23.

APPENDIX II

WEBSTER'S IMPROPRIETIES[1]

activ	*not*	active	deceipt	*not*	desate
adversity		advarsity	detachment		detachement
analogy		anawlogy	desperate		desput
angel		anegel	diamond		dimon
apron		apurn	dictionary		dicsonary
apron		apun	divert		divart
ask		ax	drain		dreen
asparagus		sparrowgrass	drought		drouth
attachment		attachement			
axle-tree		exl-tree	errand		arrant
			every		evry
backward		backard			
barefoot		bowfoot	farthing		fardin
bayonet		bagonet	faucet		fasset
beets		baits	flax		flex
beginning		beginnin	further		furder
bellows		bellosis			
beverage		beberage	gauntlet		gantlit
blunderbuss		blunderbush	guardian		guardeen
bowsprit		bolsplit	genius		genus
burst		bust	girl		gal
			going		goin
calk		cork	gown		gownd
card		kaird	gum		goom
carry		kerry			
celery		salary	height		haith, hate
certify		sartify	heinous		haneous
chare		chore	herb		yerb
chimney		chimbly	hinder		hender
churn		churm	homely		humbly
collander		cullender	human		yuman
coming		comin	humour		yumour
conceipt		consate	humourous		yumourous
confiscate		confisticate	hurricane		harrecane
coroner		crowner	hurricane		harricane
cover		kiver	huzza		whorra
cresses		crushes			
cucumber		cowcumber	jaundice		jaunders
curtsey		curche	jest		jeest
cutlass		cutlash	juvenil		juvenile
danger		daneger	kernel		kannul
dandruff		dander			

[1] See pp. 74 f. and 277 f.

lantern	*not*	lanthorn	radishes	*not*	redishes
lantern		lantorn	raisins		reesons
lest		leest	raspberry		rozberry
licorice		lickerish	receipt		resate
			rennet		runnet
mercury		marcury	resin		rozum
mercy		marcy	rheumatism		rumatiz
motiv		motive	rhubarb		rubub
muskmellon		musmillion	rinse		rense
			roof		ruf
negro		neger	ruffian		ruffin
nest		neest			
nothing		nothin	sallad		sallit
			sassafras		savafax
onion		ineyon	sillabub		sullabub
onion		eenyon	since		sence
overplus		overplush	smother		smuder
			soot		sut
panther		painter	spirit		sperit
perfect		parfect	stranger		straneger
pincers		pinchers			
plait		pleet	that		dat
popular		pople	this		dis
porringer		pornger	thou		dou
pour		poor	town		townd
practis		practise			
proposal		propozhal	vagabond		vagabone
pumpkin		punkin			
			wainscot		winchcot
quoit		quate	watermellon		watermillion
quota		quoto	whitlow		whitblow

SOME SPELLINGS WHICH ARE TO BE FOUND IN WEBSTER'S SPELLING BOOKS AND IN VARIOUS DICTIONARIES [a]

American Spelling Book	Compendious Dictionary, 1806	Dictionary of the English Language, 1807	Dictionary of the English Language, 1817	American Dictionary, quarto, 1828	American Dictionary, octavo, 1829	Dictionary of the English Language, duodecimo, 1929	Elementary Spelling Book	American Dictionary, quarto, 1841	American Dictionary, quarto, 1848	American Dictionary, quarto, 1865
. . .	fiber	do.	do.	do.	fibre / fiber	fiber / fibre	. . .	do.	do.	do.
meter	do.	do.	do.	do	metre / meter	meter	. . .	meter / metre	do.	do.
frolic / frolick	frolick	do.	do.	do.	do.	do.	. . .	do.	frolic / frolick	frolic
. . .	hillock	do.	do.	do.	hilloc	hillock	do.	do.	do.	do.
offence	offense	do.	do.	do.	do.	do.	do.	do.	do.	do.
. . .	blamable	blameable	do.	blamable	do.	do.	do.	do.	do.	do.
ratable	do.	do.	rateable	ratable	do.	do.	. . .	do.	do.	do.
enterprize	enterprize	enterprise	do.	enterprise	do.	do.	do.	do.	do.	do.
methodize	methodise	do.	do.	methodize	do.	do.	do.	do.	do.	do.
. . .	pencilled	pencilled	. . .	penciled	do.	do.	. . .	do.	do.	do.
jeweller	do.	do.	do.	jeweler	do.	do.	. . .	do.	do.	do.
instructor	instructer / instructor	instructor	do.	do.	do.	do.	do.	do.	do.	do.
. . .	sailer / sailor	do.	do.	sailor / sailer	do.	sailor	. . .	sailor / sailor	do.	sailor / sailor
. . .	plaintiff	do.	do.	plaintif	plaintiff / plaintif	plaintif	. . .	plaintif / plaintiff	plaintiff	do.

	Ed. 1	Ed. 2	Ed. 3	Ed. 4	Ed. 5	Ed. 6	Ed. 7	Ed. 8	Ed. 9	Ed. 10	Ed. 11	Ed. 12	Ed. 13	Ed. 14
. . .	sheriff	do.	do.	do.	sheriff	sheriff / sheriff	sheriff	. . .	sherif	sheriff / sherif	sherif	do.	do.	do.
determine	determin	do.	determine	do.	do.	do.	do.	do.	do.	do.	do.	do.	do.	do.
. . .	envelop	do.	do.	do.	envelop / envelope	envelop	do.	do.	envelope / envelop	envelop / envelope	envelop	do.	envelope / envelop	do.
examine	examin	do.	examine	do.	do.	do.	do.	do.	do.	do.	do.	do.	do.	do.
feather	feather / fether	do.	do.	do.	do.	feather	feather	feather / fether	feather	feather	do.	do.	feather	do.
leather	lether	do.	do.	do.	leather / lether	leather	leather	leather / lether	leather	leather	leather	do.	leather	do.
wo, woe	woe, wo	do.	do.	do.	wo	woe, wo	wo	woe, wo	woe	woe, wo	woe	do.	do.	do.
moult	molt	do.	do.	do.	do.	do.	do.	do.	do.	do.	do.	do.	do.	do.
chemist	do.	do.	do.	do.	chimist	chimist	chimist	chimist / chemist	chimist	chimist	do.	chemist	chemist	do.
cholic	colic	do.	do.	do.	do.	cholic	cholic	colic	cholic	do.	cholic	do.	do.	do.
crowd	crowd / croud	do.	do.	do.	crowd / embodied	crowd	crowd	crowd / croud	crowd / croud	crowd / croud	crowd	do.	do.	do.
. . .	imbodied	embodied	embodied	do.	imbodied	do.	do.	embodied / imbodied	embodied	embodied / imbodied	imbodied	do.	do.	do.
jail	gaol / jail	do.	do.	do.	do.	jail	jail	do.	do.	do.	jail	do.	do.	do.
gray / grey	do.	do.	do.	do.	gray	do.	do.	gray / grey	gray	gray / grey	do.	gray	do.	gray
heinous	hainous	do.	do.	do.	heinous / hainous	hainous	do.	do.	heinous / hainous	hainous	hainous	do.	heinous	do.
molasses	melasses	do.	do.	do.	molasses / melasses	melasses	do.	do.	molasses / melasses	melasses	melasses	do.	molasses	do.
plow	do.	do.	do.	do.	plough / plow	plow	do.	do.	plough / plow	plow	plow	do.	plow / plough	do.
women	wimmen	do.	women	do.	do.	women	do.	women	do.	do.	do.	do.	do.	do.
. . .	yelk / yolk	do.	yelk	do.	do.	yelk	do.	yelk / yolk	yelk	yelk	do.	yelk / yolk	do.	do.
. . .	zebra / zeber	zebra	do.	do.	do.	do.	do.	do.	do.	do.	do.	do.	do.	do.

a These words are only a few of the hundreds whose spelling was inconsistent in the various Webster books. The critics made much of these inconsistencies.

APPENDIX IV

LEXICOGRAPHIC DEVELOPMENTS

In order to illustrate the methods that Webster and the lexicographers who preceded him used, the spelling, pronunciation, etymology, definition, and illustration of the word "democracy," insofar as these features were present, are given in the following chronological arrangement. The dictionaries used were those available in the libraries of New York City. When possible, first editions [1] were chosen.

Cawdrey, 1604
democracie, (g) a commonwealth governed by the people.

Cockeram, 1623
Democracie. Rule which people have over themselves without a superiour, unlesse such as they themselves will appoint.

Phillips, 1662
Democracy, (Greek) a Government wherein the Magistrates are chosen from among the people, and by the people.

Blount, 1674
Democracy (democratia) a kind of Government of a Commonweal, wherein the people have the chief rule without any Superior or Magistrate over them, save only such as themselves choose.

E. Coles, 1701
Democracy, g. [Greek] a government whose magistrates are chosen from among and by the People.

Glossographia Anglicana Nova, 1707
Democracy, a Form of Government, where the Supreme or Legislative Power is lodged in the Common People, or Persons chose out of them.

Bullokar, 12th ed., 1719
Democracy. A Kind of Government, wherein the People bear Rule without other Superiours, saving such as they appoint.

Bailey, 1736
DEMO′CRACY [*democracie* F. *democrazia* It. *democracia*, Sp. *democratia*, L. of δημοκρασια of δήμου the people, and κρατέω to exercise power over, Gr.] a form of government where the supreme or legislature power is lodged in the common people, or persons chosen out from them.

DEMOCRACY, or a democratical government, has been presented iconologically by a woman in a mean but decent habit, to represent the condition of the common people, crown'd with a chaplet of vine leaves, wreath'd, with a branch of elm to denote union, holding in one hand a pomegranite, as an emblem of the people assembled in one body: and in the other serpents, because they are content to remain in a low state, and don't aspire to higher things. Corn lying on the

---

[1] See pp. 215 f. for titles of the works from which these items were drawn and for dates of the first editions.

ground, and sacks of corn round about her, to shew that a publick provision for the necessities of every one maintains peace and union.

J. Kersey, 5th ed., 1748

Democracy, a Government where the People bear Rule.

Johnson, 1755

DEMO'CRACY. n.s. [δημοχρατια] One of the three forms of government; that in which the sovereign power is neither lodged in one man, nor in the nobles, but in the collective body of the people.

While many of the servants, by industry and virtue, arrive at riches and esteem, then the nature of the government inclines to a *democracy*.—Temple.

The majority having the whole power of the community, may employ all that power in making laws, and executing those laws; and there the form of the government is a perfect *democracy*.—Locke.

Perry, 1775

De-moc'ra-cy, s. popular government.

Sheridan, 3d ed., 1790

DEMOCRACY, de-mok-kra-sy. s. One of the three forms of government, that in which the sovereign power is lodged in the body of the people.

Walker, 1791

DEMOCRACY, de-mok'kra-se. f. One of the three forms of government, that in which the sovereign power is lodged in the body of the people.

Elliott and Johnson, 1800

De moc ra cy, s. popular government.

Entick, edited by Murray, 1805

Democ'racy, s. a popular form of government.

Webster, 1806

Democ'racy, n. a popular form of government.

Webster, 1807, 1817

Democ'racy, n. a form of government in which the sovereign power is exercised by the people.

Webster, 1828

DEMOC'RACY, n. [Gr. δημοχρατια: δημος, people, and χρατεω, to possess, to govern.] Government by the people; a form of government in which the supreme power is lodged in the hands of the people collectively, or in which the people exercise the powers of legislation. Such was the government of Athens.

APPENDIX V
NATURE STUDY AND FABLES

The Squirrel

The squirrel is a beautiful little animal. The gray and black squirrels live in the forest and make a nest of leaves and sticks on the high branches. It is amusing to see the nimble squirrel spring from branch to branch, or run up and down the stem of a tree, and dart behind it to escape from sight. Little ground squirrels burrow in the earth. They subsist on nuts, which they hold in their paws, using them as little boys use their hands.

Of the Boy That Stole Apples

An old man found a rude boy upon one of his trees stealing apples, and desired him to come down; but the young sauce-box told him plainly he would not. "Won't you?" said the old man, "then I will fetch you down;" so he pulled up some turf or grass and threw at him; but this only made the youngster laugh, to think the old man should pretend to beat him down from the tree with grass only.

"Well, well," said the old man, "if neither words nor grass will do, I must try what virtue there is in stones;" so the old man pelted him heartily with stones, which soon made the young chap hasten down from the tree and beg the old man's pardon.

MORAL

If good words and gentle means will not reclaim the wicked, they must be dealt with in a more severe manner.

The Country Maid and Her Milk Pail

When men suffer their imagination to amuse them with the prospect of distant and uncertain improvements of their condition, they frequently sustain real losses, by their inattention to those affairs in which they are immediately concerned.

A country maid was walking very deliberately with a pail of milk upon her head, when she fell into the following train of reflections: "The money for which I shall sell this milk, will enable me to increase my stock of eggs to three hundred. These eggs, allowing for what may prove addle, and what may be destroyed by vermin, will produce at least two hundred and fifty chickens. The chickens will be fit to carry to market about Christmas, when poultry always bears a good price; so that by May Day I can not fail of having money enough to purchase a new gown. Green!—let me consider—yes, green becomes my complexion best, and green it shall be. In this dress I will go to the fair, where all the young fellows will strive to have me for a partner; but I shall perhaps refuse every one of them, and, with an air of disdain, toss from them." Transported with this triumphant thought, she could not forbear acting with her head what thus passed in her imagination, when down came the pail of milk, and with it all her imaginary happiness.[1]

[1] The above fables and engravings were included in many issues of the *Elementary Spelling Book*. The engravings appeared in the *Webster Pictorial Elementary Spelling Book* (1844 ?). They were by Anderson and Morgan. See p. 79.

BIBLIOGRAPHY

Abbot, Jacob, The Teacher. Boston, W. Pierce, 1836.

Adamson, John William. The Educational Writings of John Locke. New York, Longmans, Green & Company, 1912.

Aiken, Janet Rankin. English Present and Past. New York, The Ronald Press Company, 1930. Introduction by George Philip Krapp.

—— Why English Sounds Change. New York, The Ronald Press Company, 1929.

Alexander, Caleb. The Columbian Dictionary of the English Language. Boston, 1800.

—— The Young Ladies' and Gentleman's Spelling Book. Worcester, 1799.

American Annals of Education and Instruction, Vol. II. 1822.

"Among the Dictionaries," Eclectic Magazine, XCVII (1881), 236–47.

"American Dictionary of the English Language, An . . . by Noah Webster . . . (1859), "A Dictionary of the English Language by Joseph E. Worcester . . . (1860)," Atlantic Monthly, V (1860), 631–37.

Ayres, Harry M. "The English Language in America," Cambridge History of American Literature, Vol. IV. New York, The Macmillan Company, 1927.

Bacon, F. The Moral and Historical Works of Lord Bacon. London, Henry G. Bohn, 1854.

Baker, Franklin T. "The Vernacular," Munro's Principles of Secondary Education. New York, 1915.

Barnard's American Journal of Education, II, X, XIII, XIV, XV, XVII, 1855, '61, '64, '65, '67.

Bartlett, John Russell. A Glossary of Words and Phrases Usually Regarded as Peculiar to the United States, 4th ed., Boston, 1877.

Bascome, Edward. A History of Epidemic Pestilence from the Earliest Ages, 1495 Years before the Birth of Our Saviour to 1848. London, 1851.

Bates, Albert Carlos. Check List of Connecticut Almanacs 1709–1850. Worcester, American Antiquarian Society, 1914.

Baylies, Frances. A Historical Memoir of the Colony of New Plymouth. Boston, 1830.

Bean, C. Homer. "How English Grammar Has Been Taught in America," Education, XIV, 1914.

Beck, T. Romeyn. "Notes on Mr. Pickering's Vocabulary," Transactions of the Albany Institute, Vol. I. 1830.

Becker, Carl L. The Declaration of Independence. New York, Harcourt, Brace and Company, 1922.

—— The Heavenly City of the Eighteenth Century Philosophers. New Haven, Yale University Press, 1932.

Beer, Thomas. The Mauve Decade. Garden City, New York, Garden City Publishing Company, 1926.

"Belknap Papers," Massachusetts Historical Society Collections, Vols. II and III. Boston, Published by the Society, 1877.

Benezet, Anthony. The Pennsylvania Spelling Book. 2d ed., Philadelphia, 1779.

Benton, Joel. "An Unpublished Chapter in the Life of Webster," Magazine of American History, X (1883), pp. 52–56.

—— "The Webster Spelling Book," Magazine of American History, X (1883), 299–306.

Bergh, A. E. Writings of Thomas Jefferson. Vols. XIII, XVII, Washington, 1904.
Bewick, Thomas. Bewick's Select Fables of Aesop and Others. London, 1871.
Biglow, John. The Complete Works of Benjamin Franklin. 10 vols., New York, Putnam's Sons, 1887–88.
Bingham, Caleb. The Young Lady's Accidence, 7th ed., Boston, 1793.
Bullokar, John. The English Expositor Improved. London, 1719.
Boone, Richard G. Education in the United States. New York, D. Appleton & Company, 1890.
Bradlaugh, Charles. Biographies of Ancient and Modern Celebrated Freethinkers. Boston, J. P. Mendum, 1877.
Bradley, Henry. The Making of English. London, 1904.
Bradshaw, Henry. Collected Papers. Cambridge, University Printing Press, 1889.
Bringham, Clarence. An Account of American Almanacs and Their Value for Historical Study. Worcester, 1925. Reprinted from the Proceedings of the American Antiquarian Society.
Brinsley, John. Ludus literarius, or The Grammar School (1612), ed. by E. T. Campagnac, Liverpool, University Press, 1917.
Bristed, Charles Astor. "The English Language in America," Cambridge Essays. London, John W. Parker & Sons, 1855.
Bruce, Philip Alexander. Social Life in Virginia in the Seventeenth Century. Richmond, Whittet & Shepperson, 1907.
Burgh, James. The Art of Speaking. Boston, 1782.
Burlingame, Anne Elizabeth. Condorcet, The Torchbearer of the French Revolution. Boston, The Stratford Company, 1931.
Burton, Warren. The District School as It Was (1833), ed. by Clifton Johnson. Boston, Lee & Shepard Company, 1897.
Bury, J. B. The Idea of Progress. London, Macmillan Company, 1921.
Catholicon. London, Published for the Early English Text Society, 1881.
Channing, William Ellery. "On National Literature" (1823), Old South Leaflets, Vol. VI, No. 141, 1903.
Chase, Wayland Johnson. "The Distichs of Cato," University of Wisconsin. Studies in the Social Sciences and History, No. 7, 1922.
Clap, Thomas. The Annals or History of Yale College, 1700–1766. New Haven, 1766.
Coles, Elisha. An English Dictionary. London, 1701.
Colton, A. M. "Our Old Webster Spelling Book," Magazine of American History, XXIV (1890), pp. 465–66.
Common School Assistant, Vol. I, 1836.
Common School Journal, Vols. I, II, IV, V, VI, X, XII. 1839, '40, '42, '43, '44, '47, '49.
Connecticut Common School Journal, Vols. II, X, XI.
Craig, John. A New Universal Etymological, Technological, and Pronouncing Dictionary, 2d ed., London, George Routledge & Company, 1852.
Cross, E. A. Fundamentals in English. New York, The Macmillan Company, 1926.
Cubberley, Ellwood P. Public Education in the United States. New York, Houghton Mifflin Company, 1919.
Darton, F. J. Harvey. Children's Books in England, Five Centuries of Social Life. Cambridge University Press, 1932.
Darwin, Erasmus. Zoonomia or the Laws of Organic Life, I, 531. London, Printed for J. Johnson, 1794.
Davis, John. Travels of Four Years and a Half in the United States of America (1798–1802). New York, Henry Holt & Company, 1909.

DeBow's Review, XXVIII (1860), 561.

de la Fontainerie, François. French Liberalism and Education in the Eighteenth Century. New York and London, McGraw-Hill Book Company, Inc., 1932.

Descartes, René. Oeuvres de Descartes, Vol. VI. Paris, L. Cerf, 1897.

Dexter, Franklin Bowditch. Biographical Sketches of the Graduates of Yale College, Vol. IV. New York, Henry Holt & Company, 1907.

"Diary of Cotton Mather 1709–24," Massachusetts Historical Society Collections, Vols. VII, VIII. Boston, 1912.

Dilworth, Thomas. A New Guide to the English Tongue. Boston, 1770.

District School Journal, Vols. IV, IX, 1843, '48.

Dodsley, Robert. The Preceptor. London, 1748. 2d ed. 1754.

—— Select Fables of Aesop and Other Fabulists. London, 1765. 1st ed. 1761.

Dunlap, William. Diary, Vol. I. New York, Printed for the New York Historical Society, 1930.

DuPont de Nemours, Pierre. National Education in the United States of America (1800), ed. by Bessie Gardiner DuPont. Newark, University of Delaware Press, 1923.

Eggleston, Edward. Hoosier School Master, revised ed. 1913.

—— The Transit of Civilization from England to America in the Seventeenth Century. New York, 1901.

Elliott, John, and Johnson, Samuel, Jr. A Selecting, Pronouncing and Accented Dictionary. 1st and 2d editions, Suffield, Conn., 1800.

Ellis, A. J. An Early English Pronunciation. London, Published for the Philological Society by Asher & Company, 1869–89.

Elwyn, A. L. A Glossary of Supposed Americans. Philadelphia, 1859.

Ely, A. School Dictionary. 1830.

Emerson, Oliver Farrar. A History of the English Language. New York, 1894.

Enfield, William. Exercises in Elocution . . . intended as sequel to The Speaker. Warrington, 1780.

—— The Speaker. Philadelphia. Printed by William Wallis Woodward, 1799.

Entick, John. A Spelling Dictionary, ed. by William Crakelt. London, 1787.

Epinal Glossary, Latin and Old English of the Eighth Century, The. Trans. by W. Greggs. London, Printed for Philological and Early English Text Societies, 1883.

Evans, Charles. American Bibliography, Vols. I–XII, 1639–1799. Chicago, Privately printed for the author, 1903–34.

Fay, Bernard. The Revolutionary Spirit in France and America. New York, Harcourt, Brace and Company, 1927.

Fenning, Daniel. The Universal Spelling Book; or, A New and Easy Guide to the English Language. London, 1756.

Fleming, Sanford. Children and Puritanism. New Haven, Yale University Press, 1933.

Foerster, Norman. Reinterpretation of American Literature. New York, Harcourt, Brace and Company, 1928.

Foley, John P. The Jeffersonian Cyclopedia. New York, Funk & Wagnalls Company, 1900.

Ford, E. E. F. Notes on the Life of Noah Webster, Vols. I, II; ed. by Emily E. F. Skeel. New York, Privately printed, 1912.

Ford, Paul Leicester. The New England Primer. New York, Dodd, Mead & Company, 1897.

—— The Writings of Thomas Jefferson, VIII, 80. New York, Putnam's Sons, 1897.

Fowler, William C. The English Language. New York, Harper & Brothers, 1850. Revised 1855.

Fox, George. Instructions for Right-Spelling. Philadelphia, 1702, 1737, 1743, 1769.

Franklin, Benjamin. Scheme for a New Alphabet and a Reformed Mode of Spelling. Philadelphia, 1768.

Frazer, Sir James George. Condorcet on the Progress of the Human Mind. Oxford, Clarendon Press, 1933.

Freneau, Philip. Poems of Freneau, ed. by Hayden Clark. New York, Harcourt, Brace and Company, 1829.

Furnivall, F. J. The Babees Book. London, Published for Early Text Book Society, 1868.

Geddes, James. "Dictionaries in English and Foreign Languages," The Library Journal, LIV (1929), 843–49.

Gifford, William. The Quarterly Review, X (1814), 494–539.

Gilbert, Sir Humphrey. Queene Elizabeth's Achademy, ed. by F. J. Furnivall. London, Early English Text Society, 1869.

Gilman, A. Short Stories from the Dictionary. Chicago, The Interstate Publishing Company, 1886.

Gould, Edward Sherman. Good English or Popular Errors in Language. New York, W. J. Widdelton, 1867.

Grandgent, C. H. "From Franklin to Lowell, a Century of New England Pronunciation," Modern Language Association Publication, XIV, 207.

Hall, Captain Basil. Travels in North America in the Years 1827 and 1828. 2 vols. Philadelphia, Carey, Lee & Company, 1829.

Hansen, A. O. Liberalism and American Education in the Eighteenth Century. New York, The Macmillan Company, 1926.

Hartshorne, Hugh. Character in Human Relations. New York, Charles Scribner's Sons, 1932.

Haskins, Charles Homer. "A List of Textbooks from the Close of the Twelfth Century," Harvard Studies in Classic Philology, XX. Cambridge, 1909.

Hazard, Ebenezer. Historical Collections Consisting of State Papers and Other Authentic Documents; Intended as Materials for a History of the United States of America. Philadelphia, T. Dobson, 1792.

Hazen, Charles Downer. Contemporary American Opinion of the French Revolution. Baltimore, Johns Hopkins Press, 1897.

Heartman, C. F. Checklist of the New England Primer. New York, R. R. Bowker Company, 1934.

Hessels, Jan Hendrick. An Eighth-Century Latin, Anglo-Saxon Glossary. Cambridge, University Press, 1890.

Hockett, Homer Carey. Introduction to Research in American History. New York, The Macmillan Company, 1931.

Hoole, Charles. A New Discovery of the Old Art of Teaching School (1660). Introduction by Thiselton Mark. New York, C. W. Bardeen, 1912.

Hudson, Frederic. Journalism in the United States from 1690 to 1872. New York, Harper and Brothers Publishers, 1873.

James, Philip. Children's Books of Yesterday, ed. by G. Geoffrey Holme. London, The Studio Publications, Ind., 1933.

Jellinek, George. The Declaration of the Rights of Man and of Citizens, trans. by M. Farrand. New York, Henry Holt & Company, 1901.

Jernegan, Marcus W. "The Beginnings of Public Education in New England," School Review, XXIII, 319–30, 361–80.

Jesperson, Otto. Language. New York, Henry Holt & Company, 1922.

Jesperson, Otto. A Modern English Grammar. Part I, Heidelberg, 1909. Part II, Heidelberg, 1914.

John Adams' Works, ed. by C. F. Adams. Boston, Little, Brown & Company, 1850–56.

Johnson, Clifton. Old Time Schools and School Books. New York, The Macmillan Company, 1904.

Johnson, Samuel, Jr. A School Dictionary. New Haven, 1798.

Jones, Daniel. The Pronunciation of English. Cambridge, 1909.

Journal of the Proceedings of the Anthology Society. Boston, The Boston Athenaeum, 1910.

Judd, Wilbur Webster. "Noah Webster," Connecticut Magazine, n. d. Book of Pamphlets on Education, Teachers College, Columbia University.

Kellogg, A. E. "Contents of School Readers," The Educational Review, VIII (1894), 337–49.

Kenyon, John. American Pronunciation. Ann Arbor, George Wahr, 1930.

Kersey, John. A New English Dictionary, or A Compleat Collection of the Most Proper and Significant Words and Terms of Art Commonly Used in the Language. London, 1748.

Knickerbocker Magazine, VII (1836), 349.

Knight, Edgar Wallace. Education in the United States. New York, Ginn and Company, 1934.

Knox, Samuel. An Essay on the Best System of Education. Baltimore, Warner & Hanna, 1799.

Krapp, George P. The English Language in America. 2 vols. New York, The Century Company, 1925.

Lafitte du Courteil. Proposal to Demonstrate the Necessity of a National Institution in the United States. Philadelphia. Printed for G. Decombaz, 1797.

Laski, H. J. "Rise of Liberalism," Encyclopaedia of the Social Sciences, I, 103–24, ed. by E. A. Seligman. New York, The Macmillan Company, 1930.

Lecky, W. E. H. History of English in the Eighteenth Century. New York, D. Appleton & Company, 1892–93.

Leonard, S. A. "Doctrine of Correctness in English Usage 1700–1800," Wisconsin University Studies. Madison, 1929,

Letters of J. Downing, Major, to His Old Friend, Mr. Dwight. New York, 1834.

Lily, William. Brevissima institutio, Oxford, 1709.

Lindsay, Wallace Martin. The Corpus, Epinal, Erfurt and Leyden Glossaries. Oxford University Press, 1921.

—— Corpus glossarium. University Press, 1921.

Literary Diary of Ezra Stiles, ed. by Franklin Bowditch Dexter, 3 vols. New York, Charles Scribner's Sons, 1901.

Littlefield, George Emery. Early Schools and Schoolbooks of New England. Boston, The Club of Odd Volumes, 1904.

Locke, John. Some Thoughts Concerning Education (1693), ed. by R. H. Quick, Cambridge, University Press, 1913.

Lounsbury, T. R. History of the English Language. New York, Henry Holt & Company, 1882.

Low, Samuel. The Politician Outwitted. New York, W. Ross, 1789.

Lowth, Robert. A Short Introduction to English Grammar with Critical Notes. Philadelphia, Robert Aiken, 1775.

Lyman, Rollo LaVerne, English Grammar in American Schools before 1850. Washington, Bureau of Educational Bulletin, 1921.

Macaulay, T. B. Life of Samuel Johnson, ed. by Haber Nay Beuhler. New York, Longmans, Green & Company, 1918.

Mackenzie, Catherine. "Our Food Habits Changed by Time." New York Times Magazine, February 24, 1935, p. 14.

McKnight, George H., assisted by Bert Emsley. Modern English in the Making. New York, Appleton & Company, 1928.

Marryat, Captain Frederick. Diary in America with Remarks on Its Institutions, II, 31. Philadelphia, Carey and Hart, 1839.

Marsh, George Perkins. Lectures on the English Language. New York, Charles Scribner's Sons, 1862.

Martin, George H. The Evolution of Massachusetts Public School System. New York, 1894.

Mathews, M. M. The Beginnings of American English. Chicago, University of Chicago Press, 1931.

—— A Survey of English Dictionaries. London, Oxford University Press, 1933.

Matthews, Brander. American Character. New York, Thomas Crowell & Company, 1906.

—— Americanisms and Briticisms with Other Essays on Other Isms. New York, 1892.

Mencken, H. L. The American Language. New York, Alfred A. Knopf, 1919, 1921, 1923.

Menner, Robert J. "The Pronunciation of English in America," Atlantic Monthly, March, 1915, p. 360.

Meriwether, Colyer. Our Colonial Curriculum 1607–1776. Washington, D. C., Capital Publishing Company, 1907.

Milton, John. "On Education," Old South Leaflets, VIII, 2.

Mirror, The. No. 1–110, January 27, 1779–May 27, 1780. London, 1802.

Mitchell, Langdon. Understanding America. New York, George H. Doran Company, 1927.

Monroe, Paul. Cyclopedia of Education. New York, The Macmillan Company, 1911.

Moore, John Hamilton. The Young Gentleman and Lady's Monitor and English Teachers Assistant. London, 1784.

Mordecai, Samuel. Richmond in By-Gone Days. Richmond, West & Johnson, 1860.

Morley, John Viscount. Biographical Studies. London, The Macmillan Company, 1923.

Mulcaster, Richard. Elementarie, ed. by E. T. Campagnac. Oxford, Clarendon Press, 1925.

Murray, James A. H. The Evolution of English Lexicography. Oxford, Clarendon Press, 1900.

Neef, Joseph. Sketch of a Plan and Method of Education Founded on an Analysis of the Human Faculties and Natural Reason. Philadelphia, 1808.

Neumann, Joshua H. American Pronunciation According to Noah Webster. New York, 1924.

Nevins, Allan. American Press Opinion Washington to Coolidge, A Documentary Record of Editorial Leadership and Criticism. New York, D. C. Heath & Company, 1928.

—— American Social History as Recorded by British Travelers. New York, Henry Holt and Company, 1923.

New International Encyclopaedia, Vol. II. New York, Dodd, Mead & Company, 1923.

New York (State) Senate Documents, Vol. III, Nos. 65–97, 1851.

Ogilvie, John. The Imperial Dictionary. 2 vols. London, Blackie & Son, 1853.

Oldest English Texts, ed. by Henry Sweet. London, Early English Text Society, 1885.

"100th Anniversary of the G. & C. Merriam Company," High School Teacher, VII (1931), 395.

Parrington, V. L. Main Currents in American Thought. 3 vols. New York, Harcourt, Brace and Company, 1927–30.

Partridge, Eric. Words, Words, Words. London, Methuen & Company, Ltd., 1933.

Perry, Bliss. "The American Spirit in Literature, A Chronicle of Great Interpreters." The Chronicles of America. New Haven, Yale University Press, 1921.

Perry, William. The Only Sure Guide to the English Tongue. 7th Worcester ed., Worcester, 1793.

Pickering, John. A Vocabulary, or Collection of Words and Phrases Which Have Been Supposed to Be Peculiar to the United States of America. Boston, 1816.

Pickering, Octavius. The Life of Timothy Pickering. 4 vols. Boston, Little, Brown and Company, 1867–73.

Picket, Albert, and Picket, John. The Academician. Vol. I, Feb. 7, 1818–Jan. 29, 1820.

Porter, G. S. Laddie. New York, Grosset & Dunlap, 1913.

Price, Richard. Observations on the Importance of the American Revolution and the Means of Making It a Benefit to the World. London, Printed for T. Cadell, in the Strand, 1785.

Proceedings of the American Philological Society, III (1843), 3–37.

Read, Allan Walker. "Noah Webster's Project in 1801 for a History of American Newspapers," Journalism Quarterly, XI (1934), 258–75.

—— "The Obscenity Symbol," American Speech, IX (1934), 264–78.

—— "The Philological Society of New York, 1788," American Speech, IX (1934), 131–36.

—— "Webster's Euphemisms," Dialect Notes, VI (1934), 385–91.

Reeder, Rudolph R. The Historical Development of School Readers and Method in Teaching Reading. New York, 1900.

Reisner, Edward H. Nationalism and Education since 1789. New York, The Macmillan Company, 1922.

"Remembrances of Samuel Latham Mitchill," Library of American Literature, V (1888–90), 190.

Rosenbach, A. S. W. Early American Children's Books. Portland, Maine, Southworth Press, 1933.

Rosenthal, L. America and France. New York, Henry Holt & Company, 1882.

Royal American Magazine or Universal Repository, Vol. I, 1774.

Rush, Benjamin. Essays, Observations upon the Study of Latin and Greek. 1789.

—— Observations upon the Origin of the Malignant Bilious, or Yellow Fever in Philadelphia and upon Means of Preventing It. Philadelphia, Budd & Bartram, 1799.

—— A Plan for the Establishment of Public Schools and the Diffusion of Knowledge in Pennsylvania, to Which Are Added, Thoughts upon the Mode of Education Proper in a Republic . . . Philadelphia, Printed for Thomas Dobson, 1786.

—— Thoughts on Female Education. Philadelphia, Burhard & Hall, 1787.

Russell, T. W. "Webster, Word Arbiter for 100 Years," New York Times Magazine, April 15, 1928, p. 11.

Schapiro, J. S. Condorcet and the Rise of Liberalism. New York, Harcourt, Brace and Company, 1934.

Schlesinger, A. M. "American History and American Literary History," The Reinterpretation of American Literature, ed. by N. Foerster. New York, Harcourt, Brace and Company, 1928.

Scott, William. Lessons in Elocution. Edinburgh, C. Elliot, 1789.

Scudder, H. E. Men and Manners in America One Hundred Years Ago. New York, Scribner, Armstrong and Company, 1876.

—— Noah Webster. Boston, Houghton Mifflin Company, 1881.

Seligman, Edwin R. A., and Johnson, Alvin. Encyclopaedia of the Social Sciences. "The Rise of Liberalism," pp. 103–24. New York, The Macmillan Company, 1930.

Sherrill, Charles H. French Memories of the Eighteenth-Century America. New York, Charles Scribner's Sons, 1915.

Skeat, W. W. An Etymological Dictionary of the English Language. 4th ed. Oxford, 1910.

Slosson, E. E. "The American Spirit in Education." The Chronicles of America. New Haven, Yale University Press, 1921.

Smith, G. Hubert. "Noah Webster, the Archaeologist," American Anthropologist, XXXIII (1931), 620–24.

Smith, Nila B. American Reading Instruction. New York, Silver, Burdett and Company, 1934.

Smith, Samuel H. Remarks on Education. Printed for John Ormrod. Philadelphia, 1798.

Snow, Louis F. The College Curriculum in the United States. New York, 1907.

Sparks, Jared. The Life of George Washington. Boston, Tappan and Dennet, 1843.

"Spelling Book As a Civilizer, The." New York Evangelist, March 24, 1873.

Spiller, R. E. The Roots of National Culture. New York, The Macmillan Company, 1933.

Stedman, Arthur, and Hutchinson, Ellen Mackay. A Library of American Literature from the Earliest Settlement to the Present Time. New York, C. L. Webster and Company, 1888–90.

Steger, S. A. American Dictionaries. Baltimore, J. H. Furst Company, 1913.

Steiner, Bernard C. History of Education in Maryland. United States Bureau of Education, Bulletin No. 19, 1894.

Subscription Books Bulletin. Special number on dictionaries, V, October, 1934.

Sullivan, James. Observations upon the Government of the United States of America. Boston, Samuel Hall, 1791.

Sullivan, Mark. Our Times, Vol. II, New York, Scribner's Sons, 1927.

Swift, Jonathan. A Proposal for Correcting, Improving, and Ascertaining the English Tongue. London, 1711–12.

Tarbox, Increase N. "Noah Webster," Congregational Quarterly, VII, Pt. I (1865), 1–16.

Thompson, Everett E. "Noah Webster and Amherst College," Amherst Graduates' Quarterly, XXII (1933), 289–99.

Thornton, Richard H. An American Glossary. 2 vols. Philadelphia, 1912.

Thornton, William. Cadmus, or A Treatise on the Elements of Written Language. Philadelphia, R. Aitken and Son, 1793.

Tingelstad, Oscar Adolph. The Religious Element in American School Readers up to 1830. Chicago, Unpublished University of Chicago Thesis, 1925.

Todd, Charles. Life and Letters of Joel Barlow. New York, G. P. Putnam's Sons, 1886.

Tooke, Horne. Diversions of Purley. 2 vols. Philadelphia, W. Duane, 1806–7.

Trench, R. C. On the English Language, Past and Present. New York, Redfield, 1858.

Trollope, Mrs. Frances Milton. Domestic Manners of the Americans, Vols. I, II. London, Printed for Whittaker, Treacher & Company, 1832.

Tyler, Royall. The Contrast. Boston and New York, Houghton Mifflin Company, 1920.

Vail, Henry H. A History of the McGuffey Readers. Cleveland, The Burrows Brothers Company, 1911.

Vere, M. Schele de. Americanisms, the English of the New World. New York, 1872.

—— Studies in English. New York, C. Scribner's Sons, 1867.

Wagenknecht, Edward. "The Man behind the Dictionary," Virginia Quarterly Review, V (1929), 246–58.

Wallis, John. Grammatica linguae Anglicanae. London, 1653.

Warfel, H. R. "The Centenary of Noah Webster's Bible," New England Quarterly, VII (1934), 578–82.

Warthin, Aldred Scott. Noah Webster as Epidemiologist. Chicago, American Medical Association, 1923.

Watson, Foster. Beginnings of the Teaching of Modern Subjects in England. London, 1909.

—— Encyclopedia and Dictionary of Education. 4 vols. London, Sir I. Pitman & Sons, Ltd., 1921.

—— The English Grammar Schools to 1660; Their Curriculum and Practice. Cambridge, University Press, 1908.

—— The Old Grammar Schools. New York, G. P. Putnam's Sons, 1916.

Wayland, Francis. The Elements of Moral Science. New York, Cook & Company, 1835.

Webster, Noah. An Address Delivered at the Laying of the Corner Stone of the Building Now Erecting for the Charity Institution in Amherst, August 9, 1820. Boston, Ezra Lincoln, 1820.

—— An Address to the Citizens of Connecticut. New Haven, J. Walter, 1802.

—— An Address to the Freemen of Connecticut. Hartford, Hudson & Goodwin, 1806.

—— An Account of the Federal Procession . . . July 23, 1788. New York, 1819.

—— An American Dictionary of the English Language: Intended to exhibit, I. The Origin, Affinities and Primary Signification of English Words . . . II. The Genuine Orthography and Pronunciation of Words . . . III. Accurate and Discriminating Definitions . . . 2 vols. New York, S. Converse, 1828.

—— Same, abridged by Joseph Emerson Worcester . . . Walker's Key . . . New York, S. Converse, 1829.

—— Same, abridged by the author. New Haven, Hezekiah Howe, 1829.

—— Same. London, 1832.

—— Same. University edition. Revised . . . William G. Webster, 2 vols. Springfield, George and Charles Merriam, 1845.

—— Same, enlarged by Chauncey A. Goodrich. Springfield, George and Charles Merriam, 1848.

—— Same, pictorial quarto unabridged . . . Chauncey A. Goodrich. Springfield, Merriam Company, 1859.

—— Same, new illustrated royal quarto unabridged. Revised and enlarged . . . Chauncey A. Goodrich . . . Noah Porter . . . William A. Wheeler. Cambridge, H. Q. Houghton & Company, Springfield, G. & C. Merriam, 1865.

Webster, Noah. An American Dictionary of the English Language, abridged. National Pictorial Royal . . . William A. Wheeler . . . William G. Webster. New York, Ivison, Phinney, Blakeman & Company, 1867.

—— An American Magazine, ed. by Noah Webster. New York, Published from December, 1787 to November, 1788.

—— An American Selection of Lessons in Reading and Speaking. Calculated to improve the minds and refine the taste of youth. Philadelphia, Young and Mc-Culloch, 1787. Hartford, Hudson & Goodwin, 1788, 1789, 1792, 1794, 1795, 1796, 1799, 1802, 1805, 1808 ?, 1811, 1812 ?, 1816.

—— The American Spelling Book . . . The First Part of a Grammatical Institute of the English Language. Boston, Thomas and Andrews, 1789.

—— Attention! or, New Thoughts on a Serious Subject: Being an Enquiry into the Excise Laws of Connecticut, Hartford, Hudson & Goodwin, 1789.

—— "Bill of Mortality," Collections of the Massachusetts Historical Society, III (1794), 4–6.

—— Biography, for the Use of Schools. Hartford, Hezekiah Howe, 1830.

—— "Brief History," Morse's The American Geography. Elizabethtown, Shepard Kollock, 1789.

—— Brief History of Epidemic and Pestilential Diseases. Hartford, Hudson & Goodwin, 1799.

—— A Brief View. 1. Of Errors and Obscurities in the Common Version of the Scriptures . . . 2. Of Errors and Defects in Class-books Used in Seminaries of Learning . . . 3. A Few Plagiarisms, n. p., n. t.

—— A Collection of Essays and Fugitiv Writings, on Moral, Historical, Political and Literary Subjects. Boston, 1790.

—— A Collection of Papers on Political, Literary and Moral Subjects. New York, Webster & Clark, 1843.

—— A Collection of Papers on the Subject of Bilious Fevers, Prevalent in the United States. New York, Hopkins, Webb and Company, 1796.

—— A Compendious Dictionary of the English Language; in which five thousand words are added to the number found in the Best English compends; the Orthography is, in some instances corrected; the pronunciation marked by an accent or other suitable directions; and the definitions of many words amended and improved. New Haven, Increase Cooke & Company, 1806.

—— The Decomposition of White Lead Paint. New Haven, 1810.

—— Description of New York in 1786. New York, F. B. Patterson, 1874.

—— The Devil Is in You. Philadelphia, Mathew Carey, 1787.

—— A Dictionary of the English Language Compiled for the Use of Common Schools in the United States. New Haven, Sidney's Press, 1807.

—— Same. Hartford, George Goodwin & Sons, 1817.

—— "Discrepancies of English Orthography," Series of Books for Systematic Instruction in the English Language. 1830. Pp. 7–16.

—— Dissertations on the English Language: with Notes Historical and Critical. Boston, Isaiah Thomas & Company, 1789.

—— Dissertation on the Origin, History and Connexion of the Languages of Western Asia and of Europe. n. t.; n. p.

—— A Dissertation on the Supposed Change in the Temperature of Winter. New Haven, 1810.

—— Effects of Slavery on Morals and Industry. Hartford, Hudson and Goodwin, 1793.

—— The Elementary Primer, or First Lessons for Children. New York, 1831.

Webster, Noah. The Elementary Spelling Book, an Improvement on the American Spelling Book. Philadelphia, Kimber & Sharpless, 1829. This book appeared in numerous editions and reprints throughout the century and is still published by the American Book Company.

—— Elements of Useful Knowledge, Containing a Historical and Geographical Account of the United States: for the Use of Schools, Vol. I, Hartford, Hudson & Goodwin, 1802.

—— Vol. II, New Haven, Sidney's Press, 1804.

—— Vol. III, Containing a Historical and Geographical Account of the Empires and States in Europe, Asia and Africa, with Their Colonies. New Haven, Bronson, Walter & Company, 1806.

—— The English Ship of War Righting Herself after Twenty Years Hard Fighting! . . . or, Thirty Practical Essays Founded on Common Sense. Bristol, Printed for the editor . . . by T. Long. n. d. [1816].

—— An Examination into the Leading Principles of the Federal Constitution Proposed by the Late Convention Held at Philadelphia. Philadelphia, Prichard & Hall, 1787.

—— Experiments Respecting Dew. Cambridge, 1809.

—— A Grammatical Institute of the English Language, Part I, Hartford, Hudson & Goodwin, 1783. The parent of the Old Blue-Back Speller.

—— Part II, Containing a Plain and Comprehensive Grammar, Grounded on the True Principles and Idioms of the Language. Hartford, Hudson & Goodwin, 1784. Many editions appeared before the work was withdrawn in 1804.

—— Part III, Containing the Necessary Rules of Reading and Speaking, Hartford, Barlow & Babcock, 1785.

—— History of Animals; Being the Fourth Volume of Elements of Useful Knowledge. New Haven, Howe & Deforest, 1812.

—— History of the Present State of Banks and Insurance Companies in the United States. New York, 1802.

—— "History of the United States," Old South Leaflets, VIII, Boston (Taken from An American Selection, 1785).

—— History of the United States to Which a Brief Historical Account of Our English Is Prefixed. New Haven, 1832.

—— The Holy Bible, Contaning the Old and New Testaments in the Common Version. New Haven, Durrie & Peck, 1833.

—— The Illustrated Webster Spelling Book. London, Ward & Lock [1856].

—— An Improved Grammar of the English Language. New Haven, Hezekiah Howe, 1831.

—— Instructive and Entertaining Lessons for Youth, New Haven, S. Babcock and Durrie & Peck, 1835. This is substantially the same as "An American Selection."

—— A Journal of the Transactions and Occurrences in the Settlement of Massachusetts and the Other New-England Colonies, . . . 1630–1644. Hartford, Elisha Babcock, 1790.

—— "Letter to Dawes," Monthly Anthology and Boston Review, VII (1809), 208–12.

—— A Letter to Dr. David Ramsay, of Charleston, respecting the Errors in Johnson's Dictionary. New Haven, Oliver Steele & Company, 1807.

—— A Letter to General Hamilton, Occasioned by His Letter to President Adams. New York, 1800. (Signed "Aristides.")

—— Letter to the Governors, Instructors, and Trustees of the Universities, and Other Seminaries of Learning, in the United States, on The Errors of English Grammars. New York, George F. Hopkins, 1798.

Webster, Noah. A Letter to the Honorable John Pickering, on the Subject of His Vocabulary. Boston, West and Richardson, 1817.

—— A Letter to the Secretary of the Treasury on the Commerce and Currency of the United States. New York, 1819. The authorship of this letter has been ascribed to Webster, largely on the basis that it was signed "Aristides," a signature used by Webster in a letter to Hamilton in 1800.

—— Letters to a Young Gentleman, Commencing His Education. New Haven, Howe and Spalding, 1823.

—— The Little Franklin. New Haven, S. Babcock, 1836.

—— The Little Reader's Assistant. Hartford, Elisha Babcock, 1790. Contains a grammar, a Federal catechism, a farmers' catechism and an explanation of the general principles of government and commerce.

—— A Manual of Useful Studies; for the Instruction of Young Persons of Both Sexes, in Families and Schools. New Haven, S. Babcock, 1839.

—— Miscellaneous Papers: on Political and Commercial Subjects. Part I. An Address to the President of the United States on the Subject of His Administration.

—— Part II. An Essay on the Rights of Neutral Nations in Vindication of the Principles Asserted by the Northern Powers of Europe.

—— Part III. A Letter on the Value and Importance of the American Commerce to Great Britain.

—— Part IV. A Sketch of the History and Present State of Banks and Insurance Companies in the United States. New York, E. Beldon & Co., 1802.

—— Mistakes and Corrections. 1. Improprieties and Errors in the Common Version of the Scriptures, with Specimens of Amended Language in Webster's edition of the Bible. 2. Explanations of Prepositions in English and Other Languages. These Constitute a Very Difficult Part of Philology. 3. Errors in English Grammars. 4. Mistakes in the Hebrew Lexicon of Gesenius and in Some Derivations of Dr. Horwitz. 5. Errors in Butler's Scholar's Companion, and in Town's Analysis. 6. Errors in Richardson's Dictionary. New Haven, B. L. Hamlen, 1837.

—— The New American Spelling Book, for the Use of Primary Schools in the United States. New Haven, Durrie & Peck and S. Babcock, 1833.

—— New England Primer. Hudson, Ashbel Stoddard, 1801.

—— The New Testament in the Common Version. New Haven, S. Babcock, 1839.

—— The Noah Webster British and American Illustrated Spelling and Reading Book. London, Dean, 1858.

—— "Number of Deaths, in the Episcopal Church in New York in Each Month for Ten Years from January 1, 1786, to December 31, 1795," Connecticut Academy of Arts and Sciences, New Haven, I (1810), 97–98.

—— Observations on Language, and on the Errors of Class Books. New Haven, S. Babcock, 1839.

—— "On a Reform of Spelling," The Little Reader's Assistant, Hartford, Elisha Babcock, 1790, pp. 78–80.

—— An Oration, on the Extent and Power of Political Delusion. New Haven, 1800.

—— An Oration, Pronounced before the Citizens of New Haven, on the Anniversary of the Declaration of Independence; July, 1802. New Haven, William W. Morse, 1802.

—— An Oration, Pronounced before the Citizens of New Haven, on the Anniversary of the United States, July 4th, 1798. New Haven, T. & S. Green [1798].

Webster, Noah. An Oration, Pronounced before the Knox and Warren Branches of the Washington Benevolent Society, at Amherst. Northampton, William Butler, 1814.

—— "Origin of Mythology," Memoirs of Connecticut Academy of Arts and Sciences, New Haven, 1810, pp. 175–216.

—— The Peculiar Doctrines of the Gospel Explained and Defended. [New Haven: 1809.]

—— "Philology," New England Magazine, November, Boston, 1831, pp. 369–80.

—— A Philosophical and Practical Grammar of the English Language. New Haven, Oliver Steele & Company, 1807.

—— The Pictorial Elementary Spelling Book. New York, G. F. Cooledge. Various dates have been assigned to this publication. The copy in the Library of Congress is dated "1844" in pencil.

—— The Pirates; a tale for the Amusement and Instruction of Youth. Philadelphia, William Greer for Johnson and Warner, 1813. This tale is published along with essays from the Prompter. The author has not seen a copy. Authorship assigned to Webster by Rosenbach.

—— A Plain and Comprehensive Grammar of the English Language. Philadelphia, Printed for W. Young, 1789.

—— "Plan for the Union of the American States," Old South Leaflets, VIII, 1785. Part IV of Sketches of American Policy.

—— The Prompter; or a Commentary on Common Sayings and Subjects. Boston, Isaiah Thomas and E. T. Andrews, 1790.

—— "The Reforming of Spelling . . . An Essay on the Necessity, Advantages and Practicability of Reforming the Mode of Spelling," Old South Leaflets, VIII. First published in the Dissertations in 1789.

—— "Reply to Mr. Mellen's Remarks," Massachusetts Historical Society Collections, III, 1810.

—— Revolution in France. New York, George Bunce and Company, 1794.

—— A Rod For the Fool's Back. [New Haven, 1800.]

—— Rudiments of English Grammar; an abridgment of the Improved Grammar of the English Language. New Haven, Durrie & Peck, 1831.

—— Sentimental and Humorous Essays, conducive to Economy and Happiness. London, Tewkesbury, 1799. Substantially the same as the Prompter.

—— "A Short View of the Origin and Progress of the Science of Natural Philosophy, with Some Observations on the Advantages of Science in General," New York Magazine, Vol. I, June–July, 1790. Delivered by Webster at the public examination of the candidates for the college degree, July 23, 1778.

—— Sketches of American Policy. Hartford, Hudson & Goodwin, 1785.

—— The Teacher, a Supplement to the Elementary Spelling Book. New Haven, S. Babcock, 1837.

—— Ten Letters to Dr. Joseph Priestley, in Answer to His Letters to the Inhabitants of Northumberland. New Haven, Read & Morse, 1800.

—— "On the Theory of Vegetation," Memoirs of The American Academy of Arts and Sciences, Boston, II (1793), 178–85.

—— "Thoughts on Capital Punishment," The Christian Disciple, V (1817), 65–71.

—— Value of the Bible, and Excellence of the Christian Religion. New Haven, Durrie & Peck, 1834.

—— "Vindication of the Treaty of Amity, Commerce, and Navigation, with Great Britain." Philadelphia, Henry Tuckniss, for Mathew Carey, 1795.

Webster, Noah. Webster Genealogy. New Haven, Compiled and printed privately
    for presentation only. 1836.
—— Webster's International Dictionary. Springfield, G. & C. Merriam, 1890.
—— Webster's New International Dictionary. Springfield, G. & C. Merriam
    Company, 1909.
—— Revised. Springfield, G. & C. Merriam Company, 1934.
—— Webster's Old Spelling Book. Sanbornton, N. H. [1817].
—— Yorktown. (Historical Printing Club, 1881. Letter from Webster to Wash-
    ington and reply by Washington concerning the plan of battle at Yorktown.)
    Brooklyn, 1881.
Weeden, W. B. Economic and Social History of New England. 2 vols. Boston,
    Houghton Mifflin Company, 1890.
Wells, William Harvey. A Grammar of the English Language for the Use of
    Schools. Boston, Published by William H. Wardwell, 1848.
White, Richard Grant. Words and Their Uses, Past and Present. New York, Shel-
    don and Company, 1870.
Whitmore, William H. American Genealogist. Albany, Joel Munsell, 1868.
Wickersham, James Pyle. A History of Education in Pennsylvania. Lancaster, In-
    quirer Publishing Company, 1886.
Williams, R. O. Our Dictionary and Other English Language Topics. New York,
    Henry Holt & Company, 1890.
Winslow, Charles Edward Morey. "The Epidemiology of Noah Webster," Trans-
    actions of the Connecticut Academy of Arts and Sciences, XXXII (1934),
    21–109.
Wolff, Samuel Lee. "Scholars," Cambridge History of American Literature, Vol.
    IV, New York, G. P. Putnam's Sons, 1930.
Woodworth, Samuel. The Deed of Gift. New York, C. N. Baldwin, 1822.
Woody, Thomas. Educational Views of Benjamin Franklin. New York, McGraw-
    Hill Book Company, 1931.
Wright, Thomas. Anglo-Saxon and Old English Vocabularies. 2d ed. edited by R.
    P. Wulcker. London, 1884.
Wyld, H. C. K. The Historical Study of the Mother Tongue. New York, 1906.
—— A Short History of English. London, 1914.
—— A Short History of English. London, I. Murray, 1929.
Zunder, T. A. The Early Days of Joel Barlow. New Haven, Yale University Press,
    1934.
—— "Noah Webster as a Student Orator," Yale University Weekly, XXV, 1926.

PAMPHLETS, MOST OF WHICH APPEARED DURING THE
"WAR OF THE DICTIONARIES"

Andrews, I. W. Webster's Dictionaries. 1856.
Cobb, Lyman. A Critical Review of Noah Webster's Spelling Book. Albany, 1828.
—— A Critical Review of the Orthography of Dr. Webster's Series of Books for
    Systematic Instruction of the English Language. 1831.
Equal Justice. The Two Dictionaries. 1860.
Fowler, William Chauncey. Printed but Not Published. 1884.
Gould, E. S. & C. Orthography of Noah Webster.
Hickling, Swan & Brown. Recommendations of Worcester's Dictionaries . . . 1856.
Jenks, Hickling & Swan. A Reply to Messrs. G. & C. Merriam Attack. 1854.

Kingsley, J. L. Review of Webster's American Dictionary. 1829.

Lyman, C. S. Review of Worcester's Dictionary. 1860.

Merriam, G. & C. The Claims of Worcester's Dictionary Candidly Examined. 1854.

―――― The Dictionary of the Schoolroom. 1855.

―――― A Gross Literary Fraud Exposed . . . 1855.

―――― Have We a National Standard of English Lexicography? 1855.

―――― A National Standard. 1853.

―――― A Summary Summing of the Charges upon Noah Webster. 1854.

―――― Webster's Dictionary. 1890.

―――― Webster's Encyclopedic Dictionary. 1890.

Mr. Converse's Answer to Merriam's Attack.

New Jersey Society of Teachers and Friends of Education. Discussion On the Merits of Noah Webster's Orthography . . . 1845.

New York State Senate. Discussion of the Committee on Literature. 1851.

Poole, W. F. Dictionaries in Boston. 1855.

―――― English Orthoëpy. 1860.

―――― The Orthographical Hobgoblin. 1859.

―――― Websterian Orthography. 1857.

Porter, N. Sketch of Remarks Addressed to the Committee on Education. 1850.

Reply to Messrs. G. & C. Merriam Attack. 1854.

Sargent, E. The Critic Criticized. 1856.

Swan, W. D. The Critic Criticised. 1856.

Webster, Noah. Commendations of Dr. Noah Webster's Books. 1841.

―――― Series of Books for Systematical Instruction in the English Language. 1830–31.

―――― "State of English Philology," Commendations of Dr. N. Webster's Books. 1841.

―――― To the Friends of American Literature. 1831.

What Shall I Adopt for My School Dictionary? "A Teacher's Inquiry." Philorn.

Worcester, J. E. A Gross Literary Fraud Exposed. 1854.

Worcester's Dictionary Published in England.

Y—E, Webster's Orthography, a Reply to Dr. Noah Webster's Calumniators (1875), p. 10.

INDEX